P8-ASY-032

...tion!!

Whoops! Guess what? You're starting at the wrong end of the
comic!

...It's true! In keeping with the original Japanese format, **Bleach** is meant to
be read from right to left, starting in the
upper-right corner.

Unlike English, which is read from left
to right, Japanese is read from right to left,
meaning that action, sound effects and
word-balloon order are completely
reversed... something which can make
readers unfamiliar with Japanese feel pretty backwards themselves. For this reason,
manga or Japanese comics published in
the U.S. in English have sometimes been published "flopped"—that is, printed in exact reverse order, as though seen from the other side of a mirror.

By flopping pages, U.S. publishers can avoid confusing readers, but the
compromise is not without its downside. For one thing, a character in a
flopped manga series who once wore in the original Japanese version a T-
shirt emblazoned with "M A Y" (as in "the merry month of") now wears one
which reads "Y A M"! Additionally, many manga creators in Japan are themselves unhappy with the process, as some feel the
mirror-imaging of their art skews their original
intentions.

We are proud to bring you Tite Kubo's **Bleach**
in the original unflopped format. For now, though,
turn to the other side of the book and let the
adventure begin...!

—Editor

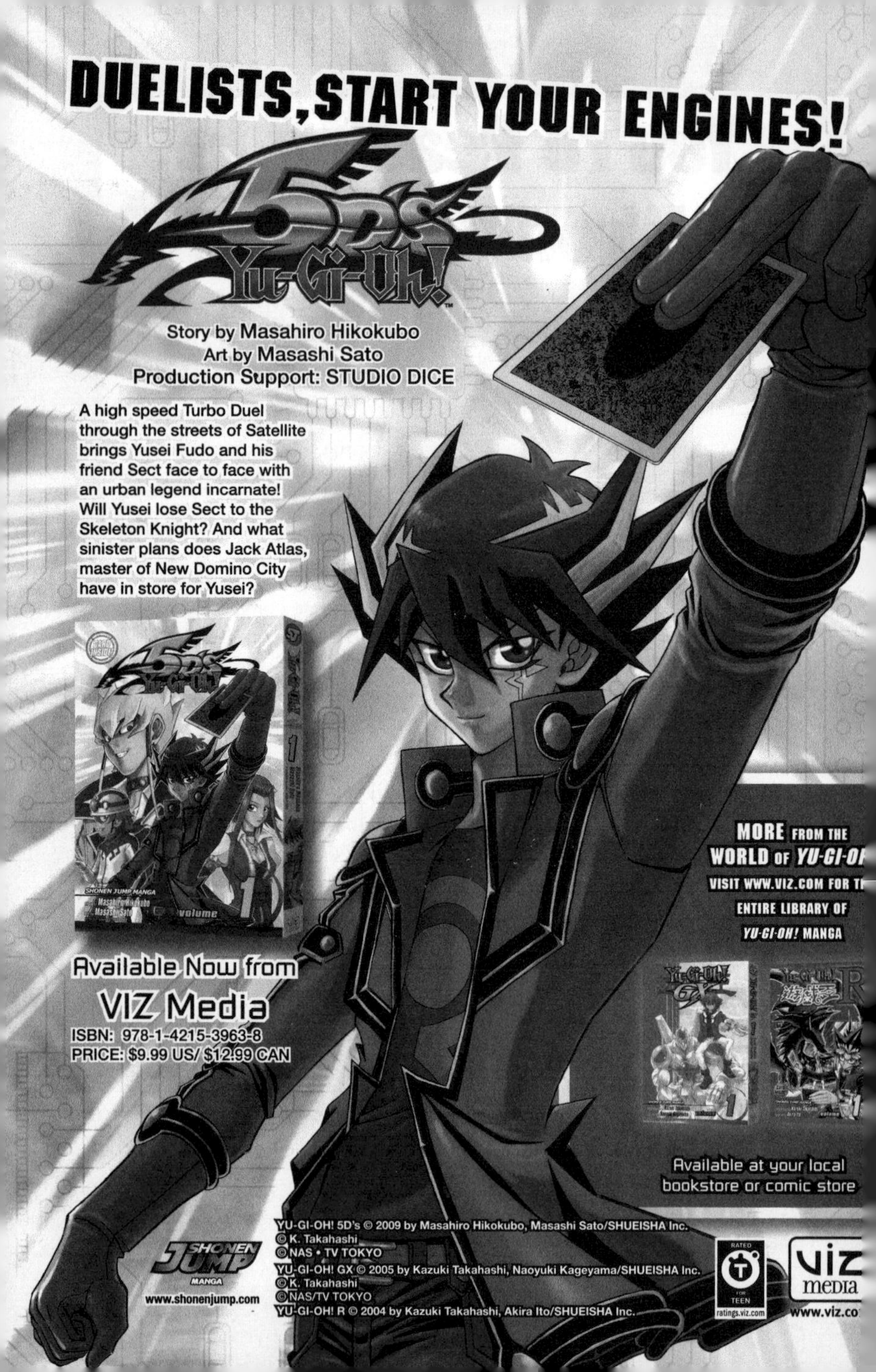
DUELISTS, START YOUR ENGINES!
5D's YU-GI-OH!™
Story by Masahiro Hikokubo
Art by Masashi Sato
Production Support: STUDIO DICE
A high speed Turbo Duel through the streets of Satellite brings Yusei Fudo and his friend Sect face to face with an urban legend incarnate! Will Yusei lose Sect to the Skeleton Knight? And what sinister plans does Jack Atlas, master of New Domino City have in store for Yusei?
Available Now from
VIZ Media
ISBN: 978-1-4215-3963-8
PRICE: $9.99 US/ $12.99 CAN
MORE FROM THE WORLD OF YU-GI-OH
VISIT WWW.VIZ.COM FOR THE ENTIRE LIBRARY OF YU-GI-OH! MANGA
Available at your local bookstore or comic store
YU-GI-OH! 5D's © 2009 by Masahiro Hikokubo, Masashi Sato/SHUEISHA Inc.
© K. Takahashi
© NAS • TV TOKYO
YU-GI-OH! GX © 2005 by Kazuki Takahashi, Naoyuki Kageyama/SHUEISHA Inc.
© K. Takahashi
© NAS/TV TOKYO
YU-GI-OH! R © 2004 by Kazuki Takahashi, Akira Ito/SHUEISHA Inc.
SHONEN JUMP MANGA
www.shonenjump.com
RATED T FOR TEEN
ratings.viz.com
viz media
www.viz.com

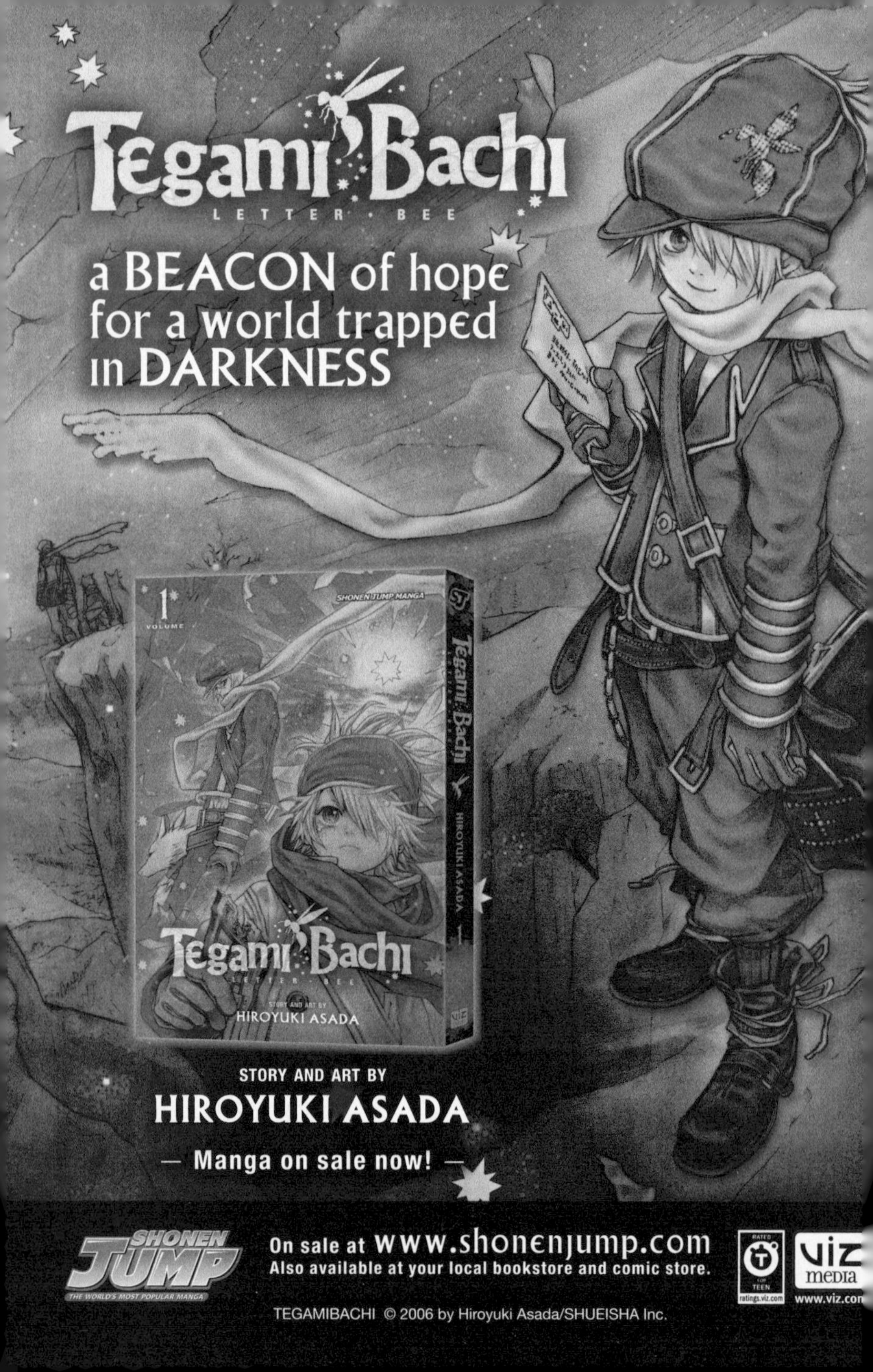
Tegami Bachi
LETTER • BEE
a BEACON of hope for a world trapped in DARKNESS
1 VOLUME
SHONEN JUMP MANGA
Tegami Bachi
LETTER • BEE
STORY AND ART BY
HIROYUKI ASADA
STORY AND ART BY
HIROYUKI ASADA
— Manga on sale now! —
SHONEN JUMP
THE WORLD'S MOST POPULAR MANGA
On sale at www.shonenjump.com
Also available at your local bookstore and comic store.
RATED T TEEN
ratings.viz.com
VIZ media
www.viz.com
TEGAMIBACHI © 2006 by Hiroyuki Asada/SHUEISHA Inc.

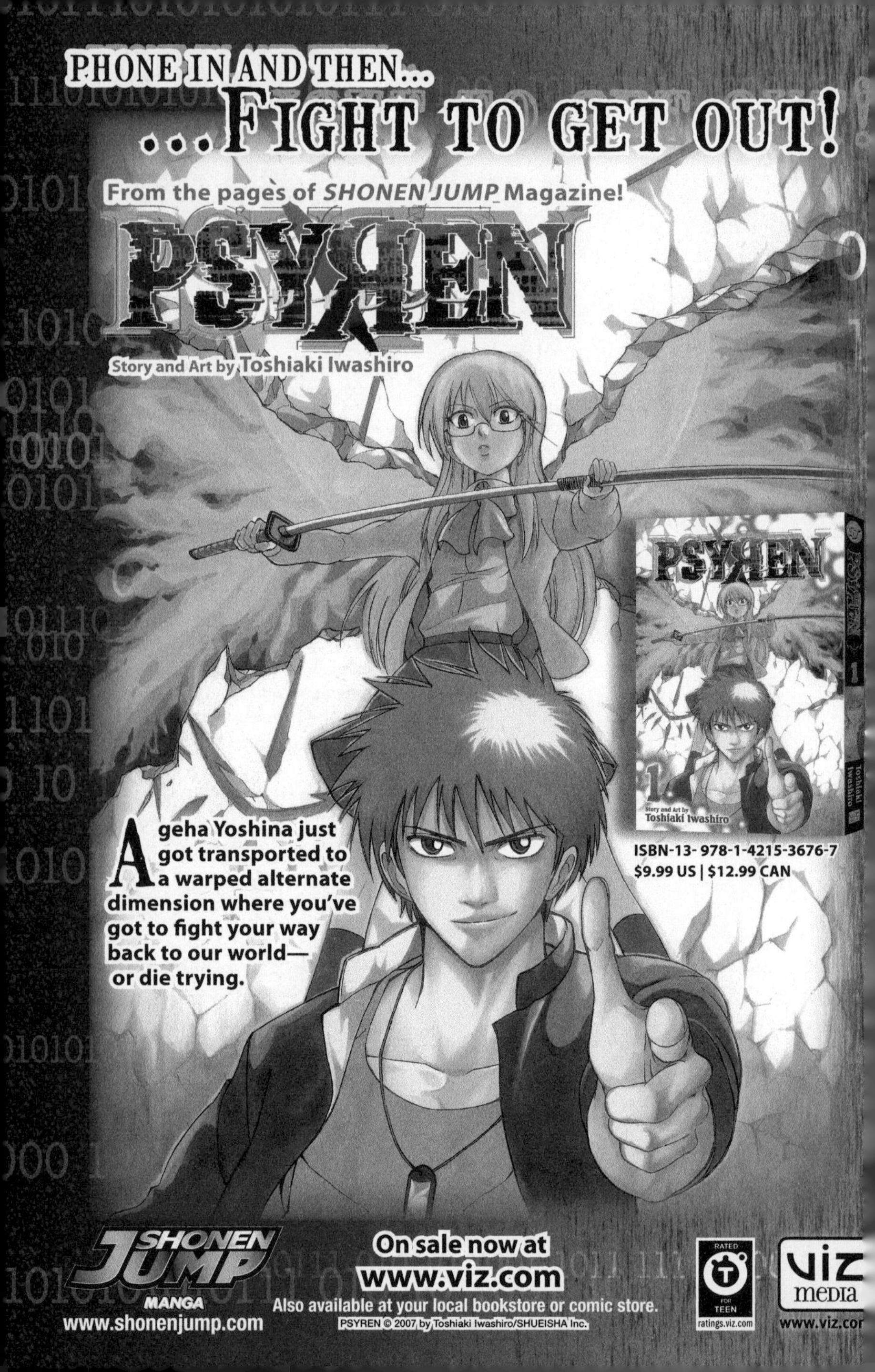
PHONE IN AND THEN...
...FIGHT TO GET OUT!
From the pages of SHONEN JUMP Magazine!
PSYREN
Story and Art by Toshiaki Iwashiro
Ageha Yoshina just got transported to a warped alternate dimension where you've got to fight your way back to our world— or die trying.
ISBN-13- 978-1-4215-3676-7
$9.99 US | $12.99 CAN
SHONEN JUMP MANGA
www.shonenjump.com
On sale now at
www.viz.com
Also available at your local bookstore or comic store.
PSYREN © 2007 by Toshiaki Iwashiro/SHUEISHA Inc.
RATED T FOR TEEN
ratings.viz.com
VIZ media
www.viz.com

Change Your Perspective

From *Akira Toriyama*, the creator of *Dr. Slump*, *COWA!* and *SandLand*

★ ★ ★ ★ ★ ★ ★

Relive Goku's quest with the new VIZBIG editions of *Dragon Ball* and *Dragon Ball Z!*

Each features:
- Three volumes in one
- Exclusive cover designs
- Color manga pages
- Larger trim size
- Color artwork
- Bonus content

DRAGON BALL
VIZBIG Edition, Volume 1

DRAGON BALL Z
VIZBIG Edition, Volume 1

Get BIG

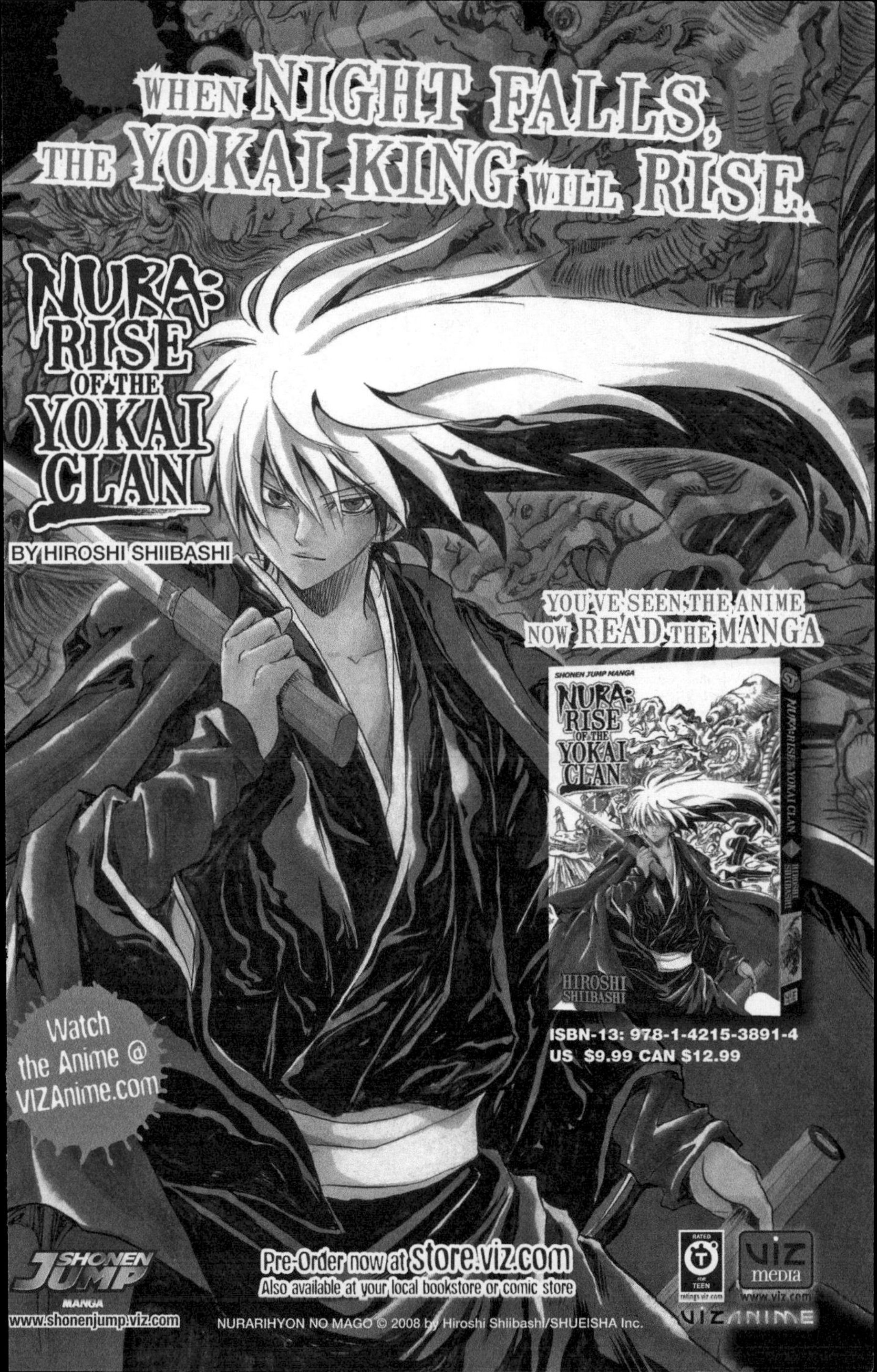
WHEN NIGHT FALLS,
THE YOKAI KING WILL RISE.
NURA: RISE OF THE YOKAI CLAN
BY HIROSHI SHIIBASHI
YOU'VE SEEN THE ANIME
NOW READ THE MANGA
SHONEN JUMP MANGA
NURA: RISE OF THE YOKAI CLAN
1
HIROSHI SHIIBASHI
ISBN-13: 978-1-4215-3891-4
US $9.99 CAN $12.99
Watch the Anime @ VIZAnime.com
SHONEN JUMP MANGA
www.shonenjump.viz.com
Pre-Order now at store.viz.com
Also available at your local bookstore or comic store
RATED T FOR TEEN
ratings.viz.com
VIZ media
www.viz.com
VIZANIME
NURARIHYON NO MAGO © 2008 by Hiroshi Shiibashi/SHUEISHA Inc.

Next Volume Preview

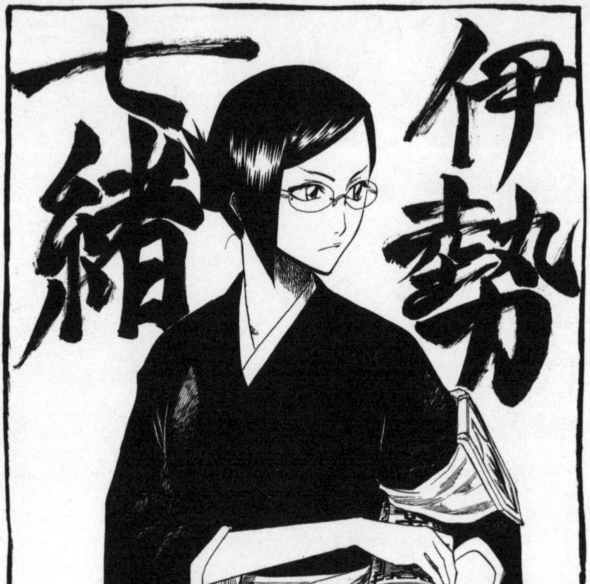
伊勢
七緒
BLEACH
ブリーチ

Chad's journey into the city of the Soul Society ended when he crossed paths with the enigmatic Captain Kyôraku. From far away, Ichigo senses Chad's weakened presence as he fights the captain of the 11th company, Kenpachi Zaraki, a man who enjoys fighting so much that he's holding himself back to make their battle last longer!

Available Now

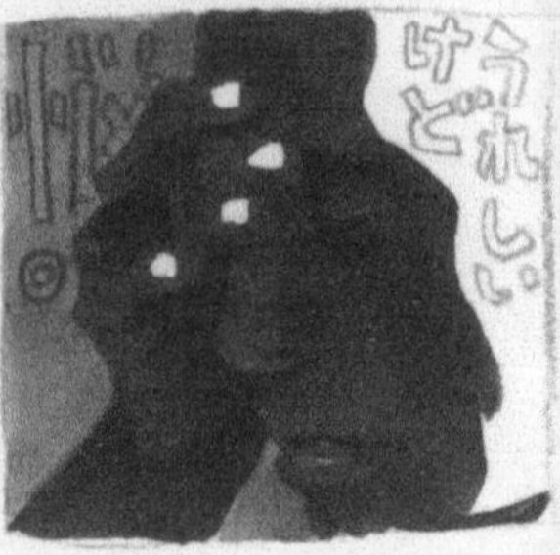

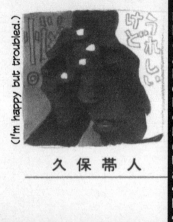

(I'm happy but troubled.)

久保帯人

Every year I participate in [*Shonen*] *Jump*'s annual JumpFesta event. This year, after leaving the stage, I looked around the convention center for the first time. A lot of fans were cheering me on from behind, but it was kind of embarrassing so I didn't look back. I really feel bad about that. But what are you supposed to do in a situation like that? Should I have waved? That doesn't seem right either...
-Tite Kubo

BLEACH is author Tite Kubo's second title. Kubo made his debut with *ZOMBIE POWDER*, a four-volume series for *WEEKLY SHONEN JUMP*. To date, *BLEACH* has been translated into numerous languages and has also inspired an animated TV series that began airing in Japan in 2004. Beginning its serialization in 2001, *BLEACH* is still a mainstay in the pages of *WEEKLY SHONEN JUMP*. In 2005, *BLEACH* was awarded the prestigious Shogakukan Manga Award in the *shonen* (boys) category.

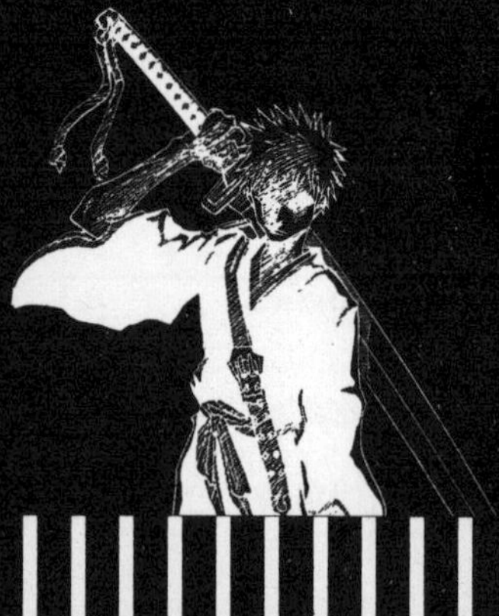

BLEACH
Vol. 12: FLOWER ON THE PRECIPICE
SHONEN JUMP Manga Edition

STORY AND ART BY
TITE KUBO

English Adaptation/Lance Caselman
Translation/Joe Yamazaki
Touch-Up Art & Lettering/Andy Ristaino
Design/Sean Lee
Editors/Kit Fox, Yuki Takagaki

Printed in the U.S.A.

Published by VIZ Media, LLC
P.O. Box 77010
San Francisco, CA 94107

10
First printing, April 2006
Tenth printing, September 2014

We think a flower on a cliff is beautiful
because we stop our feet at the cliff's edge,
unable to step out into the sky
like that fearless flower.

BLEACH12 FLOWER ON THE PRECIPICE

STARS AND

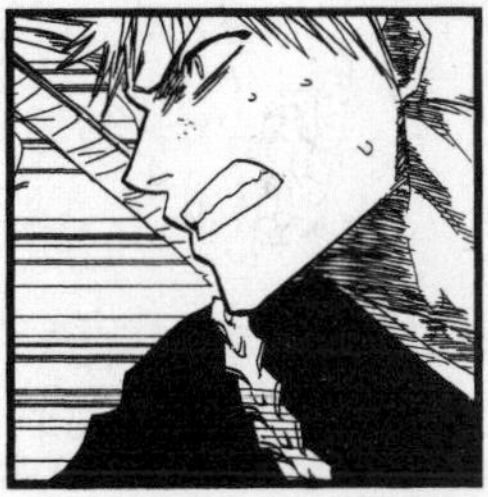

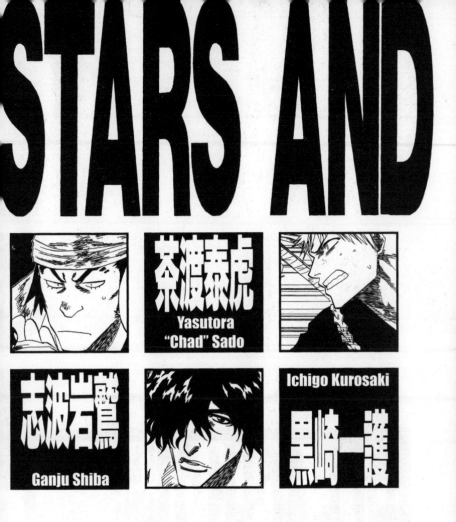

茶渡泰虎
Yasutora "Chad" Sado

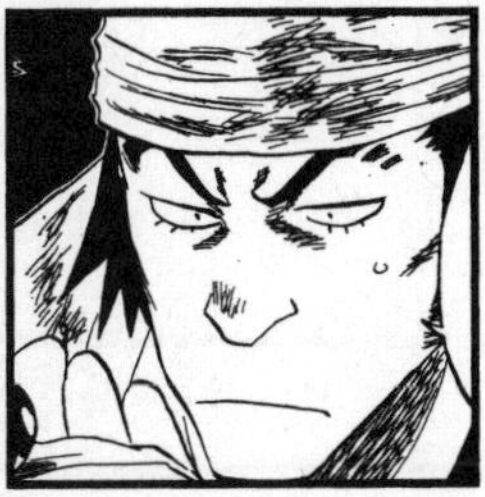

Ichigo Kurosaki
黒崎一護

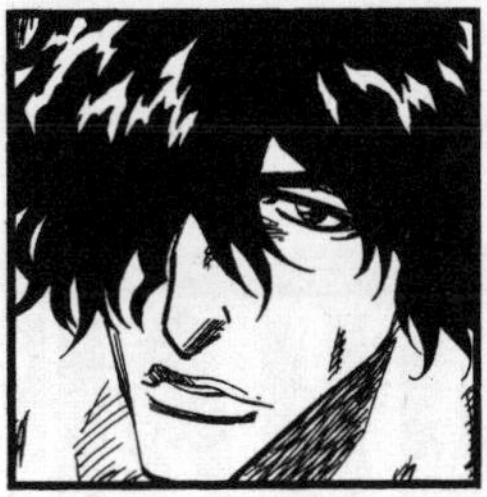

志波岩鷲
Ganju Shiba

plot

Having vowed to rescue Rukia, Ichigo and his friends go to the Soul Society and finally infiltrate the Seireitei, the city of the Soul Reapers. With the help of Soul Reaper Hanatarô Yamada, Ichigo eventually reaches the Senzaikyû where Rukia is being held. But before Ichigo can free her, his old enemy Renji arrives on the scene! Despite being terribly wounded, Ichigo defeats Renji, who makes an unexpected plea: "Save Rukia!!"

BLEACH ALL

雛森桃
Momo Hinamori

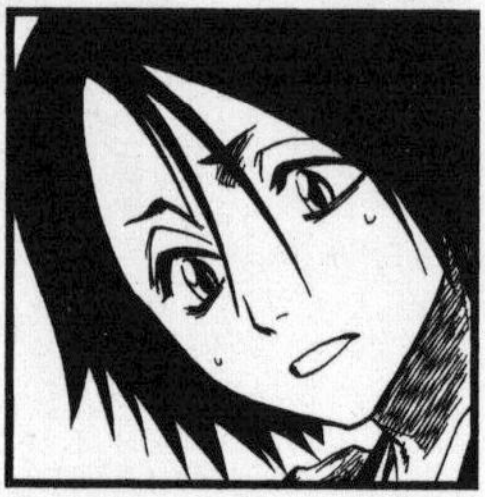

藍染惣右介
Sôsuke Aizen

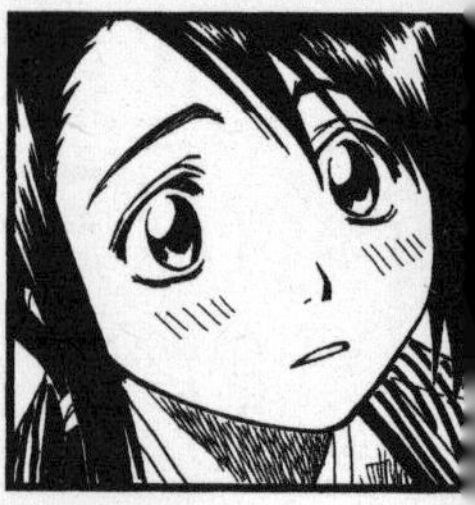

Hanatarô Yamada
山田花太郎

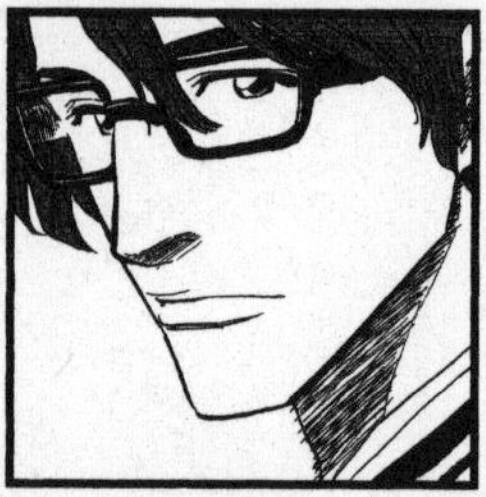

STORIES

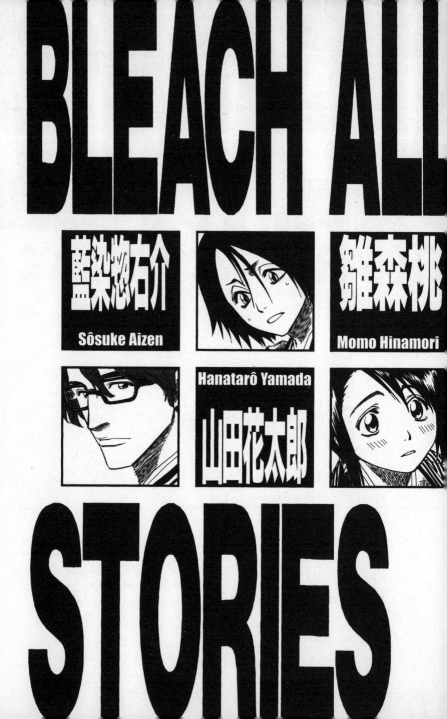

BLEACH12

FLOWER ON THE PRECIPICE

Contents

99. Dead Black War Cloud

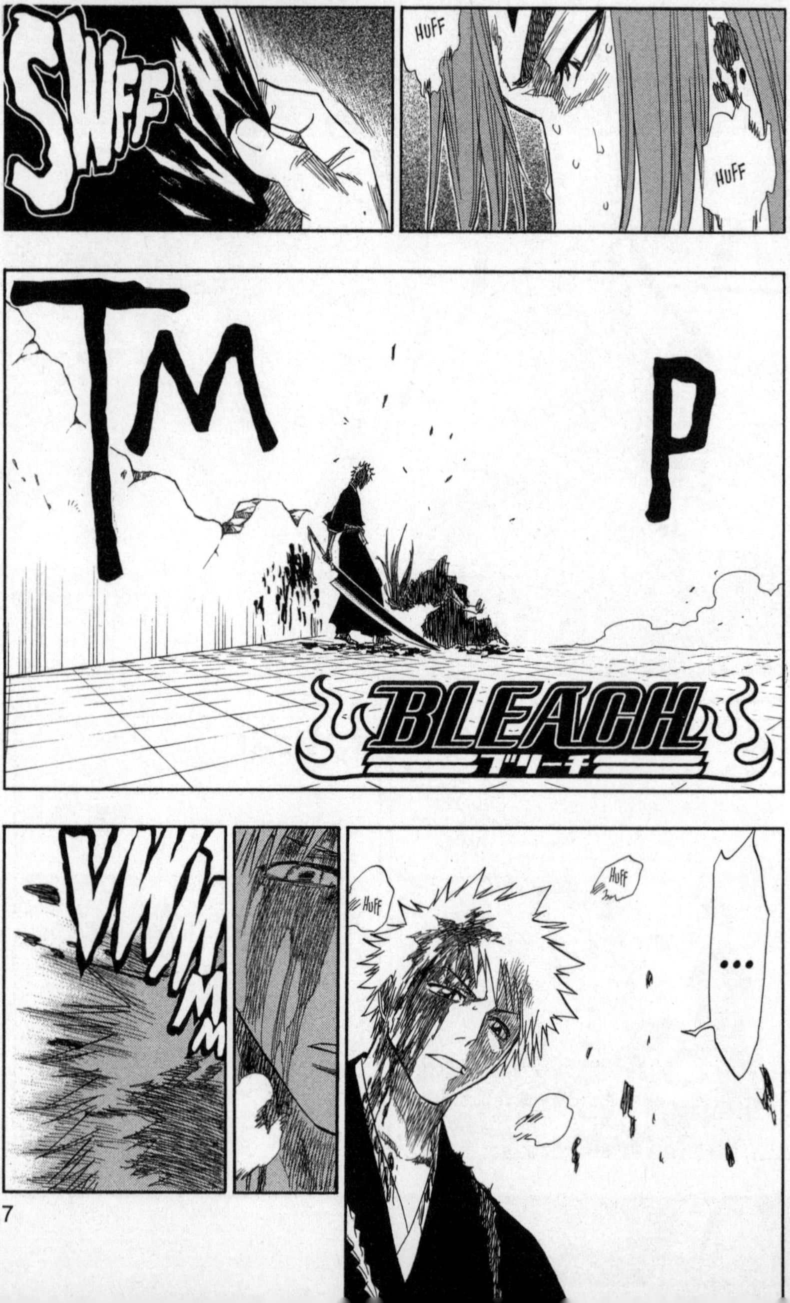
HUFF
HUFF
SWFF
TMP
BLEACH
ブリーチ
HUFF
HUFF
...
VWMMM

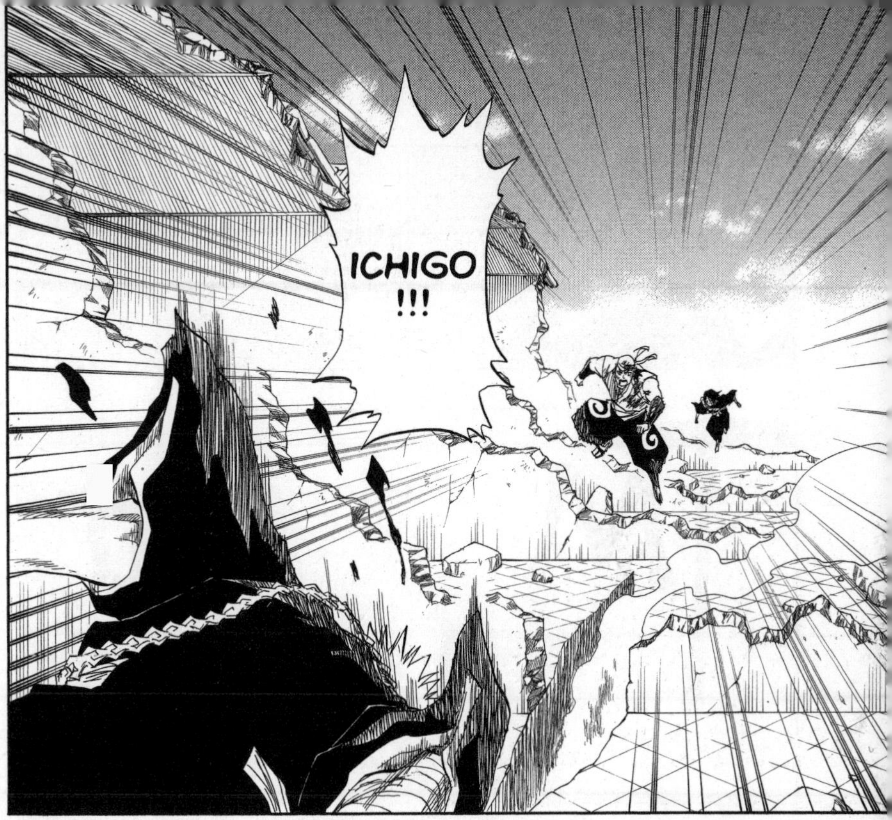
ICHIGO
!!!

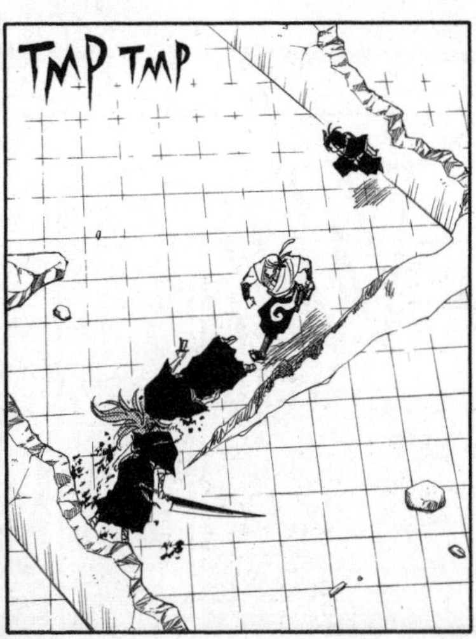
TMP TMP

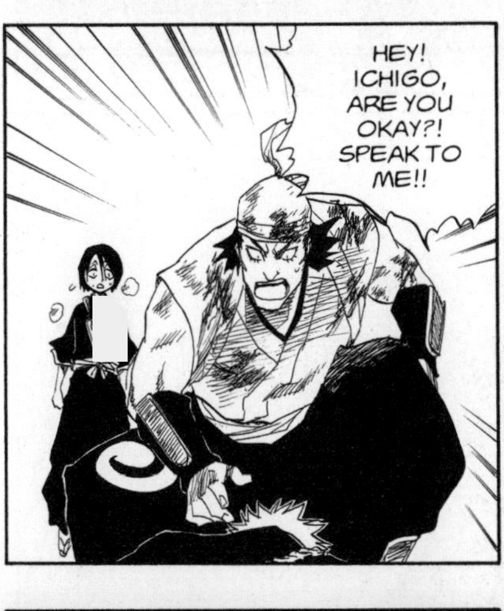
HEY! ICHIGO, ARE YOU OKAY?! SPEAK TO ME!!

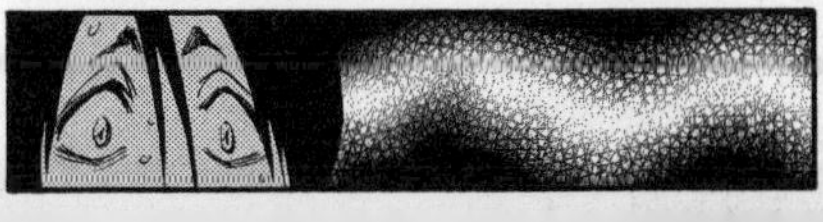

READ THIS WAY

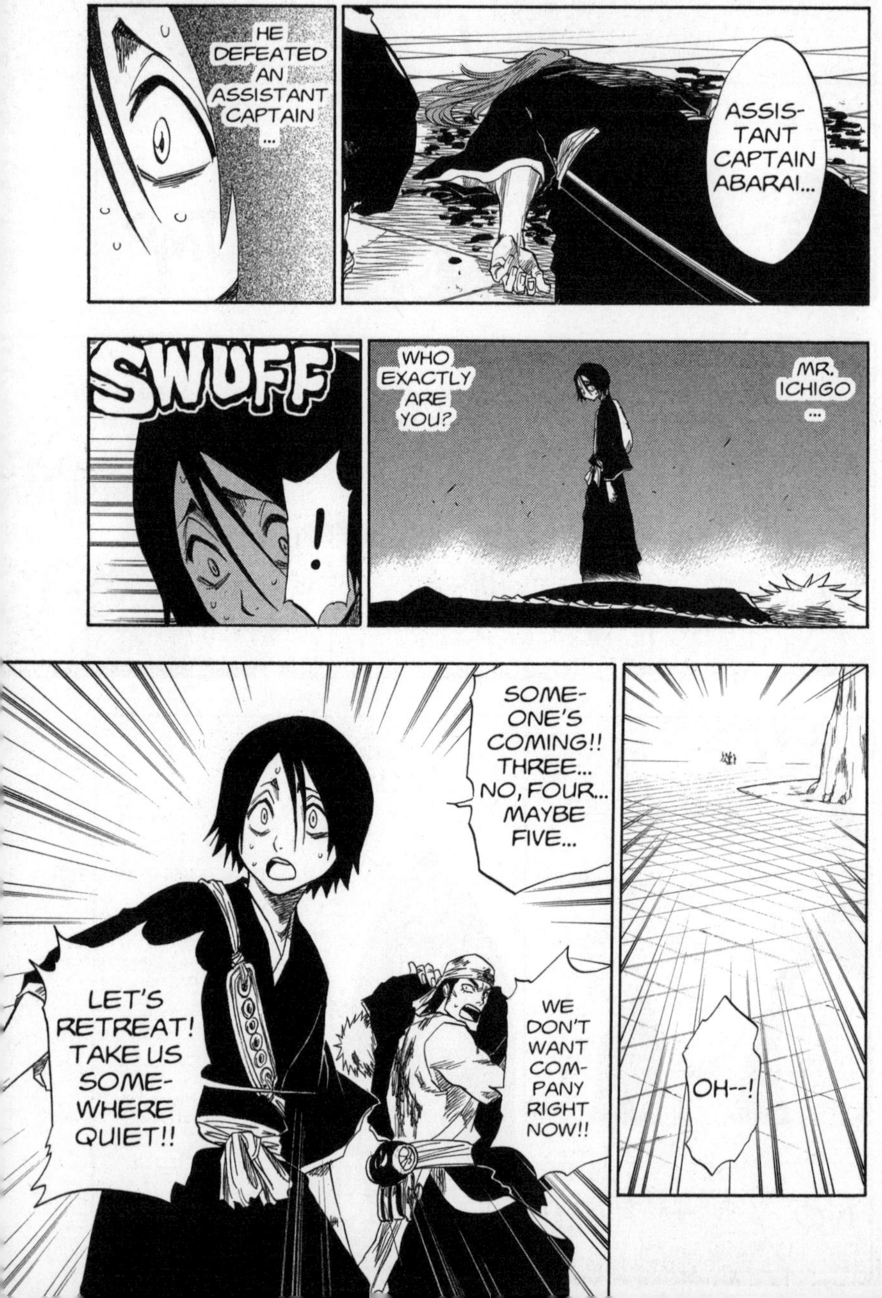
ASSIS-TANT CAPTAIN ABARAI...
HE DEFEATED AN ASSISTANT CAPTAIN...
MR. ICHIGO...
WHO EXACTLY ARE YOU?
SWUFF
!
OH--!
SOME-ONE'S COMING!! THREE... NO, FOUR... MAYBE FIVE...
WE DON'T WANT COM-PANY RIGHT NOW!!
LET'S RETREAT! TAKE US SOME-WHERE QUIET!!

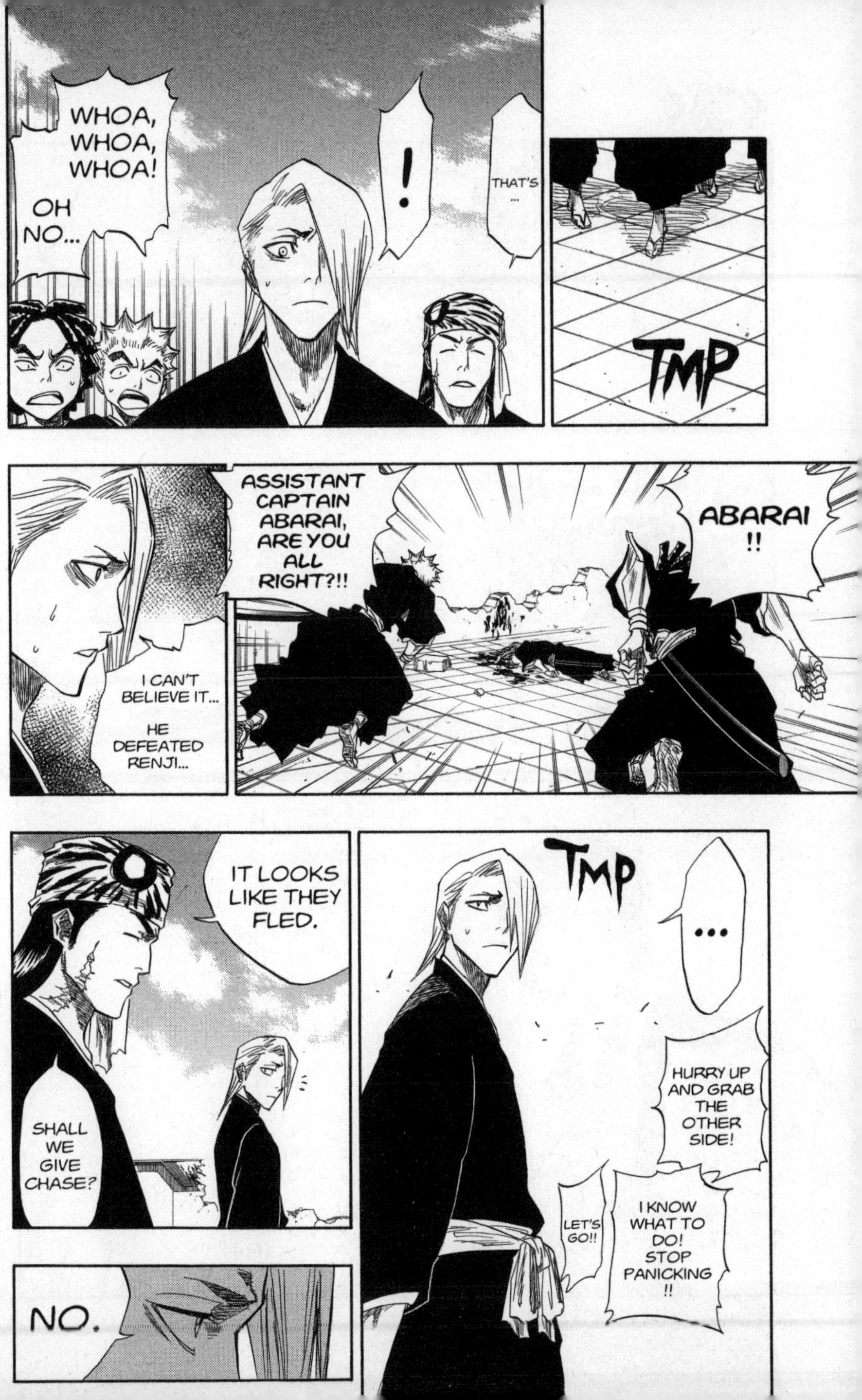
TMP
THAT'S ...
!
WHOA, WHOA, WHOA!
OH NO...
ABARAI !!
ASSISTANT CAPTAIN ABARAI, ARE YOU ALL RIGHT?!!
I CAN'T BELIEVE IT...
HE DEFEATED RENJI...
TMP
...
HURRY UP AND GRAB THE OTHER SIDE!
I KNOW WHAT TO DO! STOP PANICKING !!
LET'S GO!!
IT LOOKS LIKE THEY FLED.
SHALL WE GIVE CHASE?
NO.

READ THIS WAY

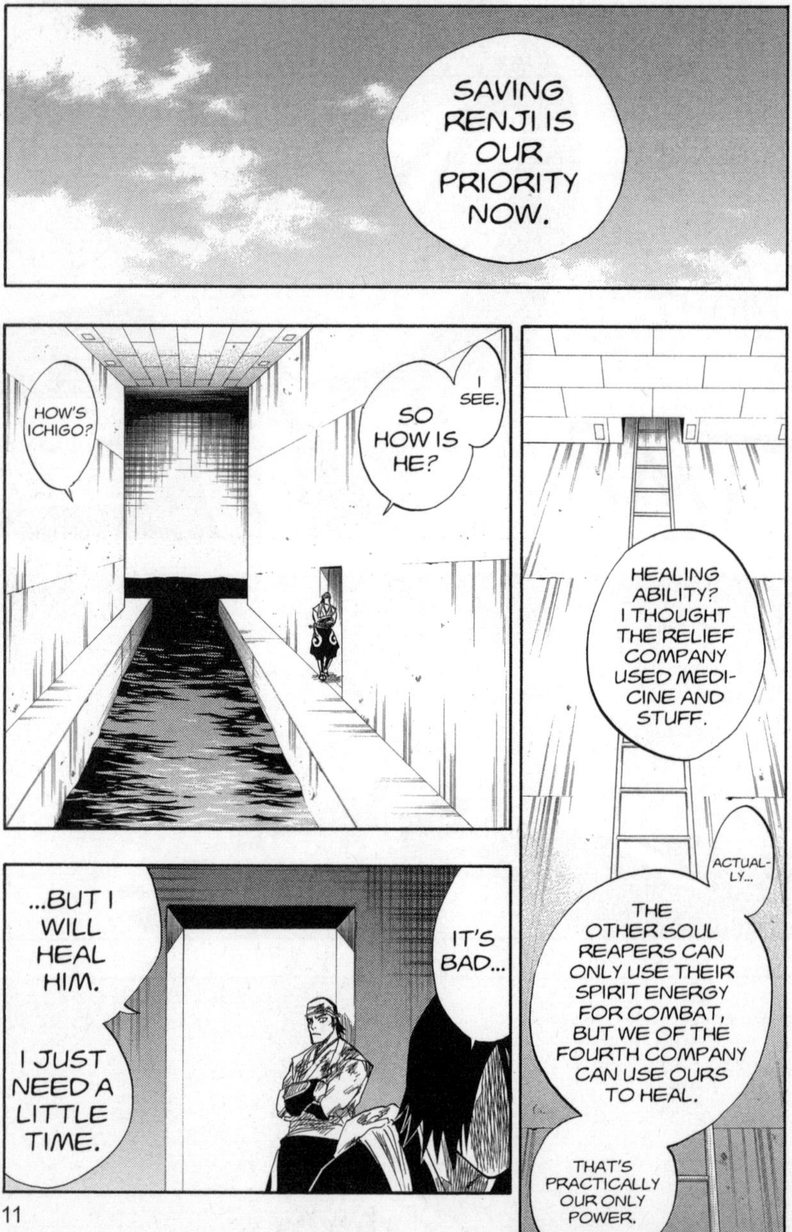
SAVING RENJI IS OUR PRIORITY NOW.
HEALING ABILITY? I THOUGHT THE RELIEF COMPANY USED MEDICINE AND STUFF.
ACTUAL-LY...
THE OTHER SOUL REAPERS CAN ONLY USE THEIR SPIRIT ENERGY FOR COMBAT, BUT WE OF THE FOURTH COMPANY CAN USE OURS TO HEAL.
THAT'S PRACTICALLY OUR ONLY POWER.
I SEE.
SO HOW IS HE?
HOW'S ICHIGO?
IT'S BAD...
...BUT I WILL HEAL HIM.
I JUST NEED A LITTLE TIME.

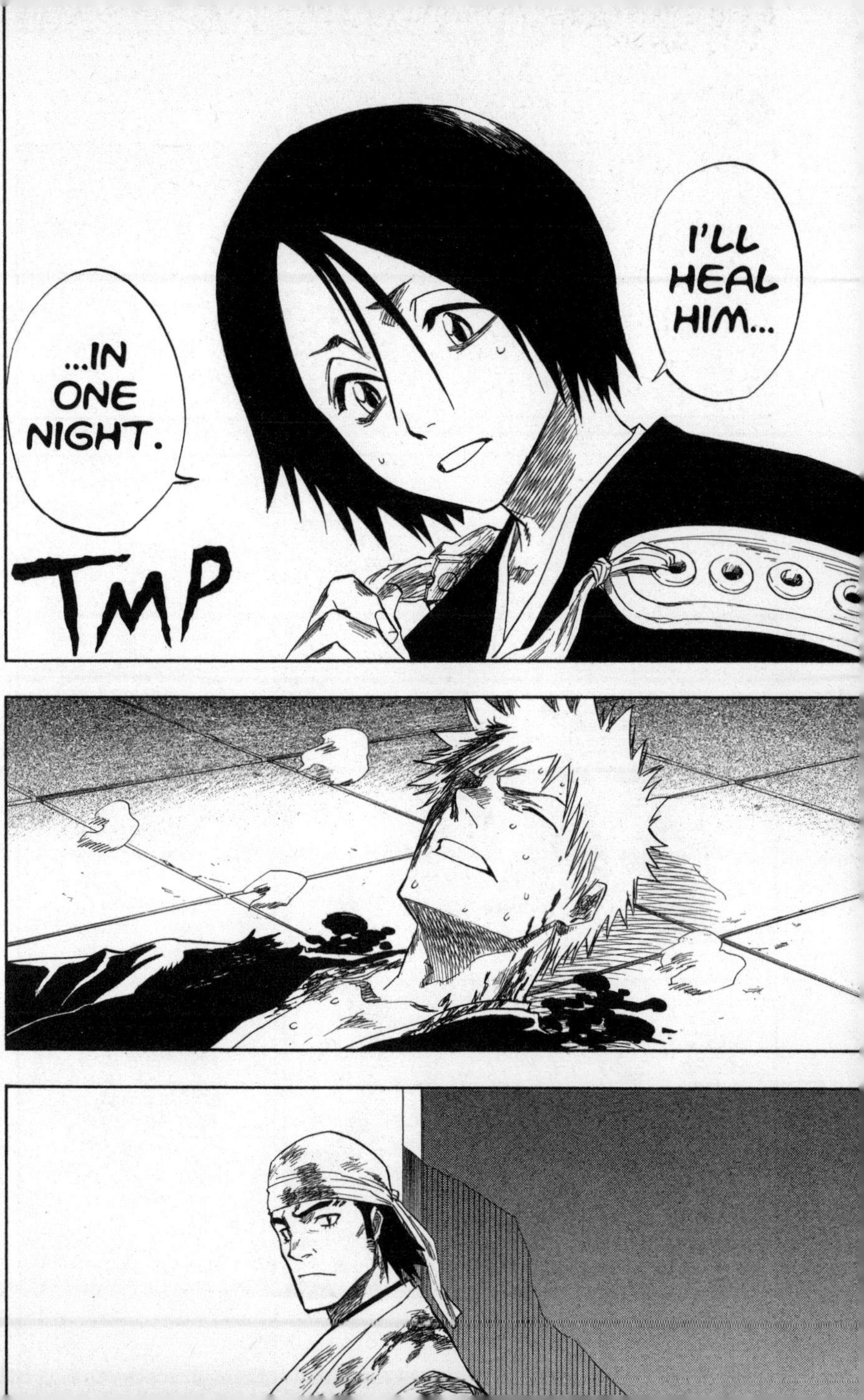
I'LL HEAL HIM...
...IN ONE NIGHT.
TMP

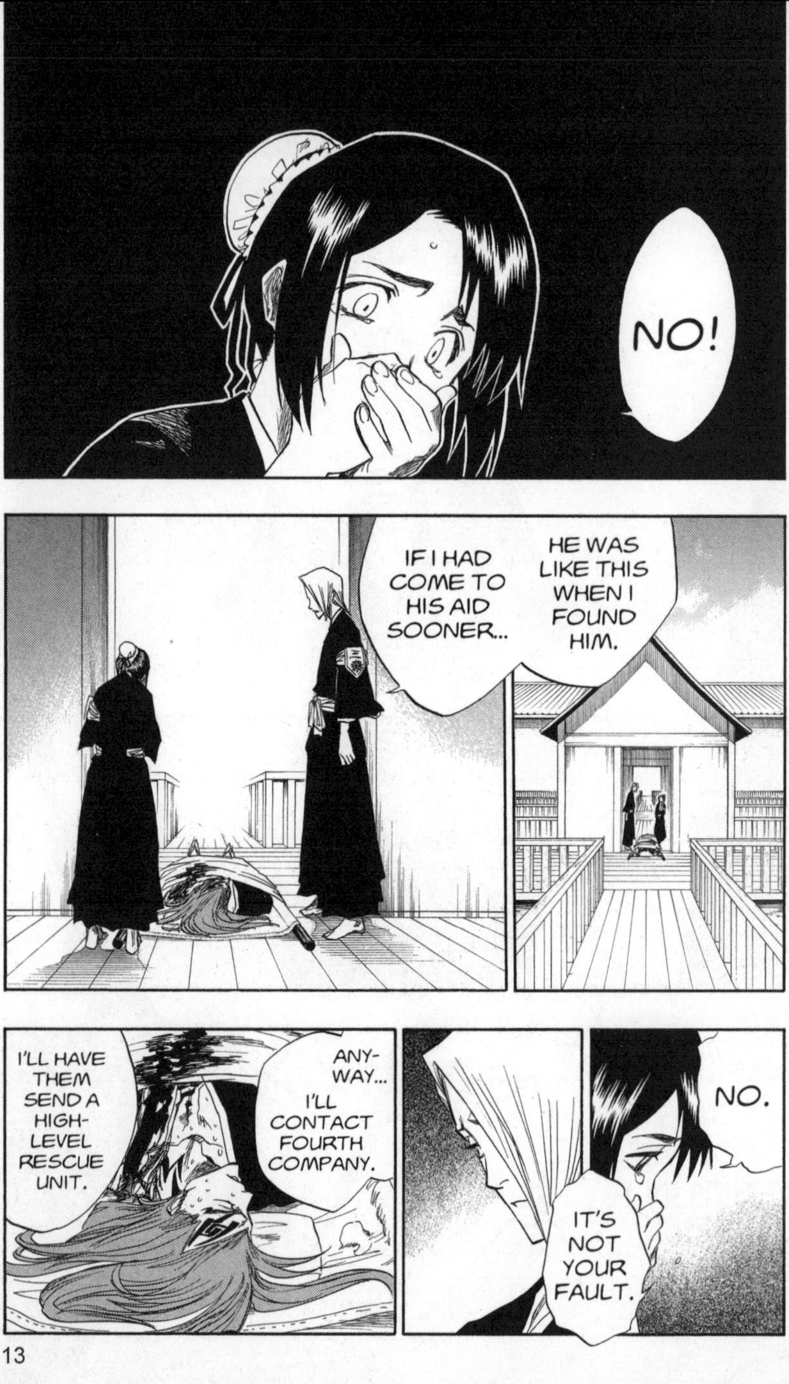
NO!
HE WAS LIKE THIS WHEN I FOUND HIM.
IF I HAD COME TO HIS AID SOONER...
NO.
IT'S NOT YOUR FAULT.
ANY-WAY... I'LL CONTACT FOURTH COMPANY.
I'LL HAVE THEM SEND A HIGH-LEVEL RESCUE UNIT.

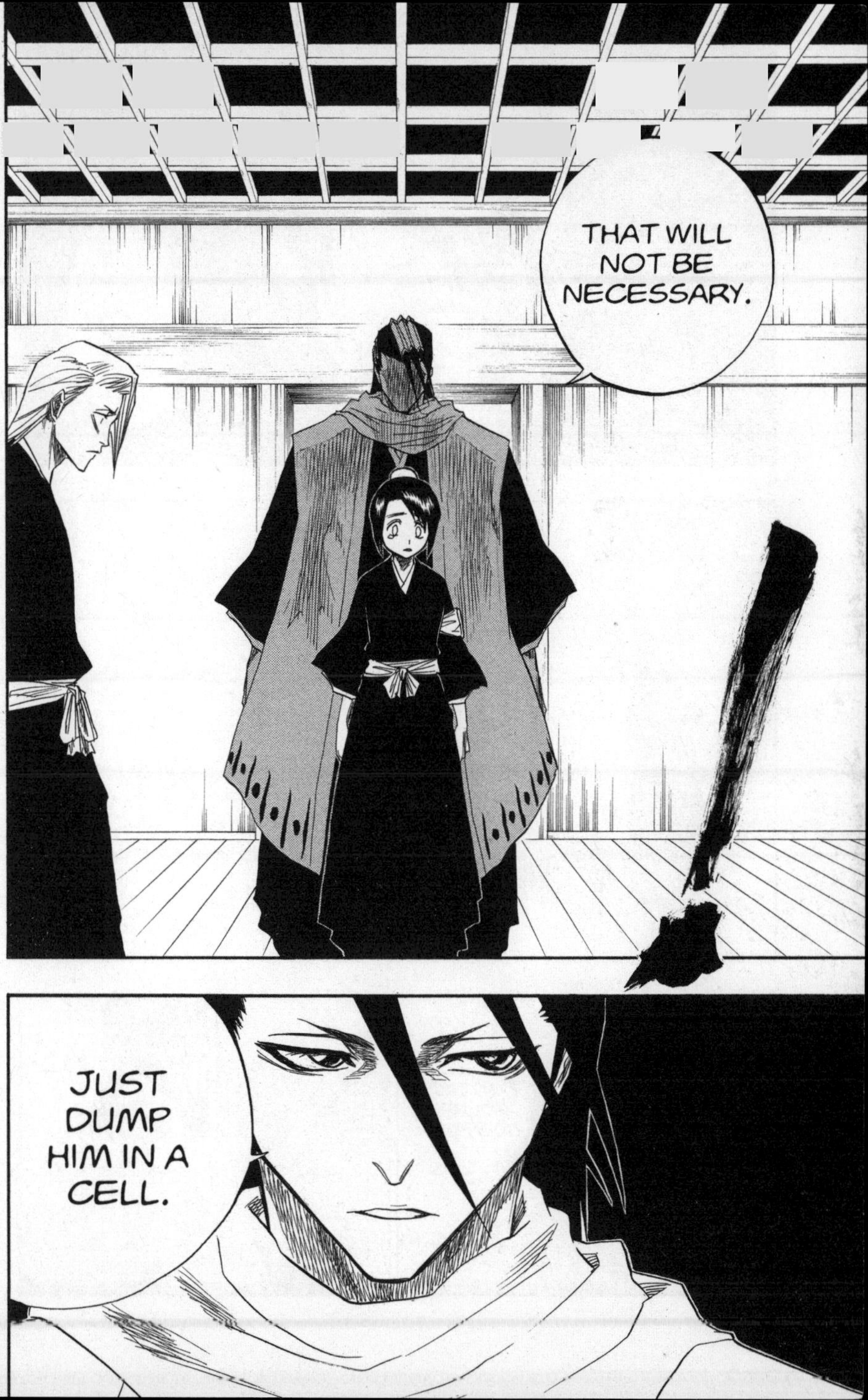
THAT WILL NOT BE NECESSARY.
JUST DUMP HIM IN A CELL.

READ THIS WAY

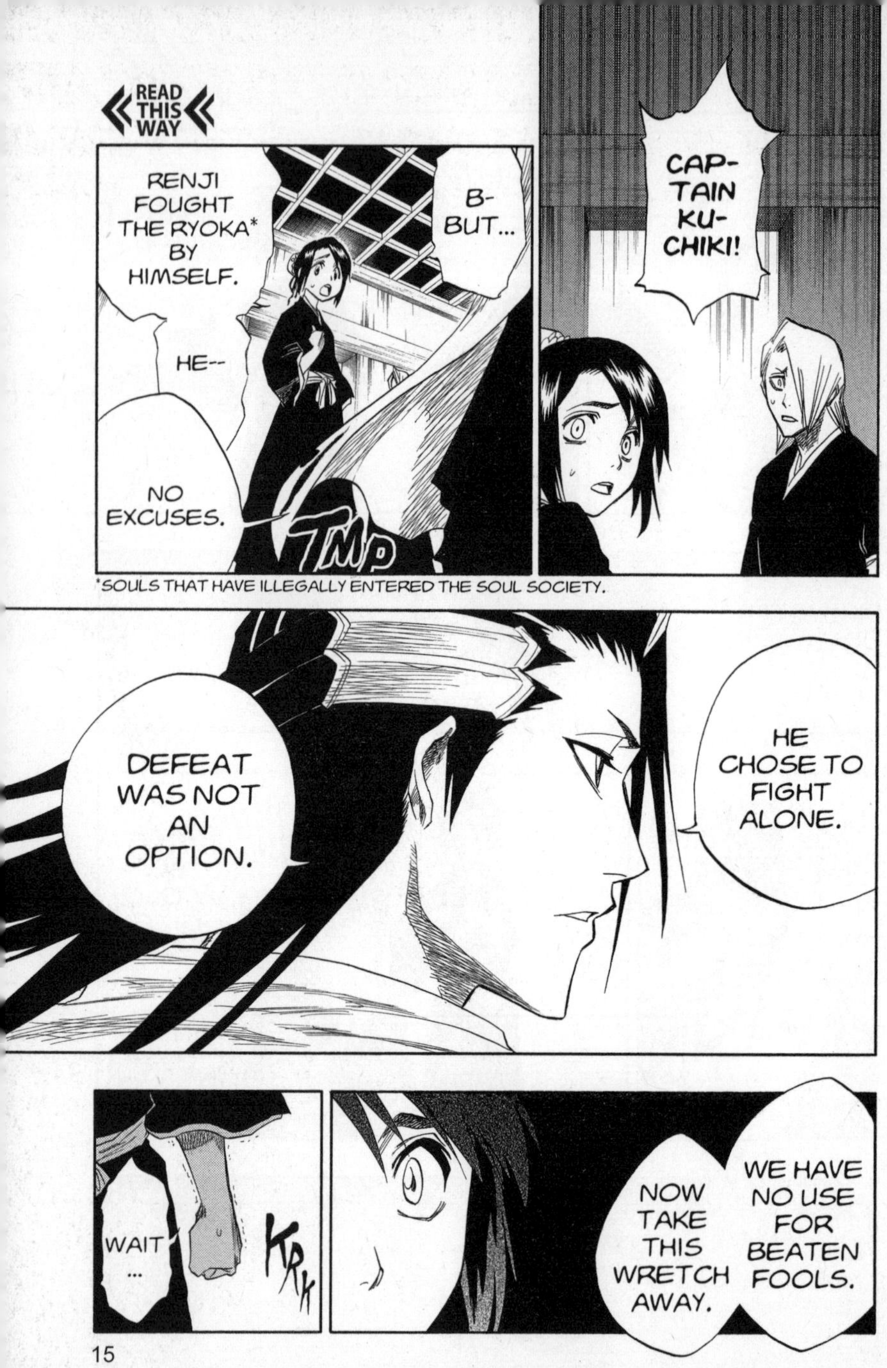
CAP-TAIN KU-CHIKI!
B-BUT...
RENJI FOUGHT THE RYOKA* BY HIMSELF.
HE--
NO EXCUSES.
TMP
HE CHOSE TO FIGHT ALONE.
DEFEAT WAS NOT AN OPTION.
WE HAVE NO USE FOR BEATEN FOOLS.
NOW TAKE THIS WRETCH AWAY.
KRK
WAIT ...

*SOULS THAT HAVE ILLEGALLY ENTERED THE SOUL SOCIETY.

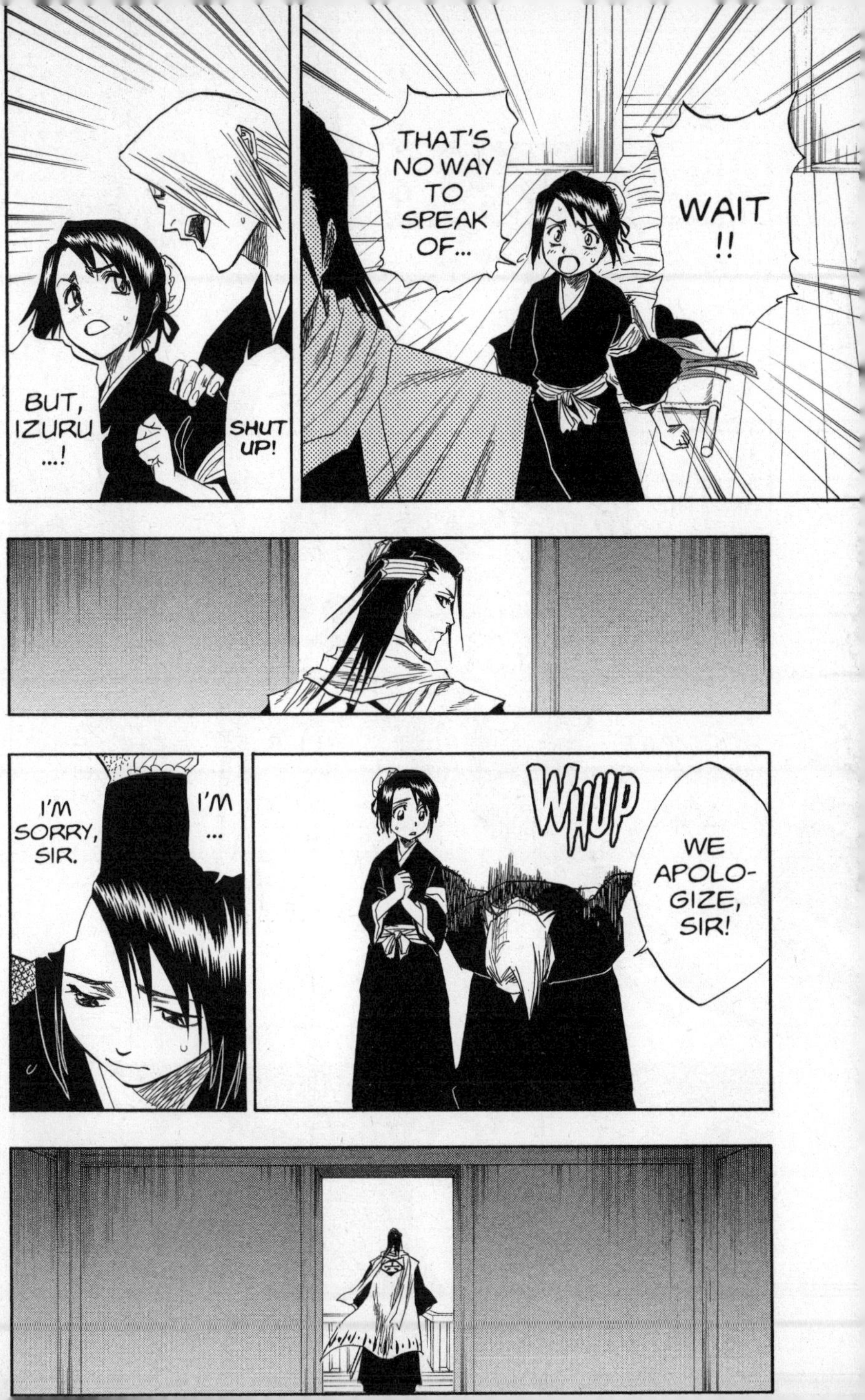
WAIT !!
THAT'S NO WAY TO SPEAK OF...
SHUT UP!
BUT, IZURU ...!
WE APOLO-GIZE, SIR!
WHUP
I'M ...
I'M SORRY, SIR.

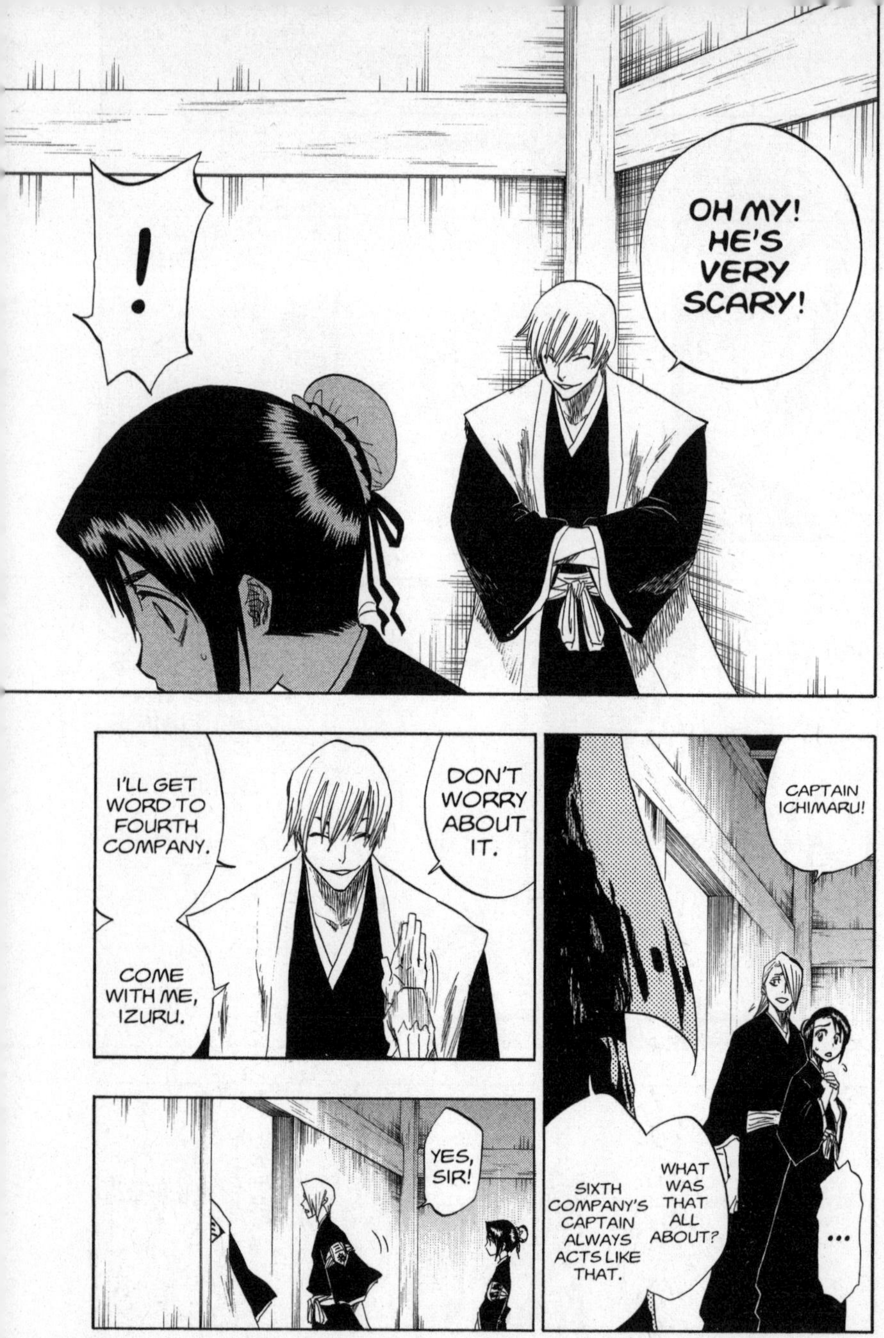
OH MY! HE'S VERY SCARY!
!
CAPTAIN ICHIMARU!
WHAT WAS THAT ALL ABOUT?
SIXTH COMPANY'S CAPTAIN ALWAYS ACTS LIKE THAT.
...
DON'T WORRY ABOUT IT.
I'LL GET WORD TO FOURTH COMPANY.
COME WITH ME, IZURU.
YES, SIR!

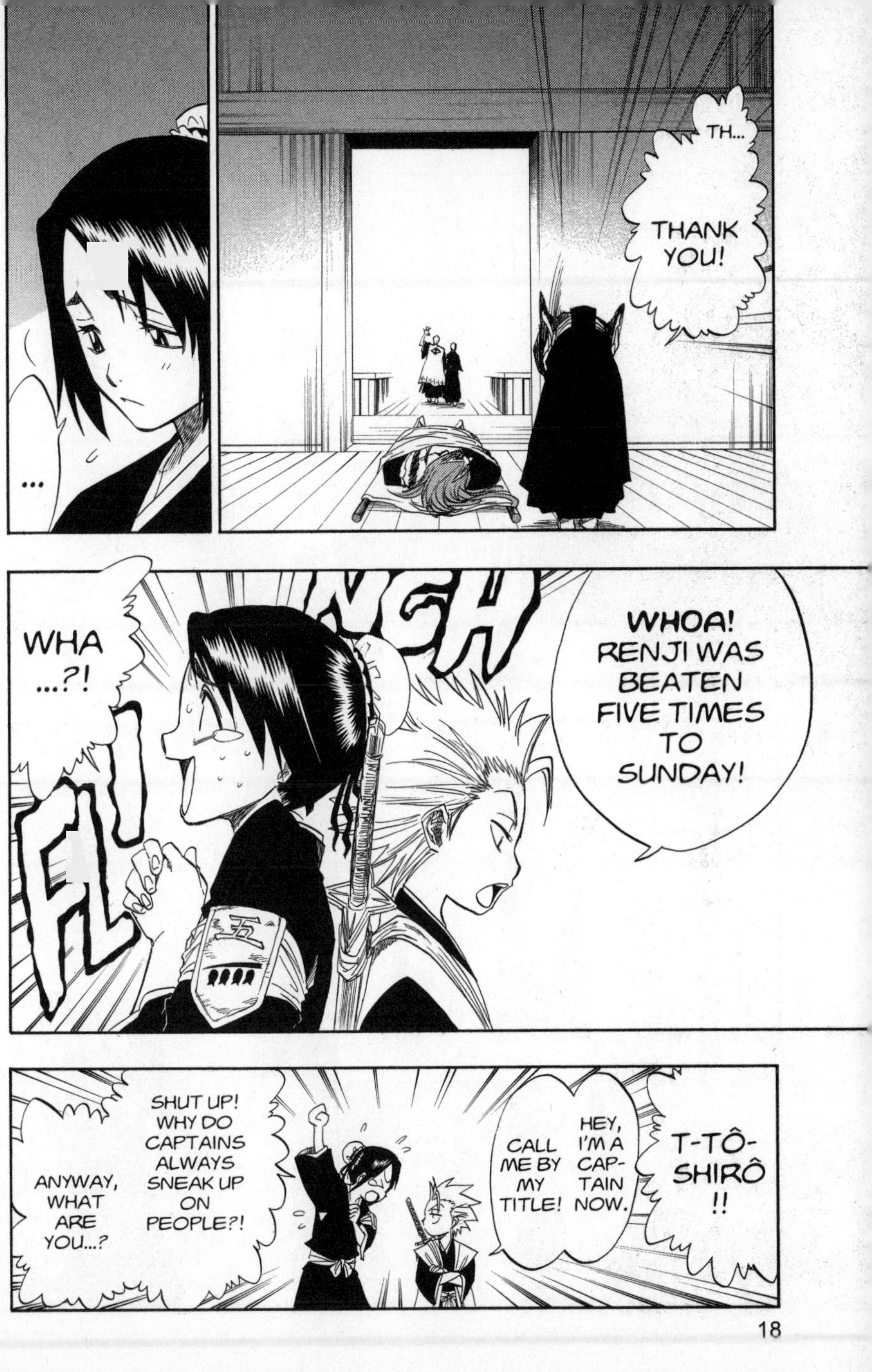
TH...
THANK YOU!
...
WHOA! RENJI WAS BEATEN FIVE TIMES TO SUNDAY!
WHA ...?!
T-TÔ-SHIRÔ !!
HEY, I'M A CAPTAIN NOW.
CALL ME BY MY TITLE!
SHUT UP! WHY DO CAPTAINS ALWAYS SNEAK UP ON PEOPLE?!
ANYWAY, WHAT ARE YOU...?

READ THIS WAY

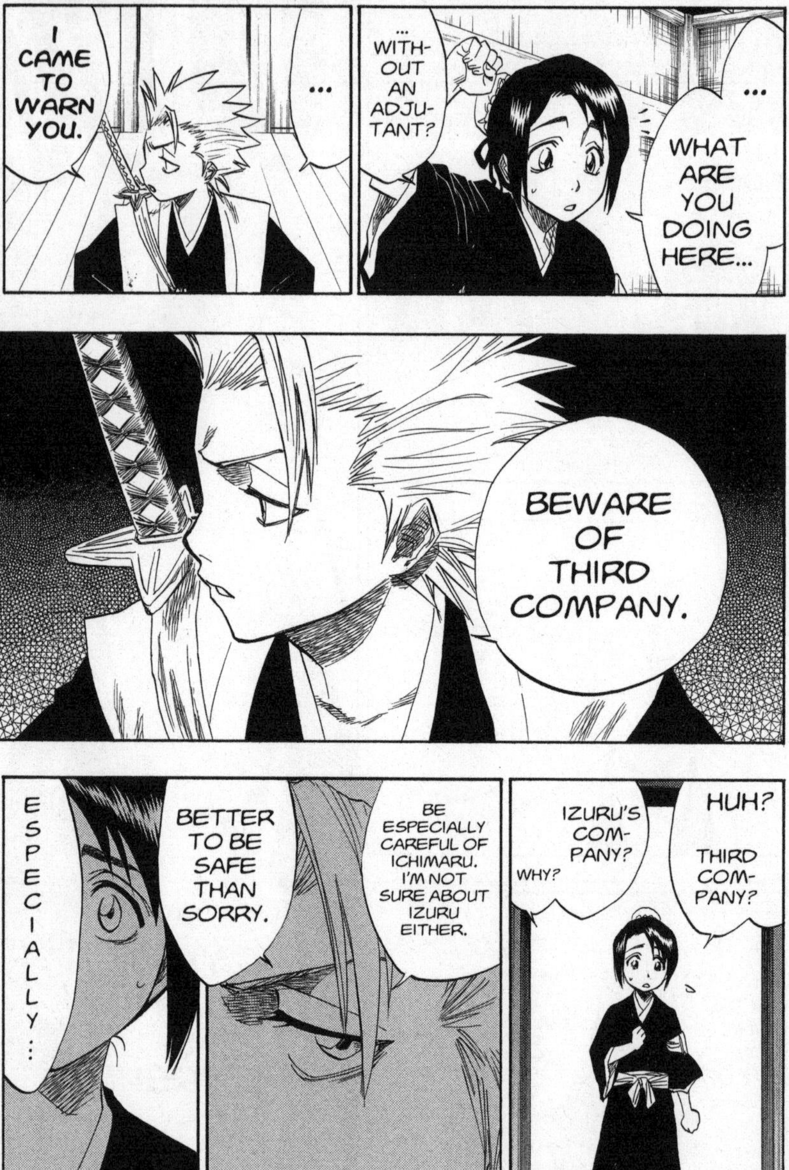
...
WHAT ARE YOU DOING HERE...
... WITH-OUT AN ADJU-TANT?
...
I CAME TO WARN YOU.
BEWARE OF THIRD COMPANY.
HUH?
THIRD COM-PANY?
IZURU'S COM-PANY?
WHY?
BE ESPECIALLY CAREFUL OF ICHIMARU. I'M NOT SURE ABOUT IZURU EITHER.
BETTER TO BE SAFE THAN SORRY.
ESPECIALLY...

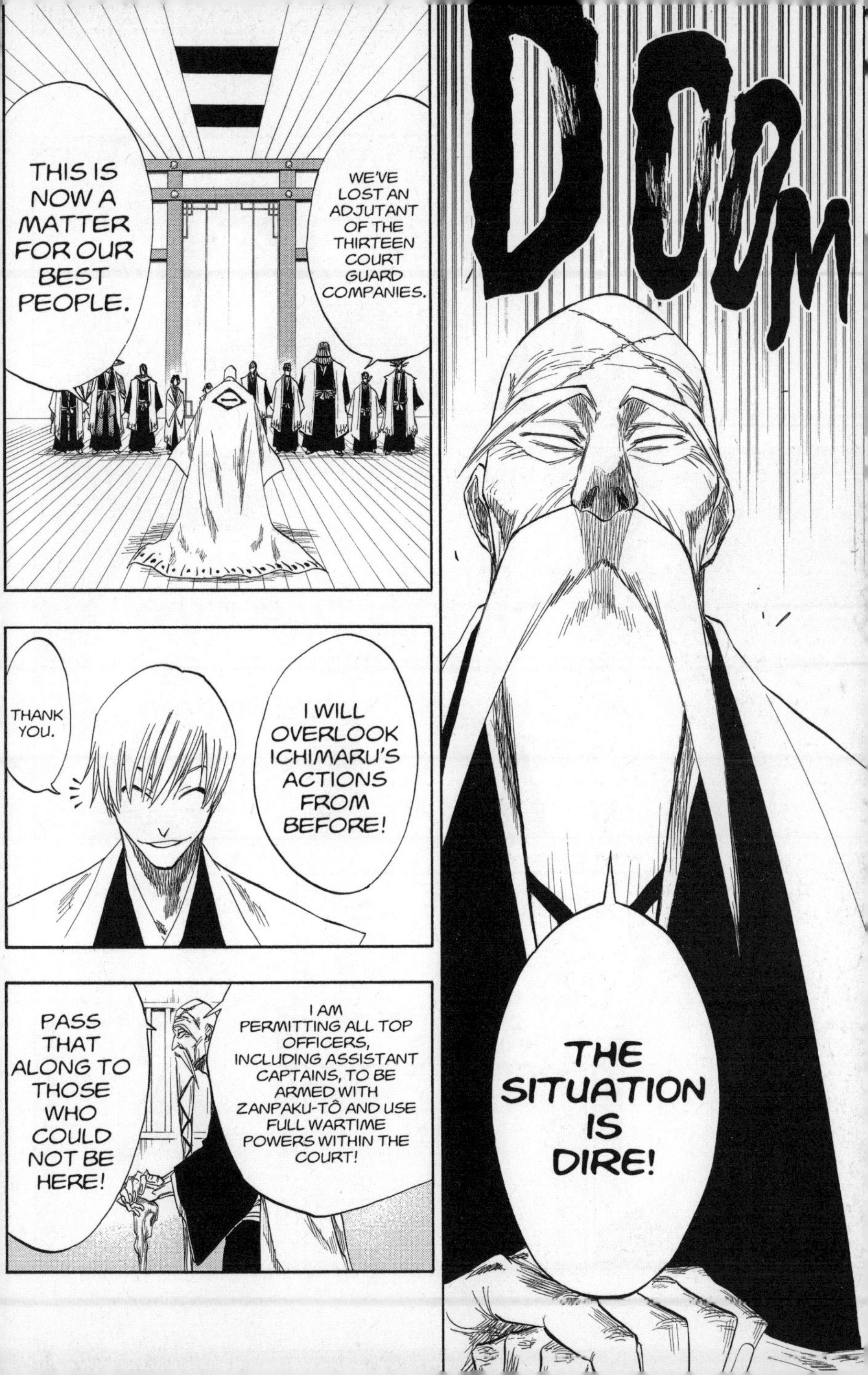
DOOM
THE SITUATION IS DIRE!
WE'VE LOST AN ADJUTANT OF THE THIRTEEN COURT GUARD COMPANIES.
THIS IS NOW A MATTER FOR OUR BEST PEOPLE.
I WILL OVERLOOK ICHIMARU'S ACTIONS FROM BEFORE!
THANK YOU.
I AM PERMITTING ALL TOP OFFICERS, INCLUDING ASSISTANT CAPTAINS, TO BE ARMED WITH ZANPAKU-TÔ AND USE FULL WARTIME POWERS WITHIN THE COURT!
PASS THAT ALONG TO THOSE WHO COULD NOT BE HERE!

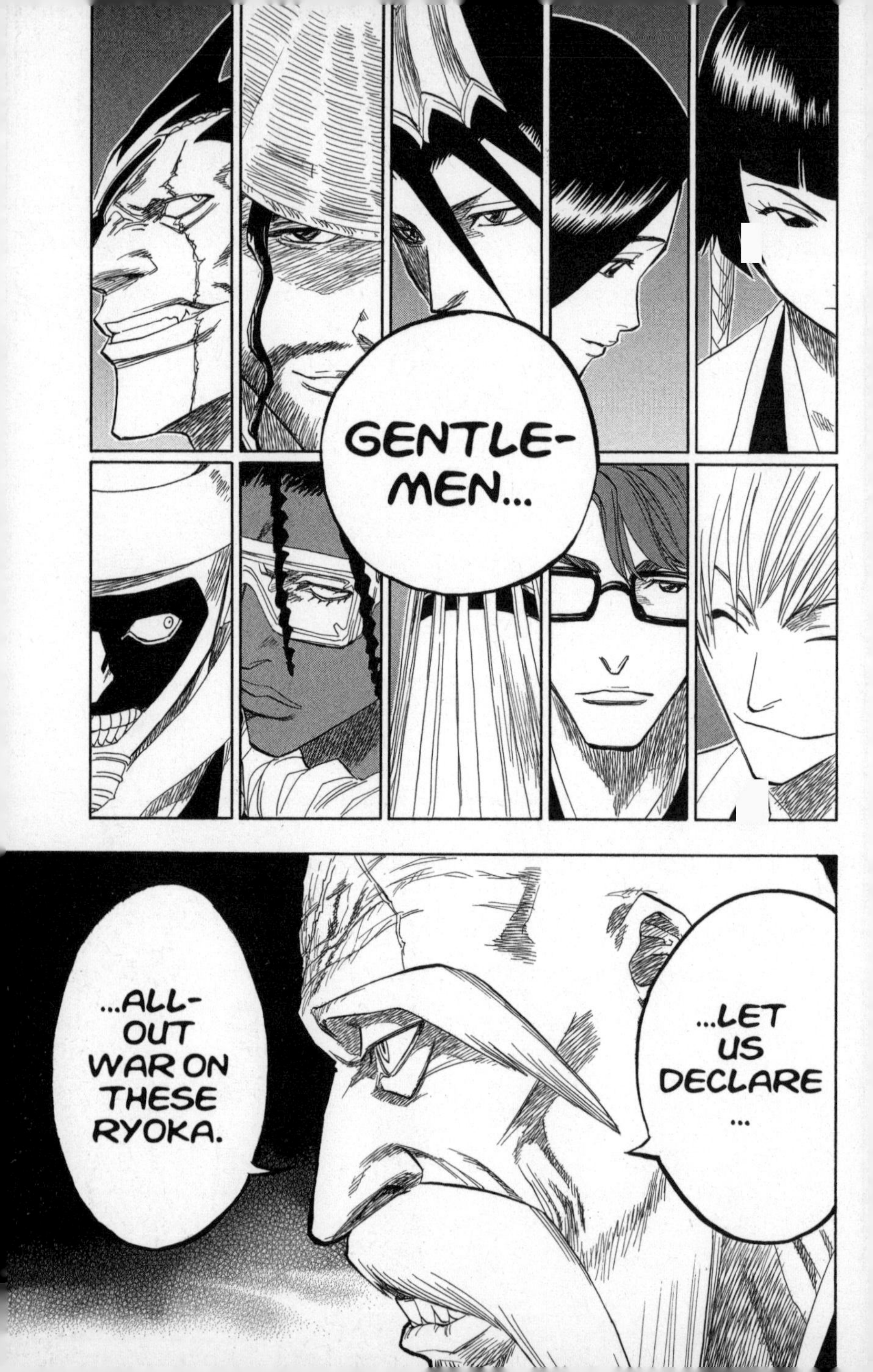
GENTLE-
MEN...
...LET US DECLARE ...
...ALL-OUT WAR ON THESE RYOKA.

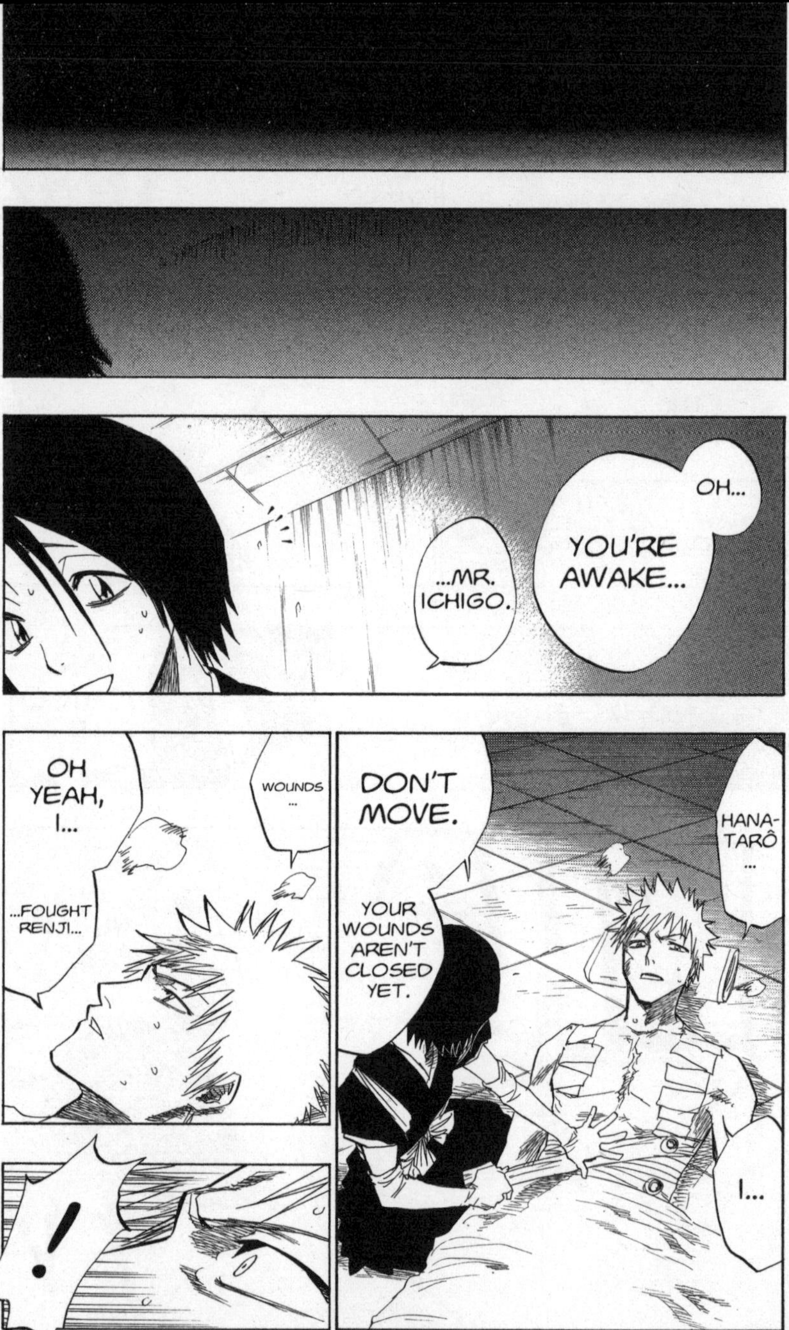
OH...
YOU'RE AWAKE...
...MR. ICHIGO.
HANA-TARÔ ...
I...
DON'T MOVE.
YOUR WOUNDS AREN'T CLOSED YET.
WOUNDS ...
OH YEAH, I...
...FOUGHT RENJI...
!

100. FLOWER ON THE PRECIPICE

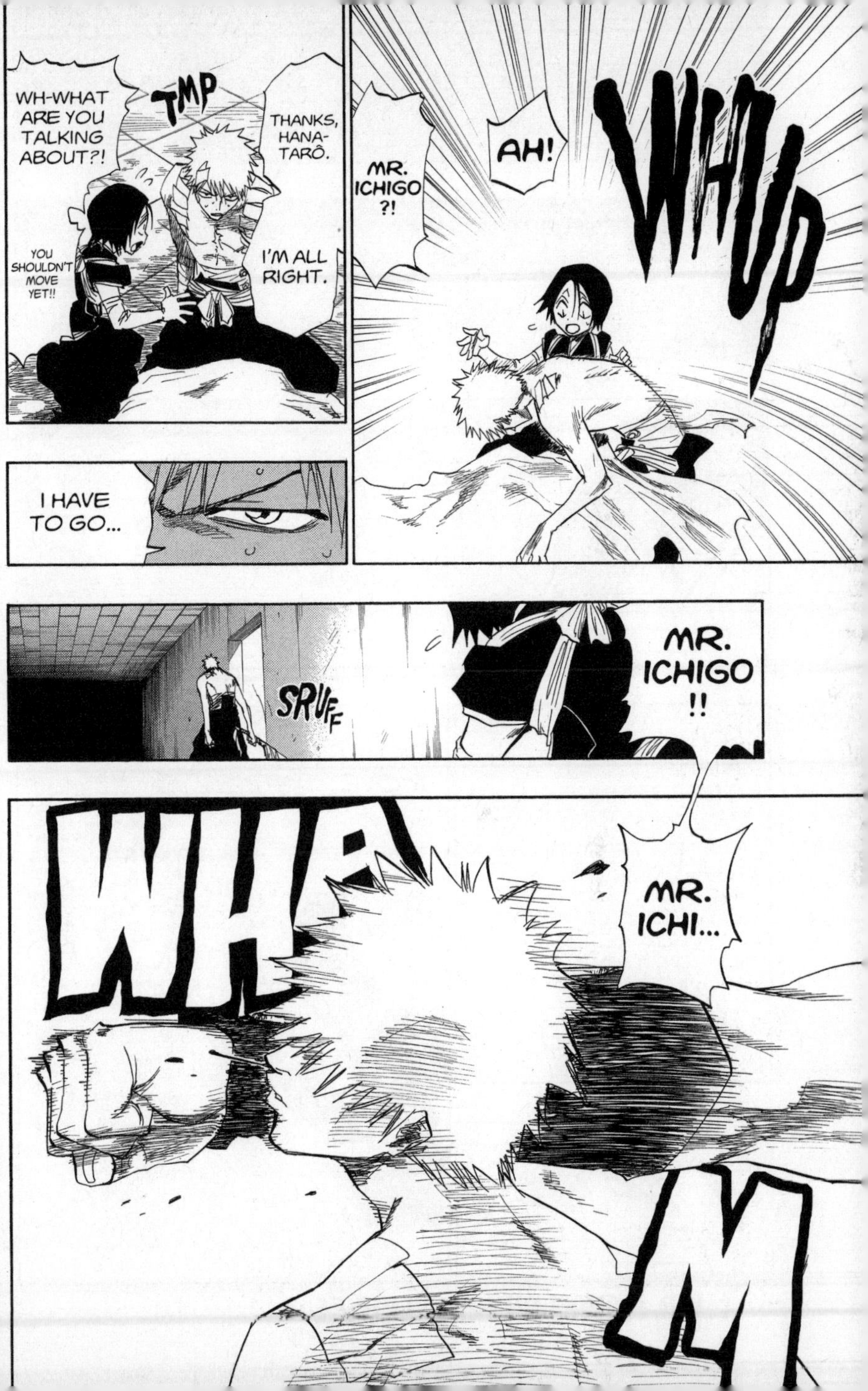
WHUP
AH!
MR. ICHIGO?!
THANKS, HANA-TARÔ.
TMP
WH-WHAT ARE YOU TALKING ABOUT?!
I'M ALL RIGHT.
YOU SHOULDN'T MOVE YET!!
I HAVE TO GO...
MR. ICHIGO!!
SRUFF
MR. ICHI...
WHAM

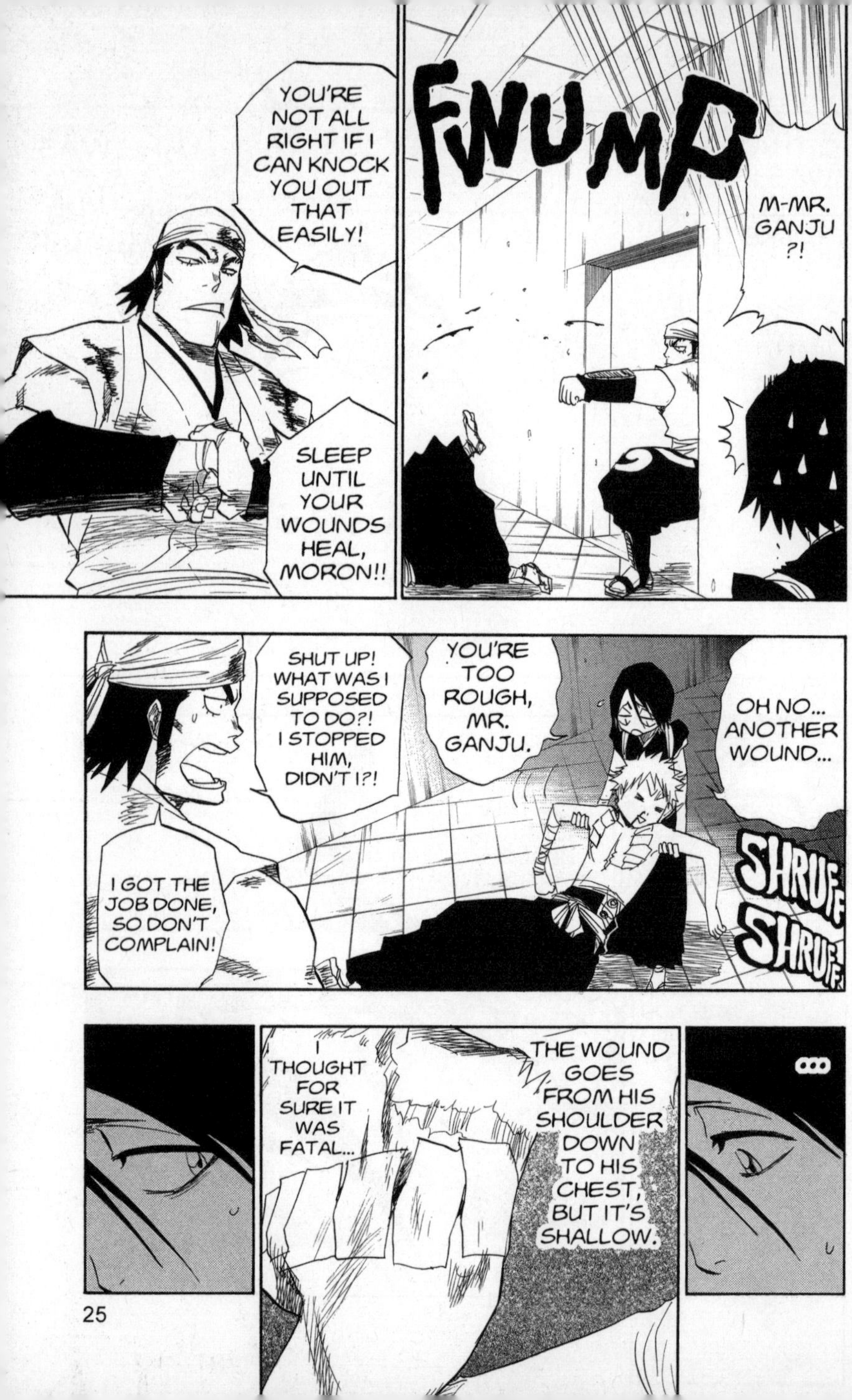
FWUMP
M-MR. GANJU?!
YOU'RE NOT ALL RIGHT IF I CAN KNOCK YOU OUT THAT EASILY!
SLEEP UNTIL YOUR WOUNDS HEAL, MORON!!
OH NO... ANOTHER WOUND...
SHRUFF SHRUFF
YOU'RE TOO ROUGH, MR. GANJU.
SHUT UP! WHAT WAS I SUPPOSED TO DO?! I STOPPED HIM, DIDN'T I?!
I GOT THE JOB DONE, SO DON'T COMPLAIN!
...
THE WOUND GOES FROM HIS SHOULDER DOWN TO HIS CHEST, BUT IT'S SHALLOW.
I THOUGHT FOR SURE IT WAS FATAL...

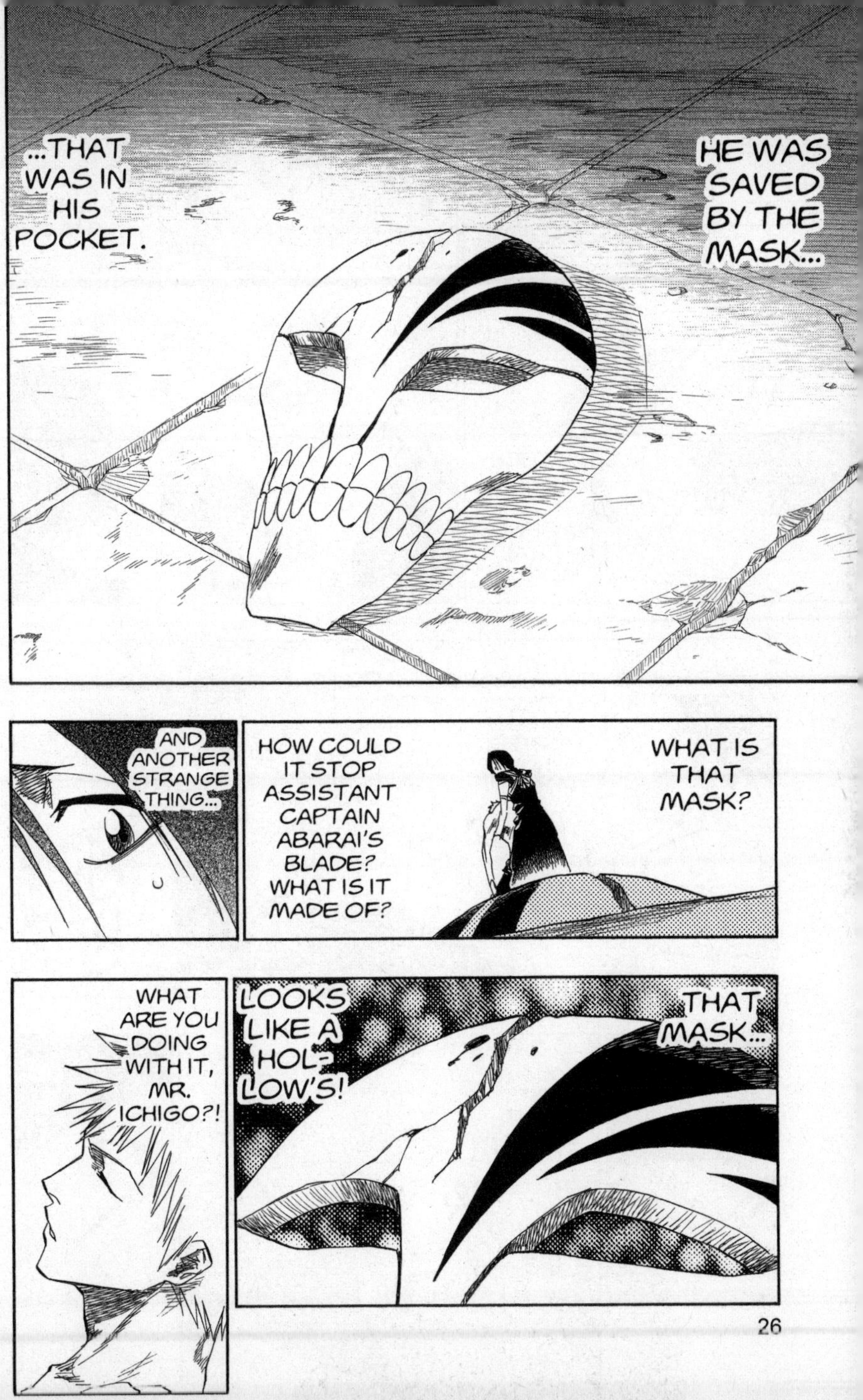
HE WAS SAVED BY THE MASK...
...THAT WAS IN HIS POCKET.
WHAT IS THAT MASK?
HOW COULD IT STOP ASSISTANT CAPTAIN ABARAI'S BLADE? WHAT IS IT MADE OF?
AND ANOTHER STRANGE THING...
THAT MASK...
LOOKS LIKE A HOL-LOW'S!
WHAT ARE YOU DOING WITH IT, MR. ICHIGO?!

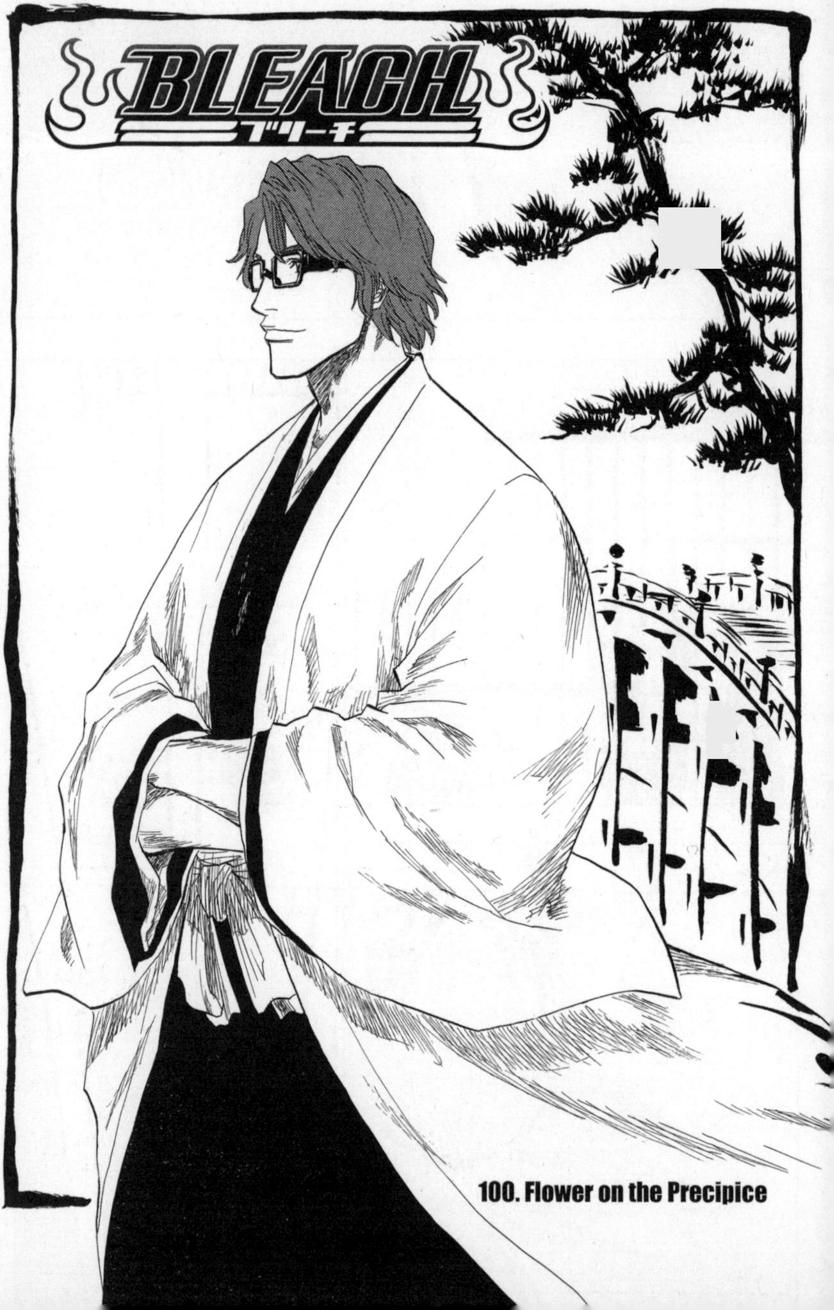
BLEACH
ブリーチ

100. Flower on the Precipice

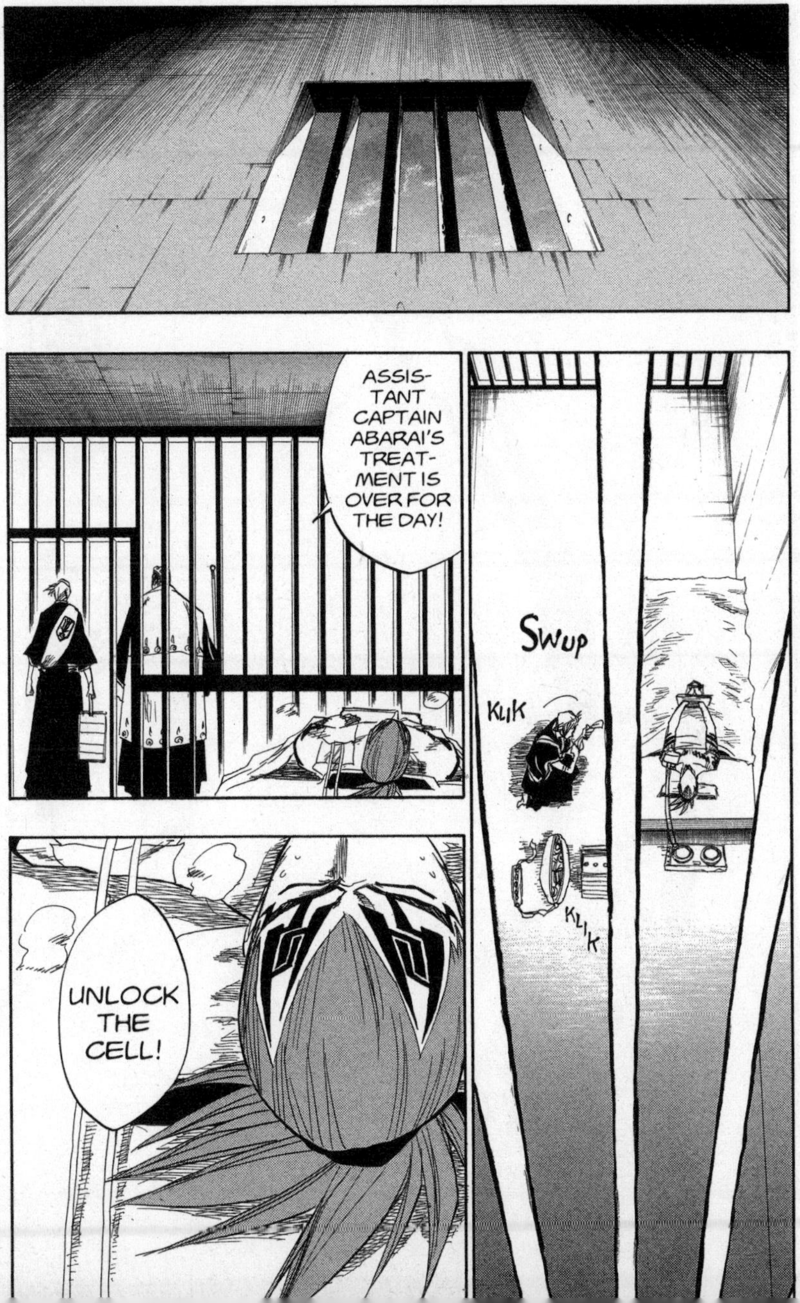
SWUP
KLIK
KLIK
ASSISTANT CAPTAIN ABARAI'S TREATMENT IS OVER FOR THE DAY!
UNLOCK THE CELL!

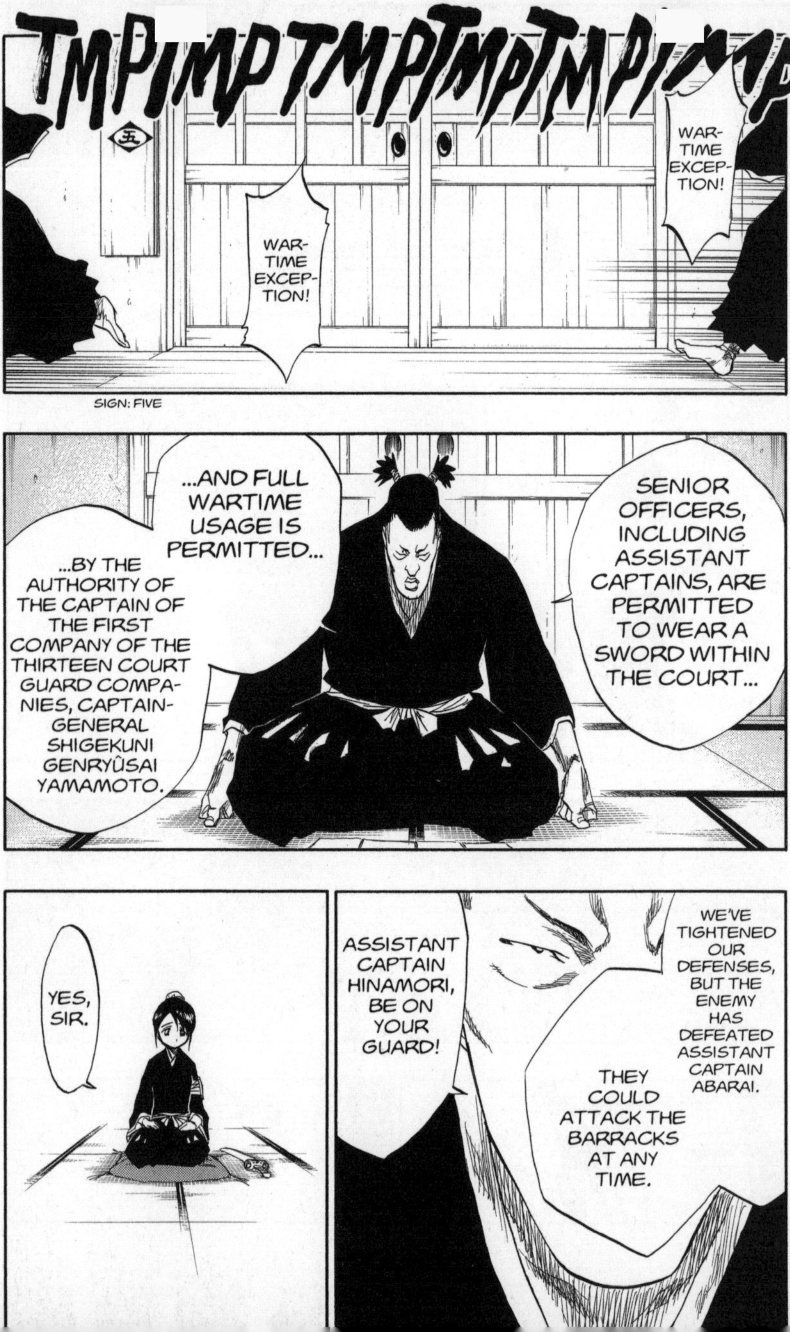
WAR-TIME EXCEP-TION!
WAR-TIME EXCEP-TION!
SIGN: FIVE
SENIOR OFFICERS, INCLUDING ASSISTANT CAPTAINS, ARE PERMITTED TO WEAR A SWORD WITHIN THE COURT...
...AND FULL WARTIME USAGE IS PERMITTED...
...BY THE AUTHORITY OF THE CAPTAIN OF THE FIRST COMPANY OF THE THIRTEEN COURT GUARD COMPA-NIES, CAPTAIN-GENERAL SHIGEKUNI GENRYÛSAI YAMAMOTO.
WE'VE TIGHTENED OUR DEFENSES, BUT THE ENEMY HAS DEFEATED ASSISTANT CAPTAIN ABARAI.
THEY COULD ATTACK THE BARRACKS AT ANY TIME.
ASSISTANT CAPTAIN HINAMORI, BE ON YOUR GUARD!
YES, SIR.

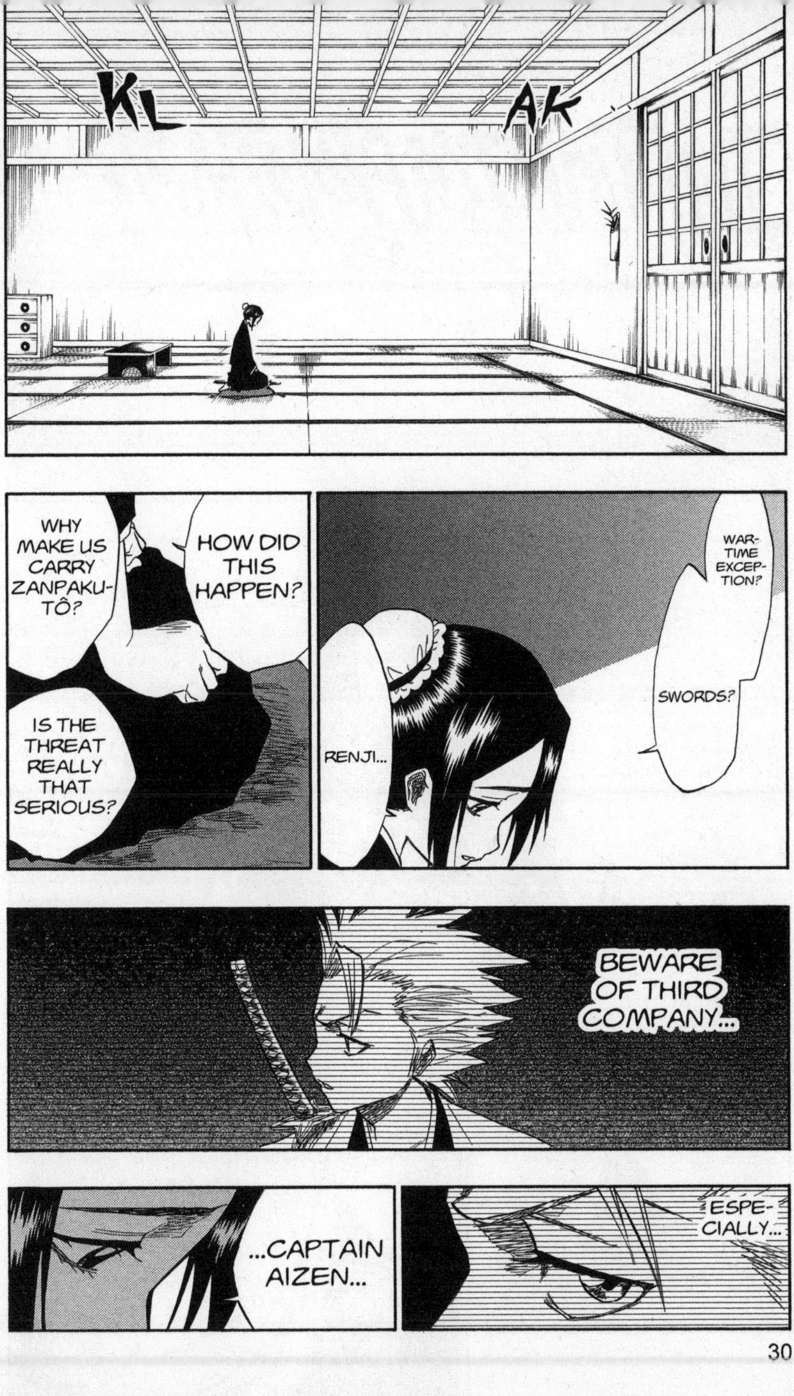
KLAK
WARTIME EXCEPTION?
SWORDS?
RENJI...
HOW DID THIS HAPPEN?
WHY MAKE US CARRY ZANPAKUTÔ?
IS THE THREAT REALLY THAT SERIOUS?
BEWARE OF THIRD COMPANY...
ESPECIALLY...
...CAPTAIN AIZEN...

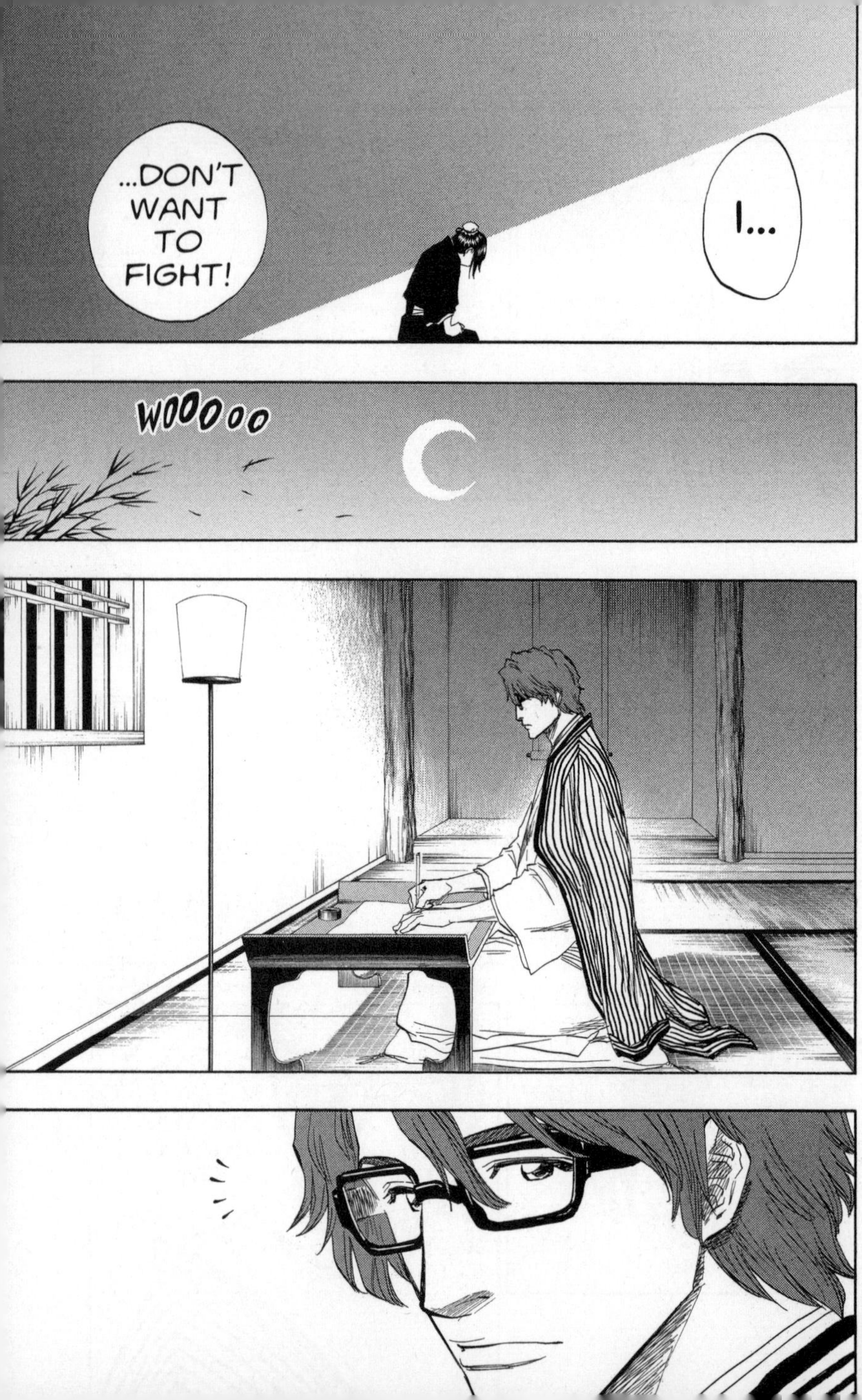
I...
...DON'T WANT TO FIGHT!
WOOOOO

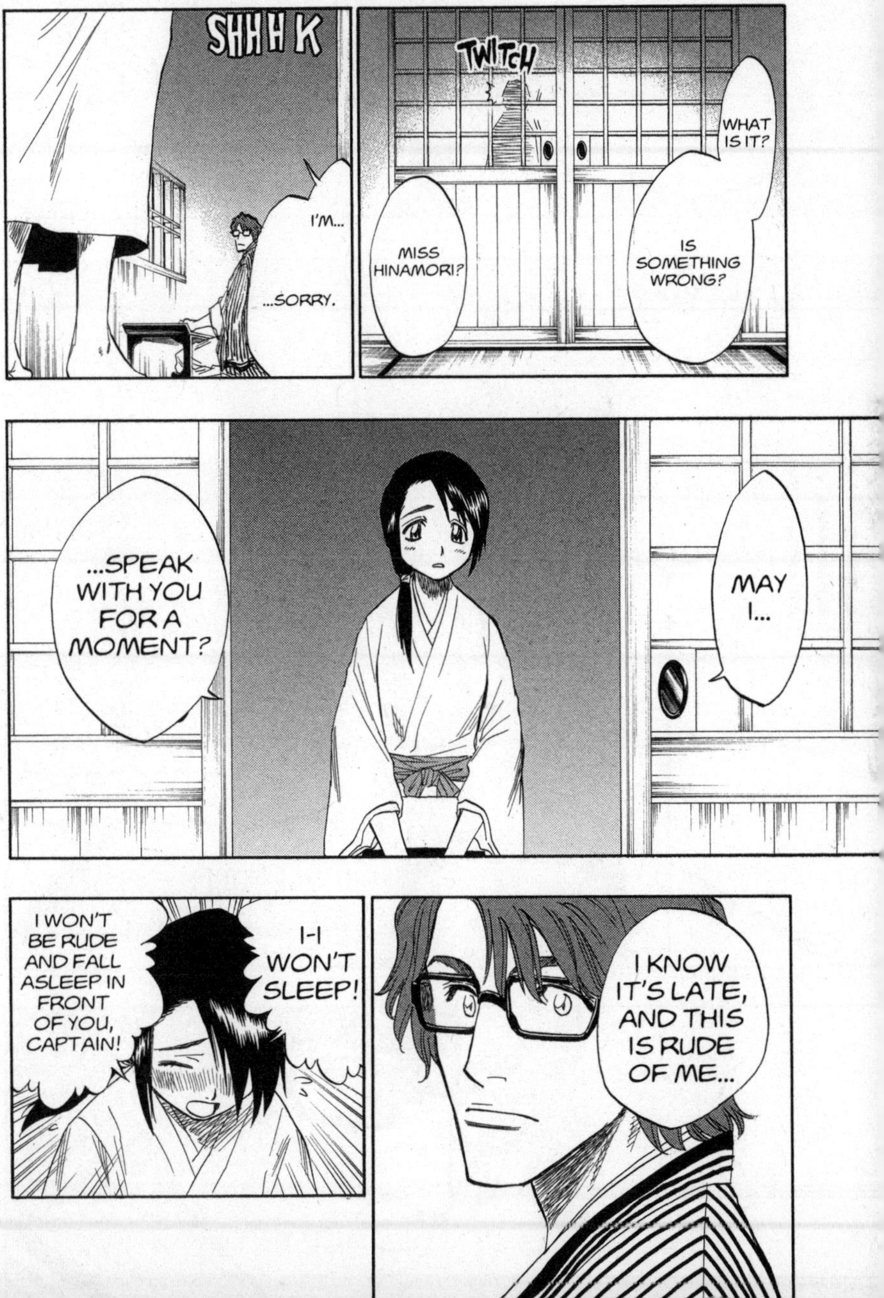
TWITCH
WHAT IS IT?
IS SOMETHING WRONG?
MISS HINAMORI?
SHHHK
I'M...
...SORRY.
MAY I...
...SPEAK WITH YOU FOR A MOMENT?
I KNOW IT'S LATE, AND THIS IS RUDE OF ME...
I-I WON'T SLEEP!
I WON'T BE RUDE AND FALL ASLEEP IN FRONT OF YOU, CAPTAIN!

READ THIS WAY

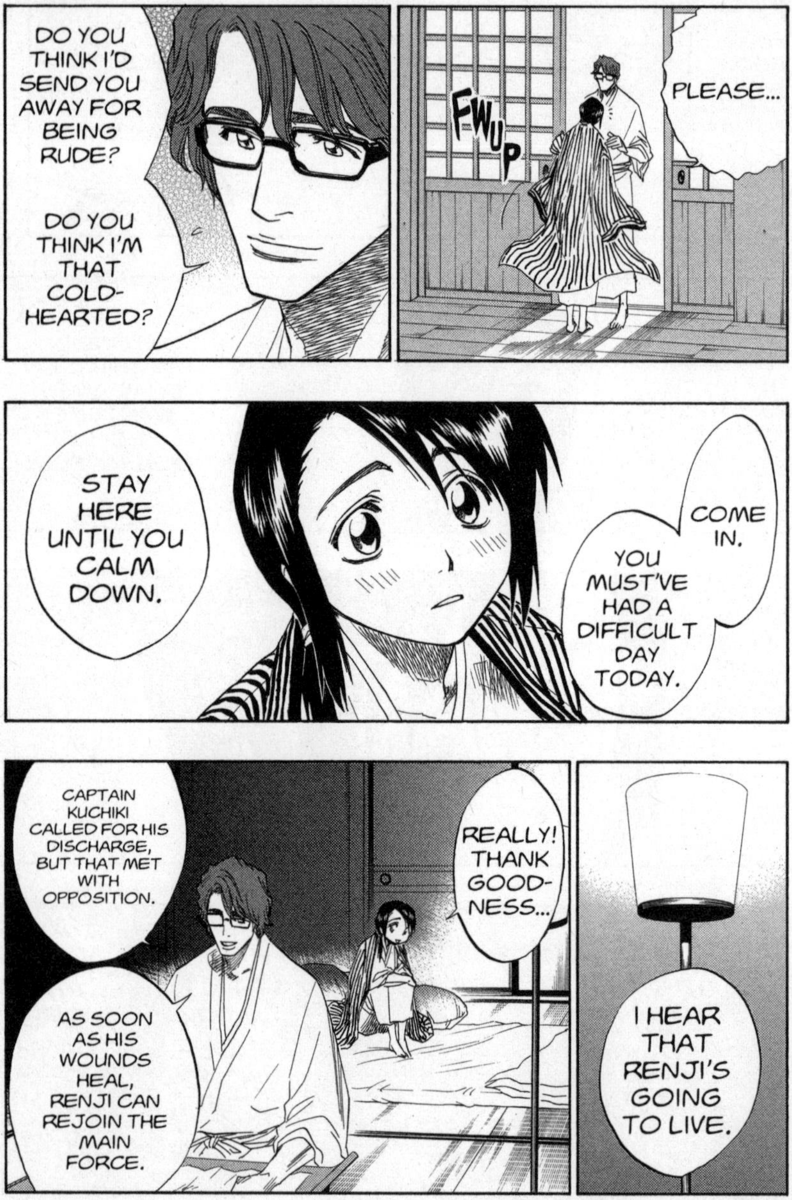
PLEASE...
FWUP
DO YOU THINK I'D SEND YOU AWAY FOR BEING RUDE?
DO YOU THINK I'M THAT COLD-HEARTED?
COME IN.
YOU MUST'VE HAD A DIFFICULT DAY TODAY.
STAY HERE UNTIL YOU CALM DOWN.
I HEAR THAT RENJI'S GOING TO LIVE.
REALLY! THANK GOOD-NESS...
CAPTAIN KUCHIKI CALLED FOR HIS DISCHARGE, BUT THAT MET WITH OPPOSITION.
AS SOON AS HIS WOUNDS HEAL, RENJI CAN REJOIN THE MAIN FORCE.

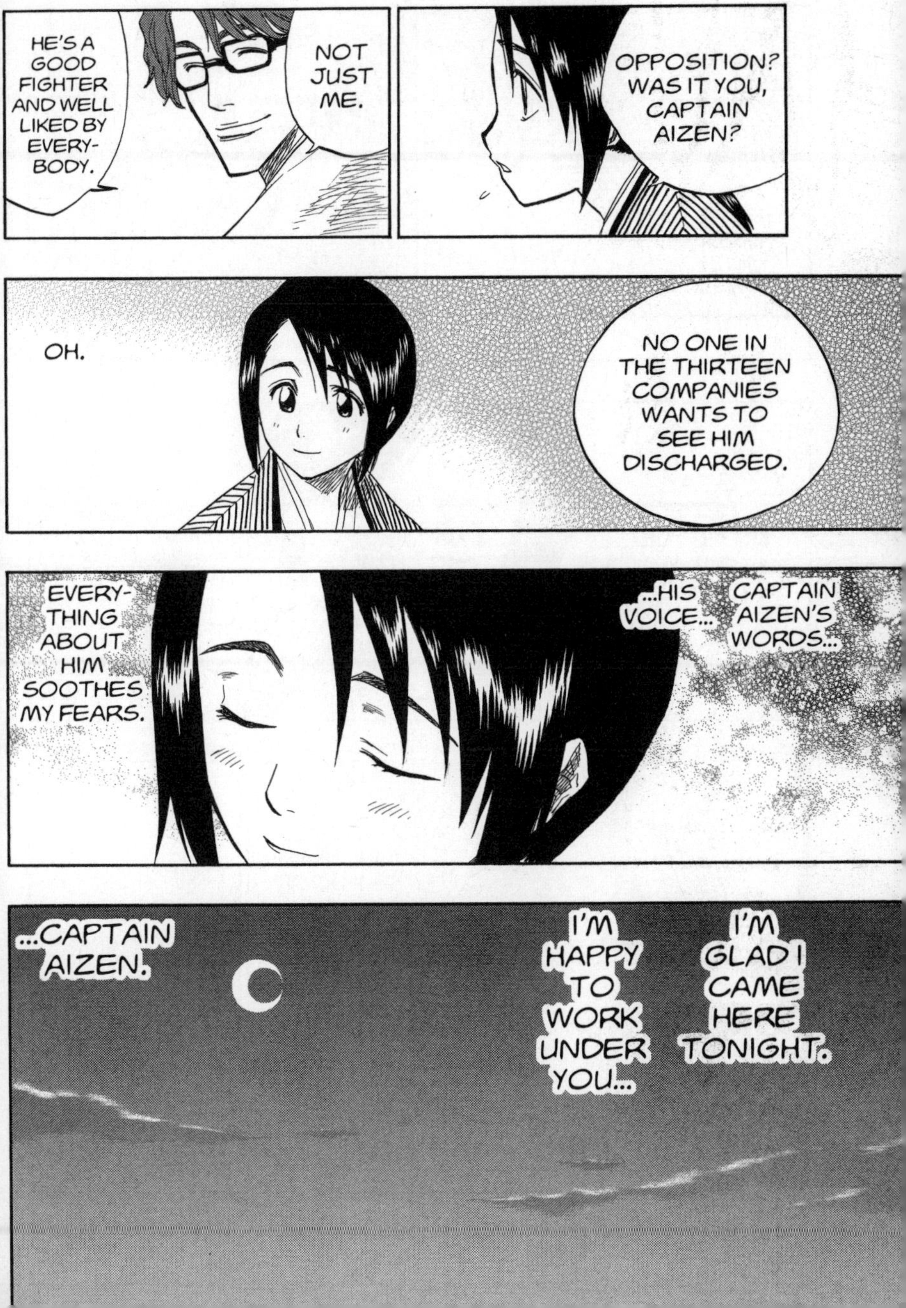
OPPOSITION? WAS IT YOU, CAPTAIN AIZEN?
NOT JUST ME.
HE'S A GOOD FIGHTER AND WELL LIKED BY EVERY-BODY.
NO ONE IN THE THIRTEEN COMPANIES WANTS TO SEE HIM DISCHARGED.
OH.
CAPTAIN AIZEN'S WORDS...
...HIS VOICE...
EVERY-THING ABOUT HIM SOOTHES MY FEARS.
I'M GLAD I CAME HERE TONIGHT.
I'M HAPPY TO WORK UNDER YOU...
...CAPTAIN AIZEN.

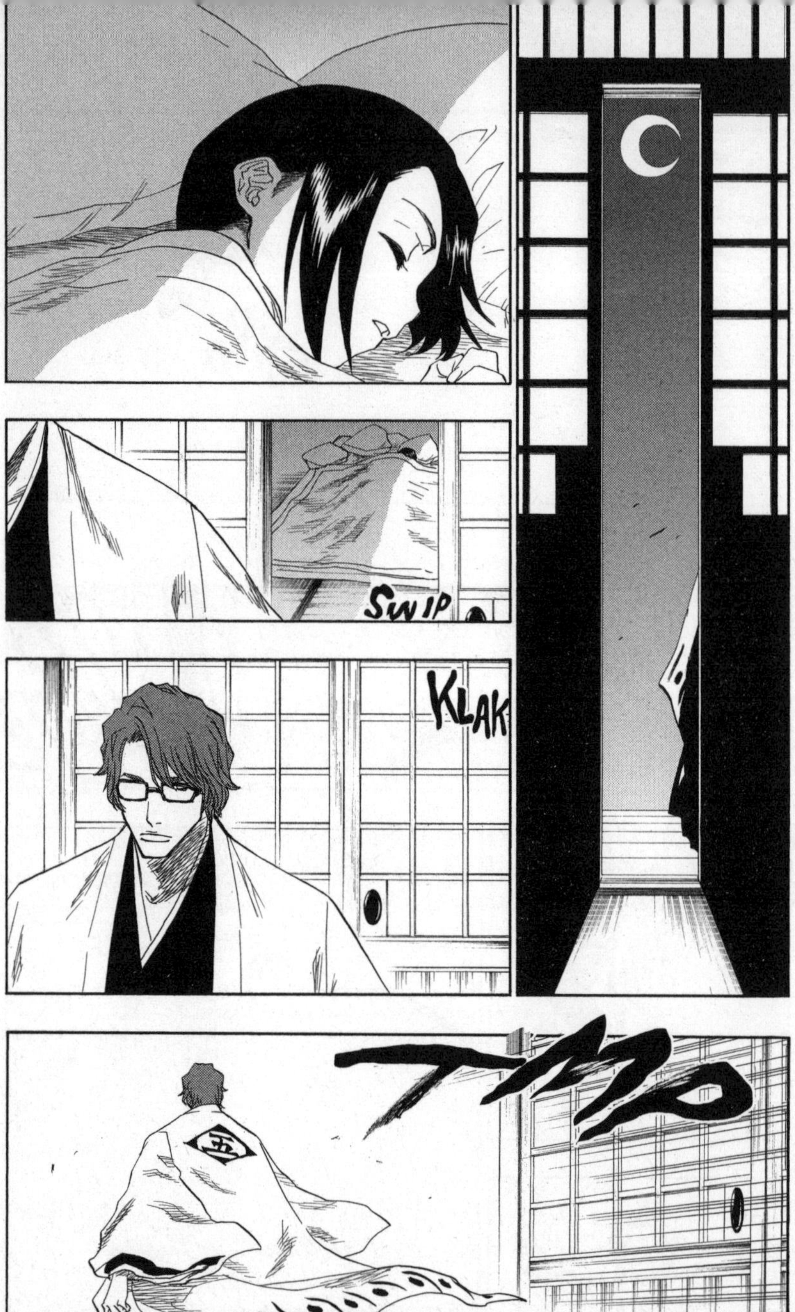
SWIP
KLAK
TAP

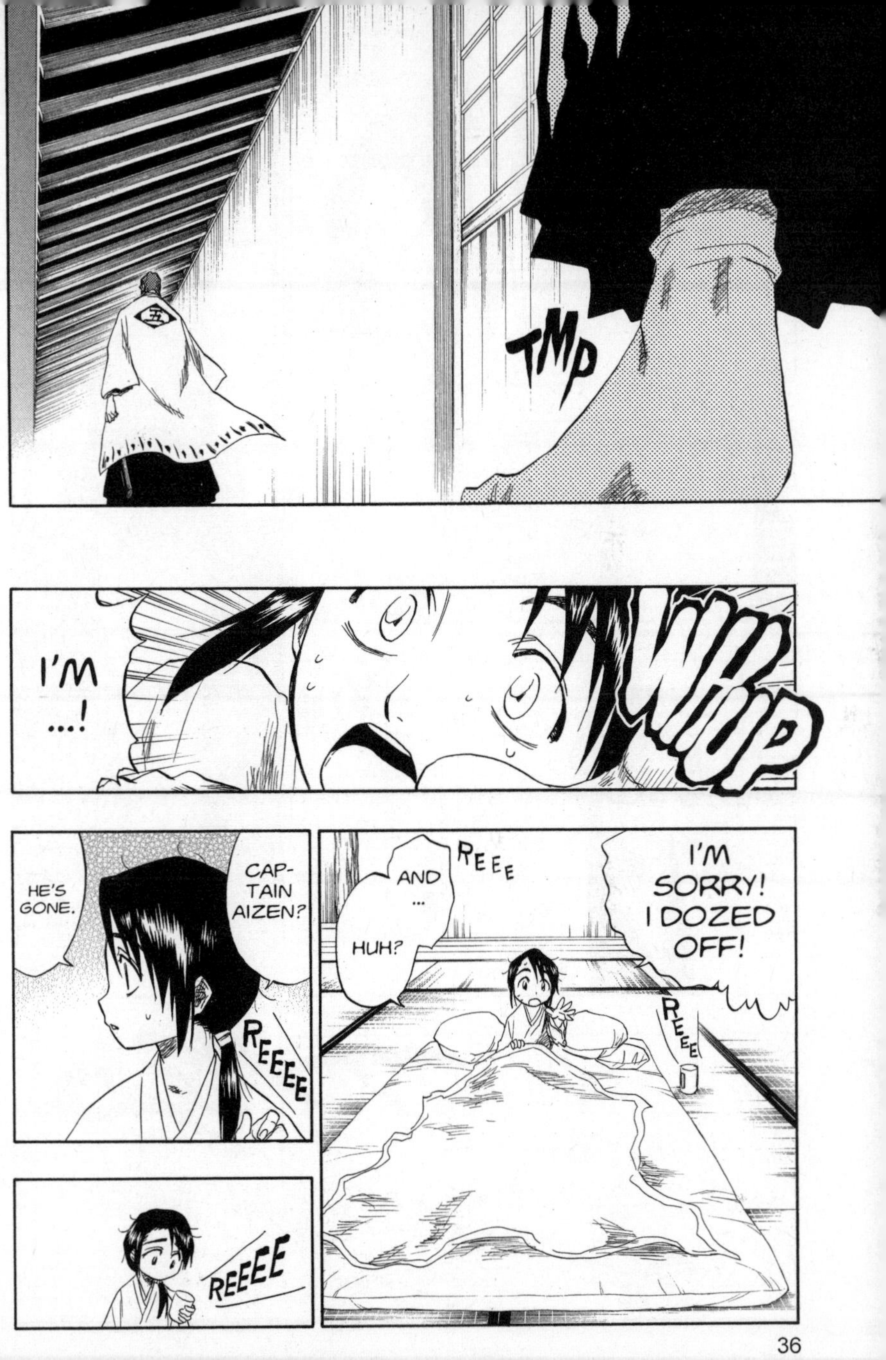
TMP
WHUP
I'M ...!
I'M SORRY! I DOZED OFF!
REEE
AND ...
HUH?
REEE
CAP-TAIN AIZEN?
HE'S GONE.
REEEEE
REEEE

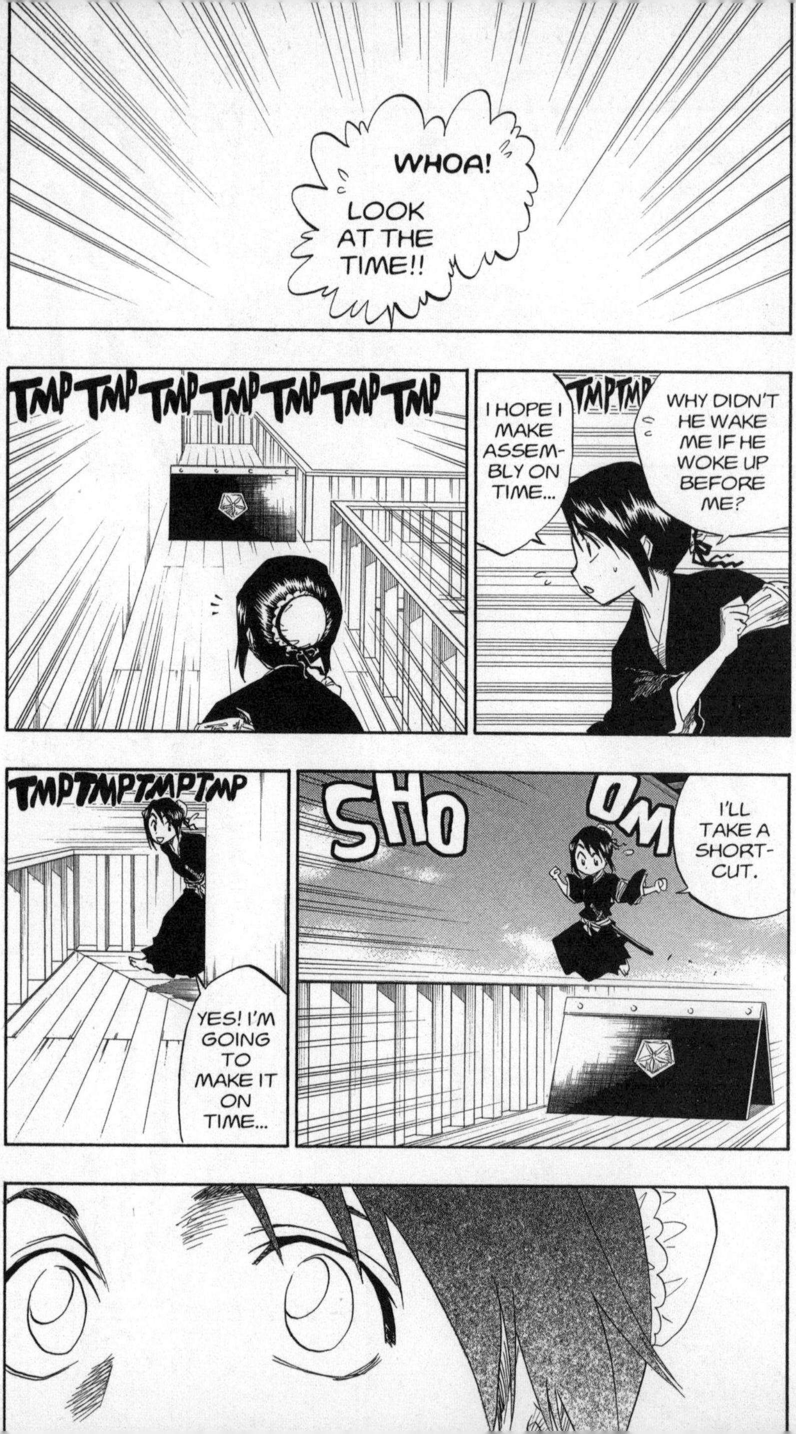
WHOA!
LOOK AT THE TIME!!
TMPTMP
WHY DIDN'T HE WAKE ME IF HE WOKE UP BEFORE ME?
I HOPE I MAKE ASSEM-BLY ON TIME...
TMP TMP TMP TMP TMP TMP TMP
SHOOM
I'LL TAKE A SHORT-CUT.
TMPTMPTMPTMP
YES! I'M GOING TO MAKE IT ON TIME...

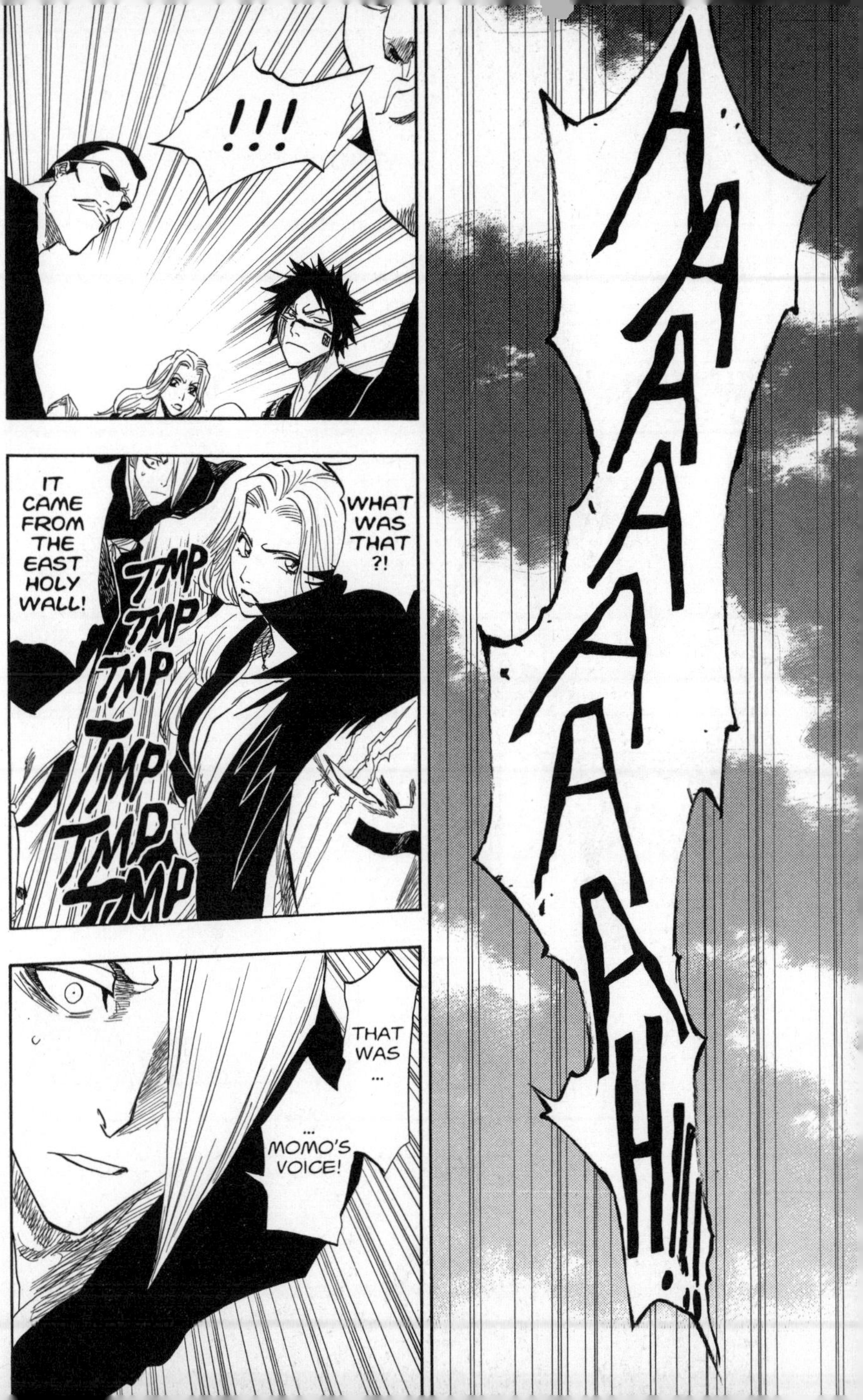
AAAAAAAH!!!
!!!
WHAT WAS THAT?!
IT CAME FROM THE EAST HOLY WALL!
TMP TMP TMP TMP TMP TMP TMP
THAT WAS...
...MOMO'S VOICE!

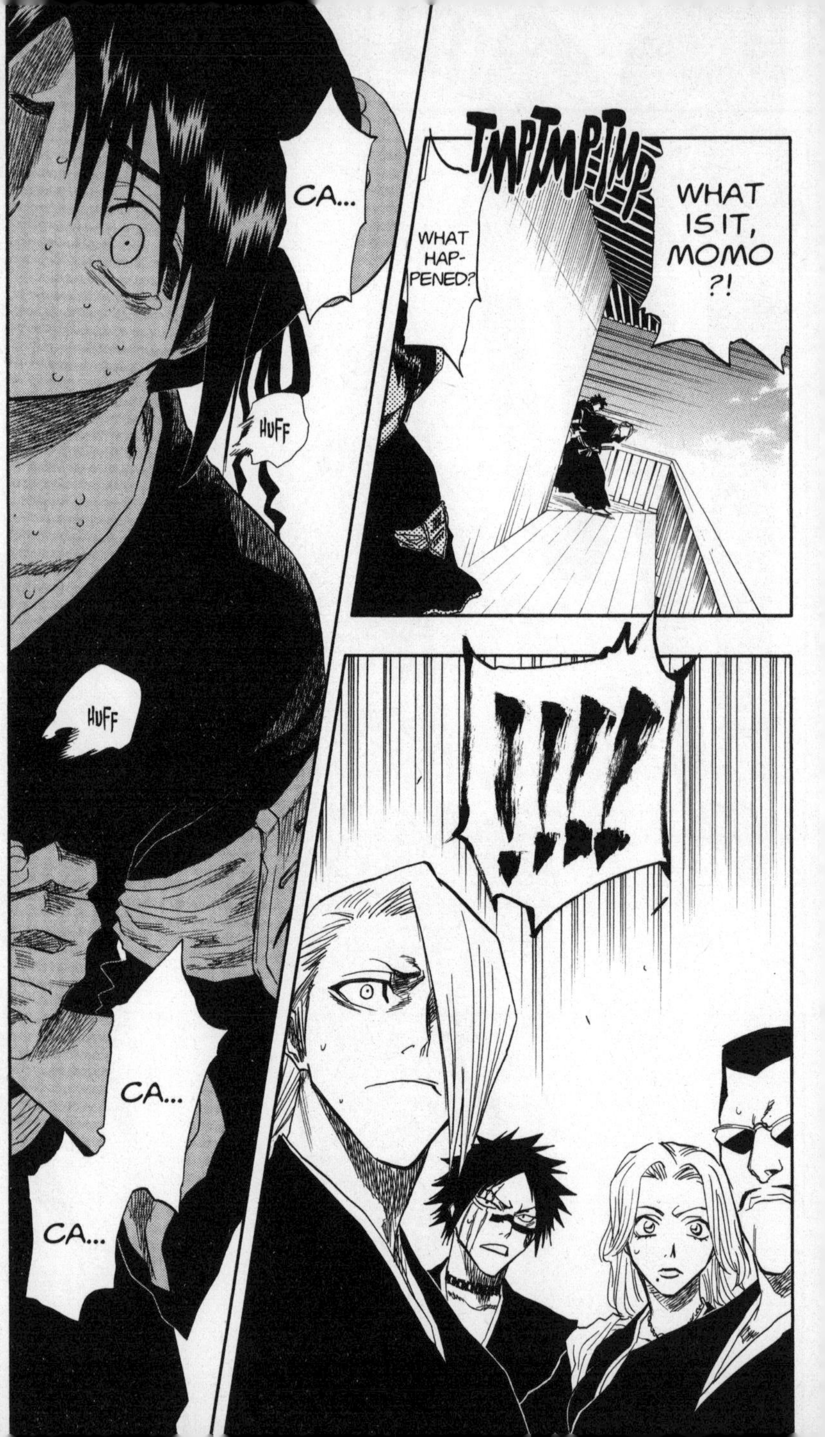
TMPTMPTMP
WHAT IS IT, MOMO?!
WHAT HAPPENED?
!!!!
CA...
HUFF
HUFF
CA...
CA...

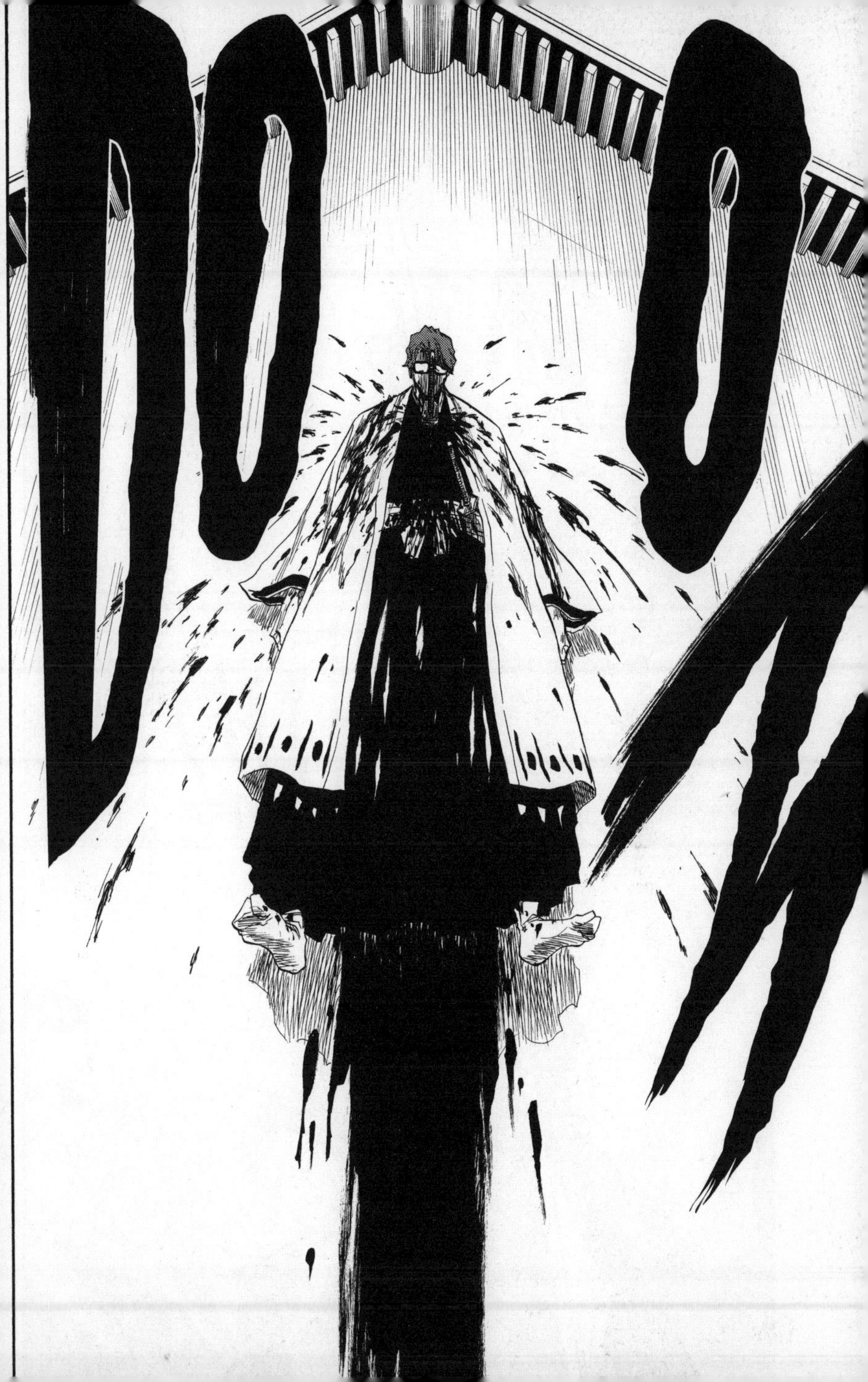
DOOM

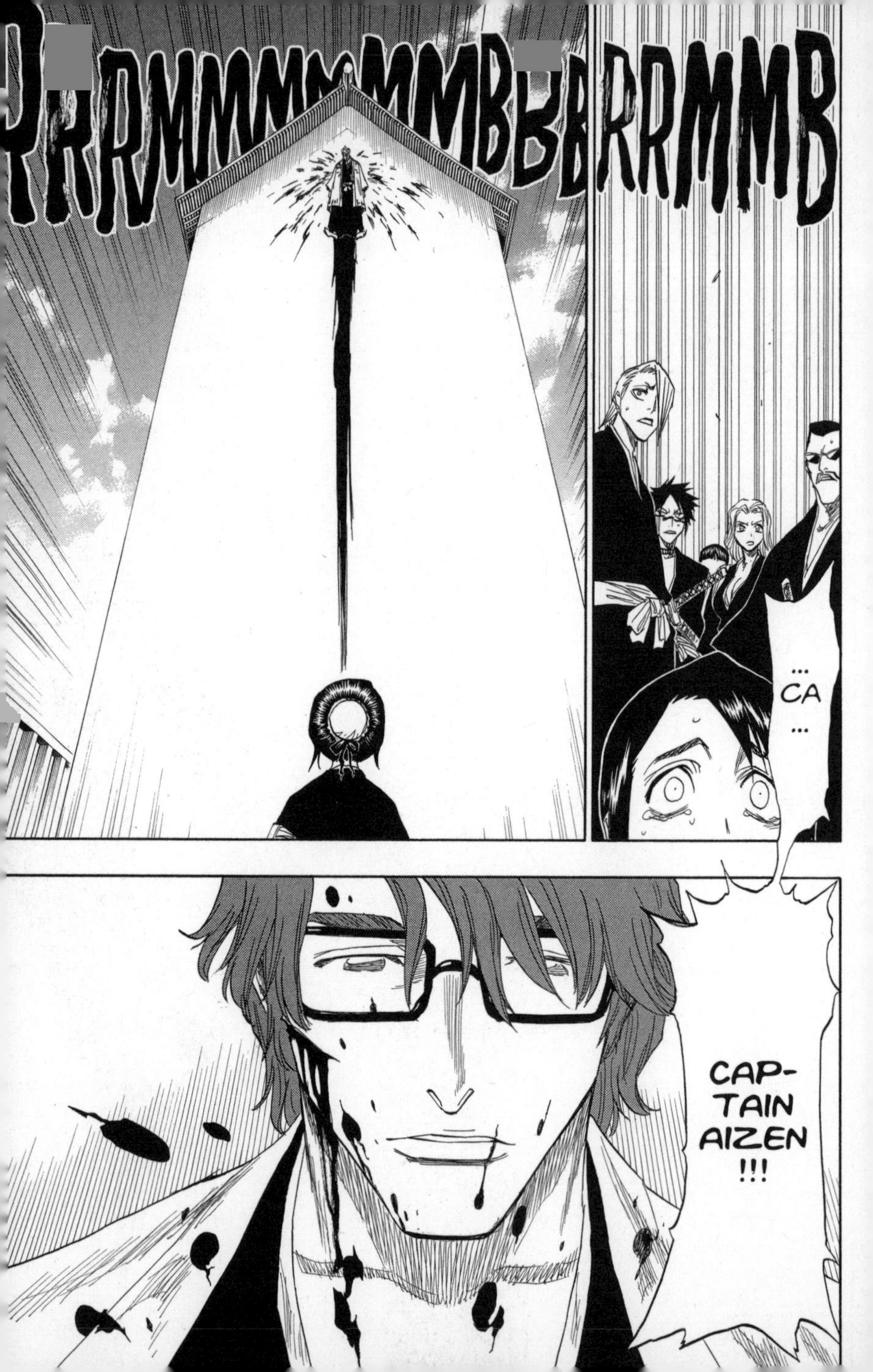
... CA ...
CAP-TAIN AIZEN !!!

101. Split Under the Red Stalk

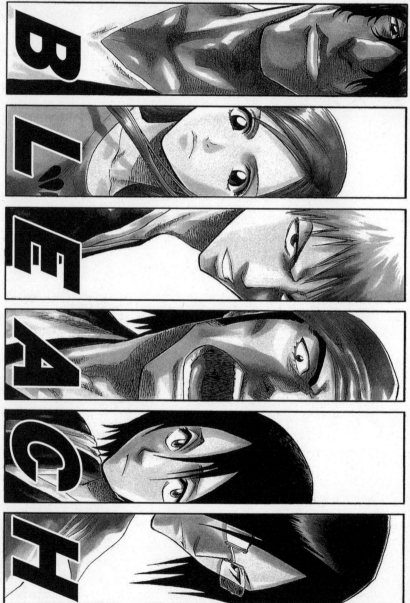

BLEACH
ブリーチ

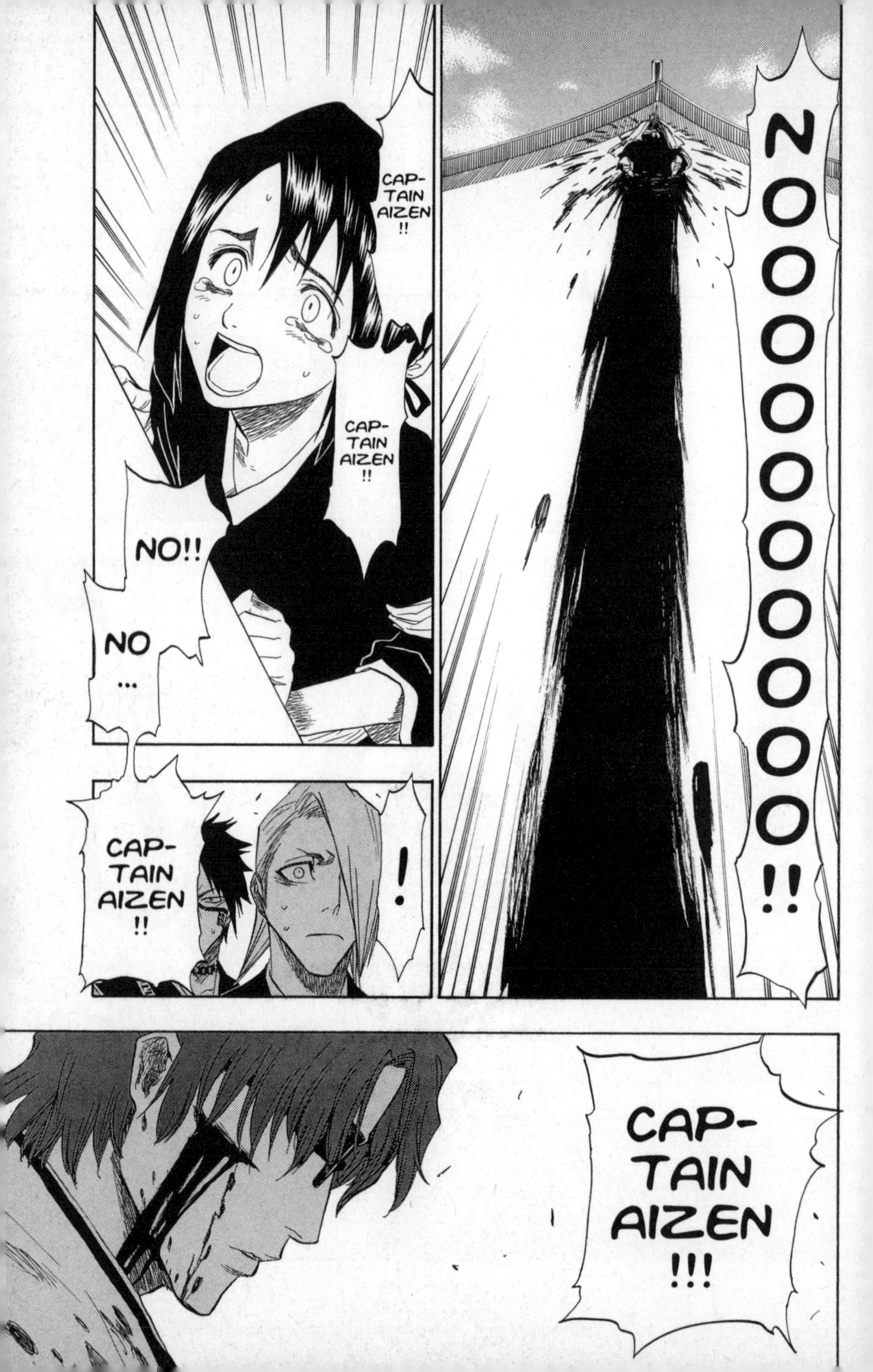
NOOOOOOOOOOO!!
CAP-TAIN AIZEN!!
CAP-TAIN AIZEN!!
NO!!
NO...
!
CAP-TAIN AIZEN!!
CAP-TAIN AIZEN!!!

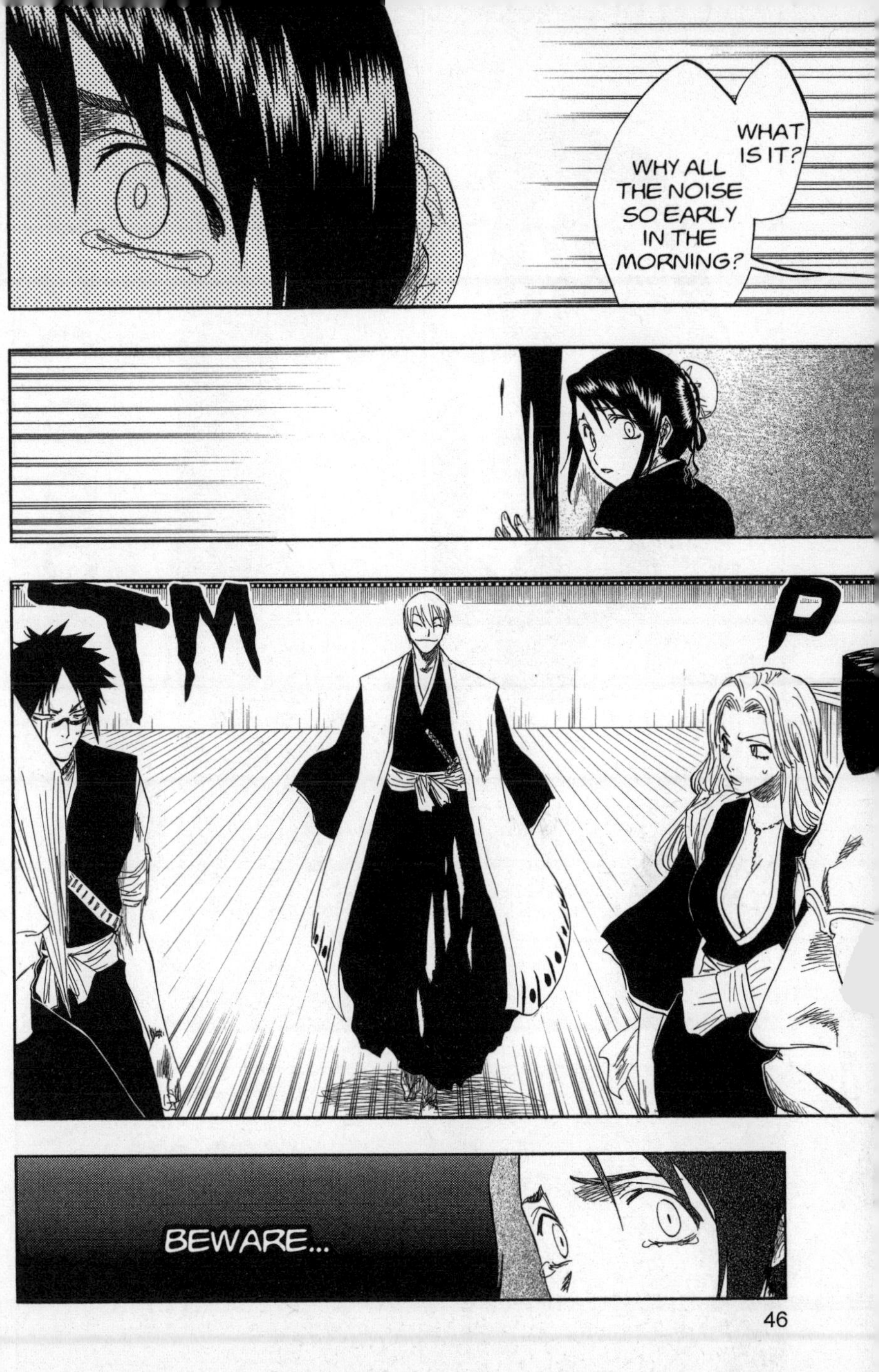
WHAT IS IT?
WHY ALL THE NOISE SO EARLY IN THE MORNING?
P
TM
BEWARE...

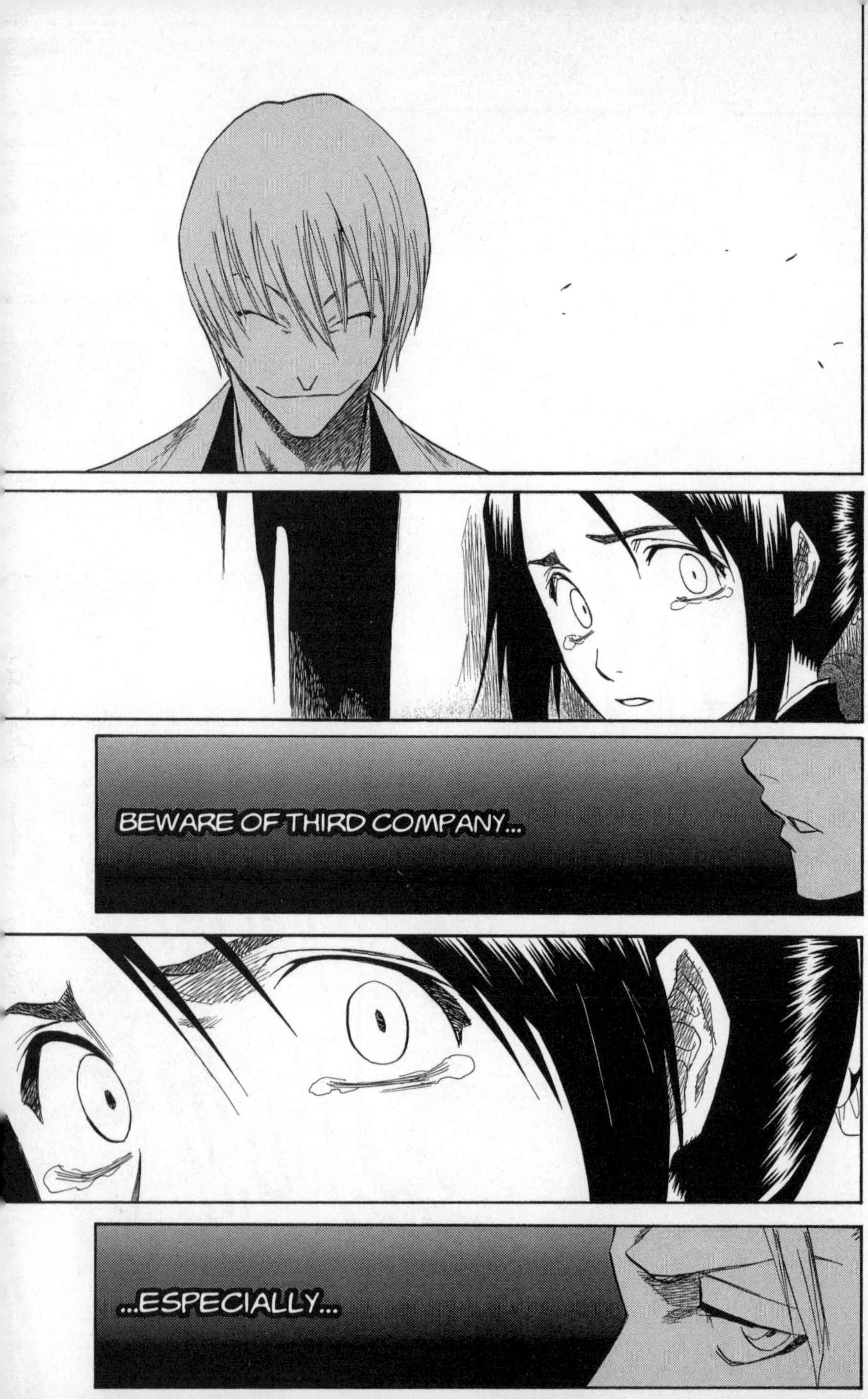
BEWARE OF THIRD COMPANY...
...ESPECIALLY...

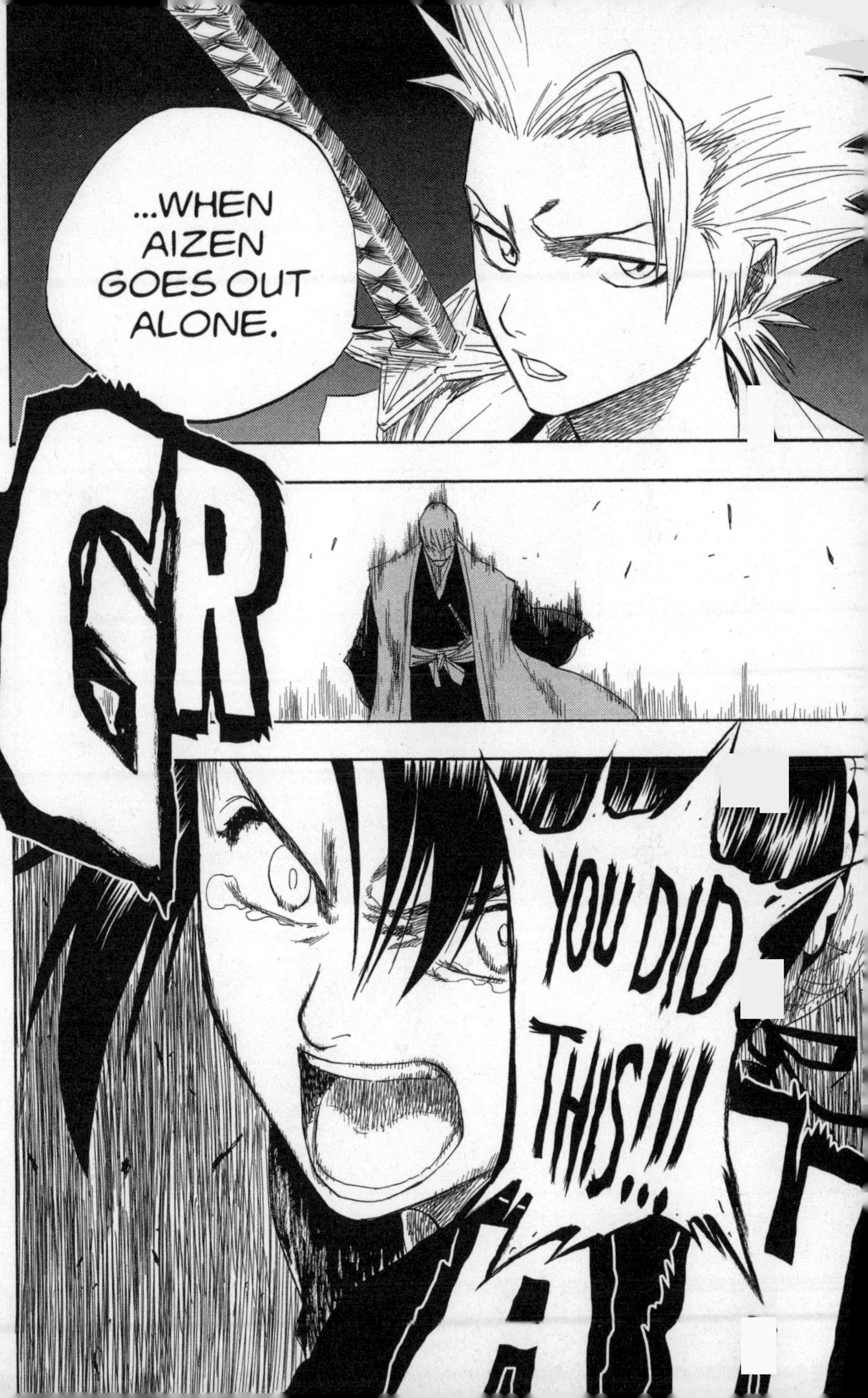
...WHEN AIZEN GOES OUT ALONE.
YOU DID THIS...!!

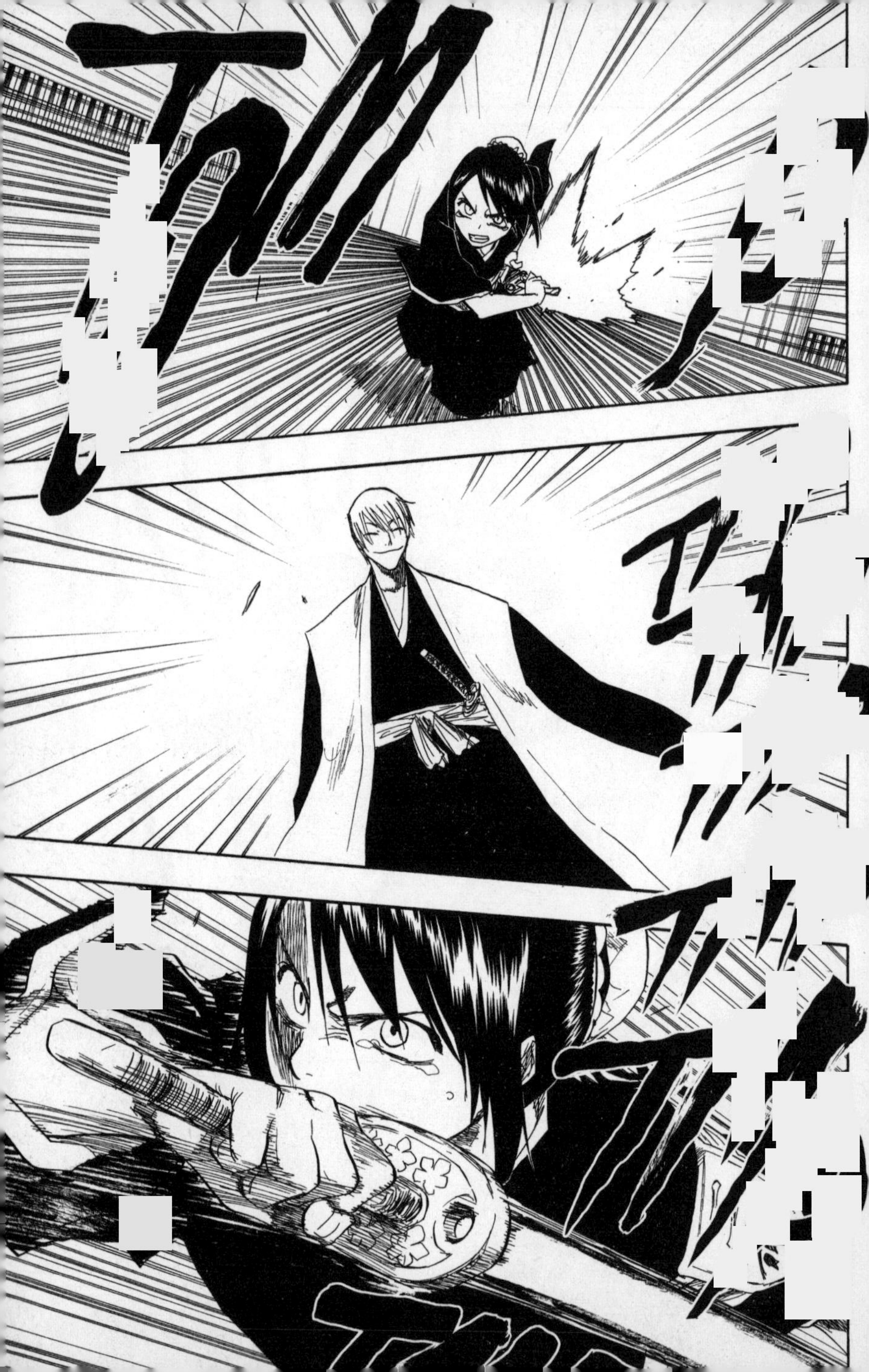

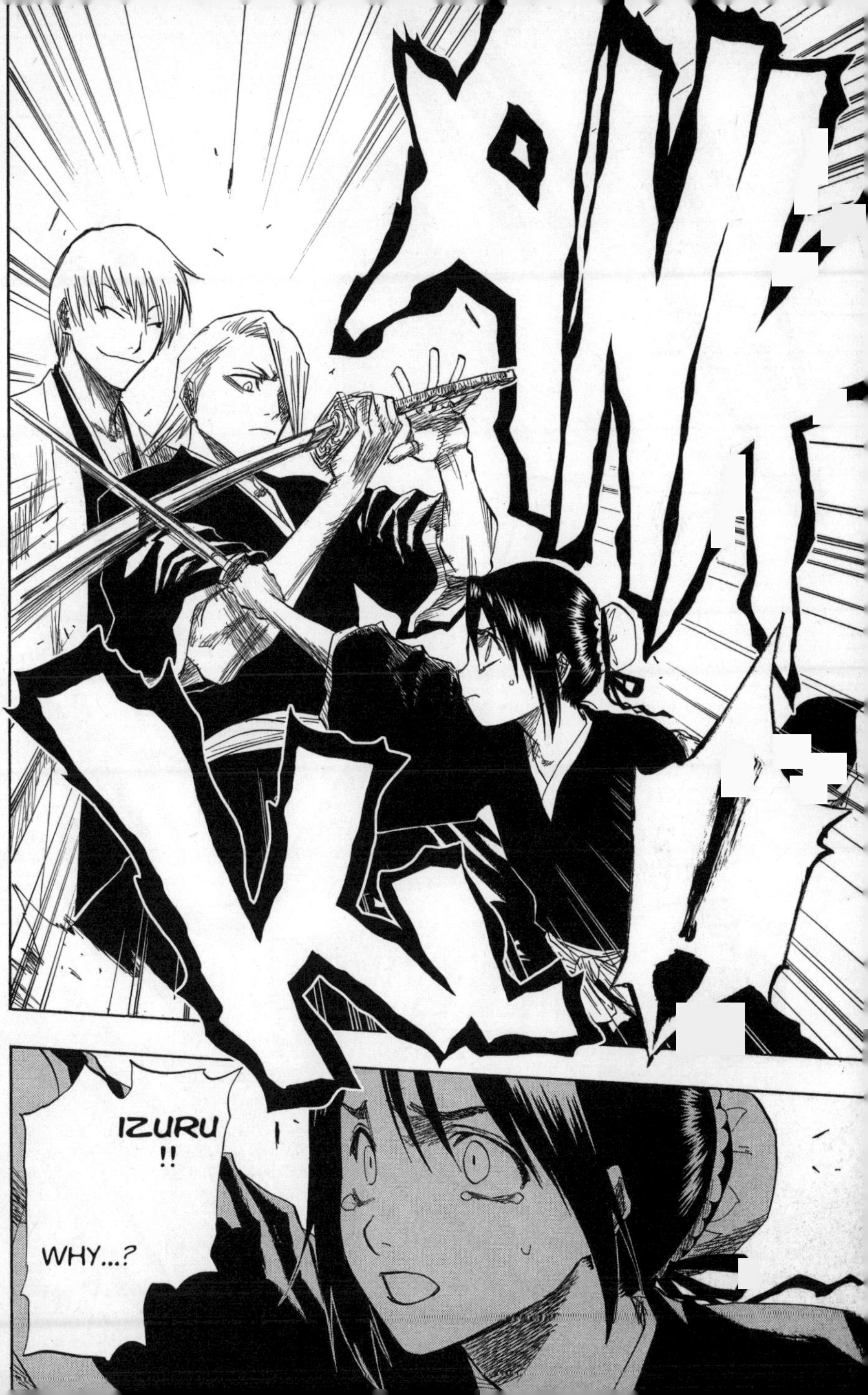
IZURU !!
WHY...?

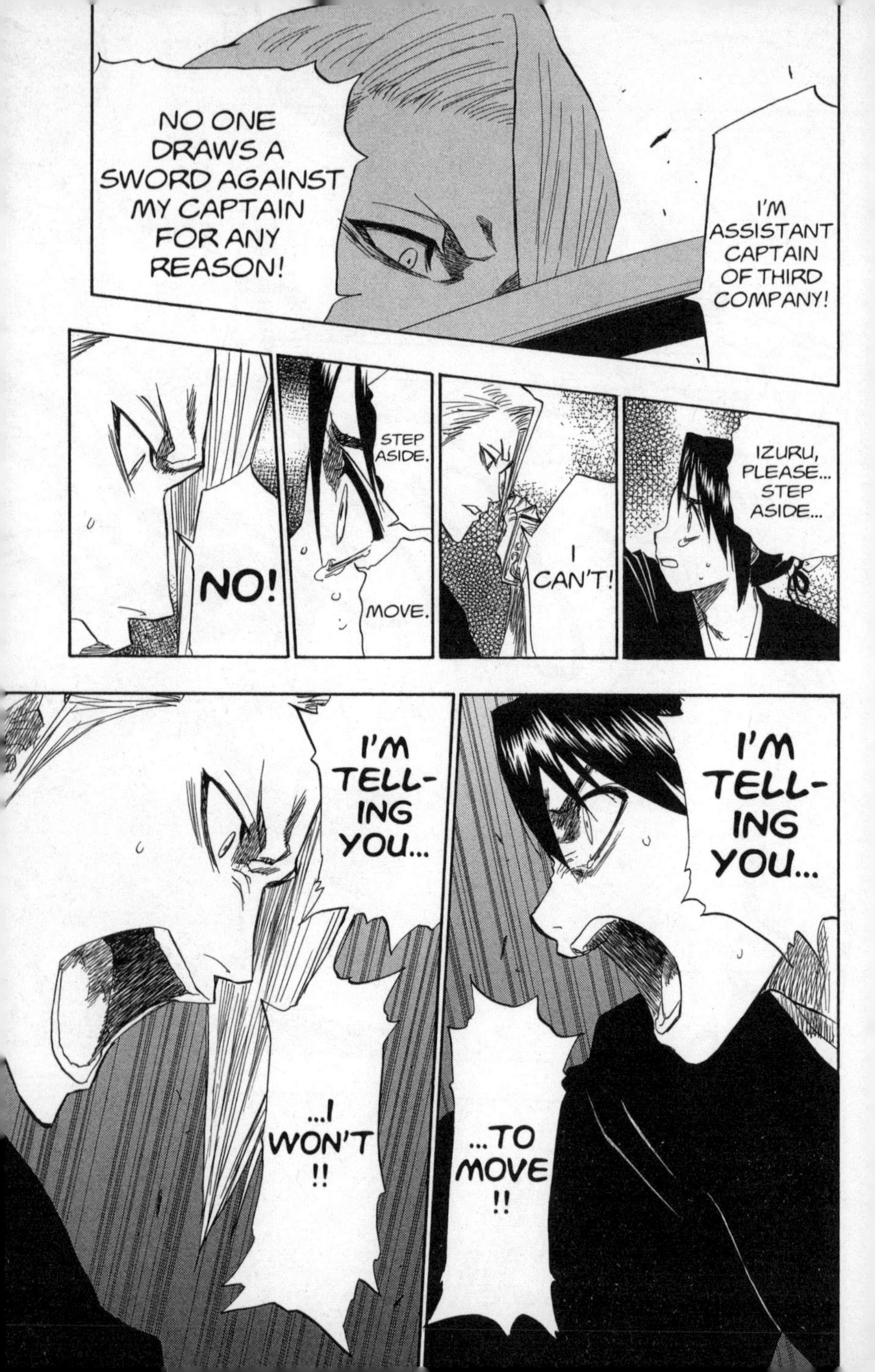
I'M ASSISTANT CAPTAIN OF THIRD COMPANY!
NO ONE DRAWS A SWORD AGAINST MY CAPTAIN FOR ANY REASON!
IZURU, PLEASE... STEP ASIDE...
I CAN'T!
STEP ASIDE.
MOVE.
NO!
I'M TELL-ING YOU...
...TO MOVE !!
I'M TELL-ING YOU...
...I WON'T !!

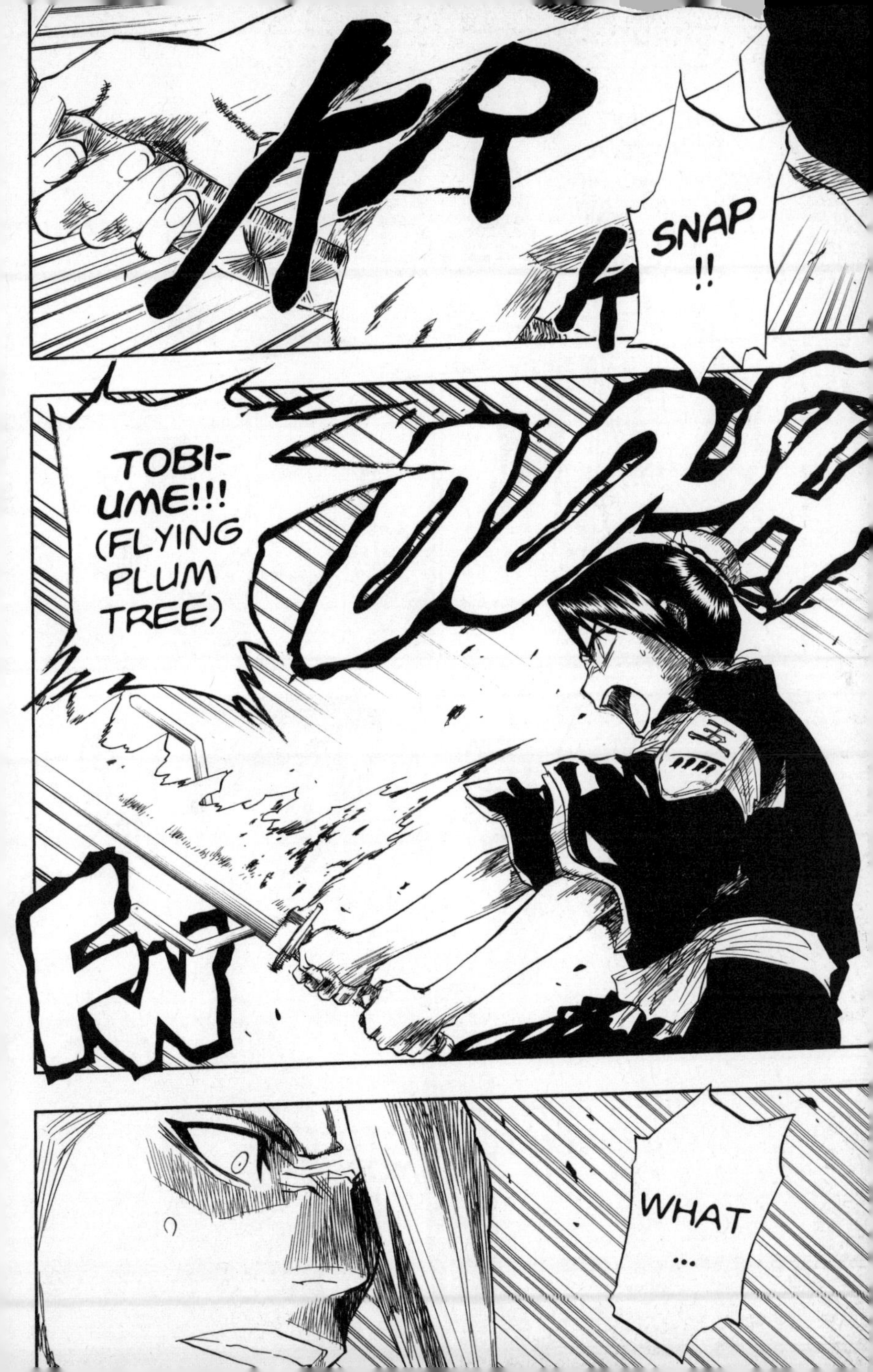
SNAP !!
TOBI-UME!!! (FLYING PLUM TREE)
WHAT ...

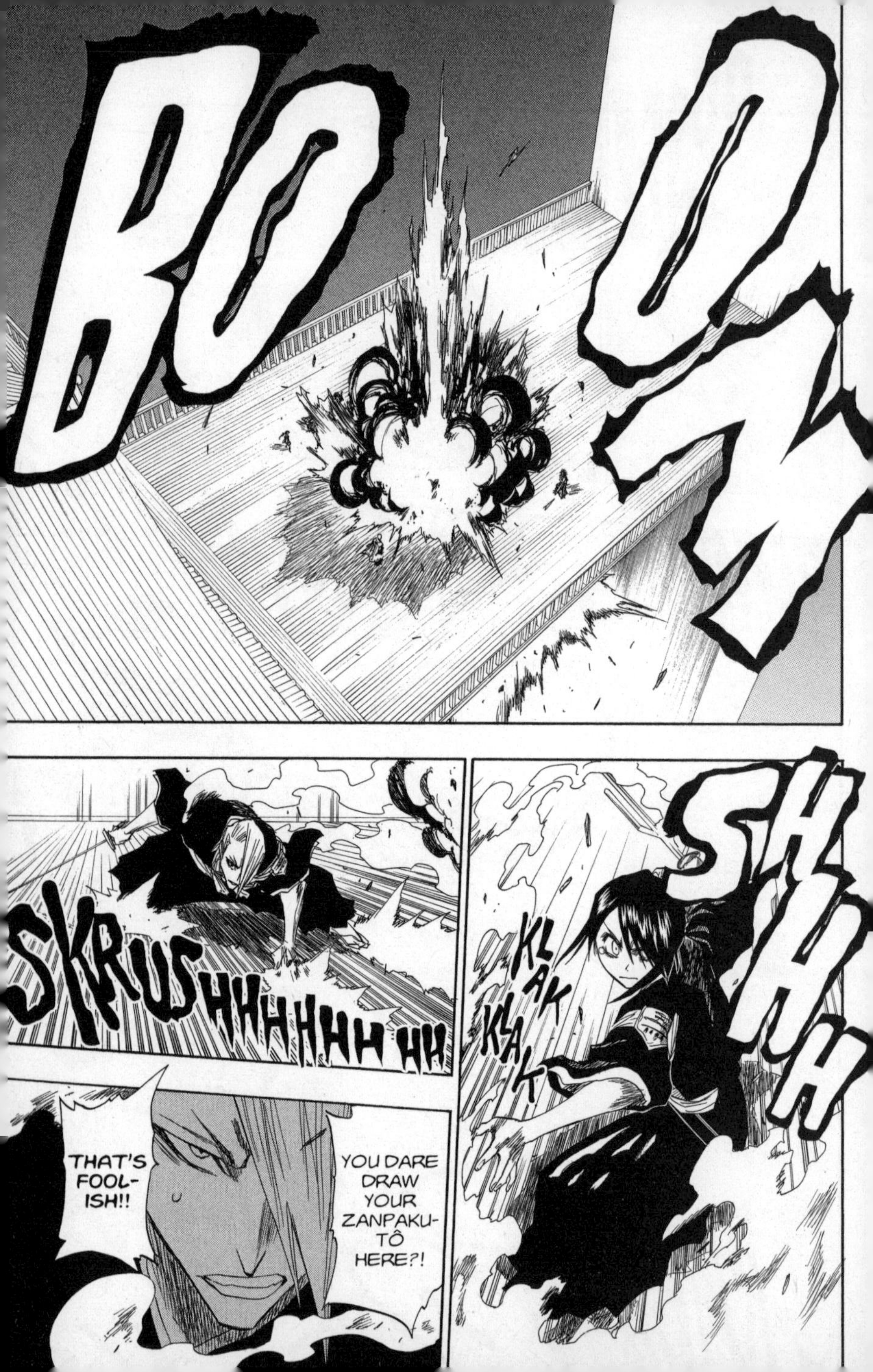
BOOM
SHHHH
KLAK KLAK
SKRUSHHHHHHHHH
YOU DARE DRAW YOUR ZANPAKU-TÔ HERE?!
THAT'S FOOL-ISH!!

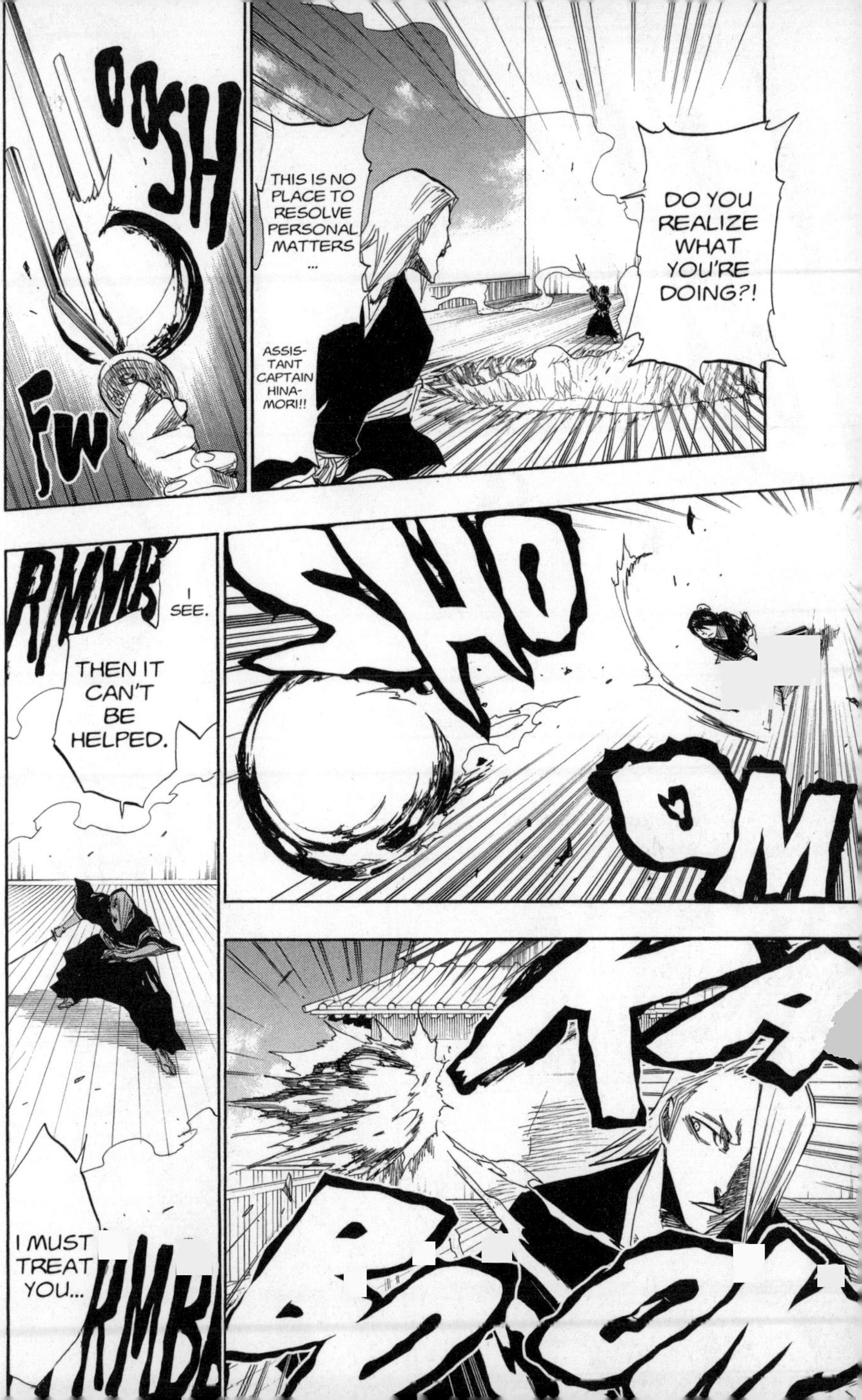
DO YOU REALIZE WHAT YOU'RE DOING?!
THIS IS NO PLACE TO RESOLVE PERSONAL MATTERS ...
ASSISTANT CAPTAIN HINAMORI!!
FWOOSH
I SEE.
THEN IT CAN'T BE HELPED.
I MUST TREAT YOU...

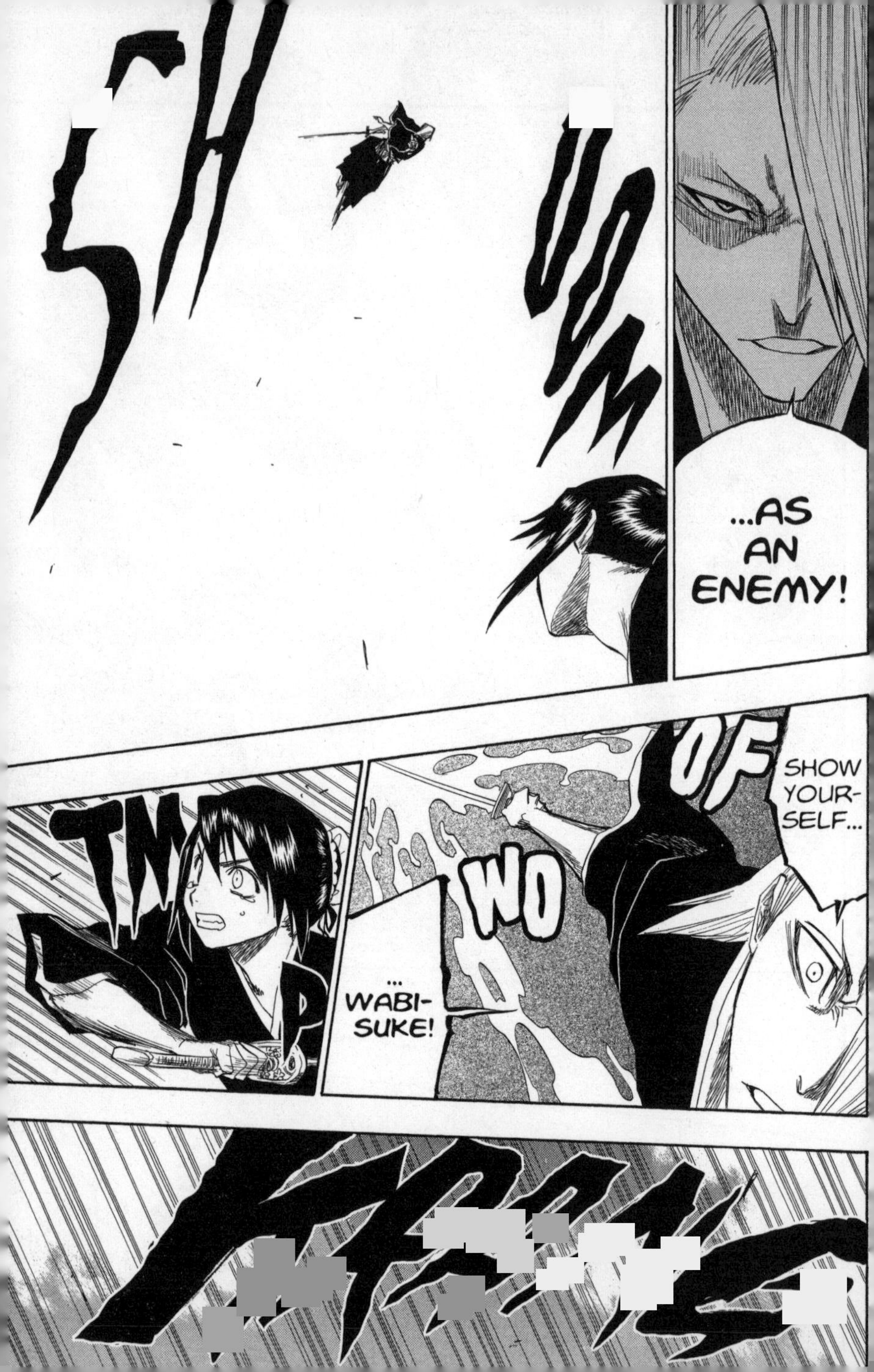
...AS AN ENEMY!
SH
OOM
SHOW YOURSELF...
OF
WO
... WABI-SUKE!
TM
P

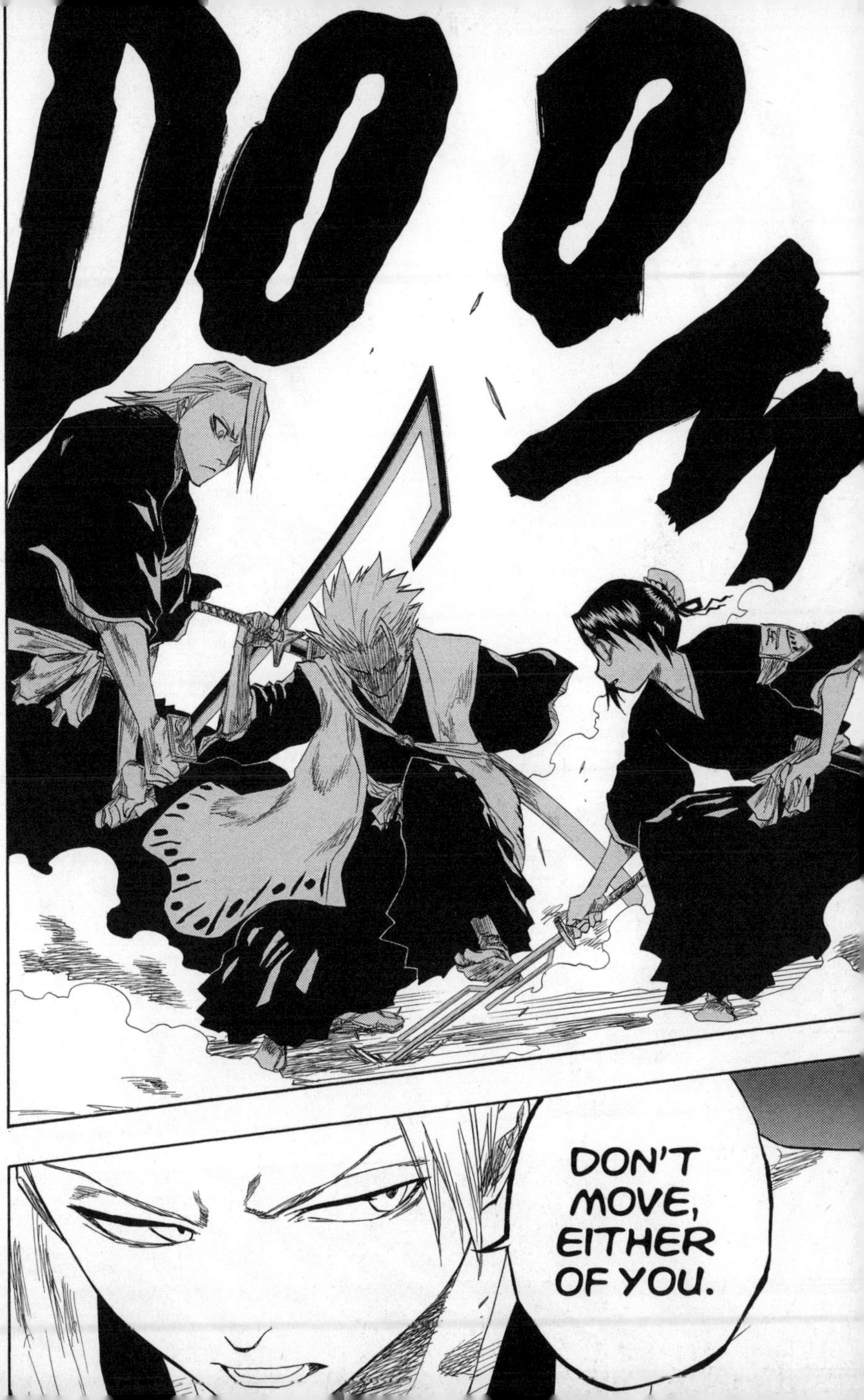
DOOM
DON'T MOVE, EITHER OF YOU.

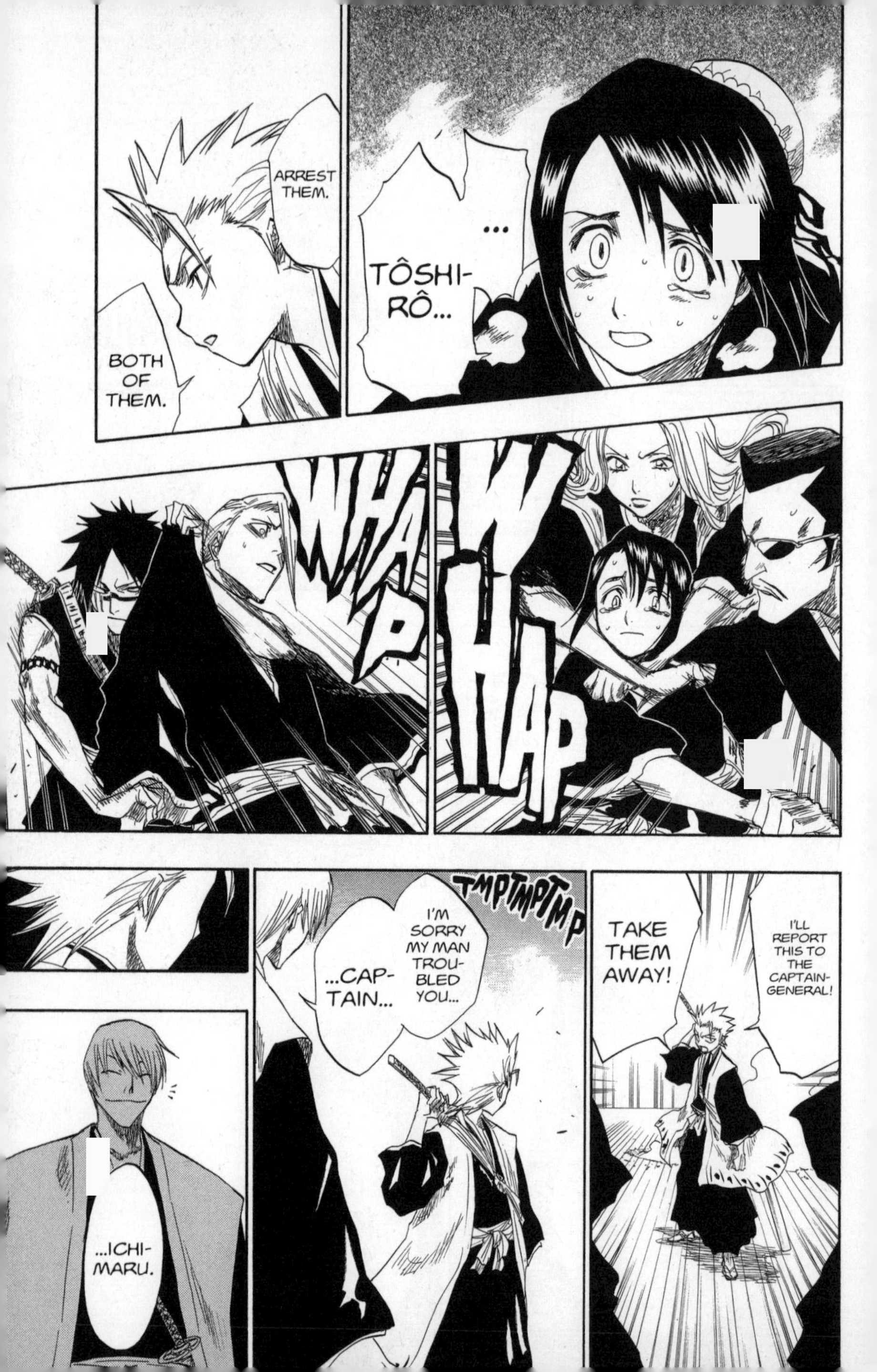
...
TÔSHI-RÔ...
ARREST THEM.
BOTH OF THEM.
WHAP
WHAP
I'LL REPORT THIS TO THE CAPTAIN-GENERAL!
TAKE THEM AWAY!
TMPTMPTMP
I'M SORRY MY MAN TROU-BLED YOU...
...CAP-TAIN...
...ICHI-MARU.

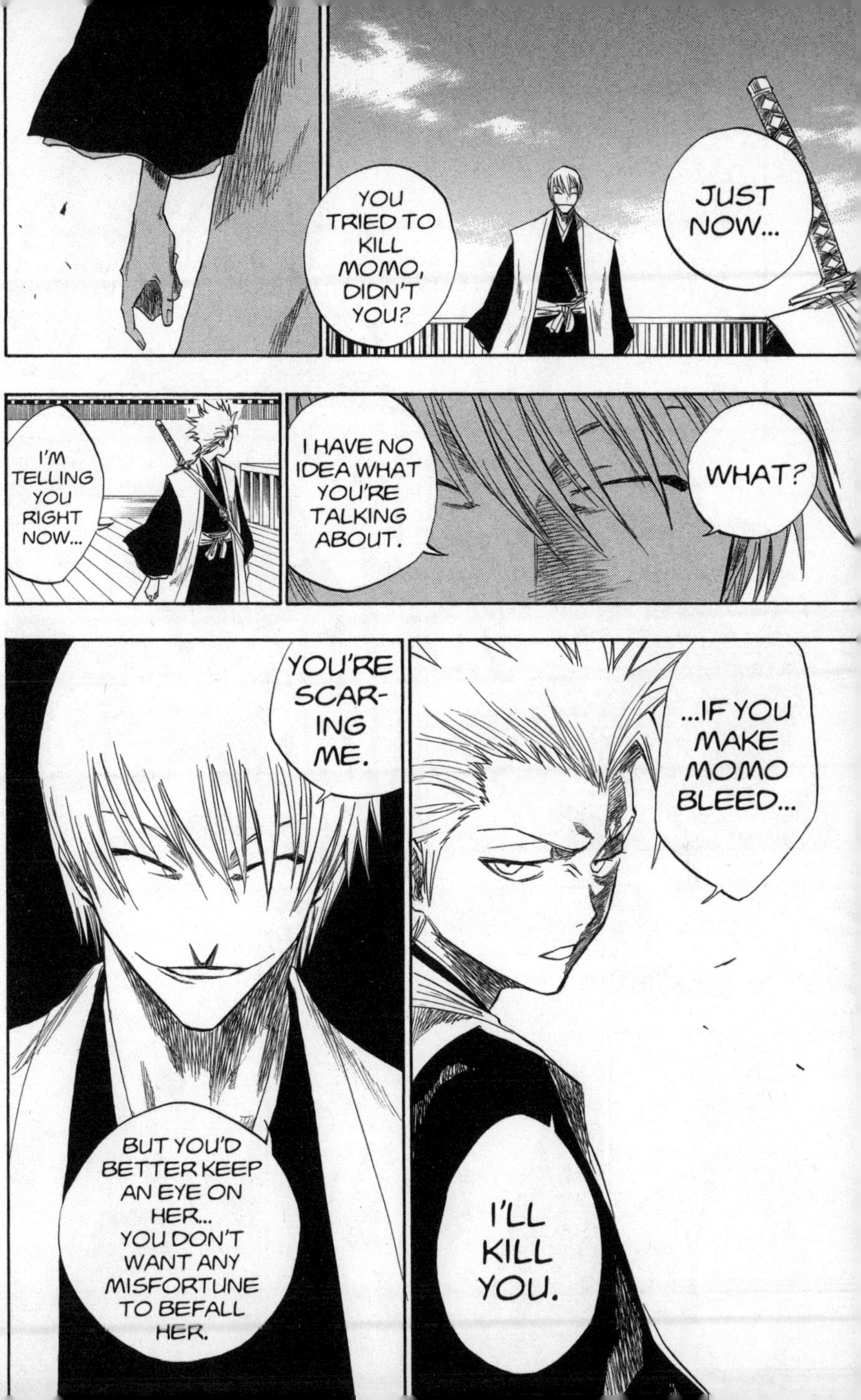
JUST NOW...
YOU TRIED TO KILL MOMO, DIDN'T YOU?
WHAT?
I HAVE NO IDEA WHAT YOU'RE TALKING ABOUT.
I'M TELLING YOU RIGHT NOW...
...IF YOU MAKE MOMO BLEED...
I'LL KILL YOU.
YOU'RE SCAR-ING ME.
BUT YOU'D BETTER KEEP AN EYE ON HER... YOU DON'T WANT ANY MISFORTUNE TO BEFALL HER.

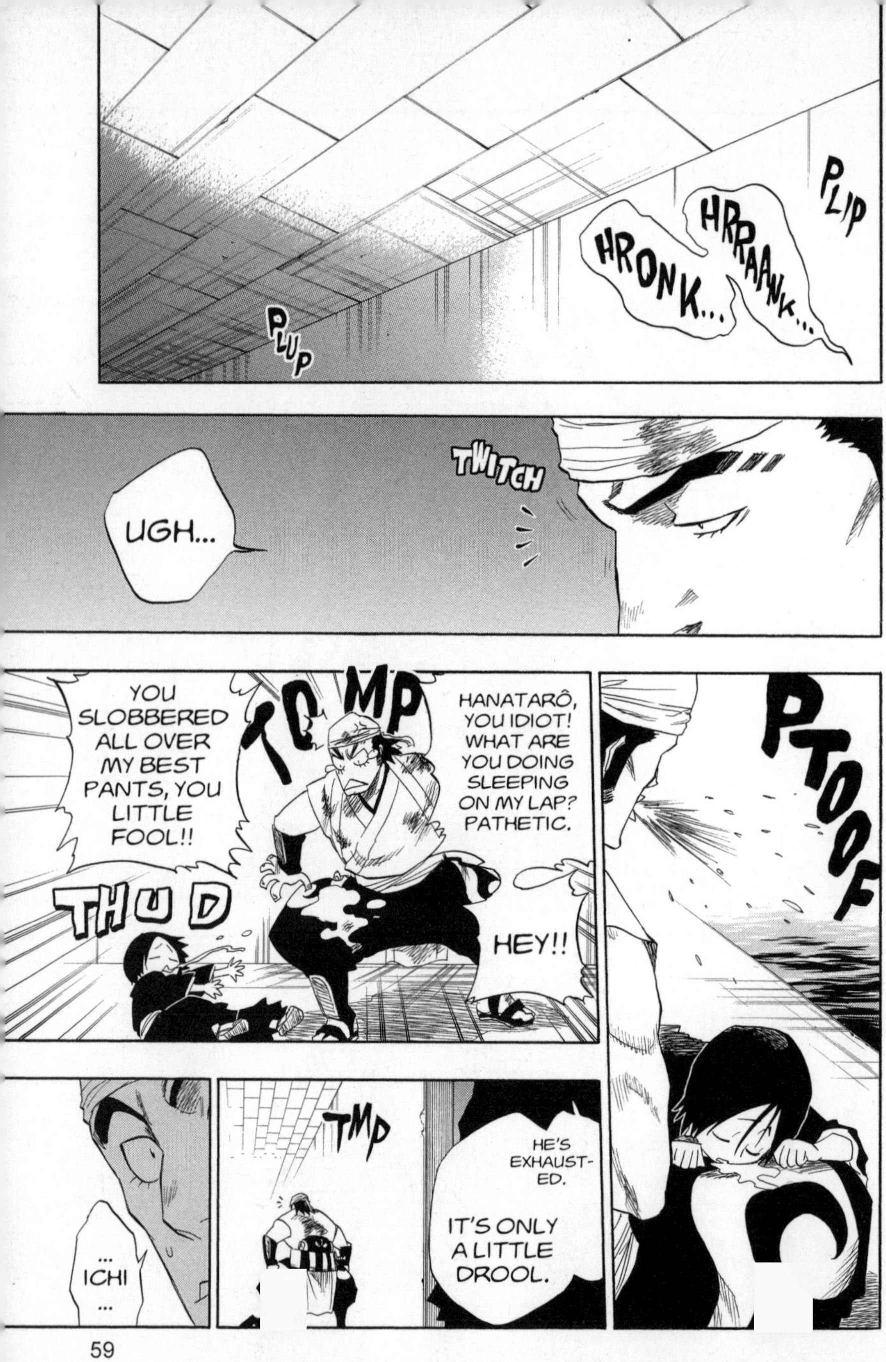
PLIP
HRRAANK...
HRONK...
PLUP
TWITCH
UGH...
PTOOF
TOMP
HANATARÔ, YOU IDIOT! WHAT ARE YOU DOING SLEEPING ON MY LAP? PATHETIC.
HEY!!
YOU SLOBBERED ALL OVER MY BEST PANTS, YOU LITTLE FOOL!!
THUD
TMP
HE'S EXHAUST-ED.
IT'S ONLY A LITTLE DROOL.
...ICHI...

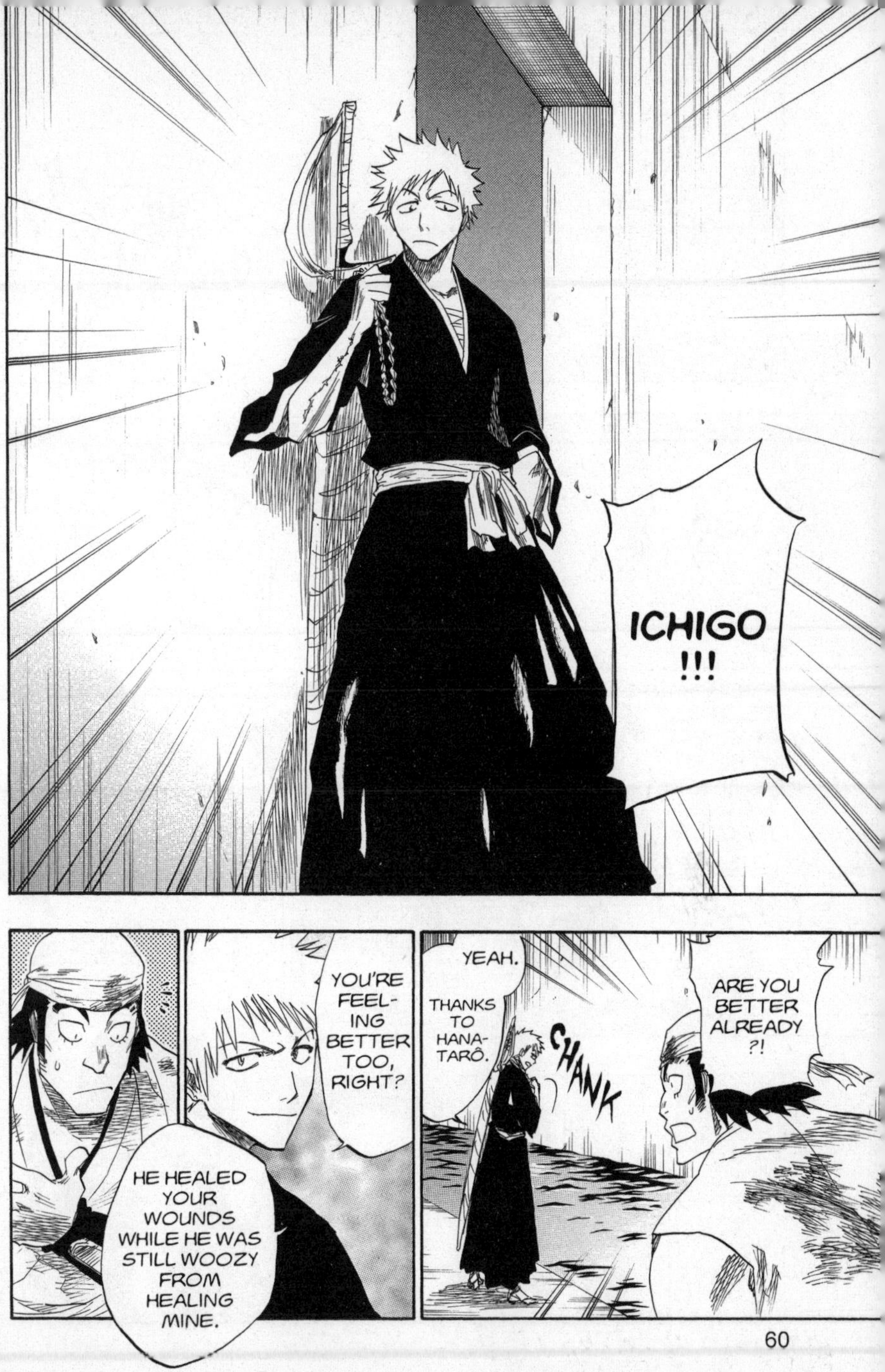
ICHIGO !!!
ARE YOU BETTER ALREADY ?!
YEAH.
THANKS TO HANA-TARÔ.
CHANK
YOU'RE FEEL-ING BETTER TOO, RIGHT?
HE HEALED YOUR WOUNDS WHILE HE WAS STILL WOOZY FROM HEALING MINE.

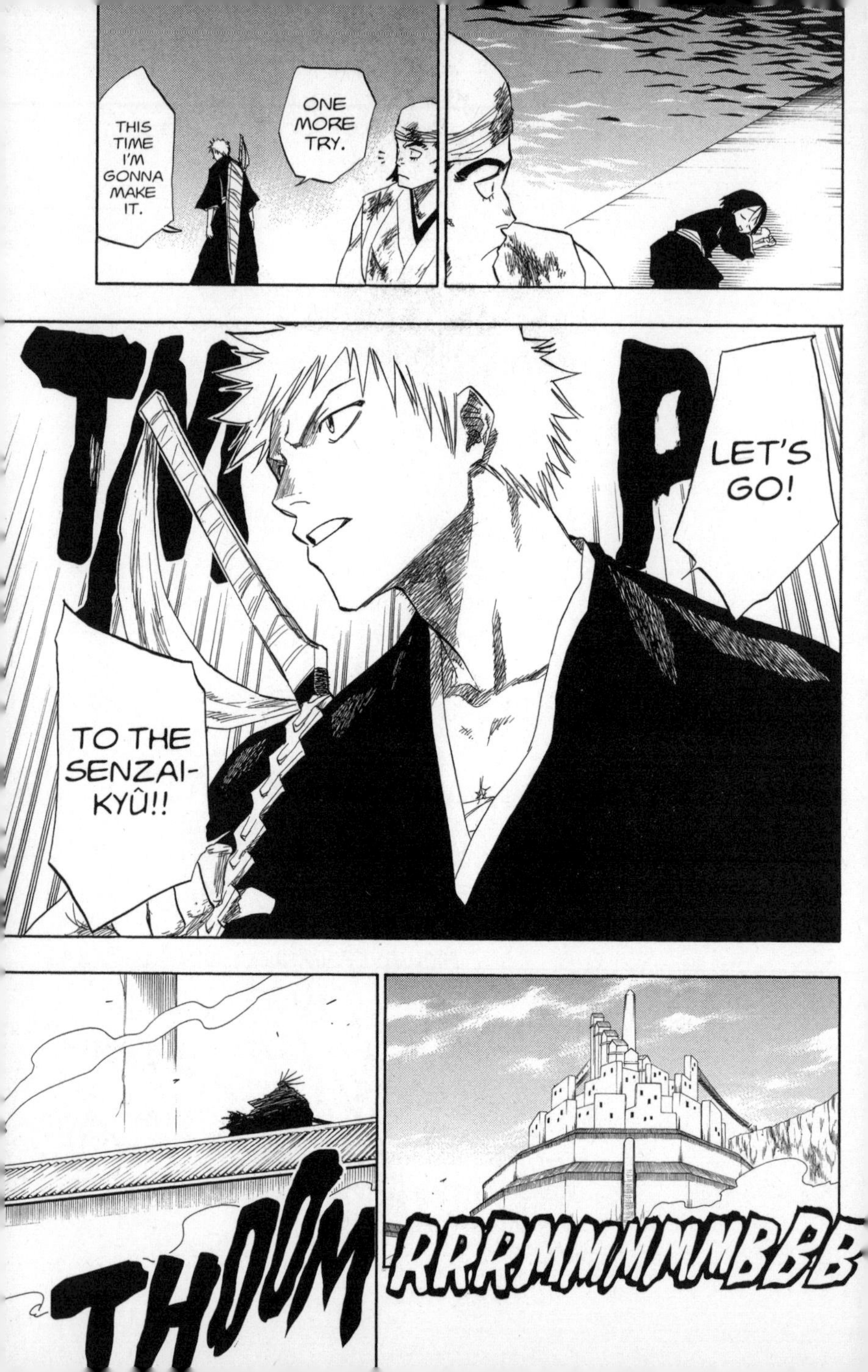
ONE MORE TRY.
THIS TIME I'M GONNA MAKE IT.
TMP
LET'S GO!
TO THE SENZAI-KYÛ!!
RRRMMMMMBBB
THOOM

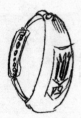

EXCLUSIVE FOURTH COMPANY RELIEF BAG

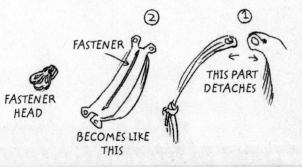

①
THIS PART DETACHES
②
FASTENER
BECOMES LIKE THIS
FASTENER HEAD

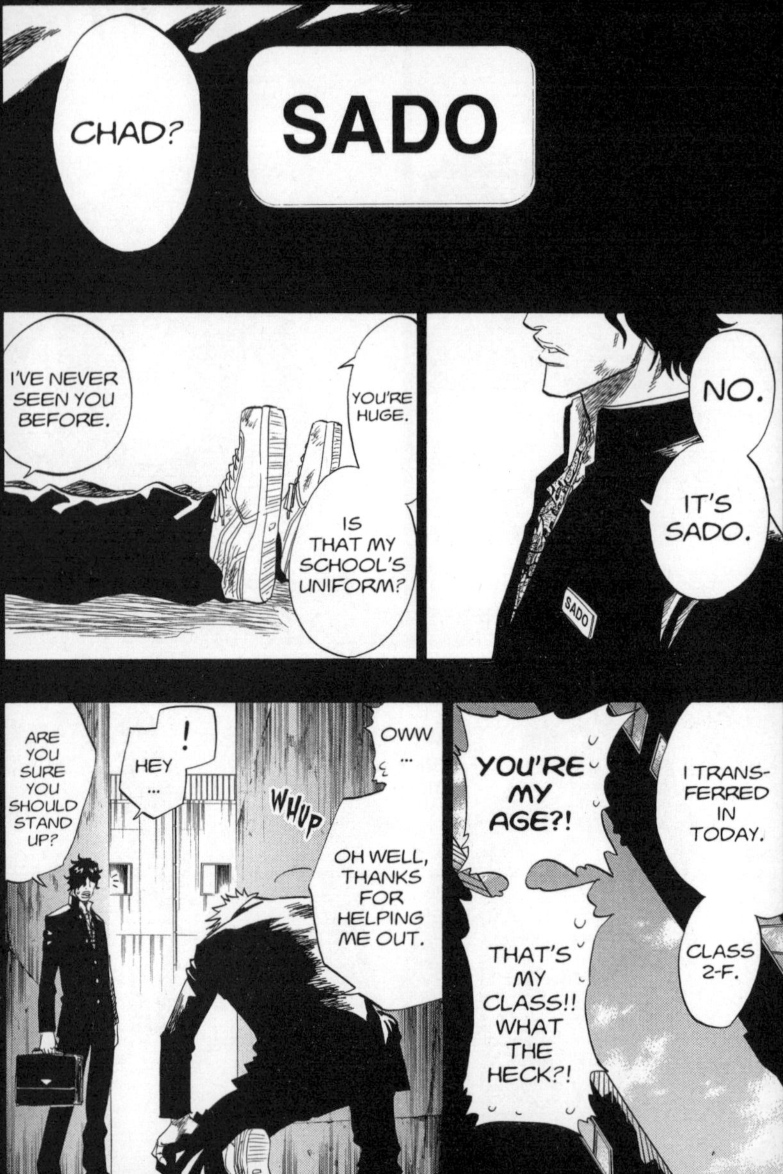
SADO
CHAD?
NO.
IT'S SADO.
SADO
YOU'RE HUGE.
IS THAT MY SCHOOL'S UNIFORM?
I'VE NEVER SEEN YOU BEFORE.
I TRANS-FERRED IN TODAY.
CLASS 2-F.
YOU'RE MY AGE?!
THAT'S MY CLASS!! WHAT THE HECK?!
OWW ...
WHUP
OH WELL, THANKS FOR HELPING ME OUT.
!
HEY ...
ARE YOU SURE YOU SHOULD STAND UP?

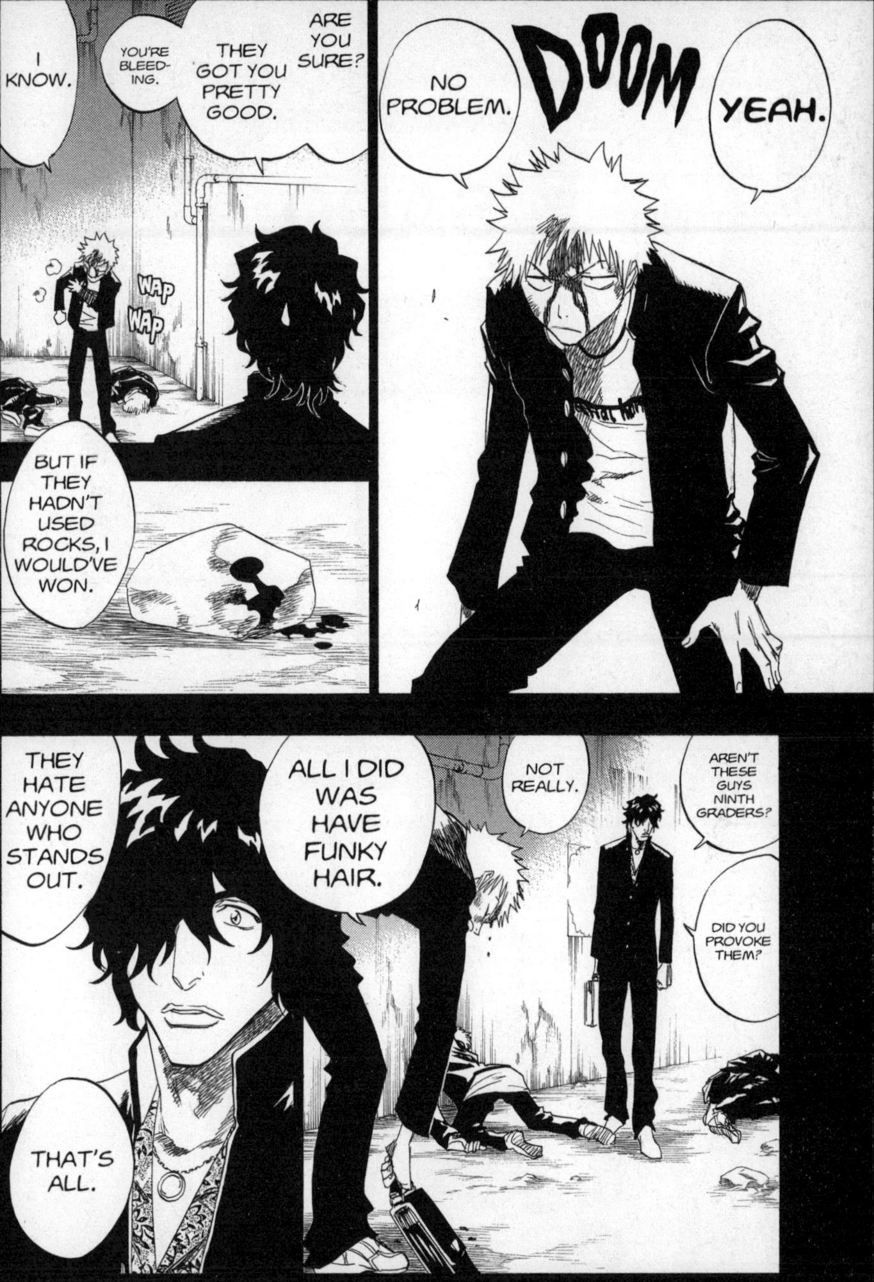
YEAH.
DOOM
NO PROBLEM.
ARE YOU SURE?
THEY GOT YOU PRETTY GOOD.
YOU'RE BLEEDING.
I KNOW.
WAP
WAP
BUT IF THEY HADN'T USED ROCKS, I WOULD'VE WON.
AREN'T THESE GUYS NINTH GRADERS?
NOT REALLY.
DID YOU PROVOKE THEM?
ALL I DID WAS HAVE FUNKY HAIR.
THEY HATE ANYONE WHO STANDS OUT.
THAT'S ALL.

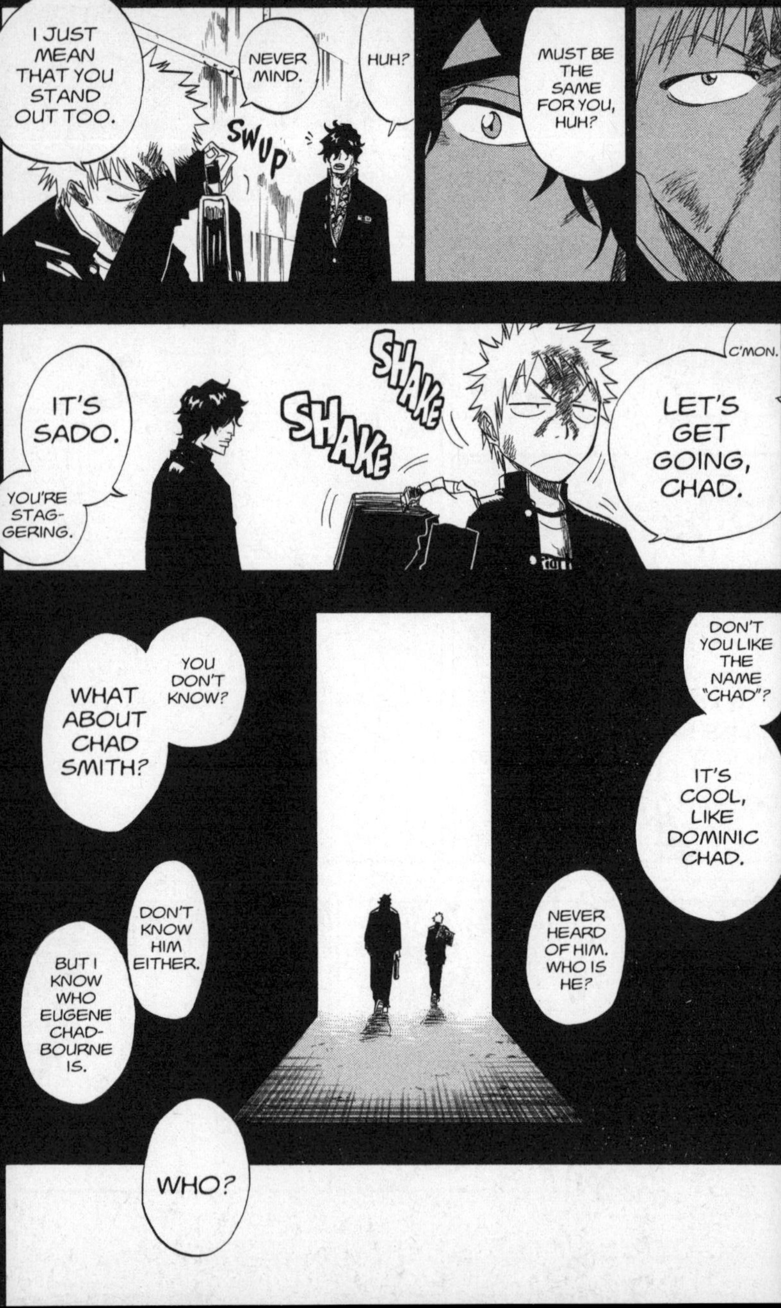
MUST BE THE SAME FOR YOU, HUH?
HUH?
NEVER MIND.
I JUST MEAN THAT YOU STAND OUT TOO.
SWUP
C'MON.
LET'S GET GOING, CHAD.
SHAKE
SHAKE
IT'S SADO.
YOU'RE STAG-GERING.
DON'T YOU LIKE THE NAME "CHAD"?
IT'S COOL, LIKE DOMINIC CHAD.
YOU DON'T KNOW?
WHAT ABOUT CHAD SMITH?
NEVER HEARD OF HIM. WHO IS HE?
DON'T KNOW HIM EITHER.
BUT I KNOW WHO EUGENE CHAD-BOURNE IS.
WHO?

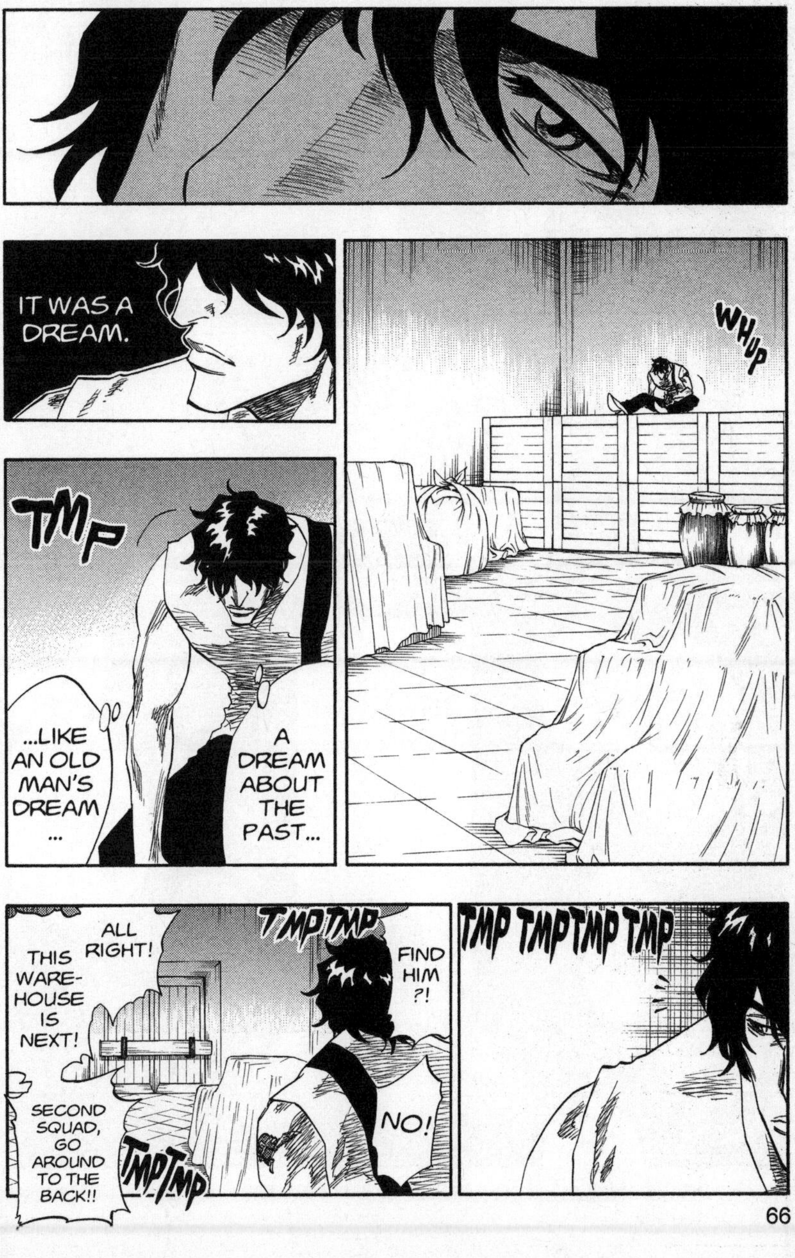
WHUP
IT WAS A DREAM.
TMP
A DREAM ABOUT THE PAST...
...LIKE AN OLD MAN'S DREAM...
TMP TMPTMP TMP
TMPTMP
FIND HIM?!
ALL RIGHT!
THIS WAREHOUSE IS NEXT!
NO!
SECOND SQUAD, GO AROUND TO THE BACK!!
TMPTMP

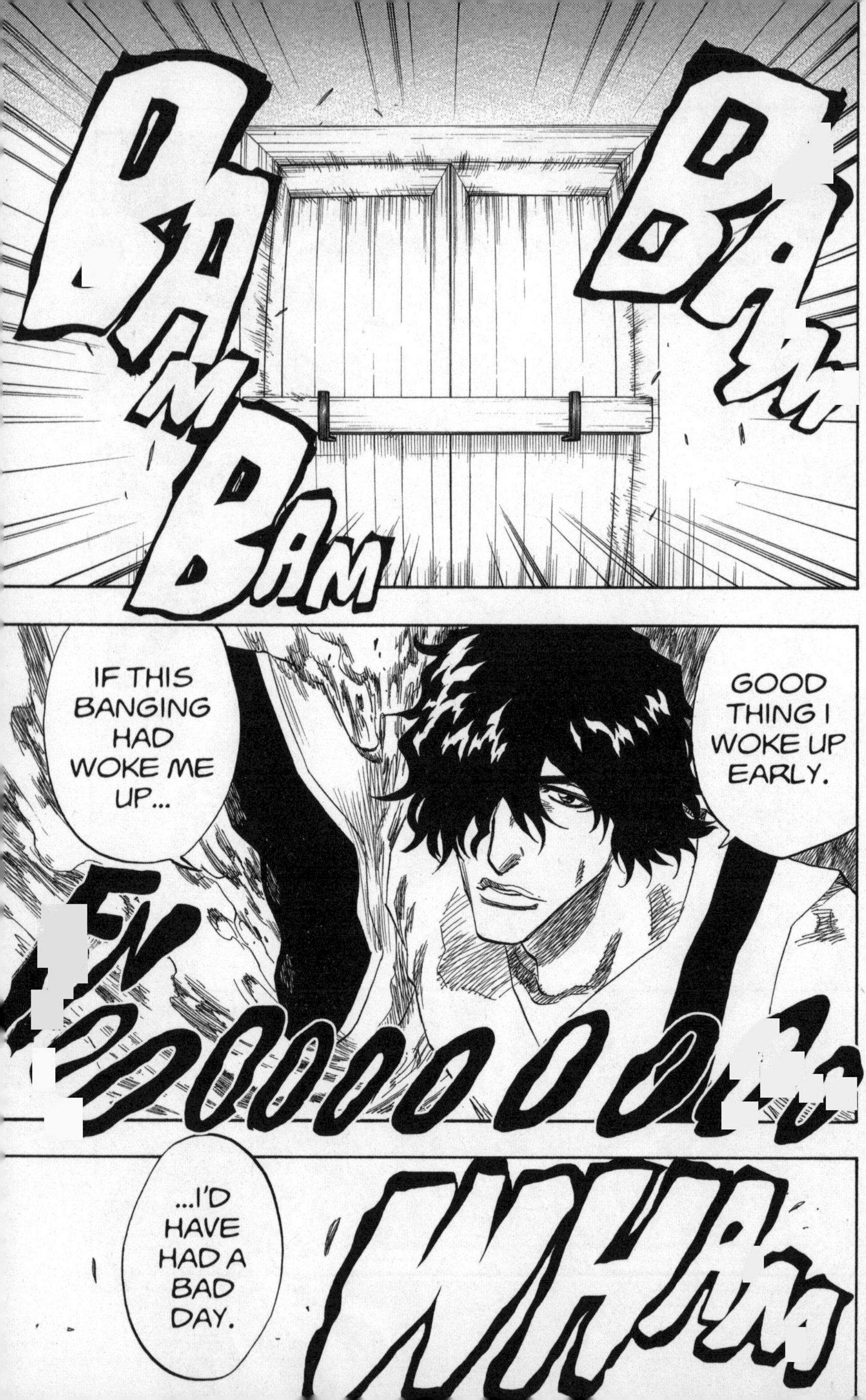
BAM
BAM BAM
GOOD THING I WOKE UP EARLY.
IF THIS BANGING HAD WOKE ME UP...
...I'D HAVE HAD A BAD DAY.

102. Nobody Wins

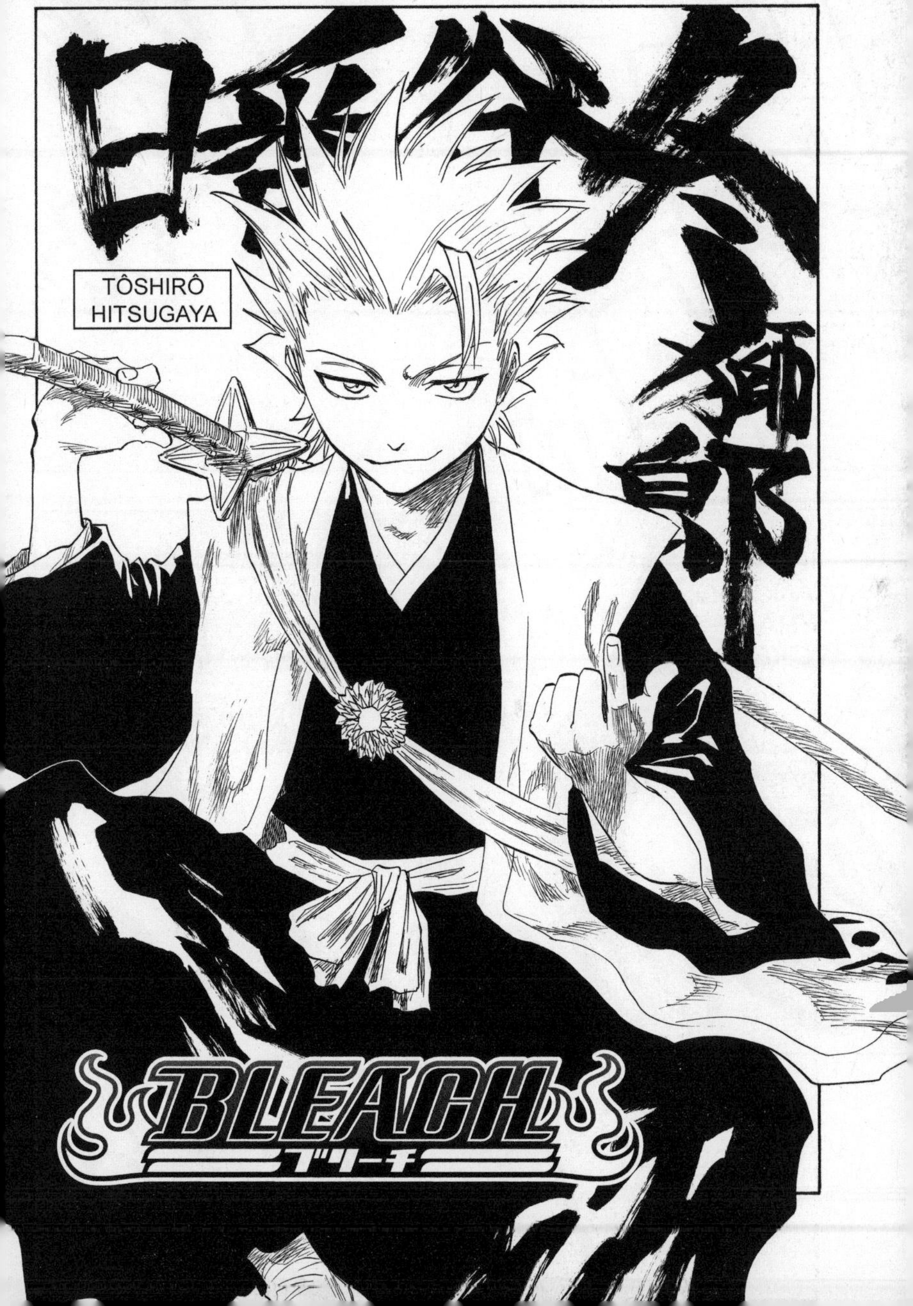
TÔSHIRÔ
HITSUGAYA
BLEACH
ブリーチ

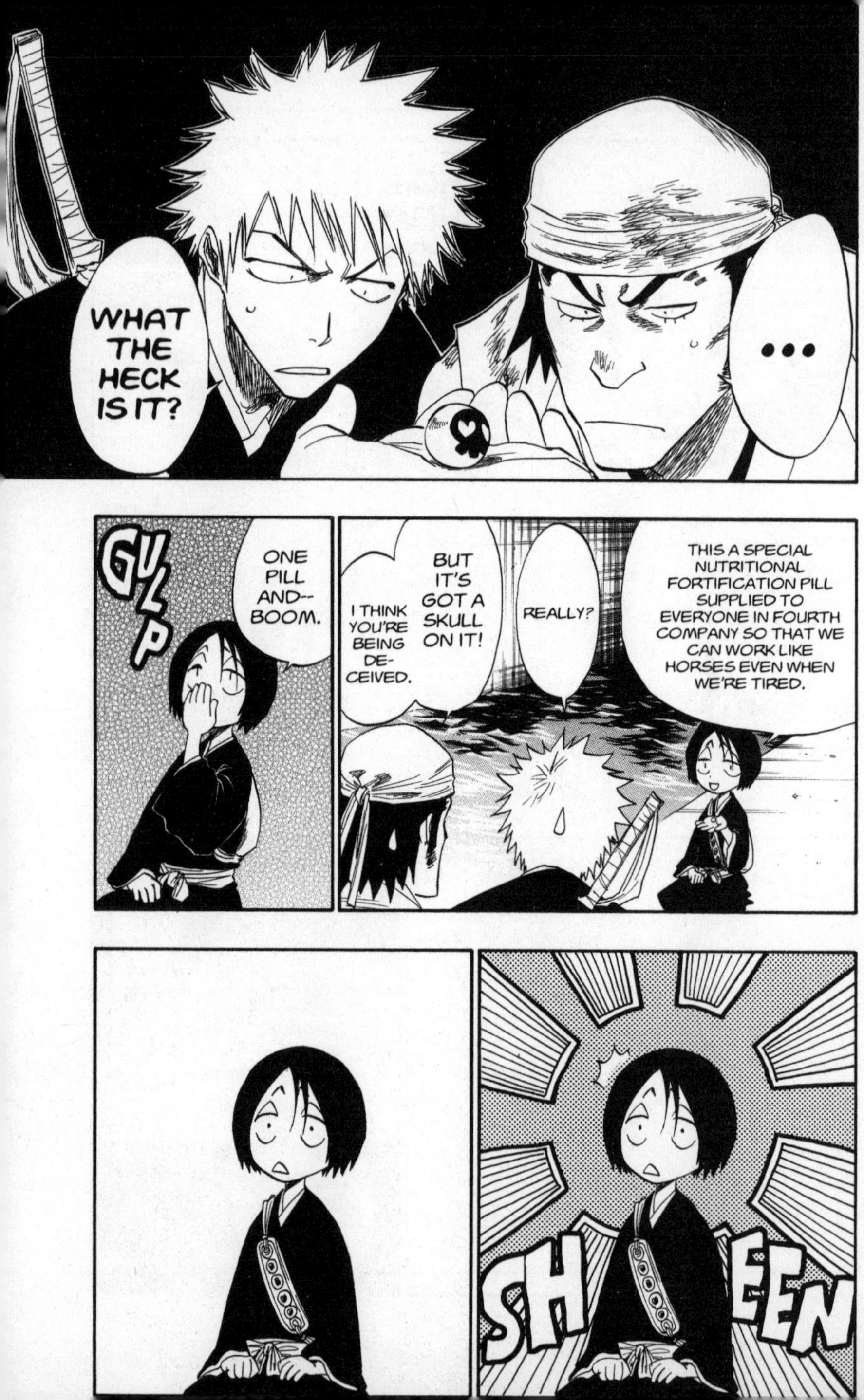
•••
WHAT THE HECK IS IT?
THIS A SPECIAL NUTRITIONAL FORTIFICATION PILL SUPPLIED TO EVERYONE IN FOURTH COMPANY SO THAT WE CAN WORK LIKE HORSES EVEN WHEN WE'RE TIRED.
REALLY?
BUT IT'S GOT A SKULL ON IT!
I THINK YOU'RE BEING DE-CEIVED.
ONE PILL AND-- BOOM.
GULP
SH EEN

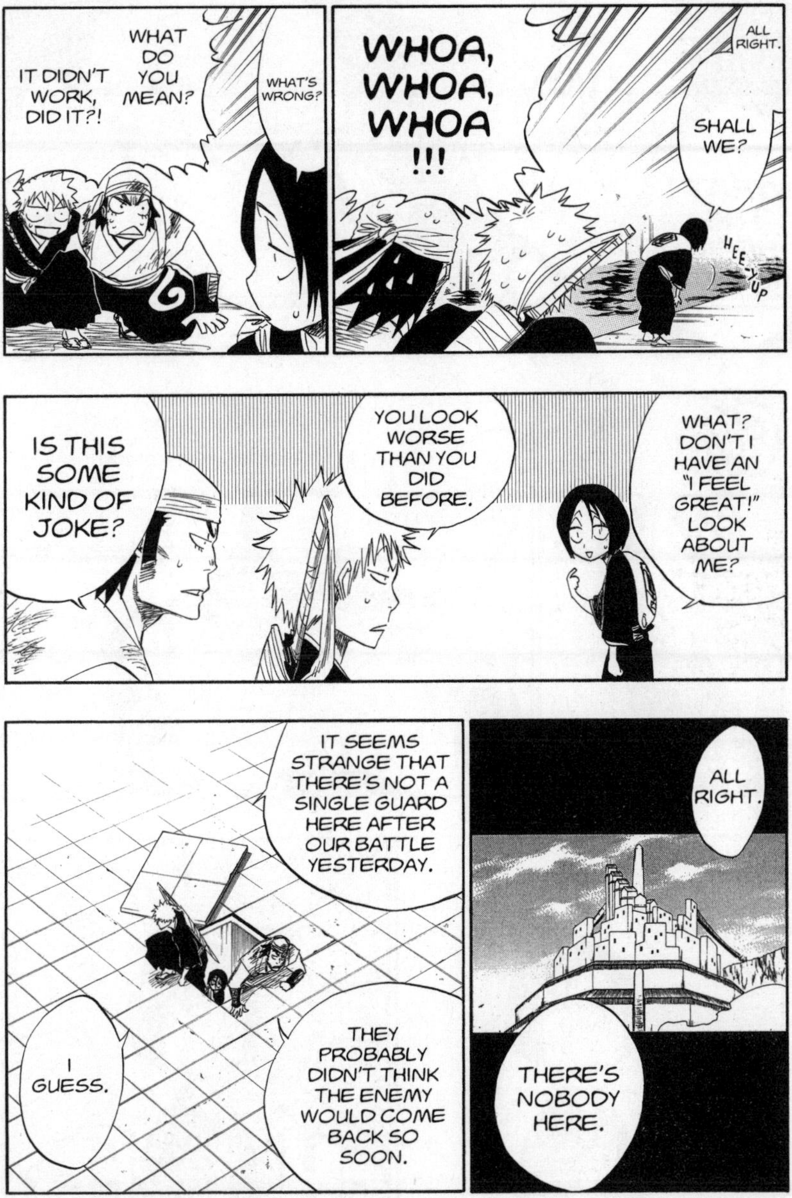
ALL RIGHT.
SHALL WE?
HEE-YUP
WHOA, WHOA, WHOA!!!
WHAT'S WRONG?
WHAT DO YOU MEAN?
IT DIDN'T WORK, DID IT?!
WHAT? DON'T I HAVE AN "I FEEL GREAT!" LOOK ABOUT ME?
YOU LOOK WORSE THAN YOU DID BEFORE.
IS THIS SOME KIND OF JOKE?
ALL RIGHT.
THERE'S NOBODY HERE.
IT SEEMS STRANGE THAT THERE'S NOT A SINGLE GUARD HERE AFTER OUR BATTLE YESTERDAY.
THEY PROBABLY DIDN'T THINK THE ENEMY WOULD COME BACK SO SOON.
I GUESS.

READ THIS WAY

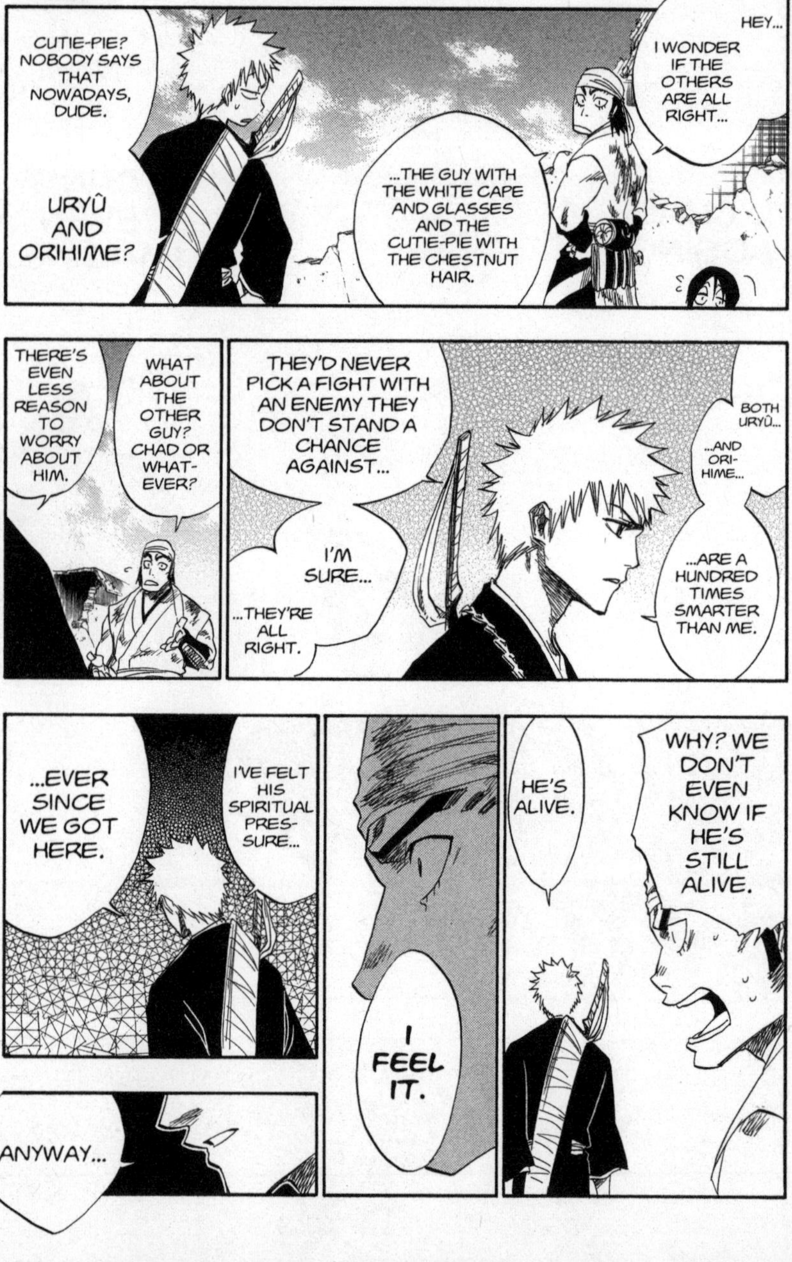
HEY... I WONDER IF THE OTHERS ARE ALL RIGHT...
...THE GUY WITH THE WHITE CAPE AND GLASSES AND THE CUTIE-PIE WITH THE CHESTNUT HAIR.
CUTIE-PIE? NOBODY SAYS THAT NOWADAYS, DUDE.
URYÛ AND ORIHIME?
BOTH URYÛ...
...AND ORI-HIME...
...ARE A HUNDRED TIMES SMARTER THAN ME.
THEY'D NEVER PICK A FIGHT WITH AN ENEMY THEY DON'T STAND A CHANCE AGAINST...
I'M SURE...
...THEY'RE ALL RIGHT.
WHAT ABOUT THE OTHER GUY? CHAD OR WHAT-EVER?
THERE'S EVEN LESS REASON TO WORRY ABOUT HIM.
WHY? WE DON'T EVEN KNOW IF HE'S STILL ALIVE.
HE'S ALIVE.
I FEEL IT.
I'VE FELT HIS SPIRITUAL PRES-SURE...
...EVER SINCE WE GOT HERE.
ANYWAY...

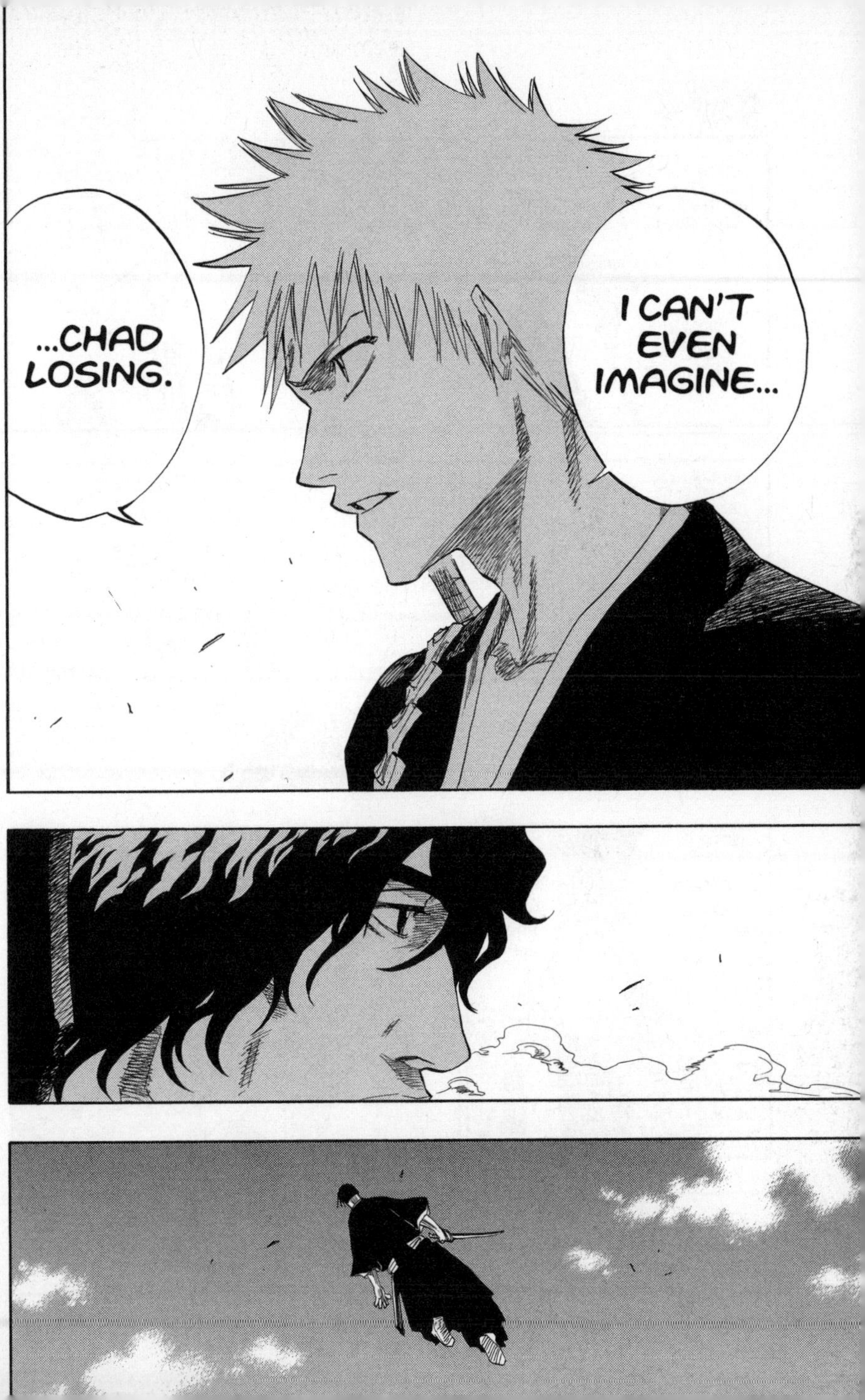
I CAN'T EVEN IMAGINE...
...CHAD LOSING.

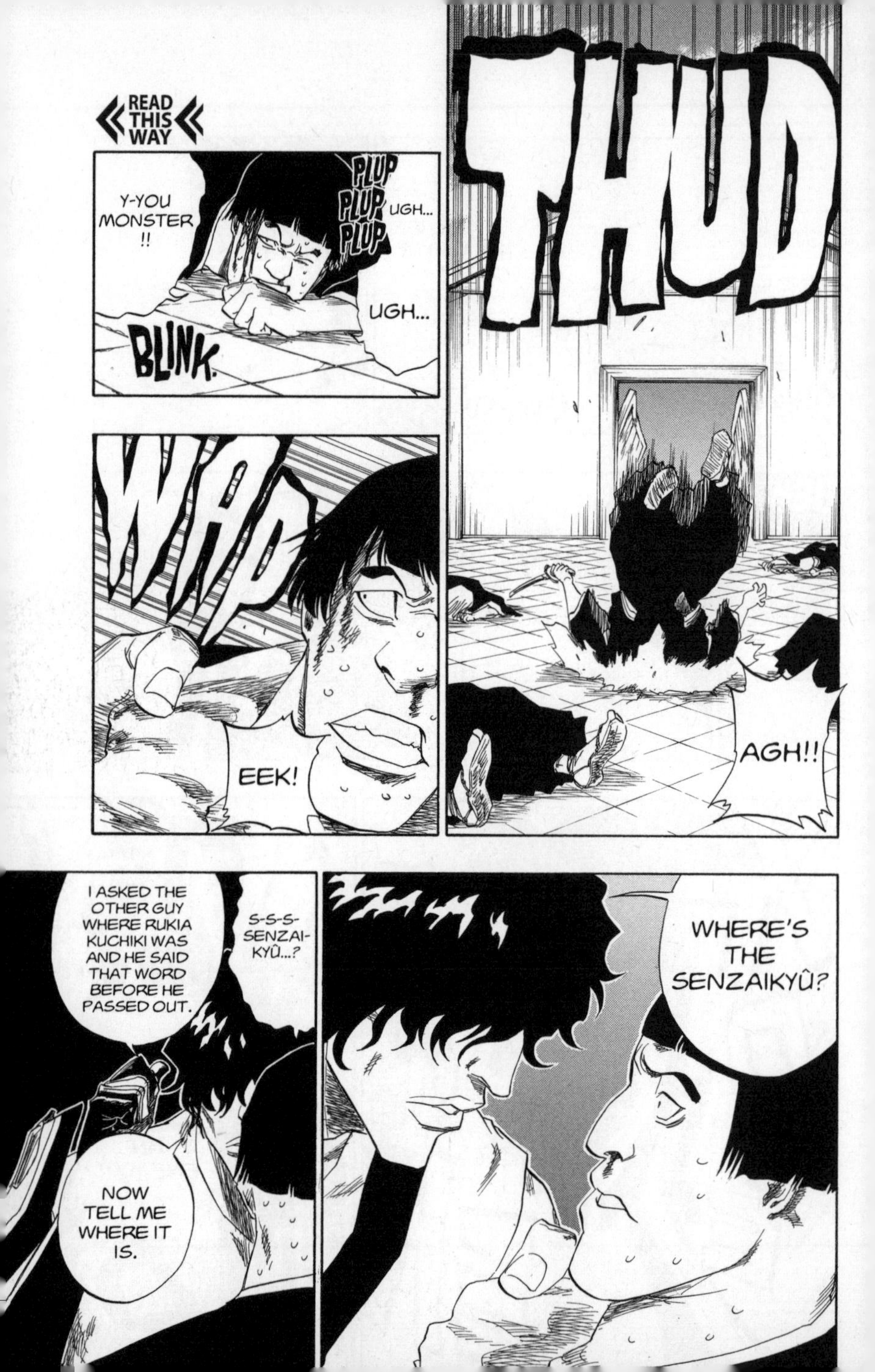
READ THIS WAY
THUD
AGH!!
PLUP PLUP PLUP
UGH...
Y-YOU MONSTER !!
UGH...
BLINK.
WHAP
EEK!
WHERE'S THE SENZAIKYÛ?
S-S-S-SENZAIKYÛ...?
I ASKED THE OTHER GUY WHERE RUKIA KUCHIKI WAS AND HE SAID THAT WORD BEFORE HE PASSED OUT.
NOW TELL ME WHERE IT IS.

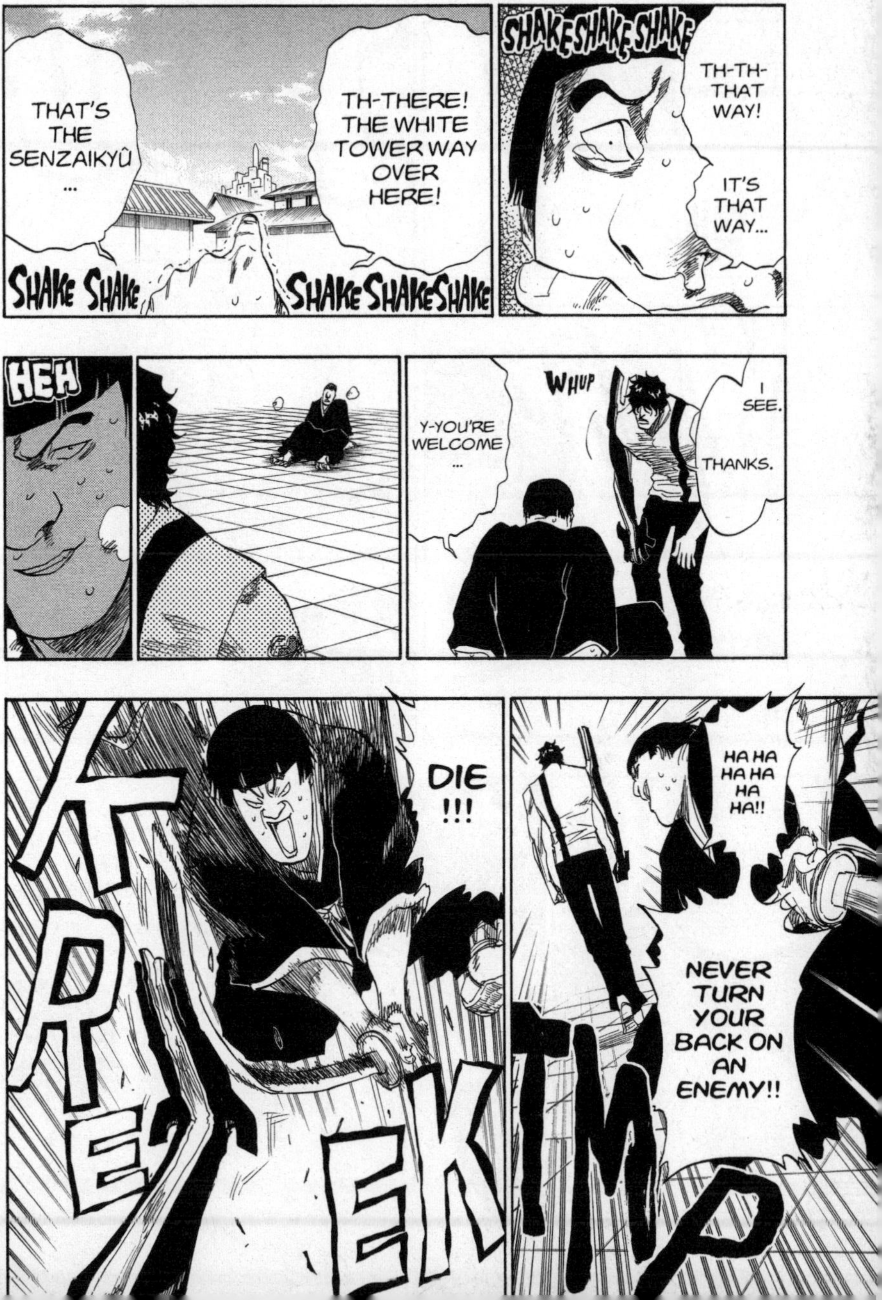
SHAKE SHAKE SHAKE
TH-TH-THAT WAY!
IT'S THAT WAY...
TH-THERE! THE WHITE TOWER WAY OVER HERE!
THAT'S THE SENZAIKYŪ...
SHAKE SHAKE SHAKE
SHAKE SHAKE
I SEE.
THANKS.
WHUP
Y-YOU'RE WELCOME...
HEH
HA HA HA HA HA HA!!
NEVER TURN YOUR BACK ON AN ENEMY!!
TMP
DIE!!!
KREEK

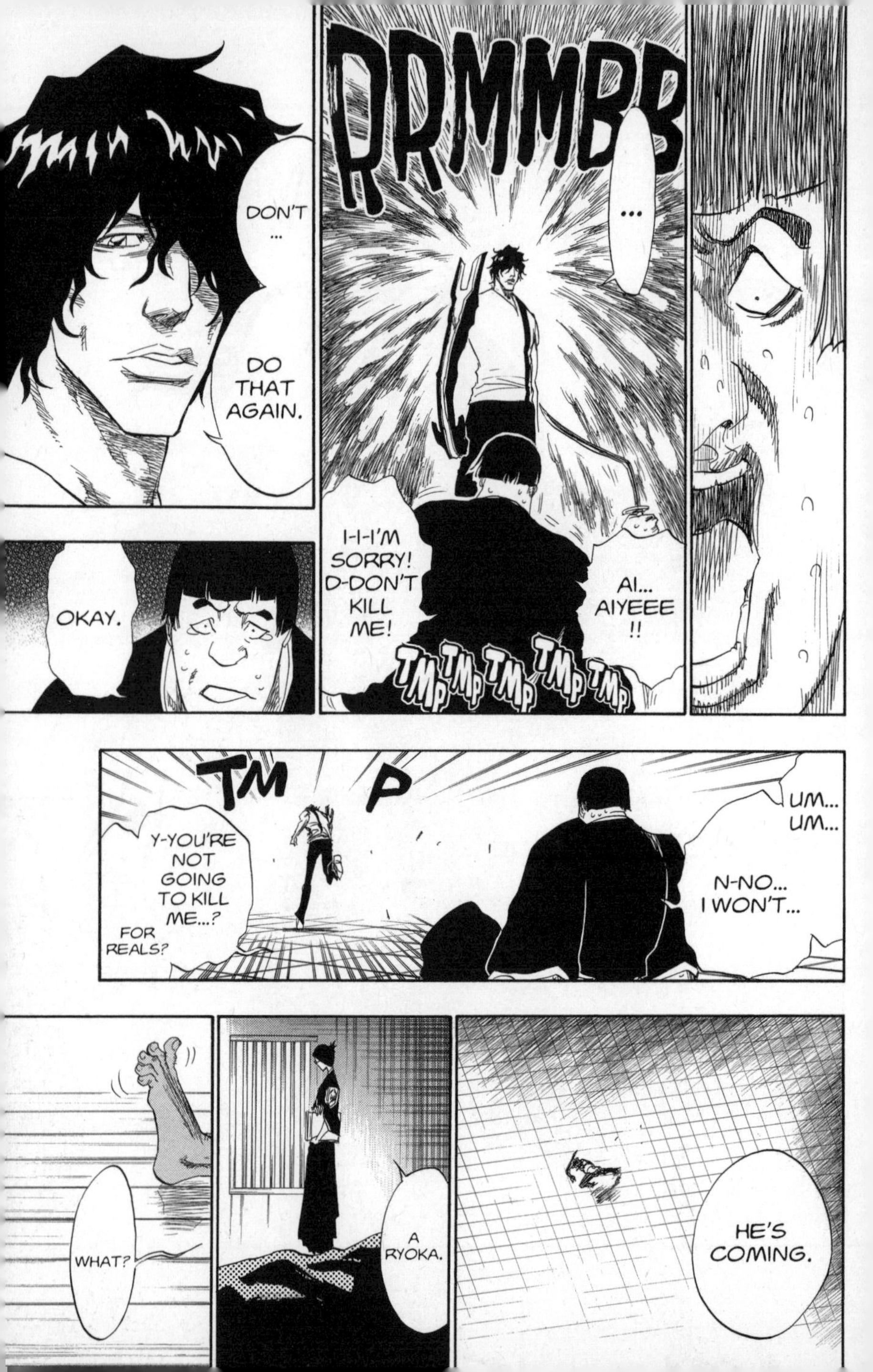
DRMMBB
...
AI... AIYEEE !!
I-I-I'M SORRY! D-DON'T KILL ME!
TMP TMP TMP TMP TMP
DON'T ...
DO THAT AGAIN.
OKAY.
UM... UM...
N-NO... I WON'T...
TM P
Y-YOU'RE NOT GOING TO KILL ME...?
FOR REALS?
HE'S COMING.
A RYOKA.
WHAT?

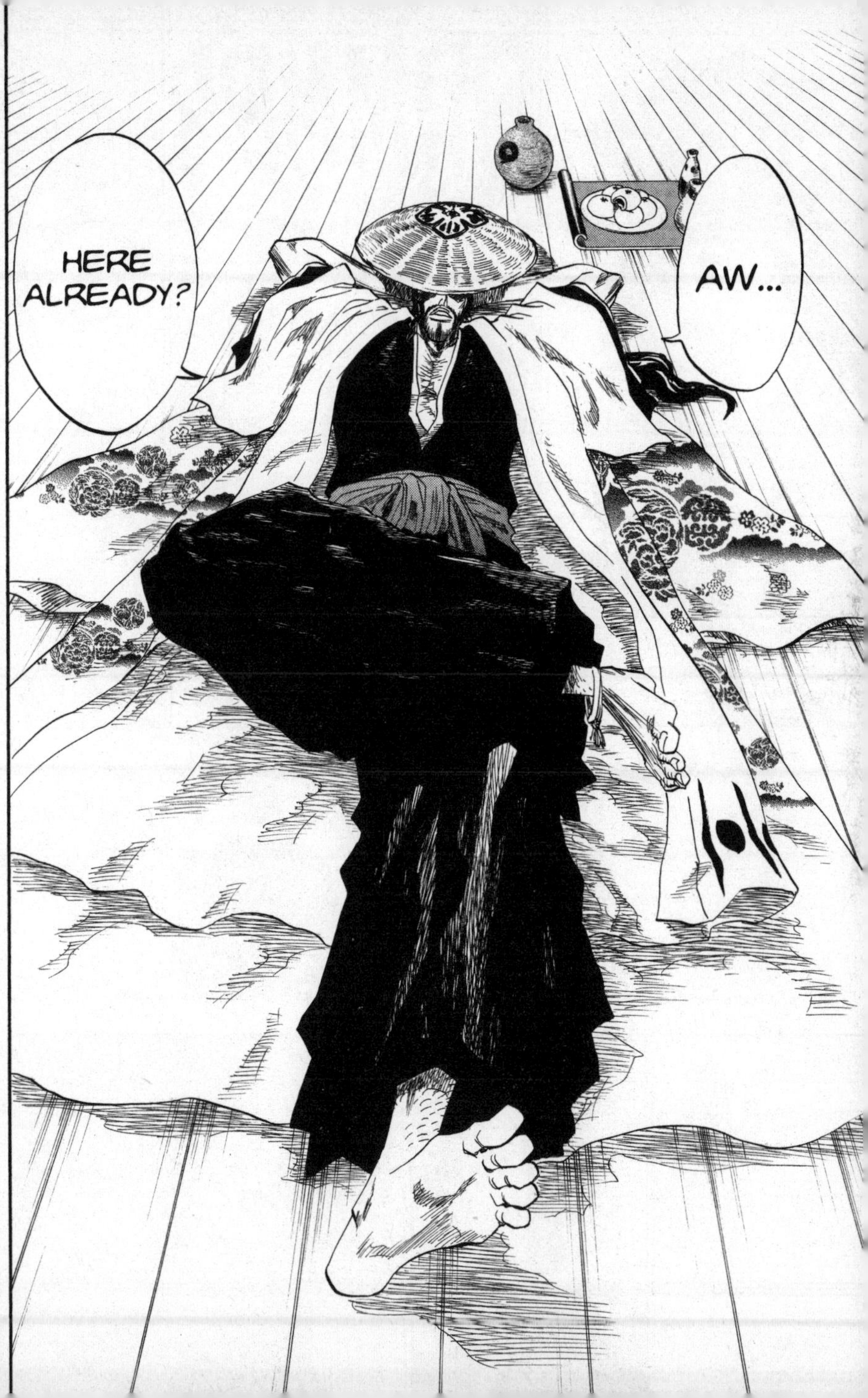
AW...
HERE ALREADY?

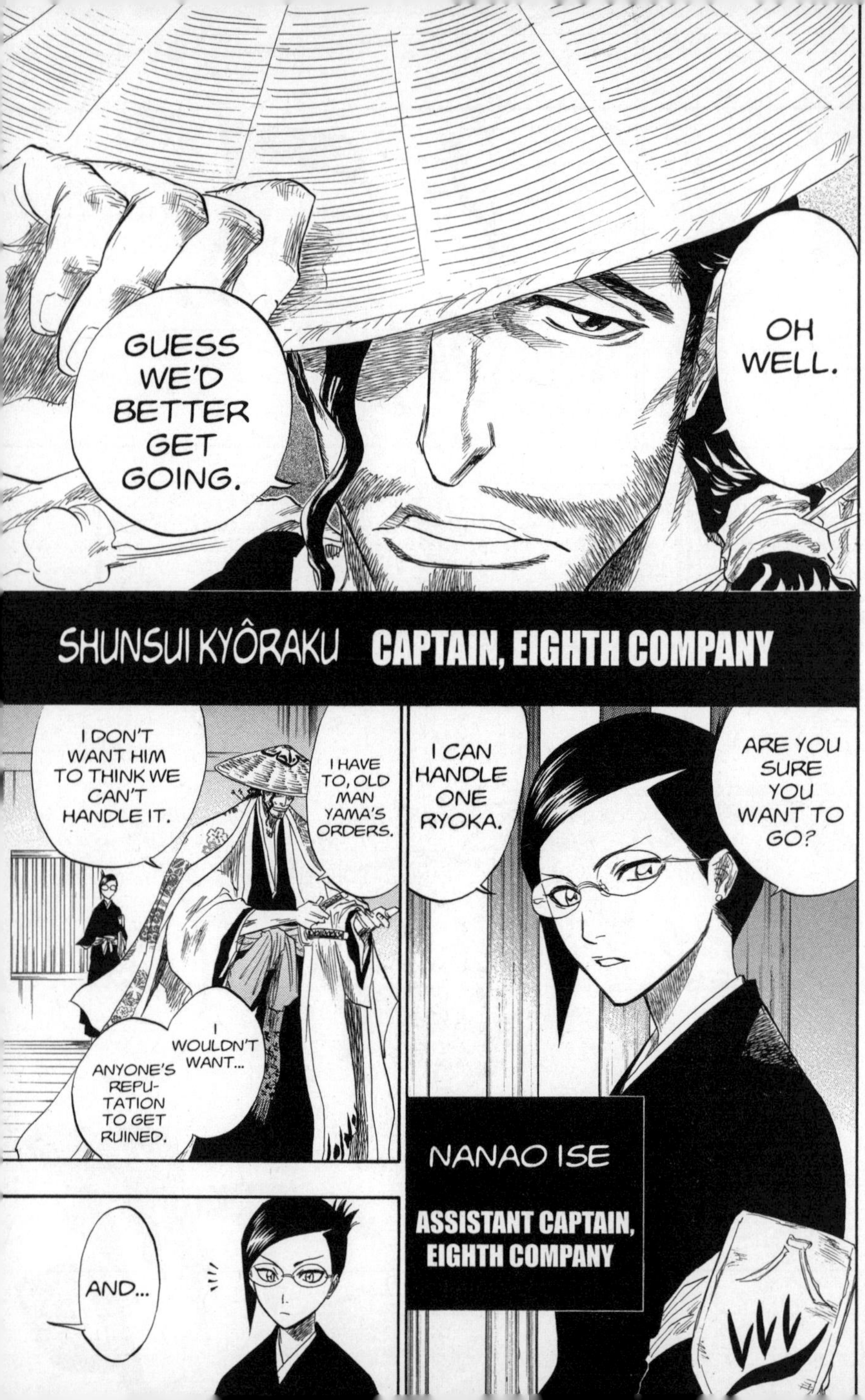
OH WELL.
GUESS WE'D BETTER GET GOING.
SHUNSUI KYÔRAKU
CAPTAIN, EIGHTH COMPANY
ARE YOU SURE YOU WANT TO GO?
I CAN HANDLE ONE RYOKA.
NANAO ISE
ASSISTANT CAPTAIN, EIGHTH COMPANY
I HAVE TO, OLD MAN YAMA'S ORDERS.
I DON'T WANT HIM TO THINK WE CAN'T HANDLE IT.
I WOULDN'T WANT...
ANYONE'S REPU-TATION TO GET RUINED.
AND...

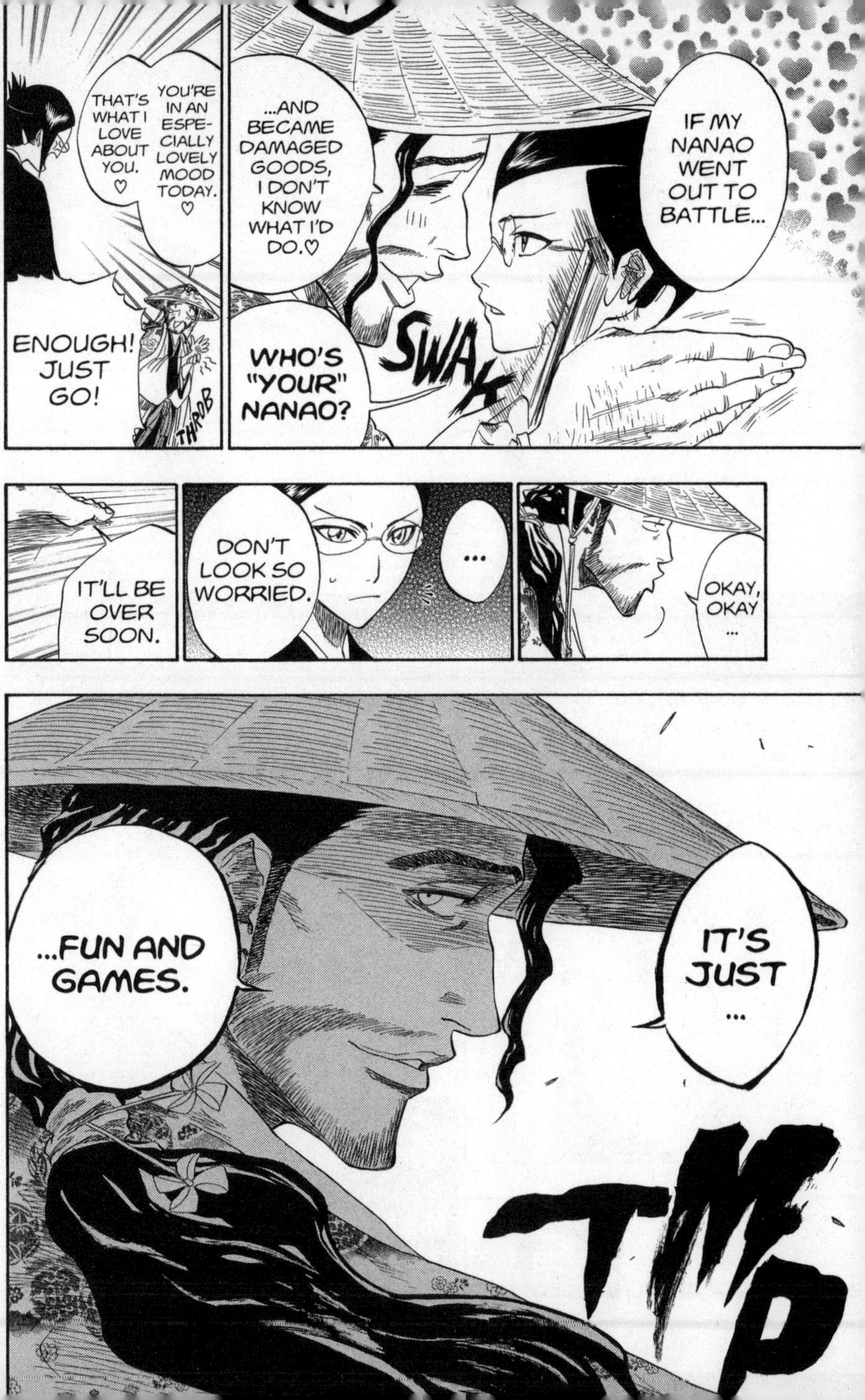
IF MY NANAO WENT OUT TO BATTLE...
...AND BECAME DAMAGED GOODS, I DON'T KNOW WHAT I'D DO.♡
SWAK
WHO'S "YOUR" NANAO?
YOU'RE IN AN ESPE-CIALLY LOVELY MOOD TODAY.♡
THAT'S WHAT I LOVE ABOUT YOU.♡
ENOUGH! JUST GO!
THROB
OKAY, OKAY ...
...
DON'T LOOK SO WORRIED.
IT'LL BE OVER SOON.
IT'S JUST ...
...FUN AND GAMES.
TMP

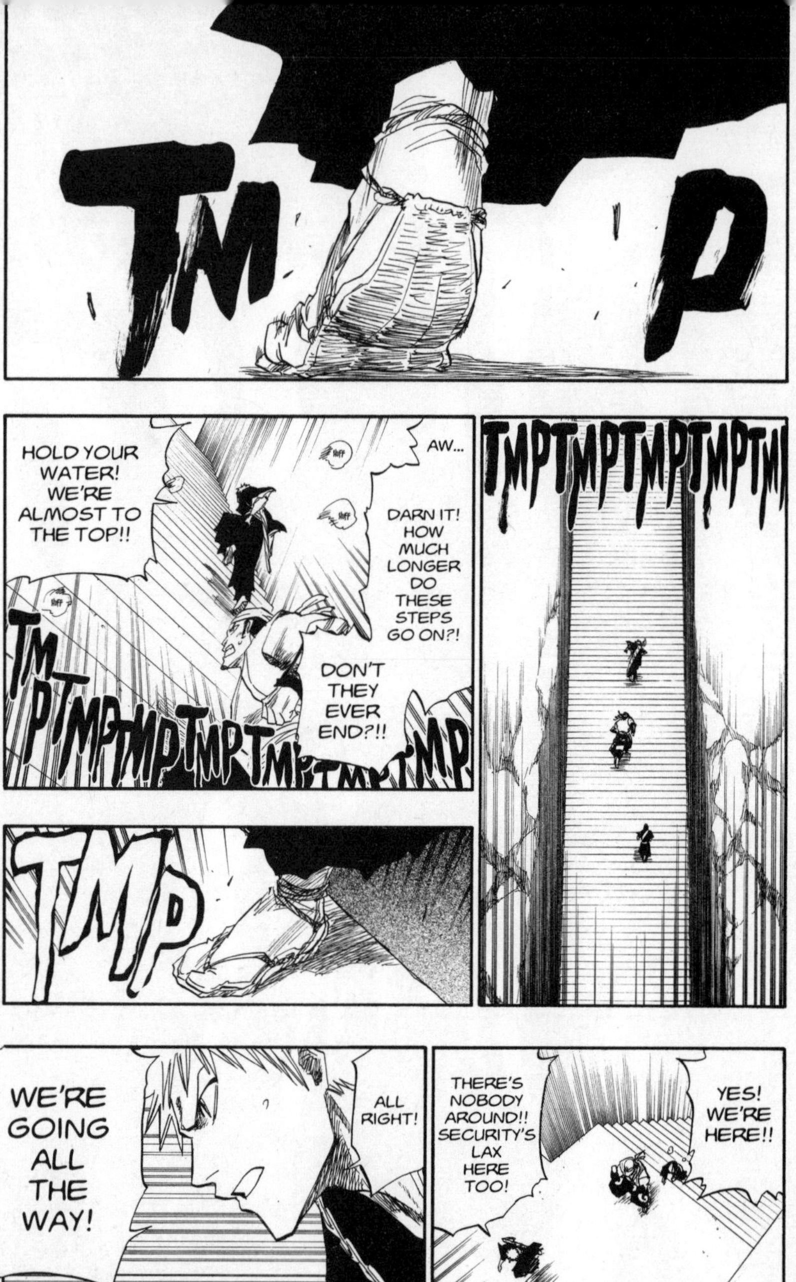
TMP
TMPTMPTMPTMPTM
AW...
DARN IT! HOW MUCH LONGER DO THESE STEPS GO ON?!
DON'T THEY EVER END?!!
HOLD YOUR WATER! WE'RE ALMOST TO THE TOP!!
TMPTMPTMPTMPTMPTMPTMP
TMP
YES! WE'RE HERE!!
THERE'S NOBODY AROUND!! SECURITY'S LAX HERE TOO!
ALL RIGHT!
WE'RE GOING ALL THE WAY!

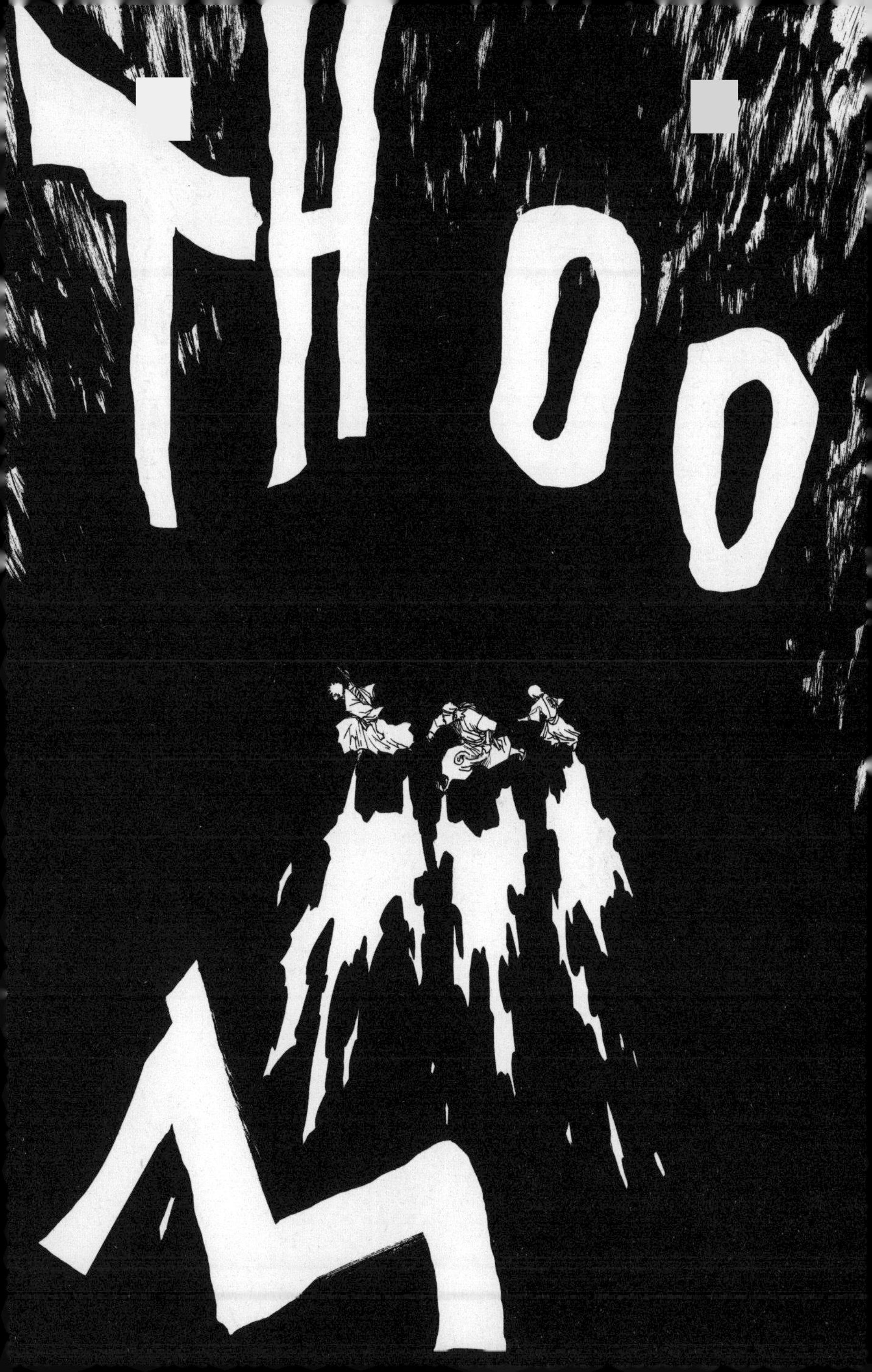
THOO

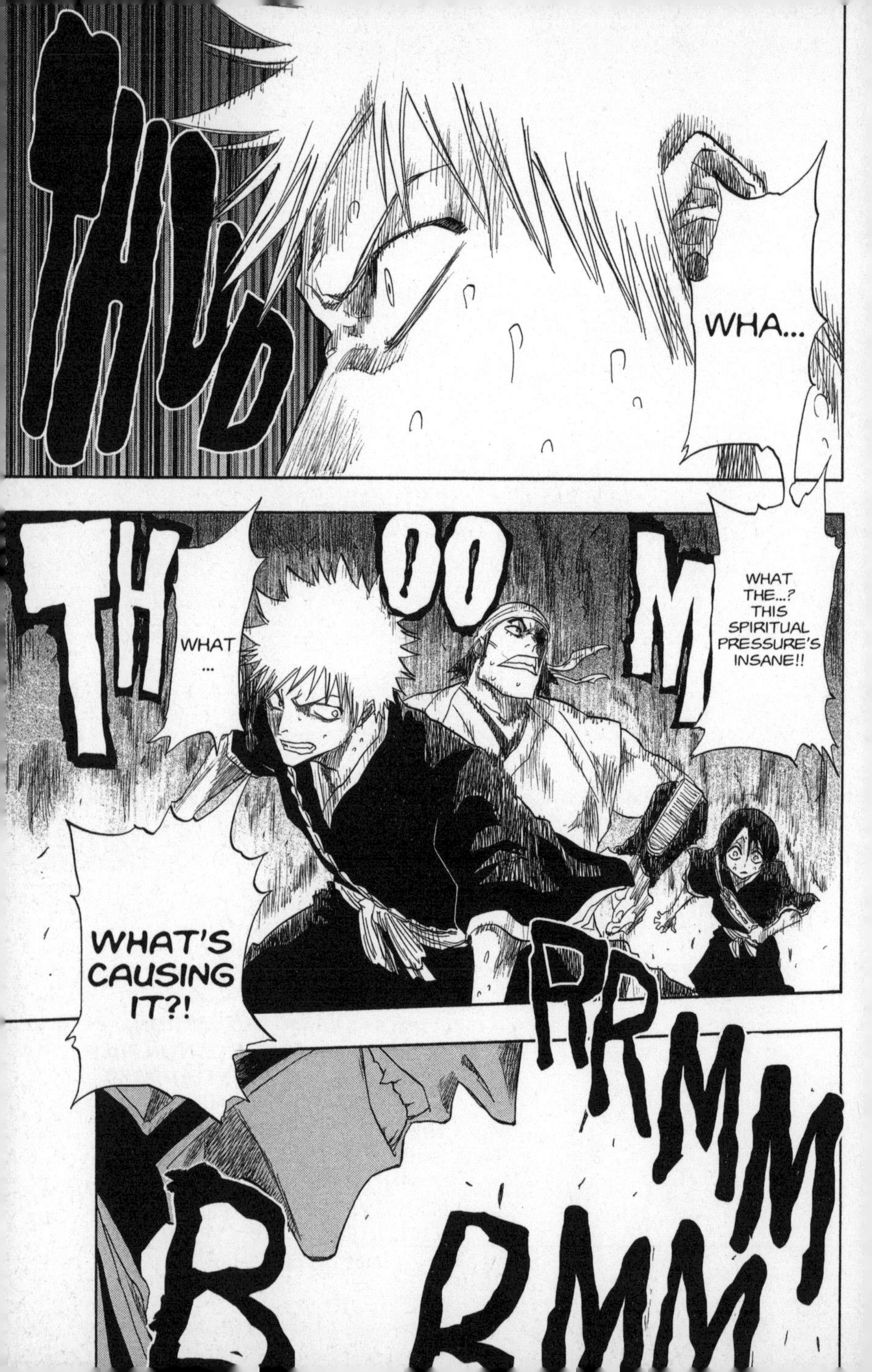
WHA...
THUD
WHAT THE...? THIS SPIRITUAL PRESSURE'S INSANE!!
THOOM
WHAT ...
WHAT'S CAUSING IT?!
RRMM
BRMM

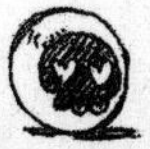

SPECIAL HANATARÔ VERSION NUTRITIONAL FORTIFICATION PILL! HANATARÔ THINKS IT'S STANDARD ISSUE FOR FOURTH COMPANY, BUT WHAT HE'S HOLDING IS SOMETHING HIS SUPERIORS CREATED AS A PRANK. IT'S DIFFERENT FROM THE MEDICINE THE OTHER MEMBERS OF HIS COMPANY CARRY. IT'S ACTIVE INGREDIENT IS FLOUR.

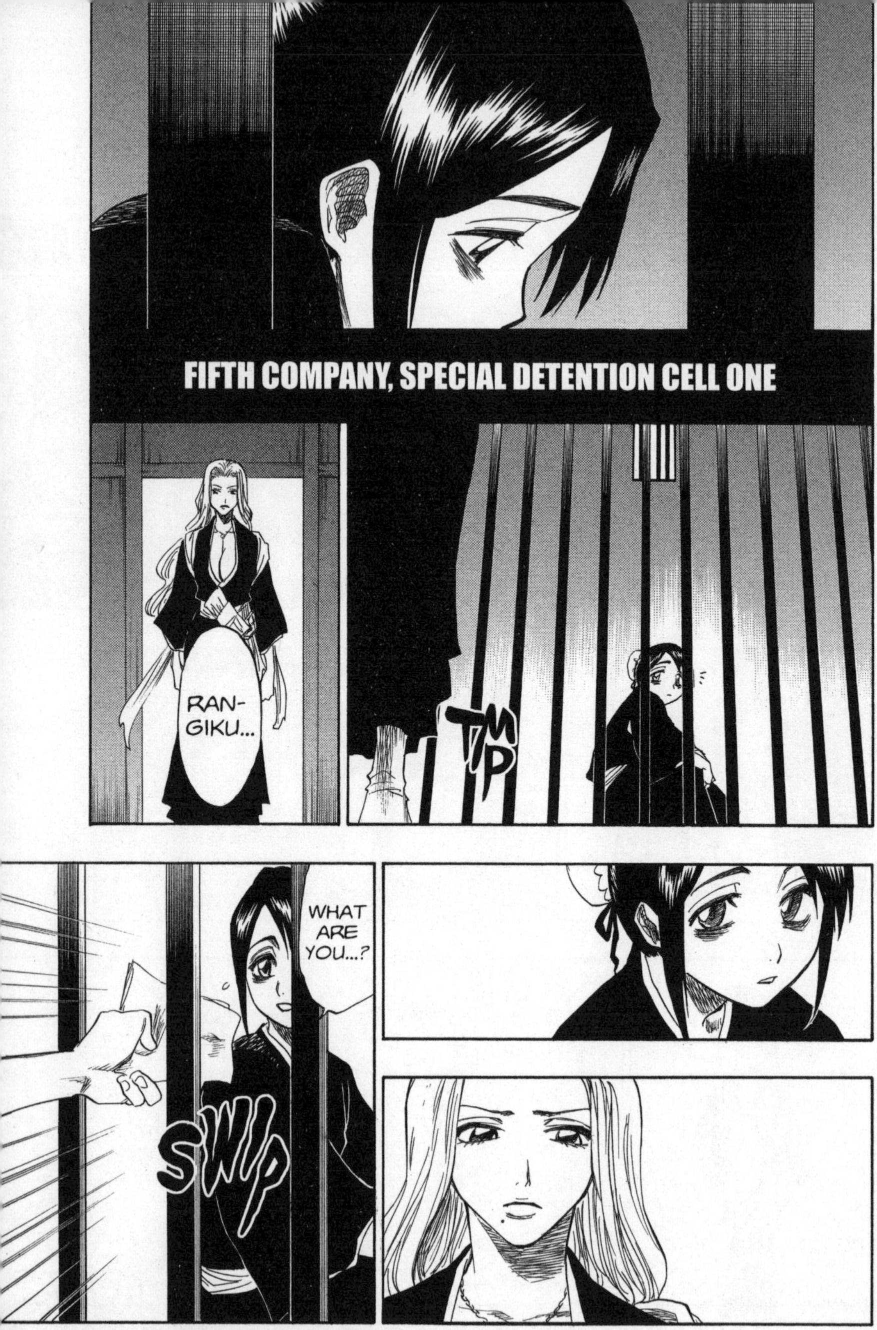
FIFTH COMPANY, SPECIAL DETENTION CELL ONE
TMP
RAN-GIKU...
WHAT ARE YOU...?
SWIP

103. Dominion

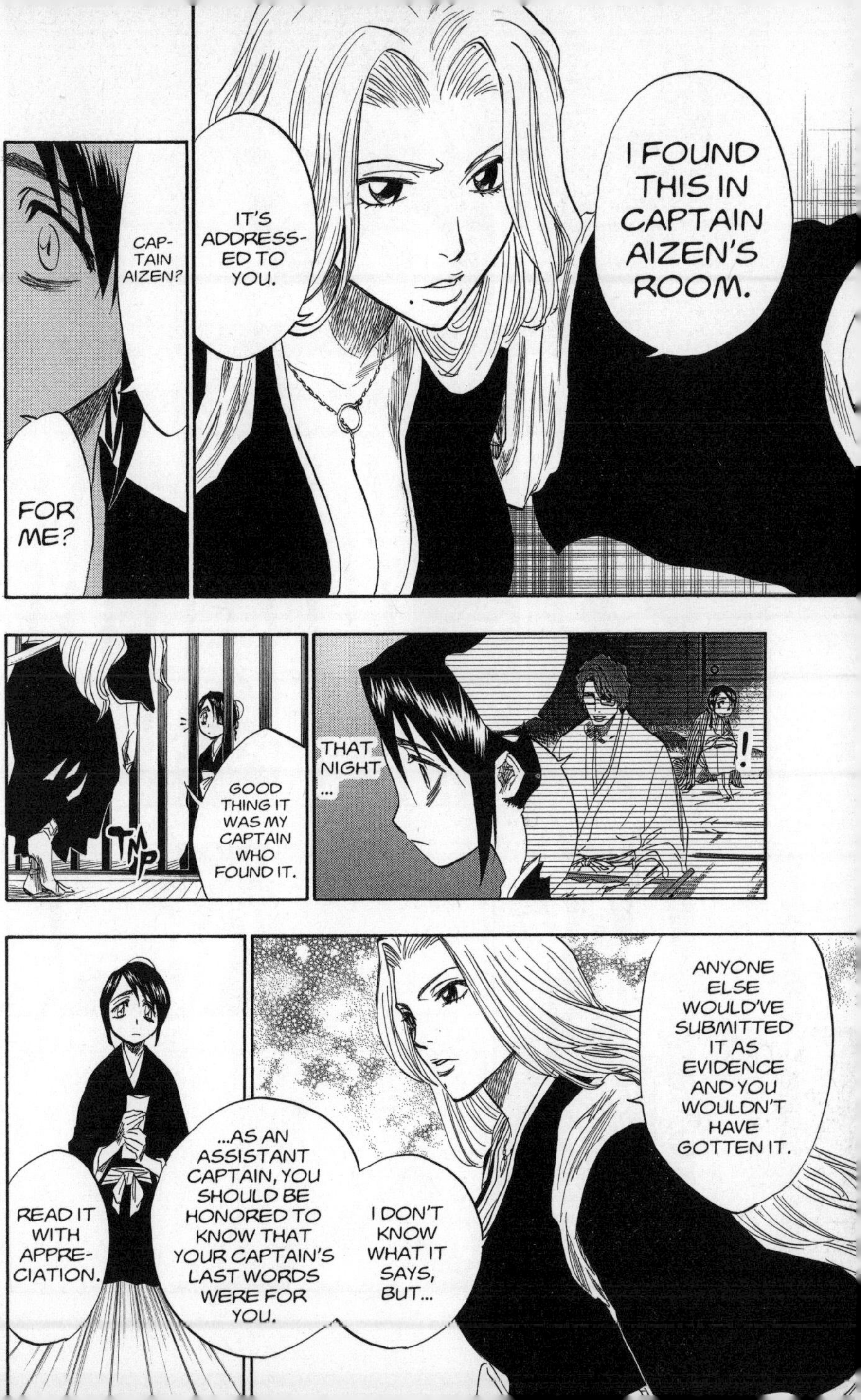
I FOUND THIS IN CAPTAIN AIZEN'S ROOM.
IT'S ADDRESSED TO YOU.
CAPTAIN AIZEN?
FOR ME?
THAT NIGHT...
GOOD THING IT WAS MY CAPTAIN WHO FOUND IT.
TMP
ANYONE ELSE WOULD'VE SUBMITTED IT AS EVIDENCE AND YOU WOULDN'T HAVE GOTTEN IT.
I DON'T KNOW WHAT IT SAYS, BUT...
...AS AN ASSISTANT CAPTAIN, YOU SHOULD BE HONORED TO KNOW THAT YOUR CAPTAIN'S LAST WORDS WERE FOR YOU.
READ IT WITH APPRECIATION.

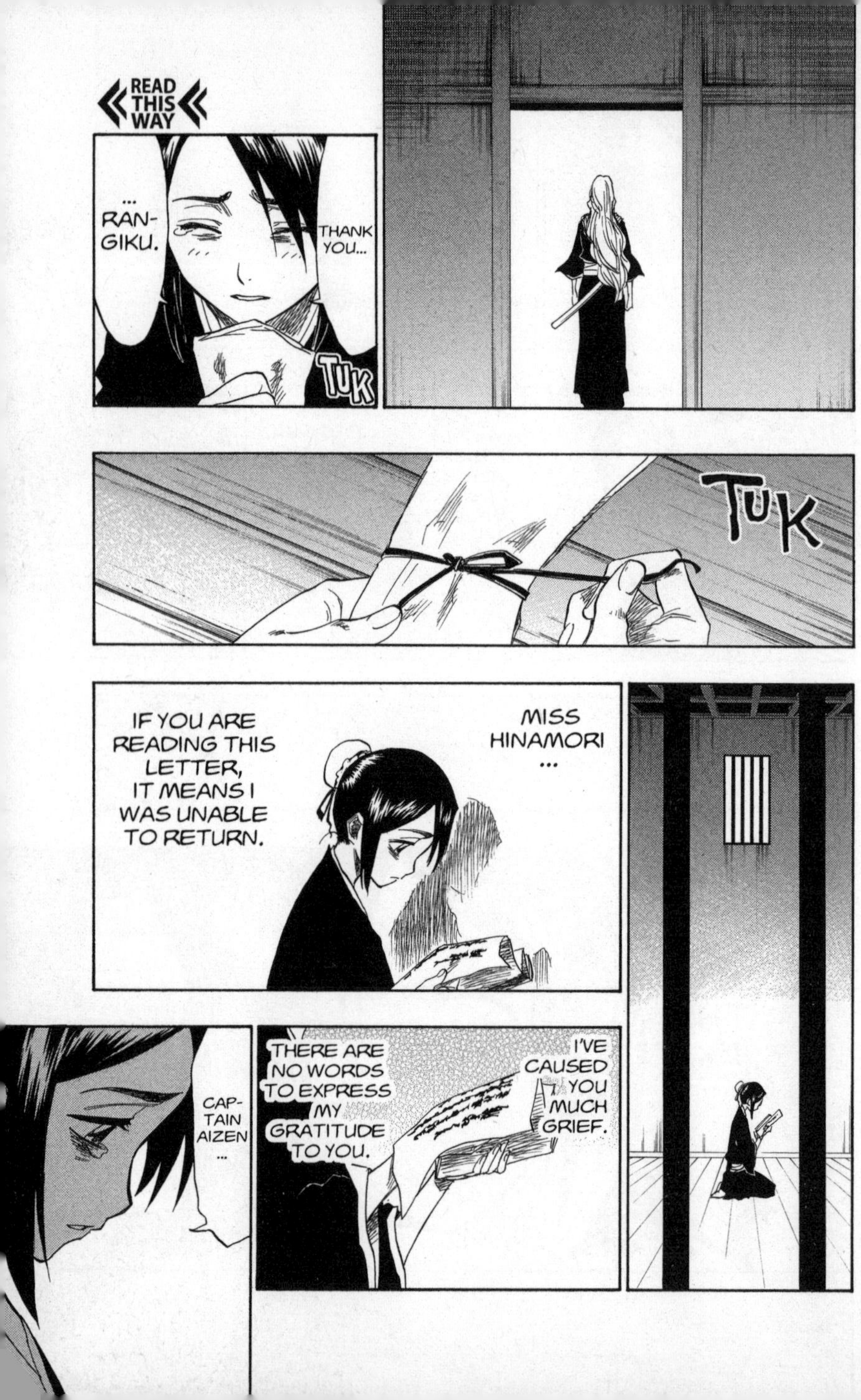
READ THIS WAY
THANK YOU...
... RAN-GIKU.
TUK
TUK
MISS HINAMORI ...
IF YOU ARE READING THIS LETTER, IT MEANS I WAS UNABLE TO RETURN.
I'VE CAUSED YOU MUCH GRIEF.
THERE ARE NO WORDS TO EXPRESS MY GRATITUDE TO YOU.
CAP-TAIN AIZEN ...

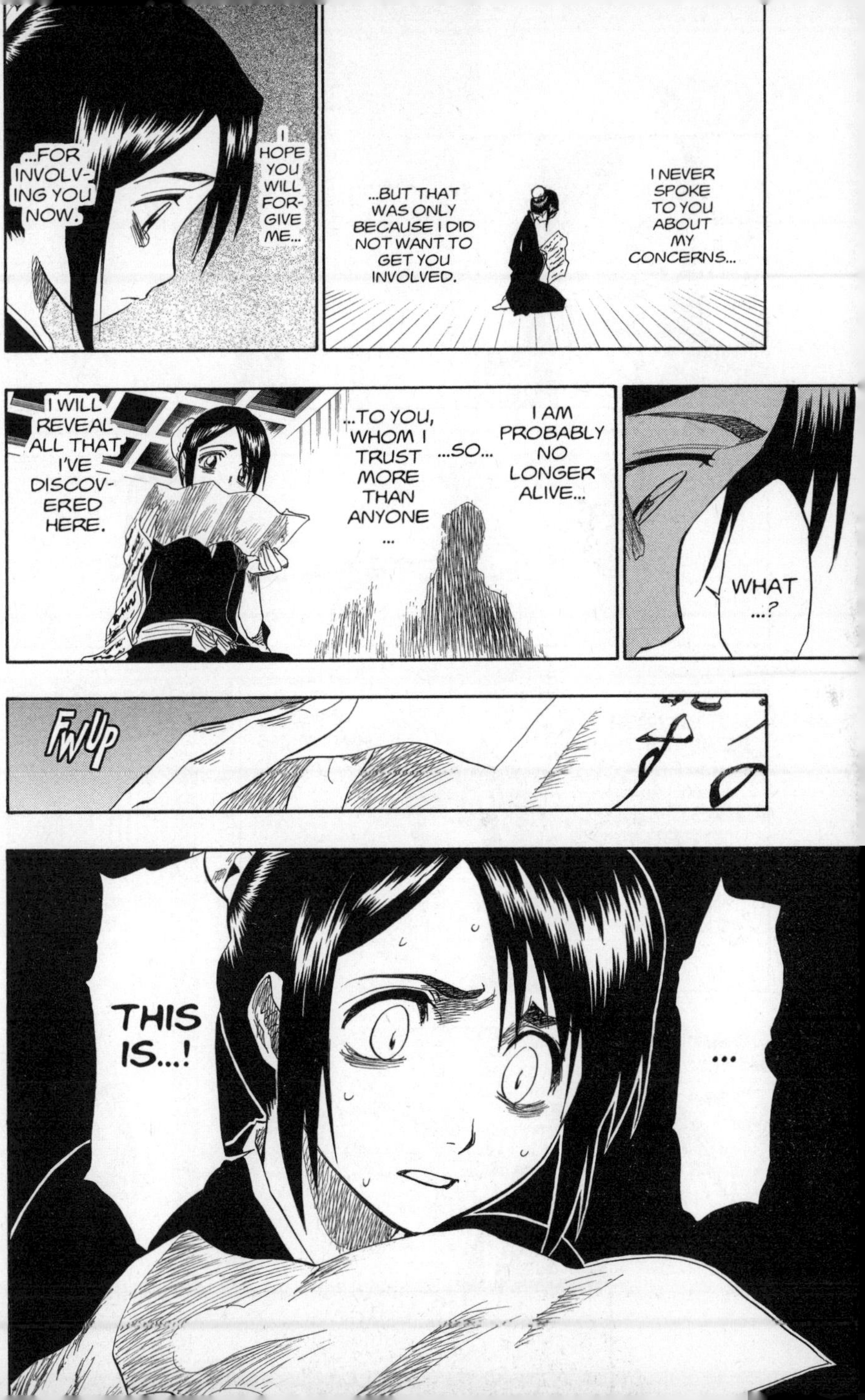
I NEVER SPOKE TO YOU ABOUT MY CONCERNS...
...BUT THAT WAS ONLY BECAUSE I DID NOT WANT TO GET YOU INVOLVED.
I HOPE YOU WILL FOR-GIVE ME...
...FOR INVOLV-ING YOU NOW.
WHAT ...?
I AM PROBABLY NO LONGER ALIVE...
...SO...
...TO YOU, WHOM I TRUST MORE THAN ANYONE ...
I WILL REVEAL ALL THAT I'VE DISCOV-ERED HERE.
FWUP
...
THIS IS...!

103. Dominion

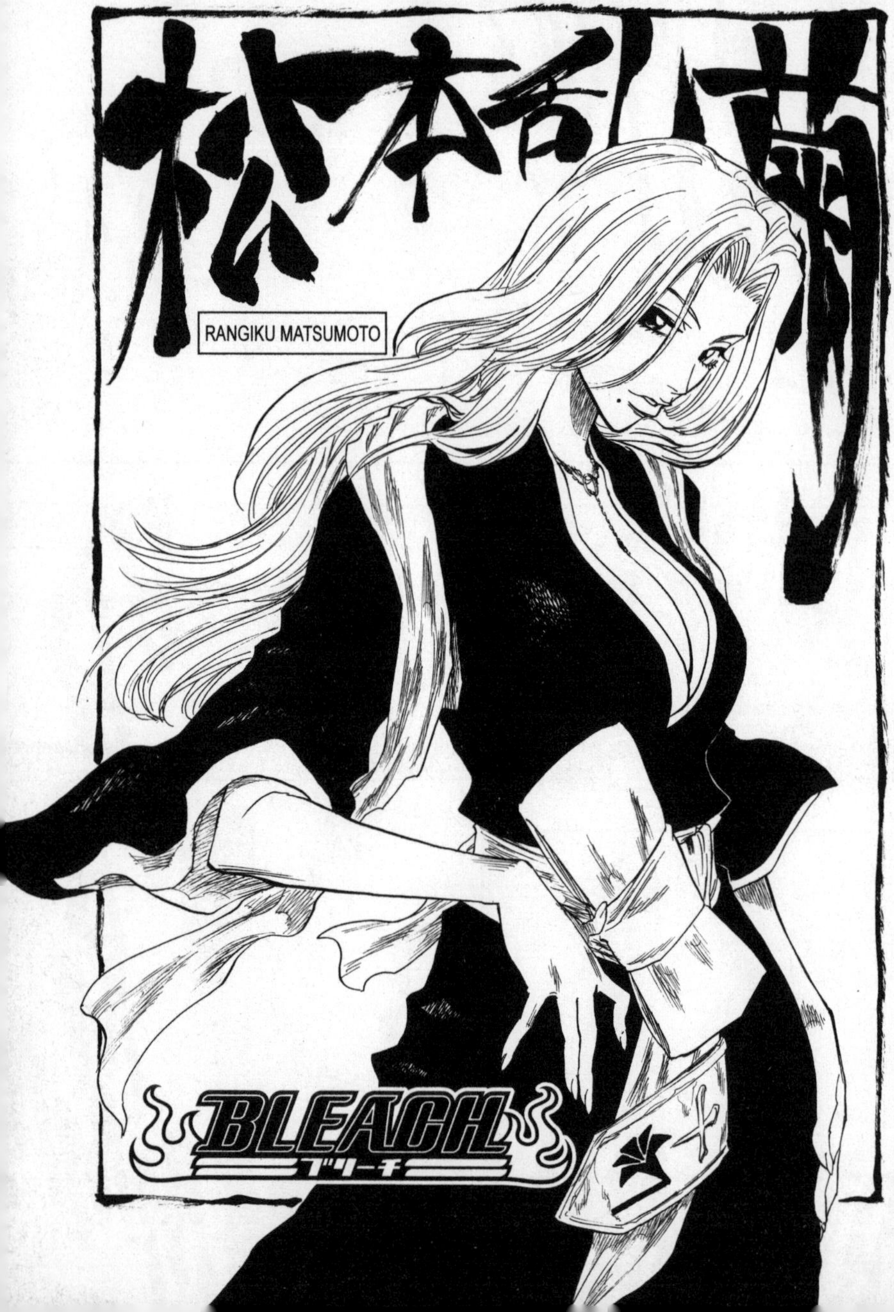
松本乱菊
RANGIKU MATSUMOTO
BLEACH
ブリーチ

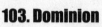

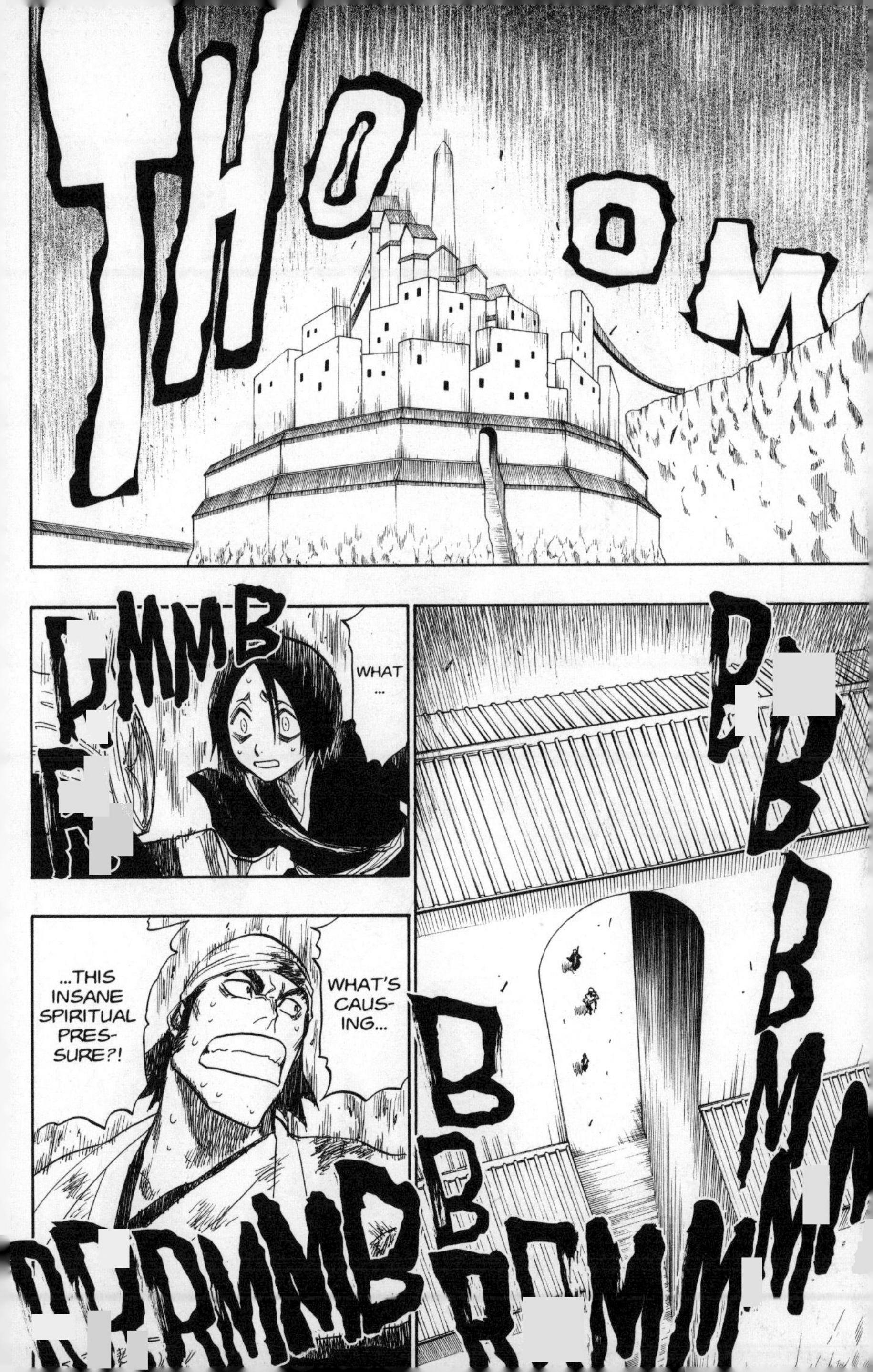
THOOM
WHAT ...
WHAT'S CAUSING...
...THIS INSANE SPIRITUAL PRESSURE?!

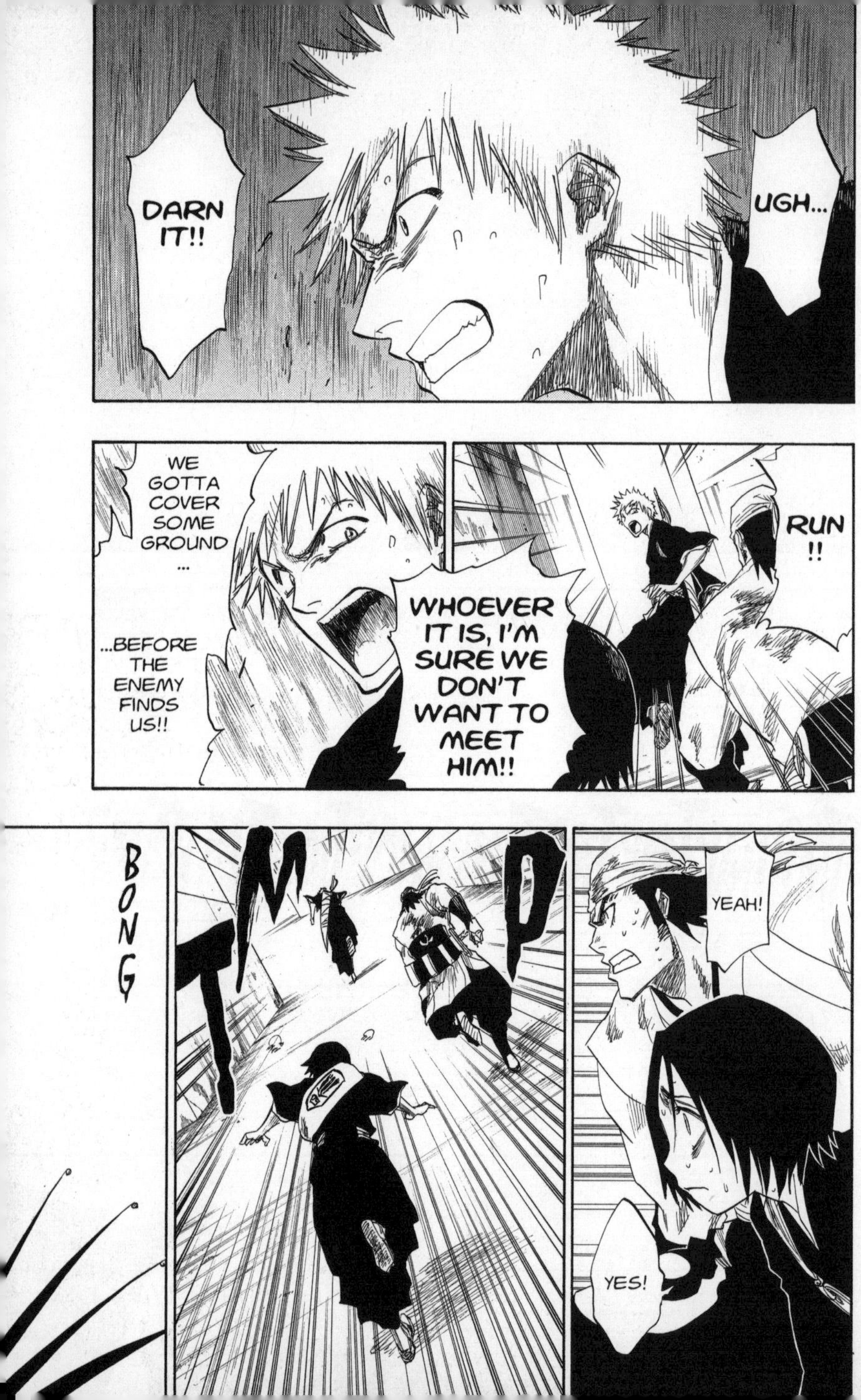
UGH...
DARN IT!!
RUN !!
WHOEVER IT IS, I'M SURE WE DON'T WANT TO MEET HIM!!
WE GOTTA COVER SOME GROUND...
...BEFORE THE ENEMY FINDS US!!
YEAH!
YES!
TMP
BONG

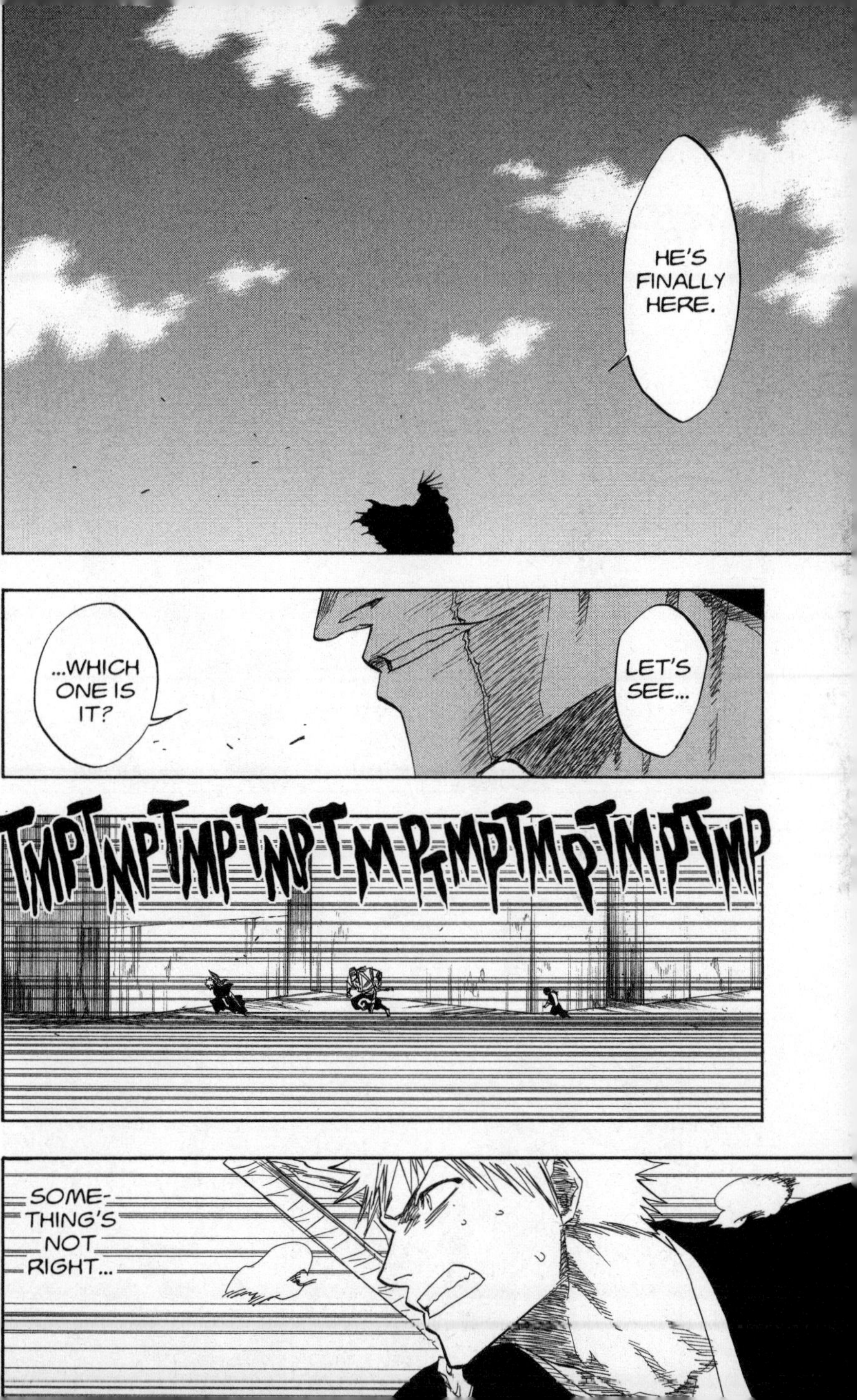
HE'S FINALLY HERE.
LET'S SEE...
...WHICH ONE IS IT?
TMPTMPTMPTMPTMPTMPTMPTMPTMP
SOME-THING'S NOT RIGHT...

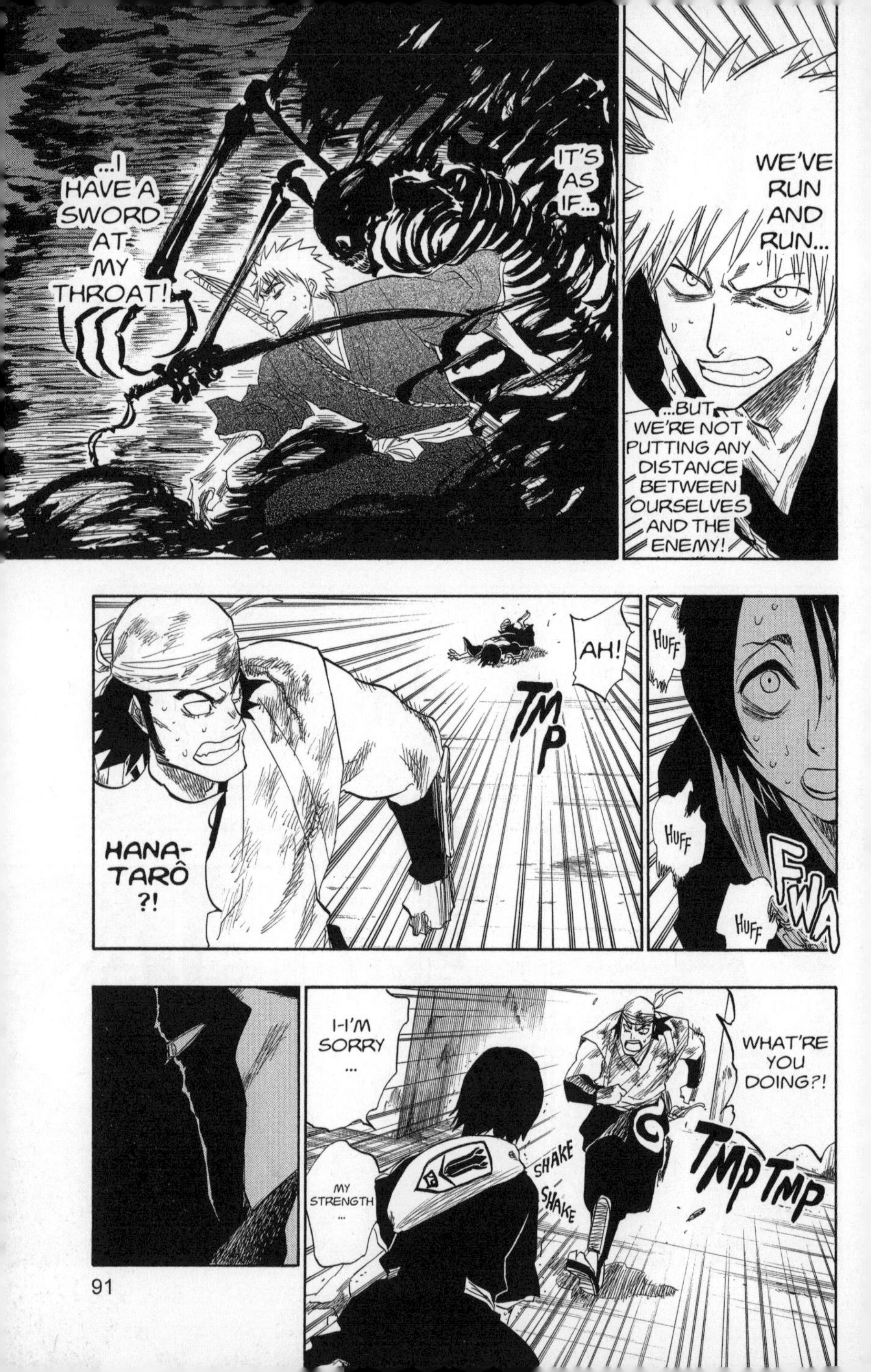
WE'VE RUN AND RUN...
...BUT WE'RE NOT PUTTING ANY DISTANCE BETWEEN OURSELVES AND THE ENEMY!
IT'S AS IF...
...I HAVE A SWORD AT MY THROAT!
HUFF
HUFF
HUFF
FWA
AH!
TMP
HANA-TARÔ ?!
WHAT'RE YOU DOING?!
TMP TMP
I-I'M SORRY ...
SHAKE SHAKE
MY STRENGTH ...

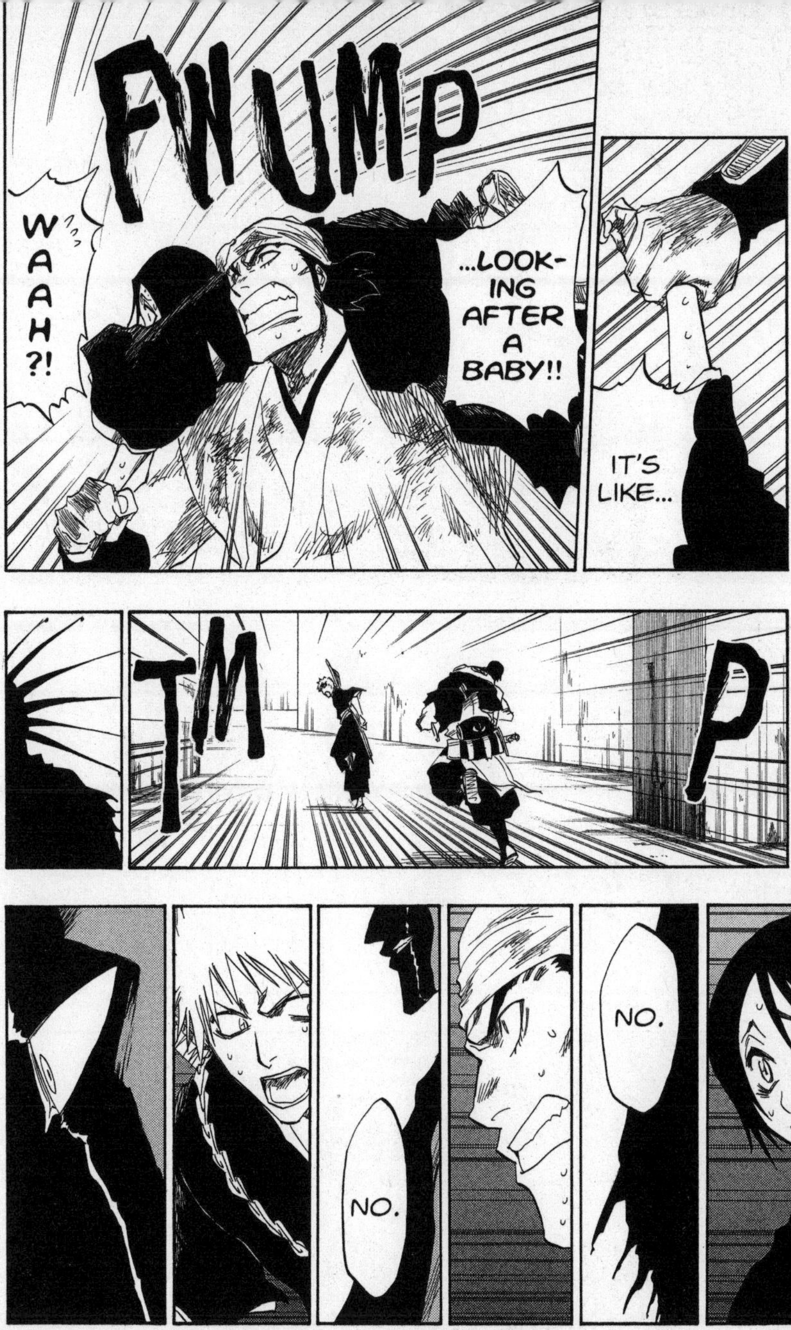
IT'S LIKE...
FWUMP
...LOOKING-ING AFTER A BABY!!
WAAAH?!
TMP
NO.
NO.

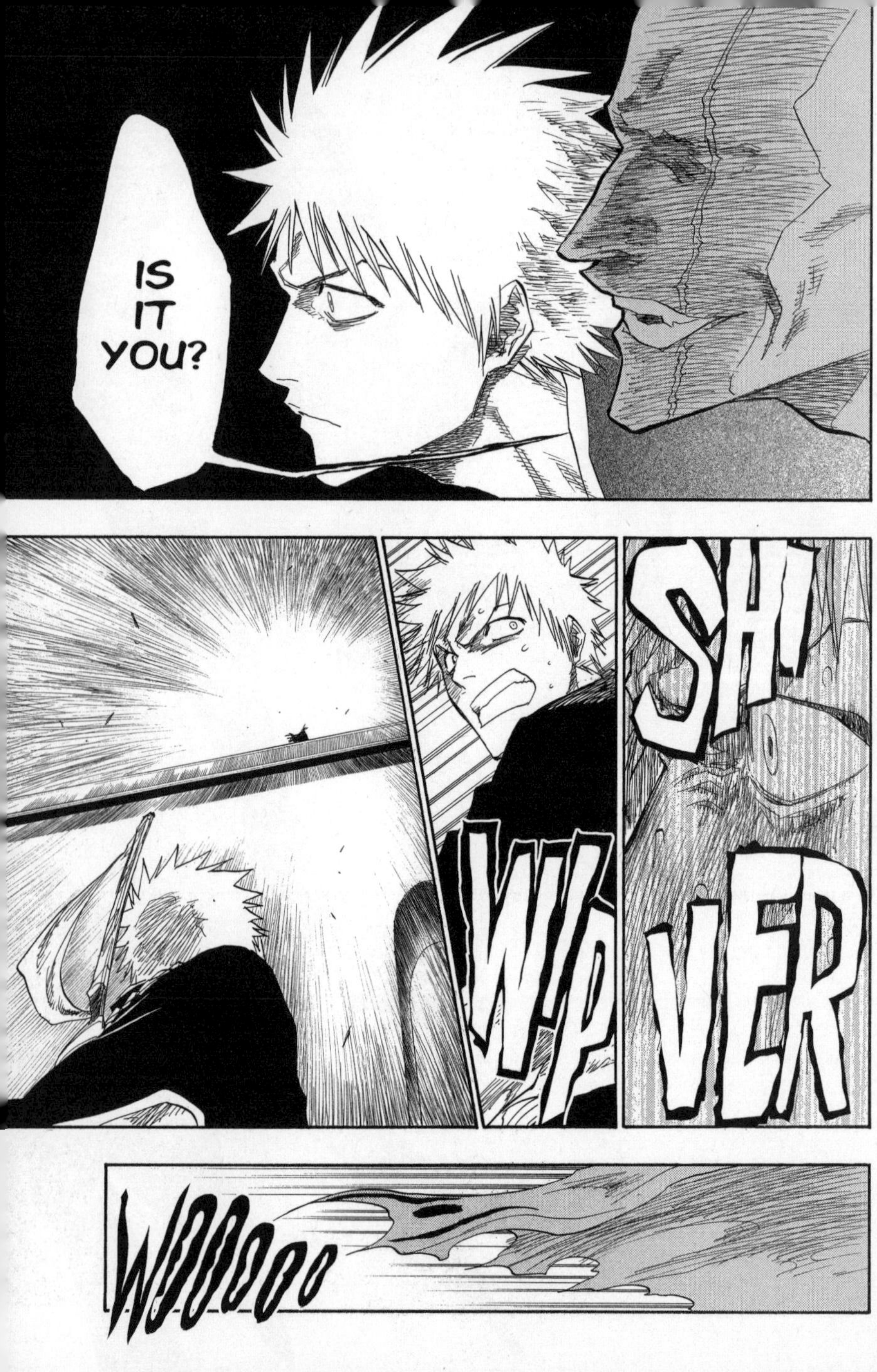
IS IT YOU?
SHIVER
WIP
WOOOOOO

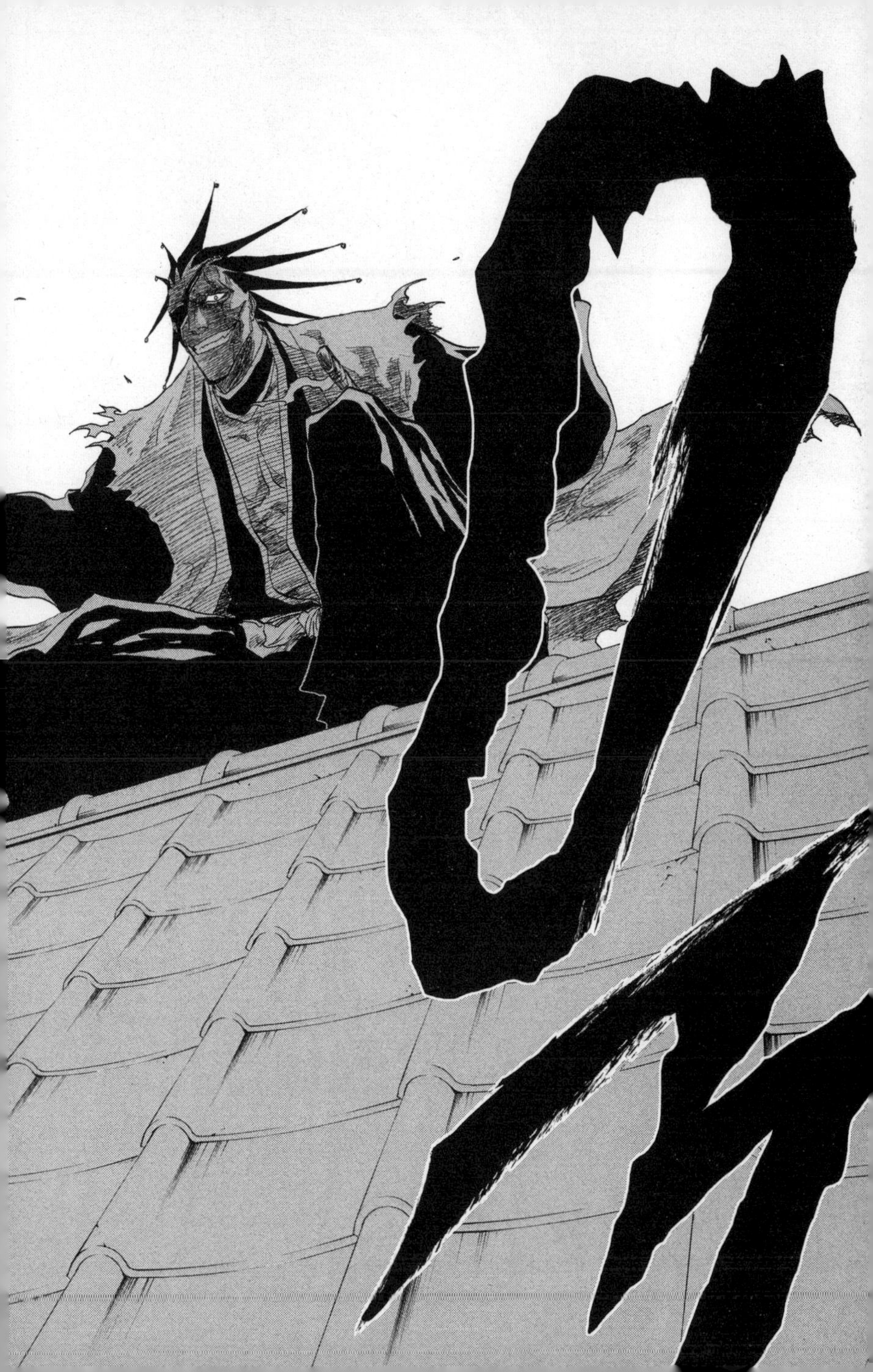

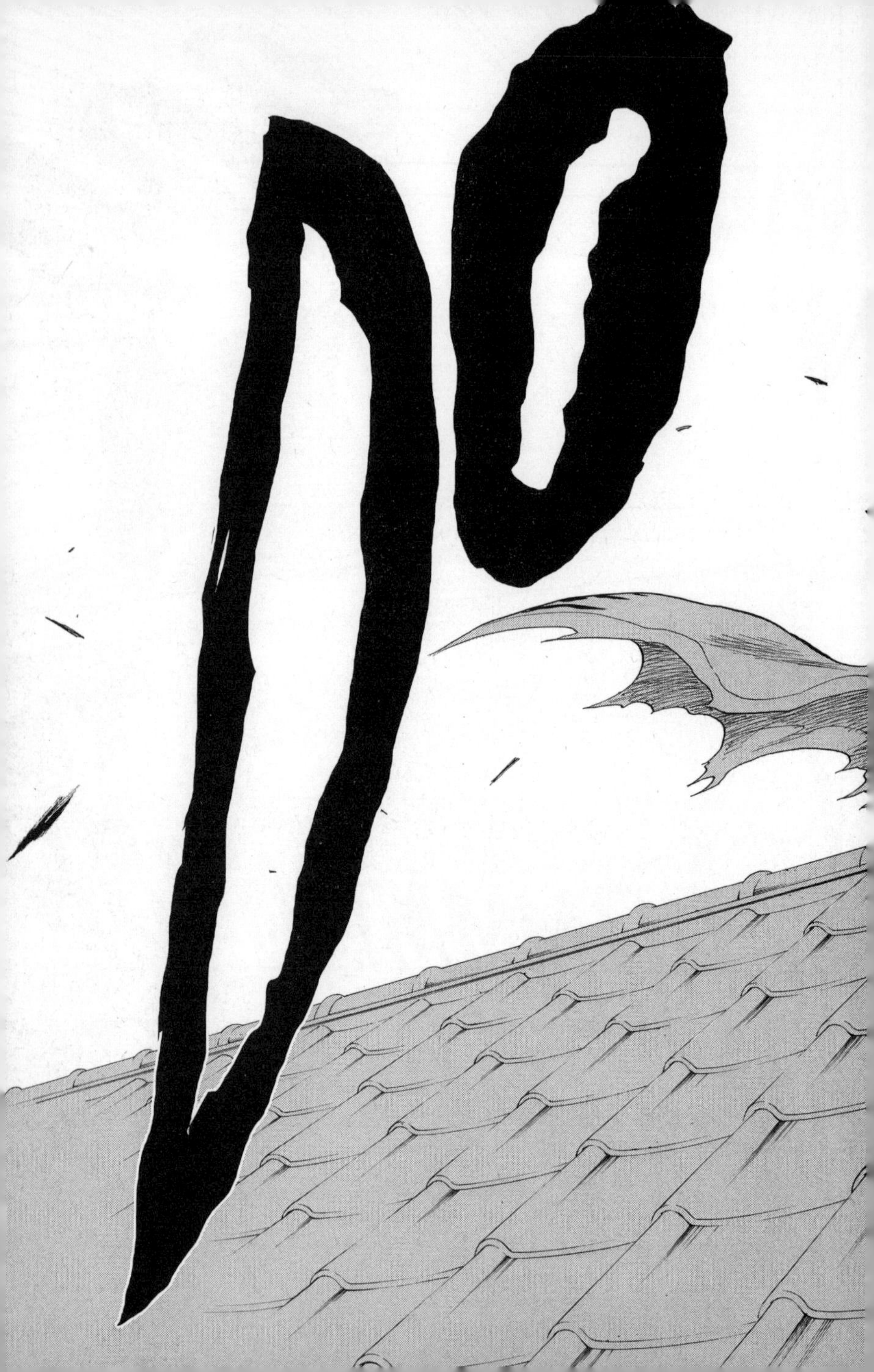

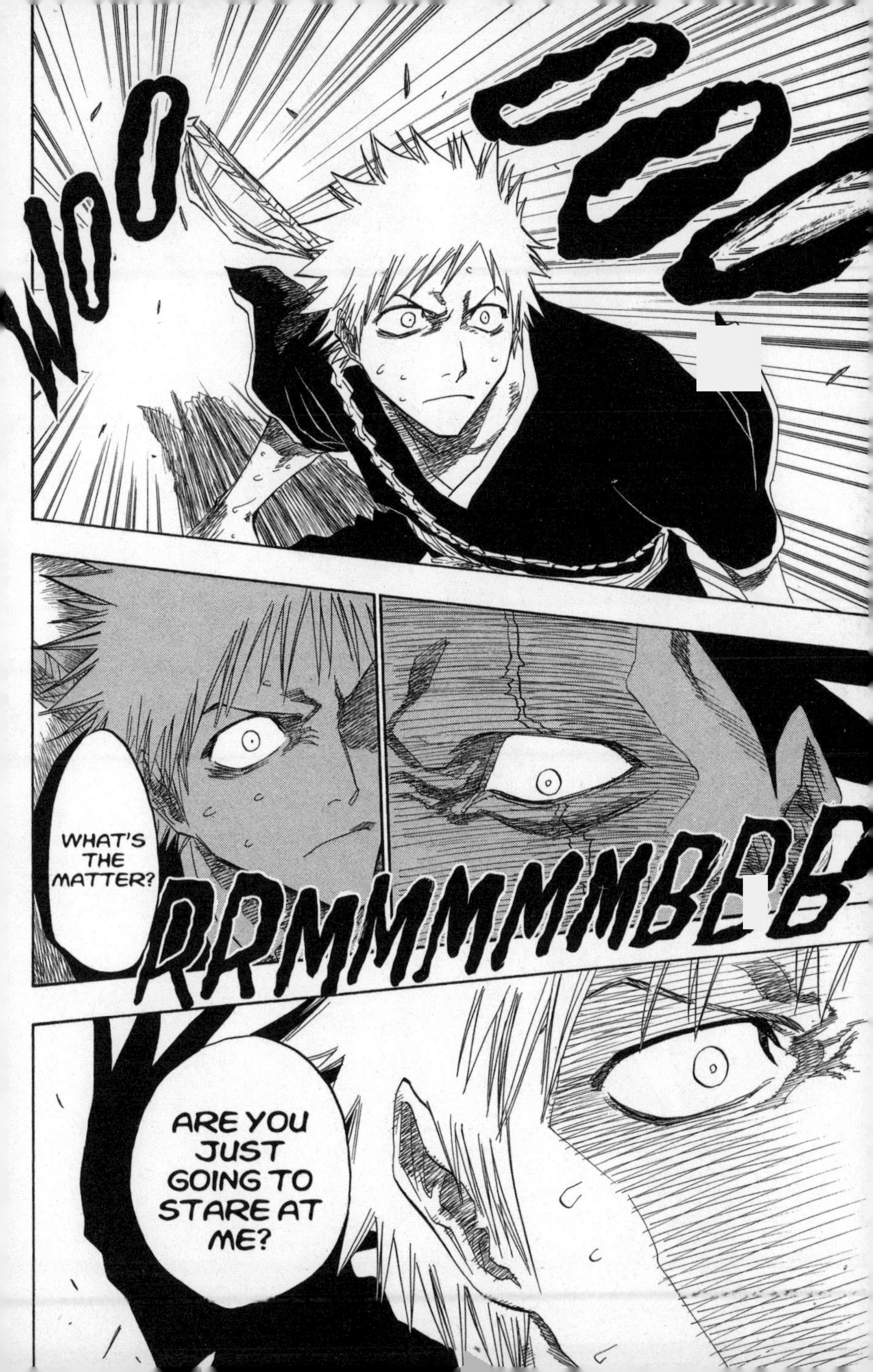
WOOOOOO
RRMMMMMMBBB
WHAT'S THE MATTER?
ARE YOU JUST GOING TO STARE AT ME?

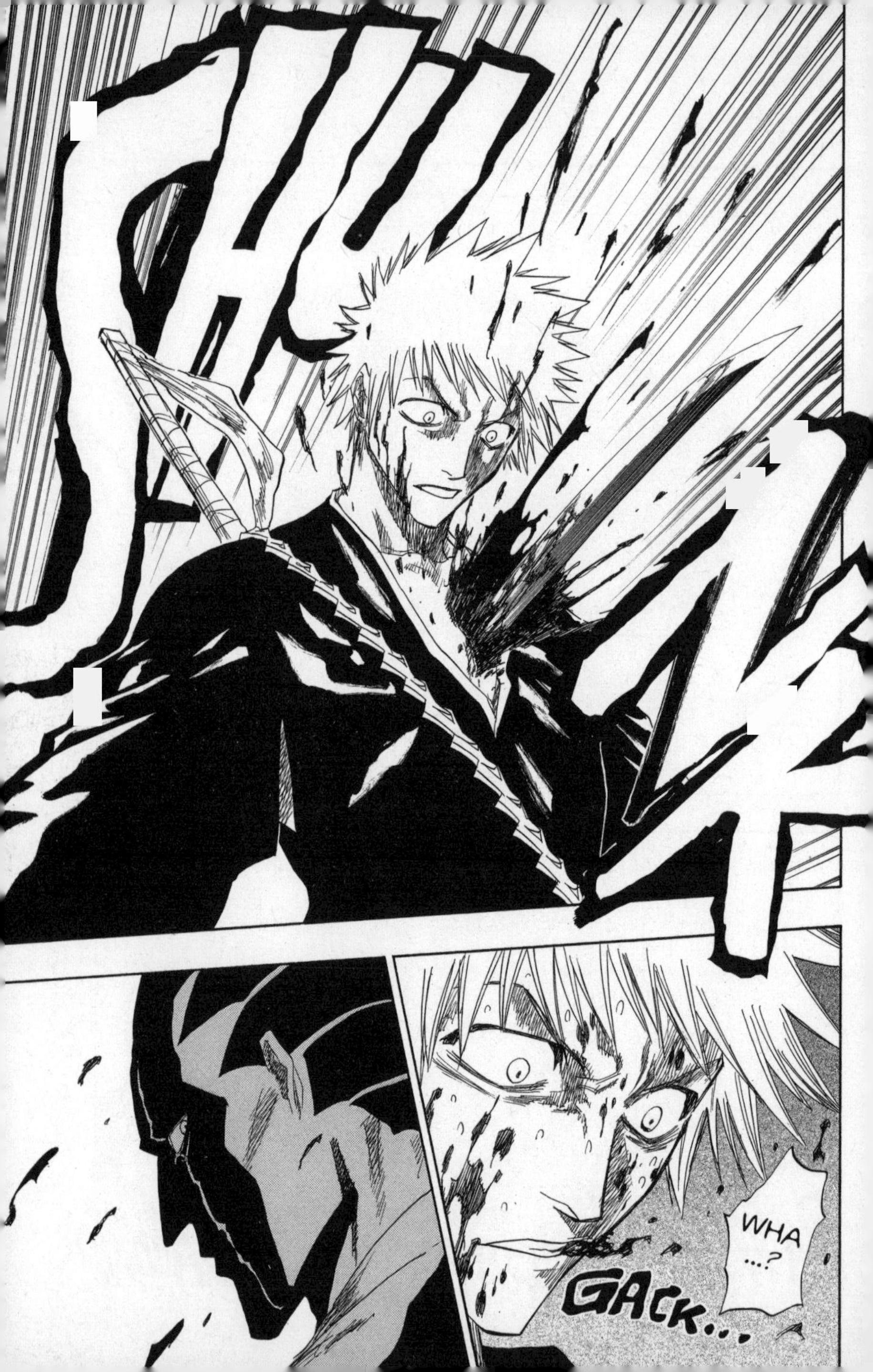
WHA ...?
GACK...

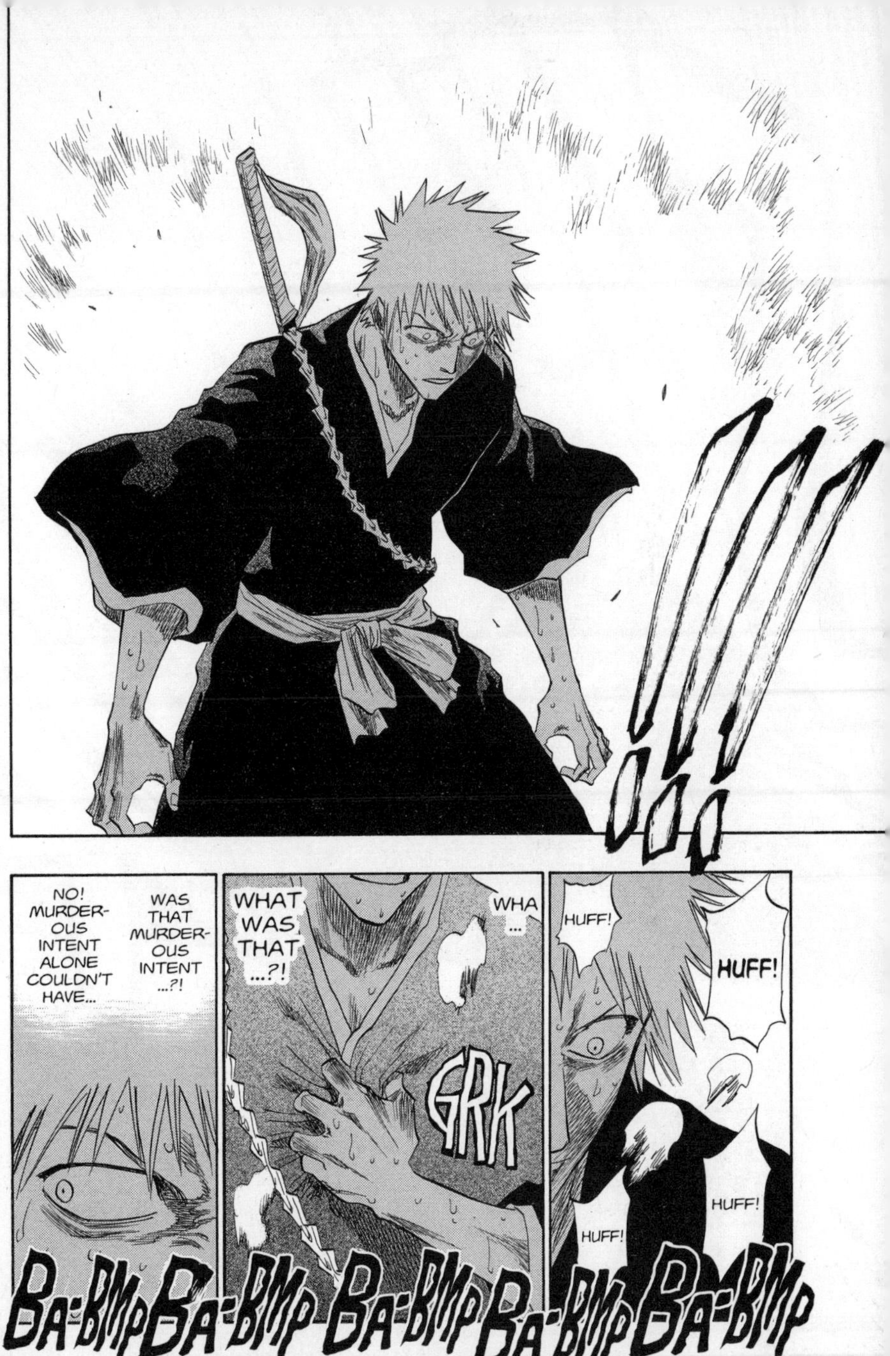
HUFF!
HUFF!
HUFF!
HUFF!
WHA...
WHAT WAS THAT...?!
GRK
WAS THAT MURDEROUS INTENT...?!
NO! MURDEROUS INTENT ALONE COULDN'T HAVE...
BA-BMP BA-BMP BA-BMP BA-BMP BA-BMP

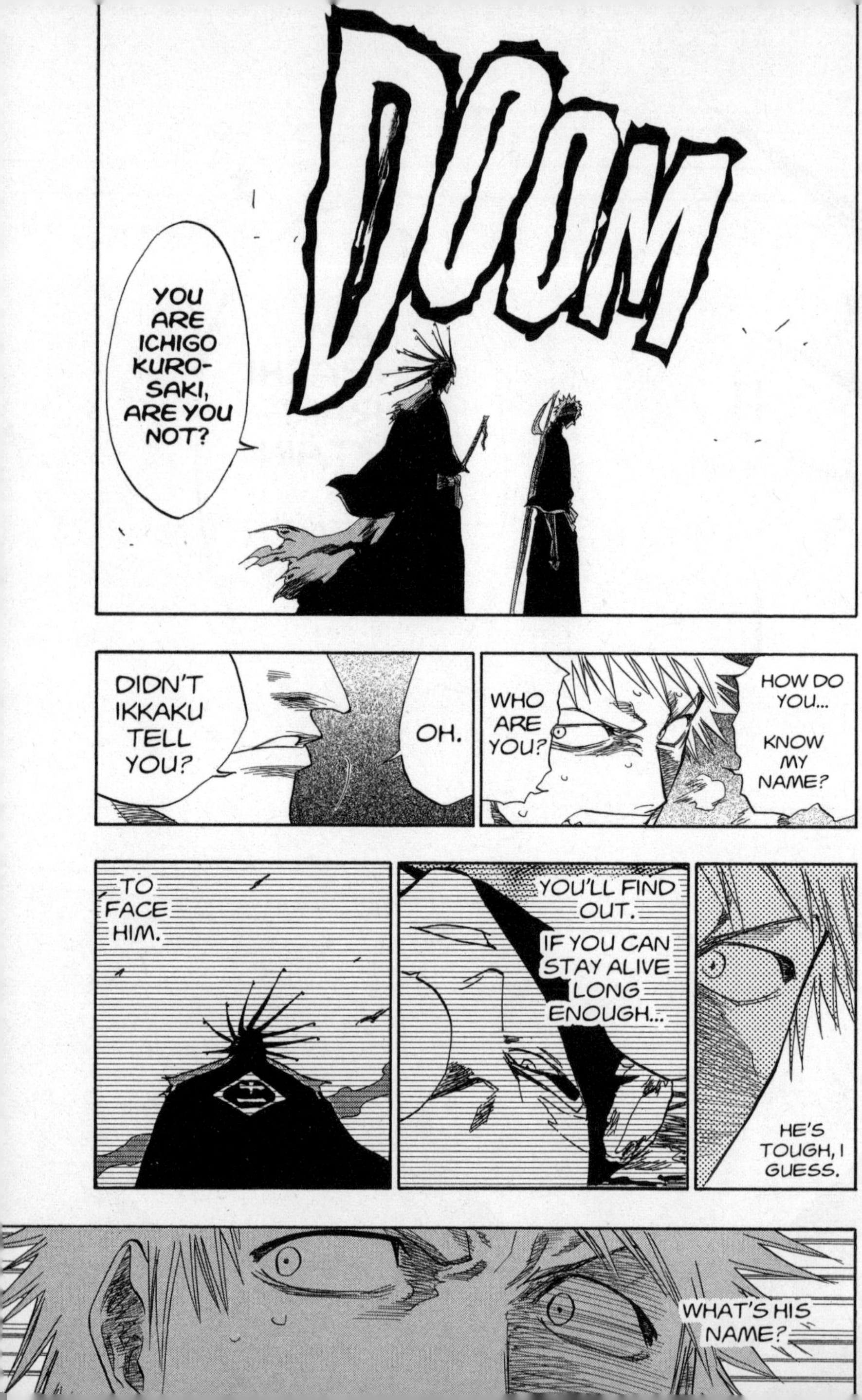
DOOM
YOU ARE ICHIGO KURO-SAKI, ARE YOU NOT?
HOW DO YOU...
KNOW MY NAME?
WHO ARE YOU?
OH.
DIDN'T IKKAKU TELL YOU?
HE'S TOUGH, I GUESS.
YOU'LL FIND OUT.
IF YOU CAN STAY ALIVE LONG ENOUGH...
TO FACE HIM.
WHAT'S HIS NAME?

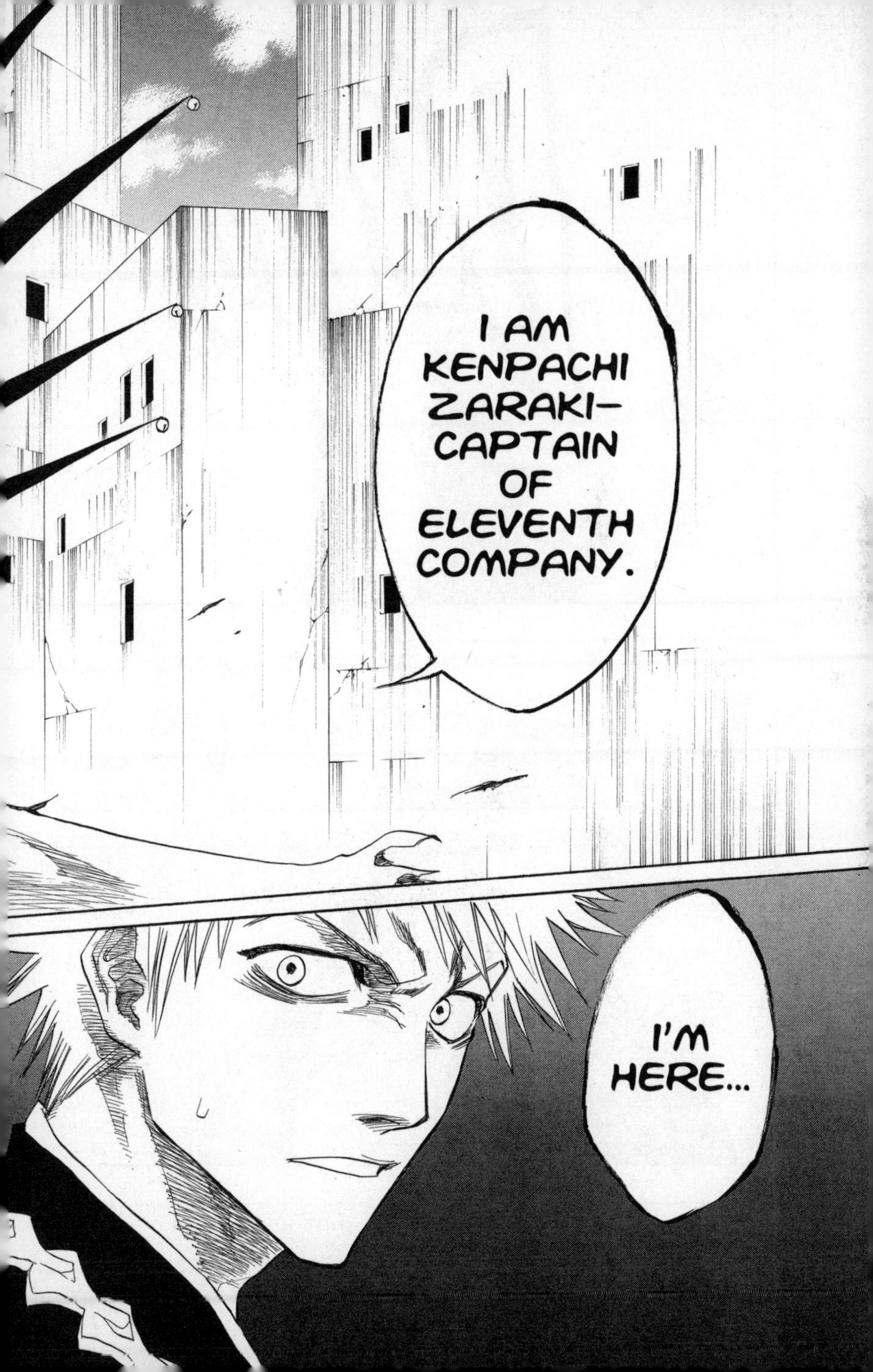
I AM KENPACHI ZARAKI– CAPTAIN OF ELEVENTH COMPANY.
I'M HERE...

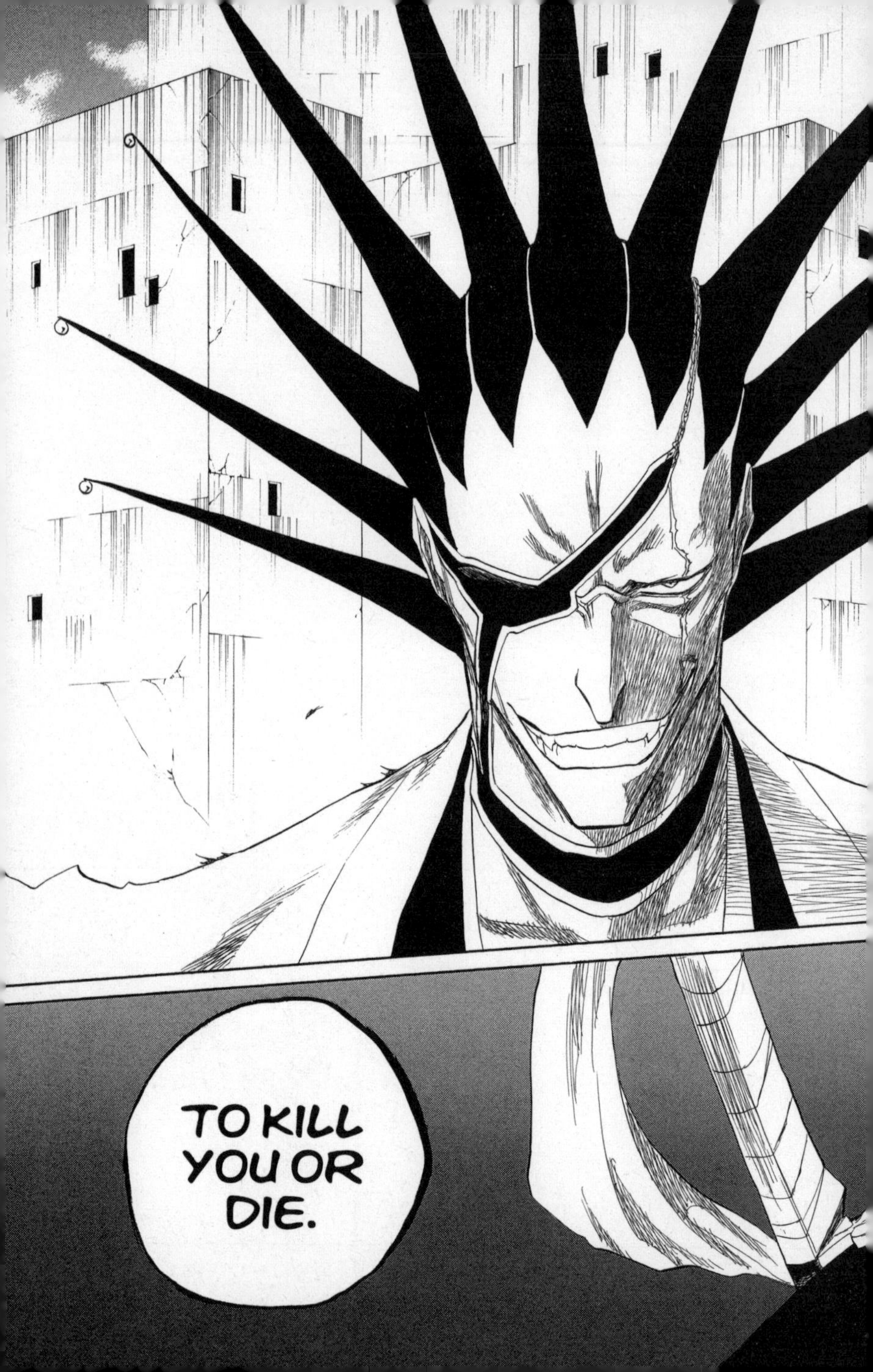
TO KILL YOU OR DIE.

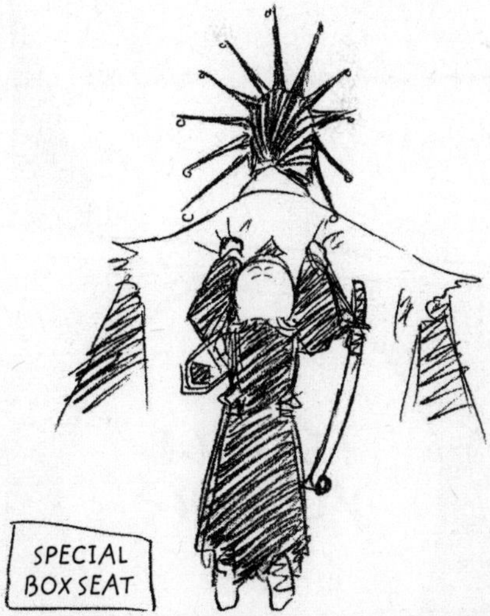
SPECIAL BOX SEAT

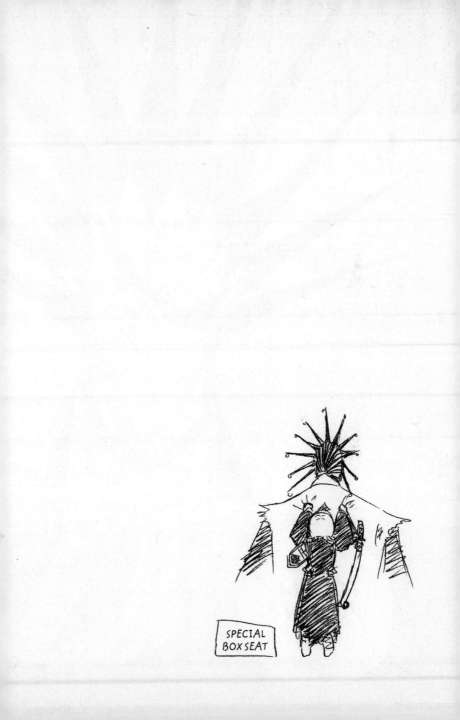

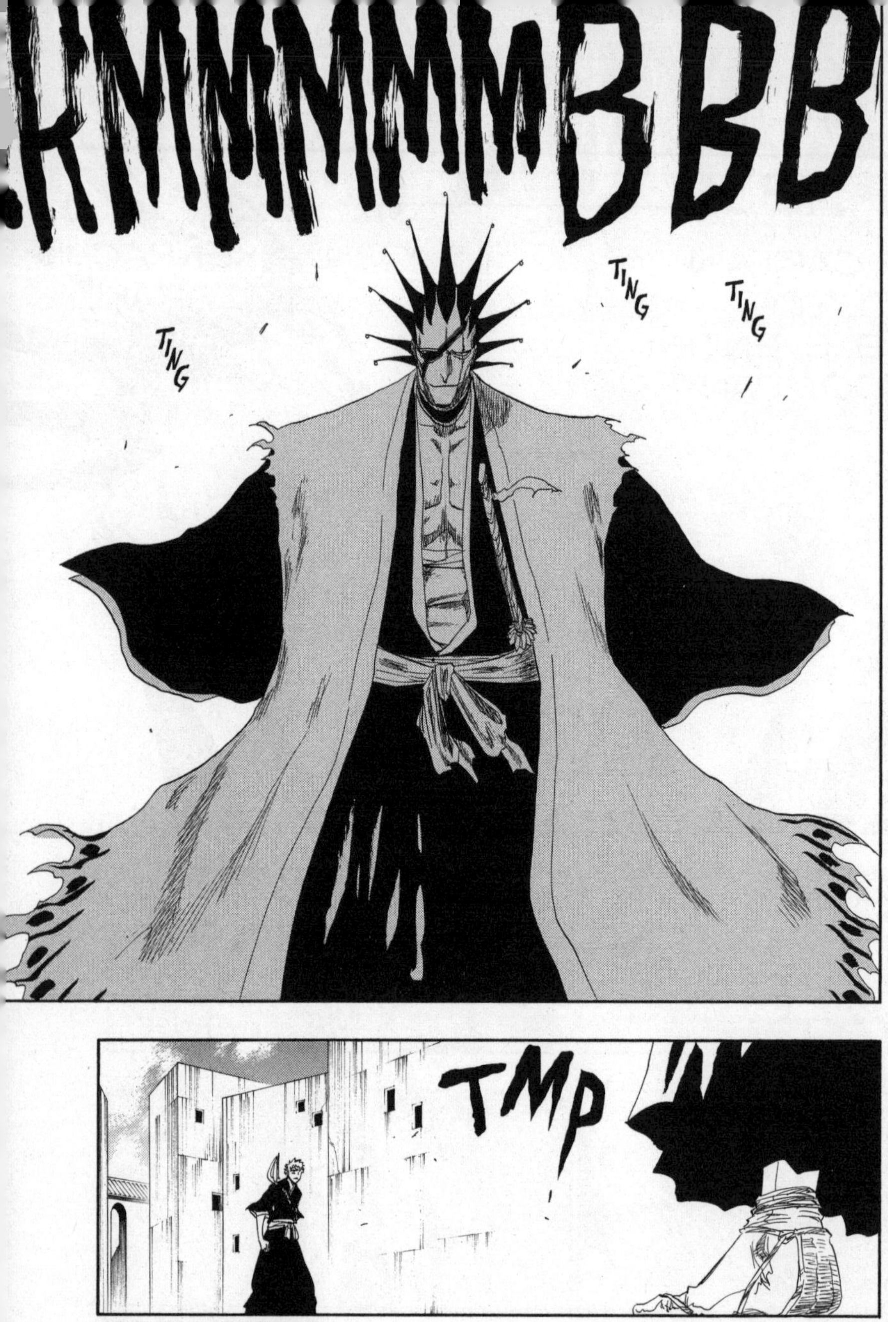
HMMMMMBBB
TING
TING
TING
TMP

104. The Undead

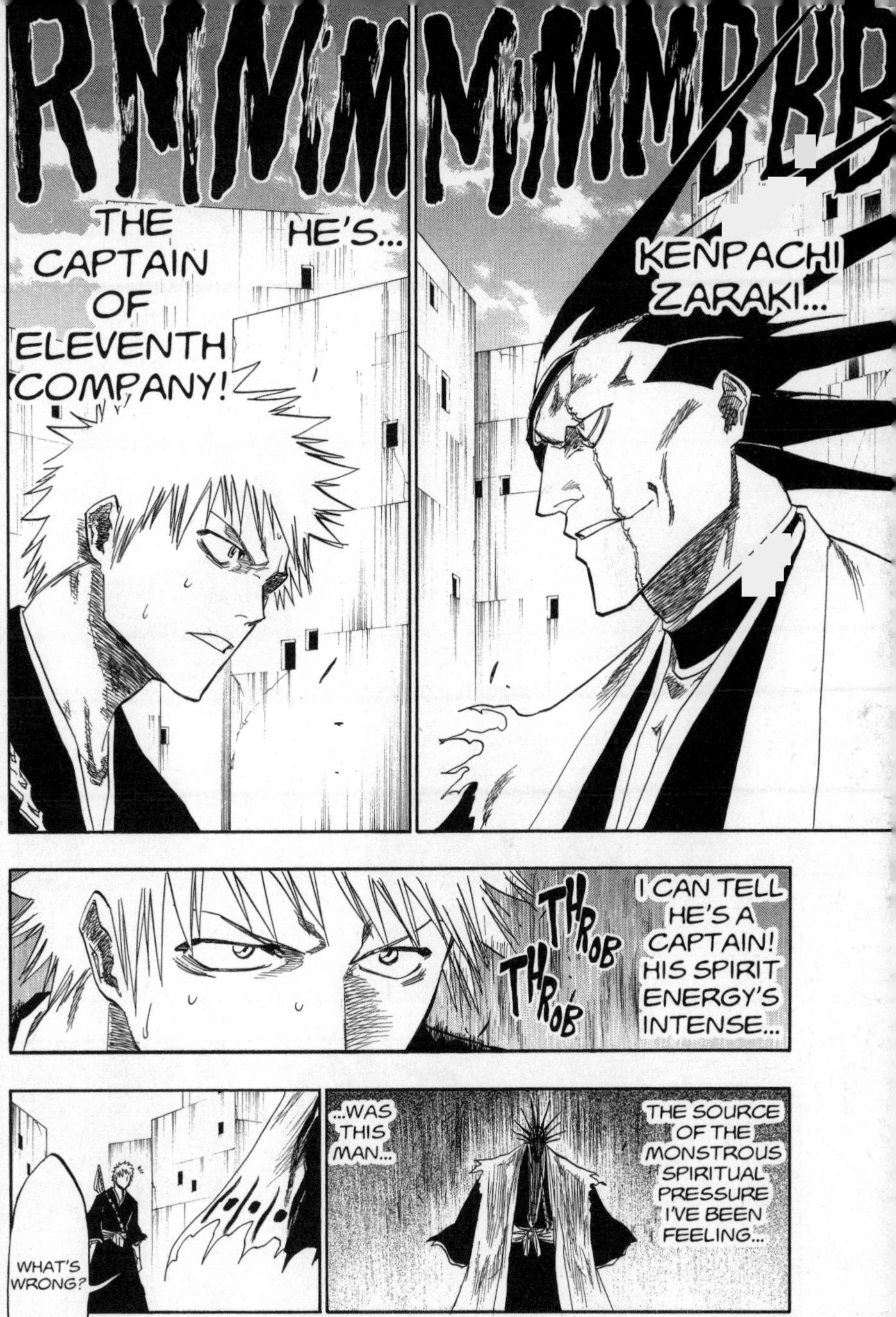
RMMMMMMBB
KENPACHI ZARAKI...
HE'S...
THE CAPTAIN OF ELEVENTH COMPANY!
I CAN TELL HE'S A CAPTAIN! HIS SPIRIT ENERGY'S INTENSE...
THROB
THROB
THE SOURCE OF THE MONSTROUS SPIRITUAL PRESSURE I'VE BEEN FEELING...
...WAS THIS MAN...
WHAT'S WRONG?

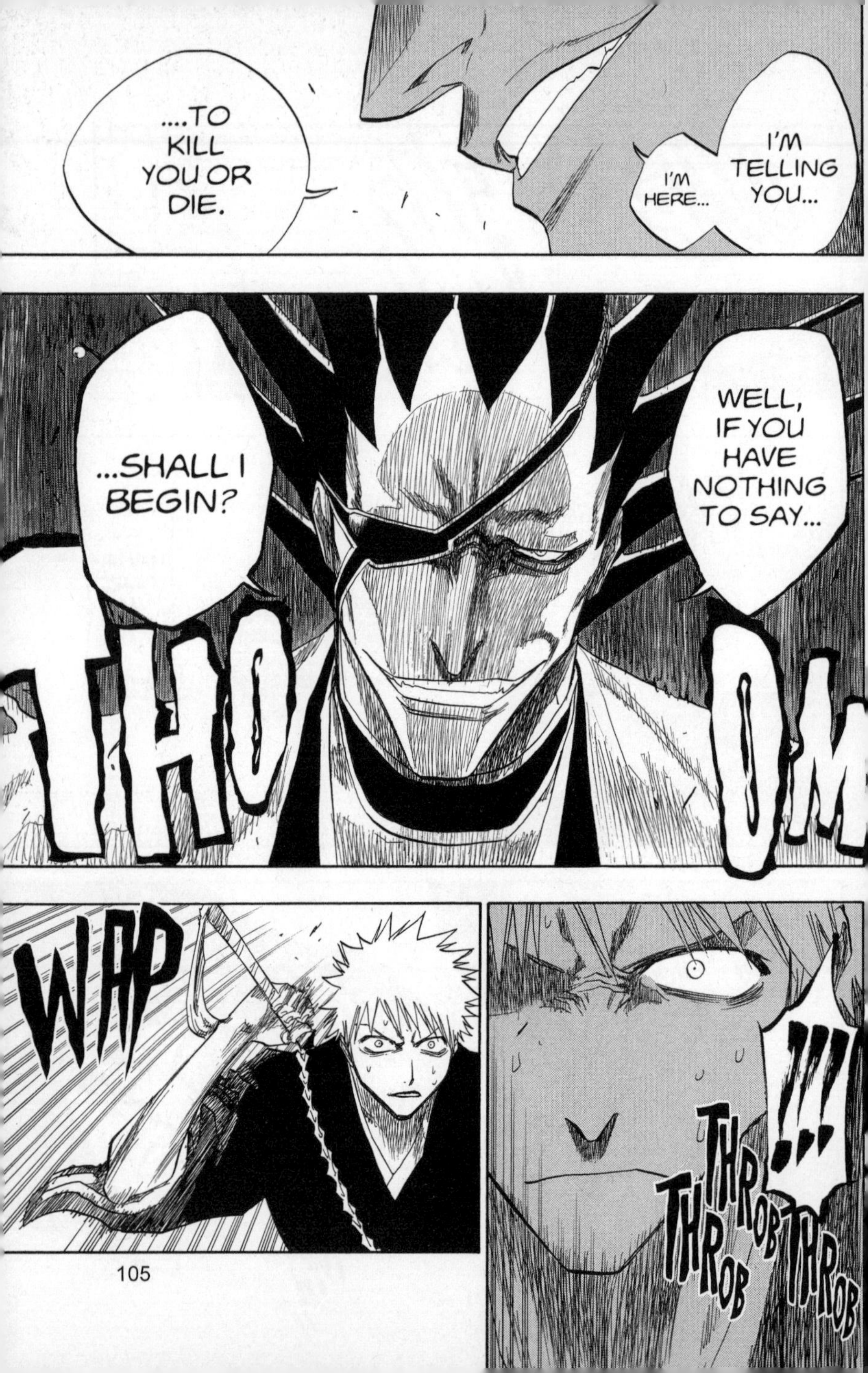
I'M TELLING YOU...
I'M HERE...
....TO KILL YOU OR DIE.
WELL, IF YOU HAVE NOTHING TO SAY...
...SHALL I BEGIN?
THOOM
!!!
THROB THROB THROB THROB
WAP

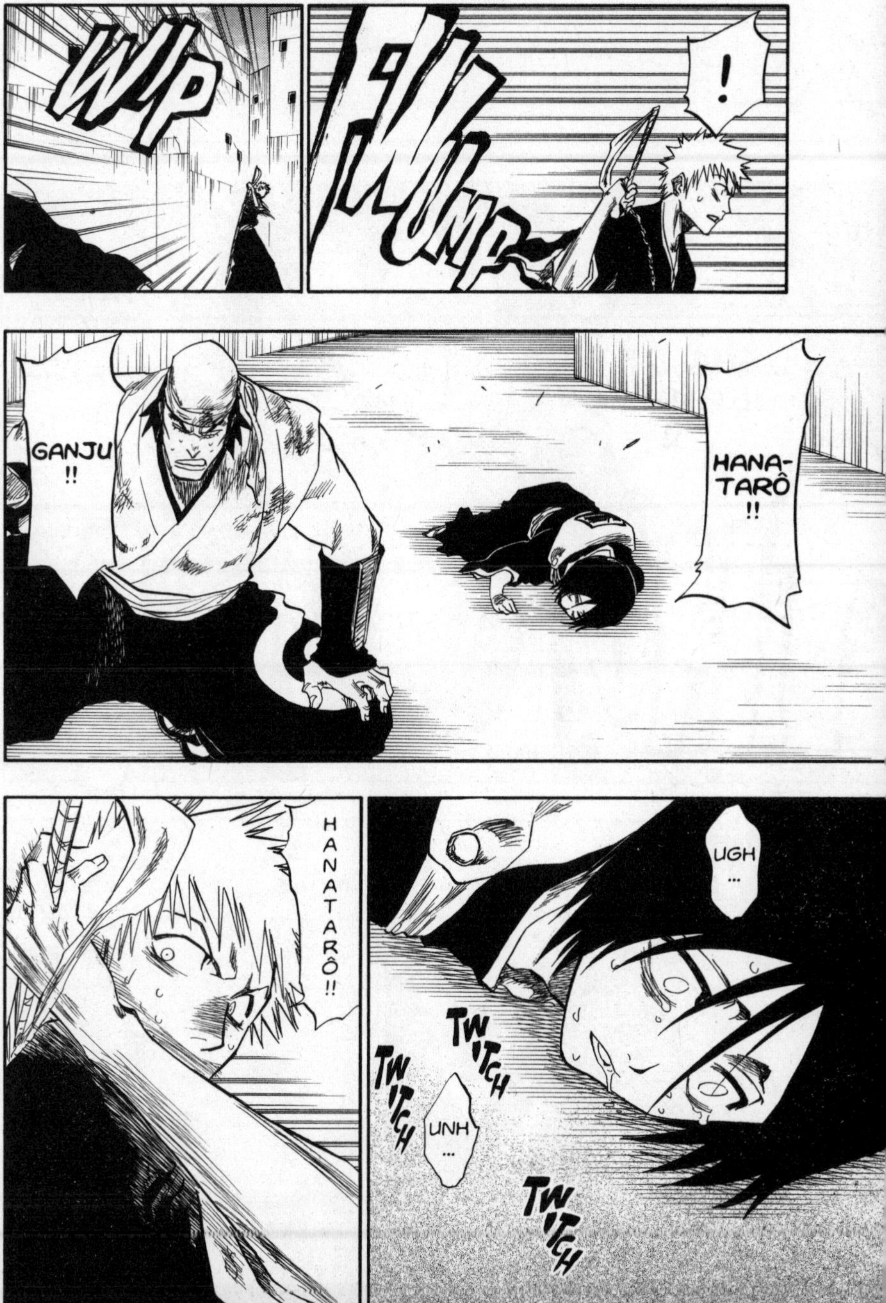
!
FWUMP
WIP
HANA-TARÔ!!
GANJU!!
UGH...
TWITCH
TWITCH
UNH...
TWITCH
HANATARÔ!!

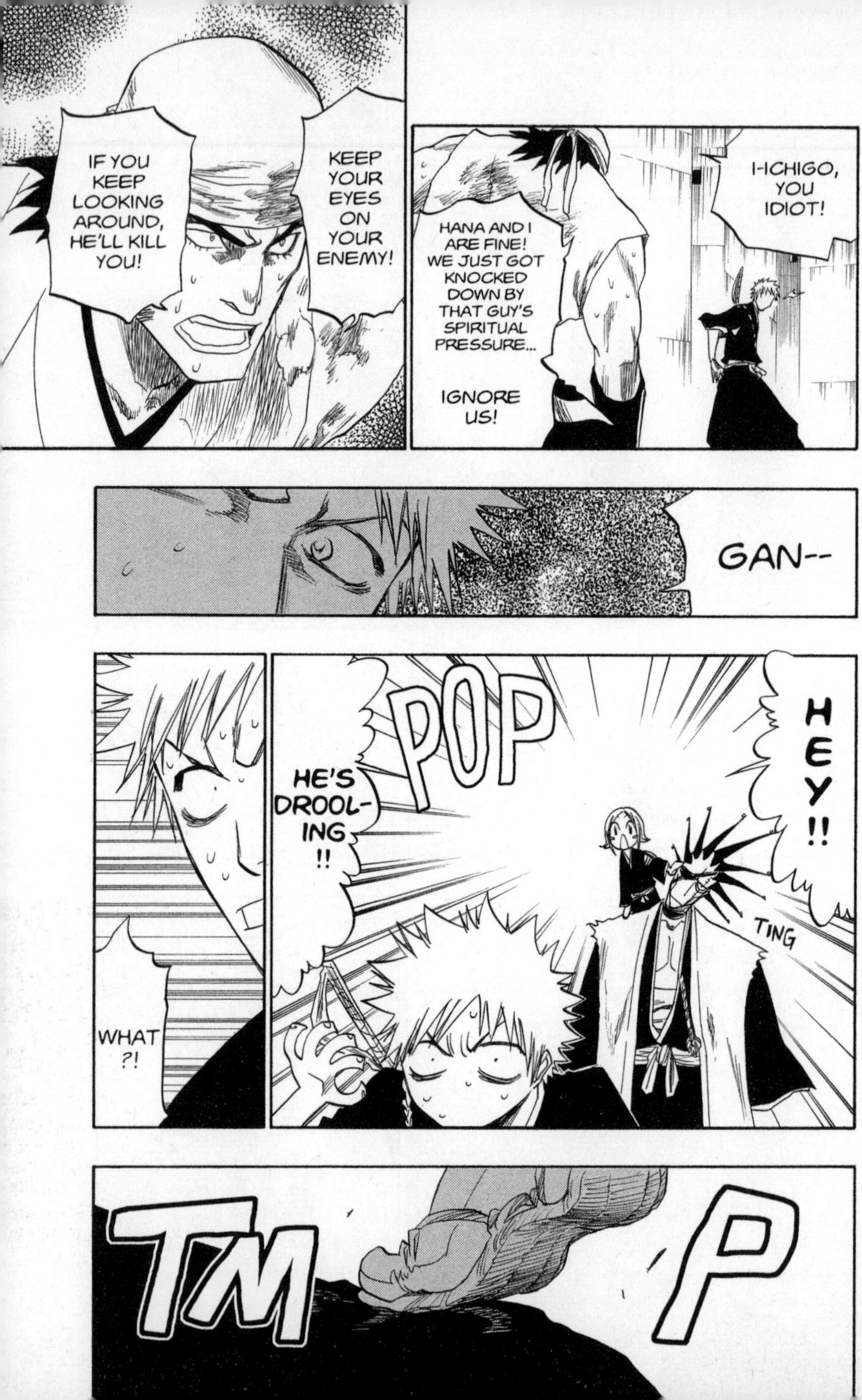

I-ICHIGO, YOU IDIOT!
HANA AND I ARE FINE! WE JUST GOT KNOCKED DOWN BY THAT GUY'S SPIRITUAL PRESSURE...
IGNORE US!
KEEP YOUR EYES ON YOUR ENEMY!
IF YOU KEEP LOOKING AROUND, HE'LL KILL YOU!
GAN--
HEY!!
POP
HE'S DROOL-ING!!
TING
WHAT?!
TMP

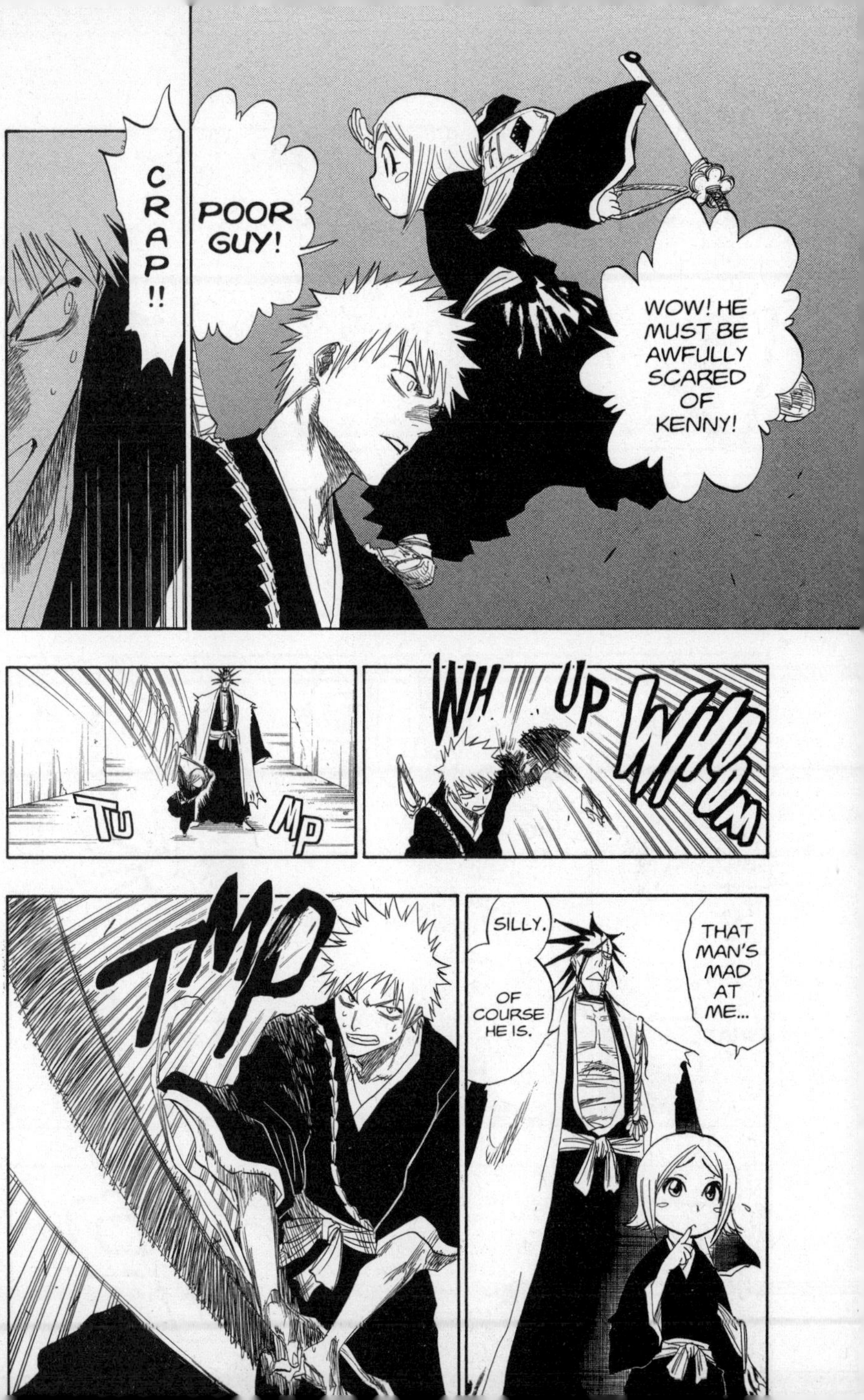
WOW! HE MUST BE AWFULLY SCARED OF KENNY!
POOR GUY!
CRAP!!
WH UP
WHOOM
TU MP
THAT MAN'S MAD AT ME...
SILLY.
OF COURSE HE IS.
TMP

READ THIS WAY

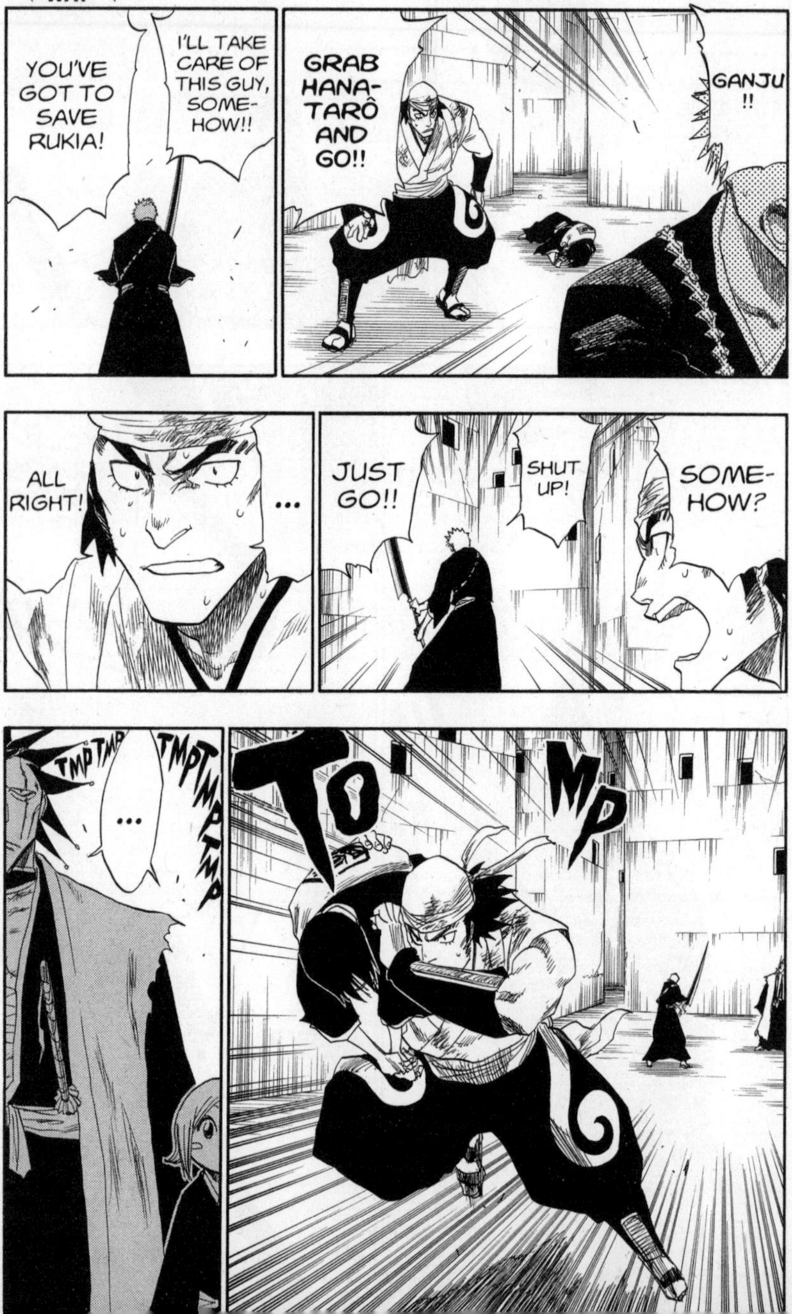
GANJU!!
GRAB HANA-TARÔ AND GO!!
I'LL TAKE CARE OF THIS GUY, SOME-HOW!!
YOU'VE GOT TO SAVE RUKIA!
SOME-HOW?
SHUT UP!
JUST GO!!
...
ALL RIGHT!
TOMP
TMPTMPTMPTMP
...
TMPTMP

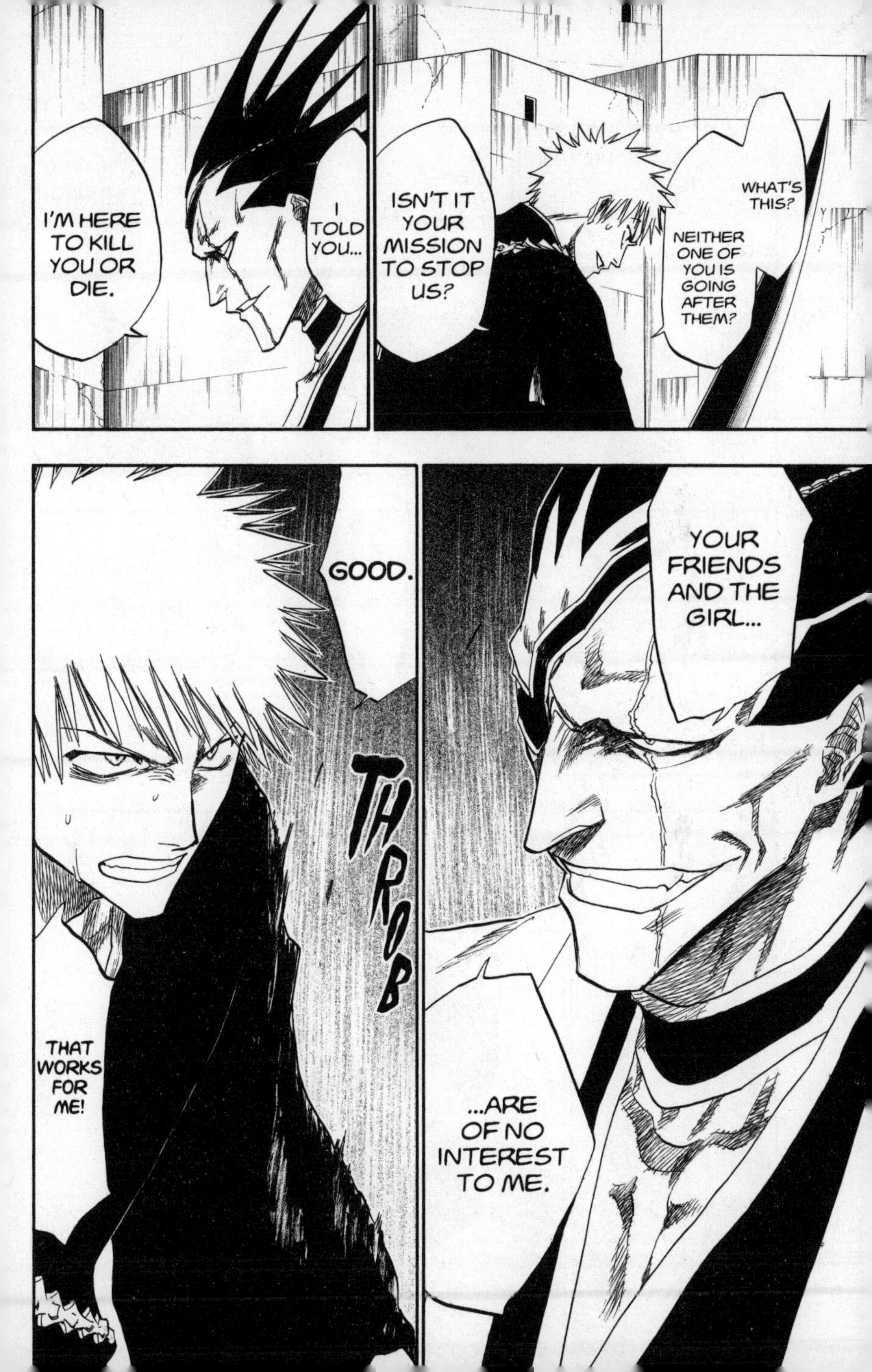
WHAT'S THIS?
NEITHER ONE OF YOU IS GOING AFTER THEM?
ISN'T IT YOUR MISSION TO STOP US?
I TOLD YOU...
I'M HERE TO KILL YOU OR DIE.
YOUR FRIENDS AND THE GIRL...
...ARE OF NO INTEREST TO ME.
GOOD.
THROB
THAT WORKS FOR ME!

104. The Undead

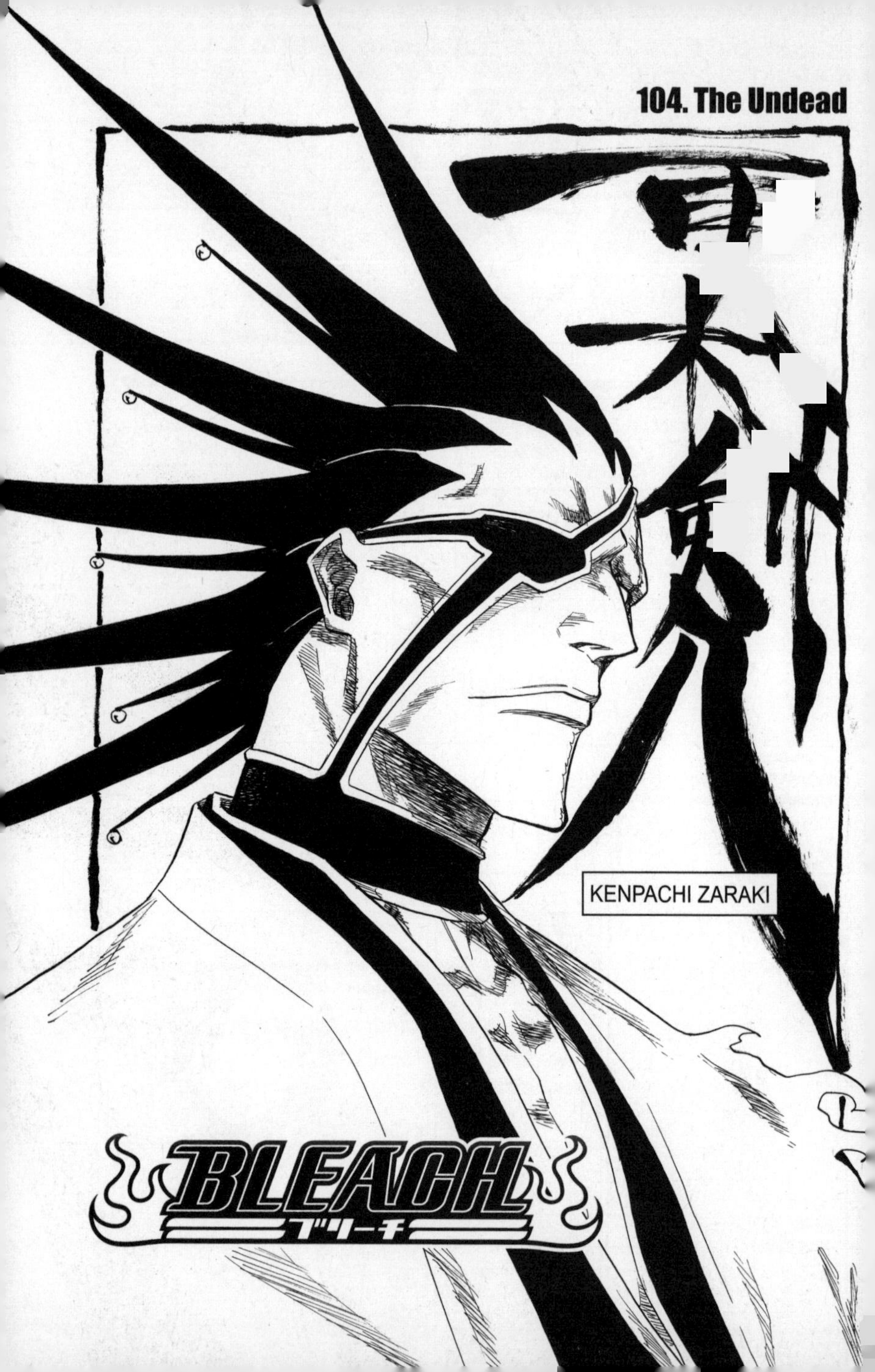
KENPACHI ZARAKI
BLEACH
ブリーチ

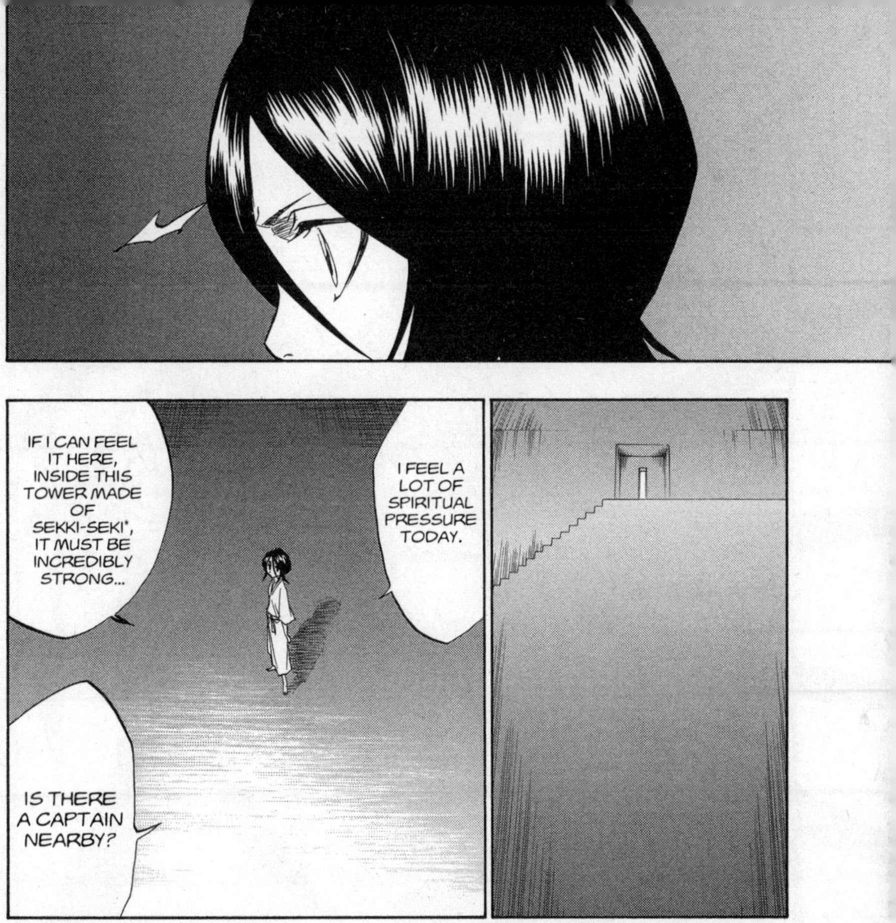
I FEEL A LOT OF SPIRITUAL PRESSURE TODAY.
IF I CAN FEEL IT HERE, INSIDE THIS TOWER MADE OF SEKKI-SEKI*, IT MUST BE INCREDIBLY STRONG...
IS THERE A CAPTAIN NEARBY?

* AN ORE THAT PROVIDES INSULATION AGAINST REISHI AND SPIRIT ENERGY.

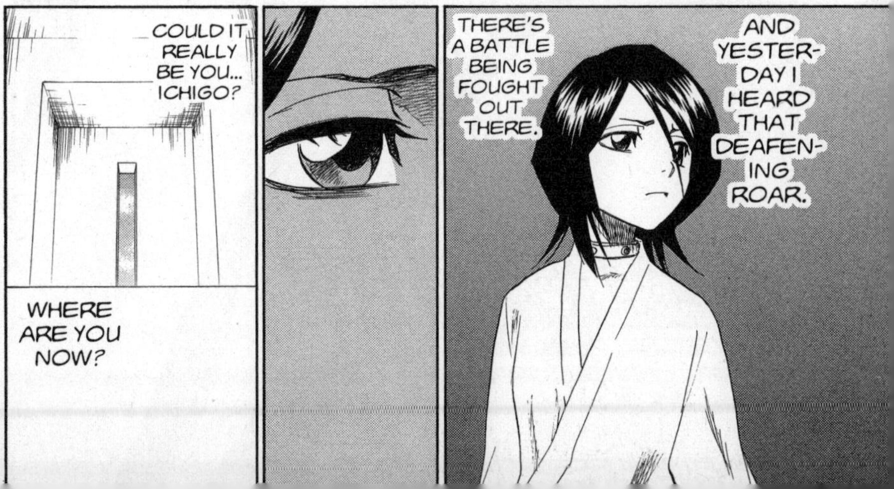
AND YESTER-DAY I HEARD THAT DEAFEN-ING ROAR.
THERE'S A BATTLE BEING FOUGHT OUT THERE.
COULD IT REALLY BE YOU... ICHIGO?
WHERE ARE YOU NOW?

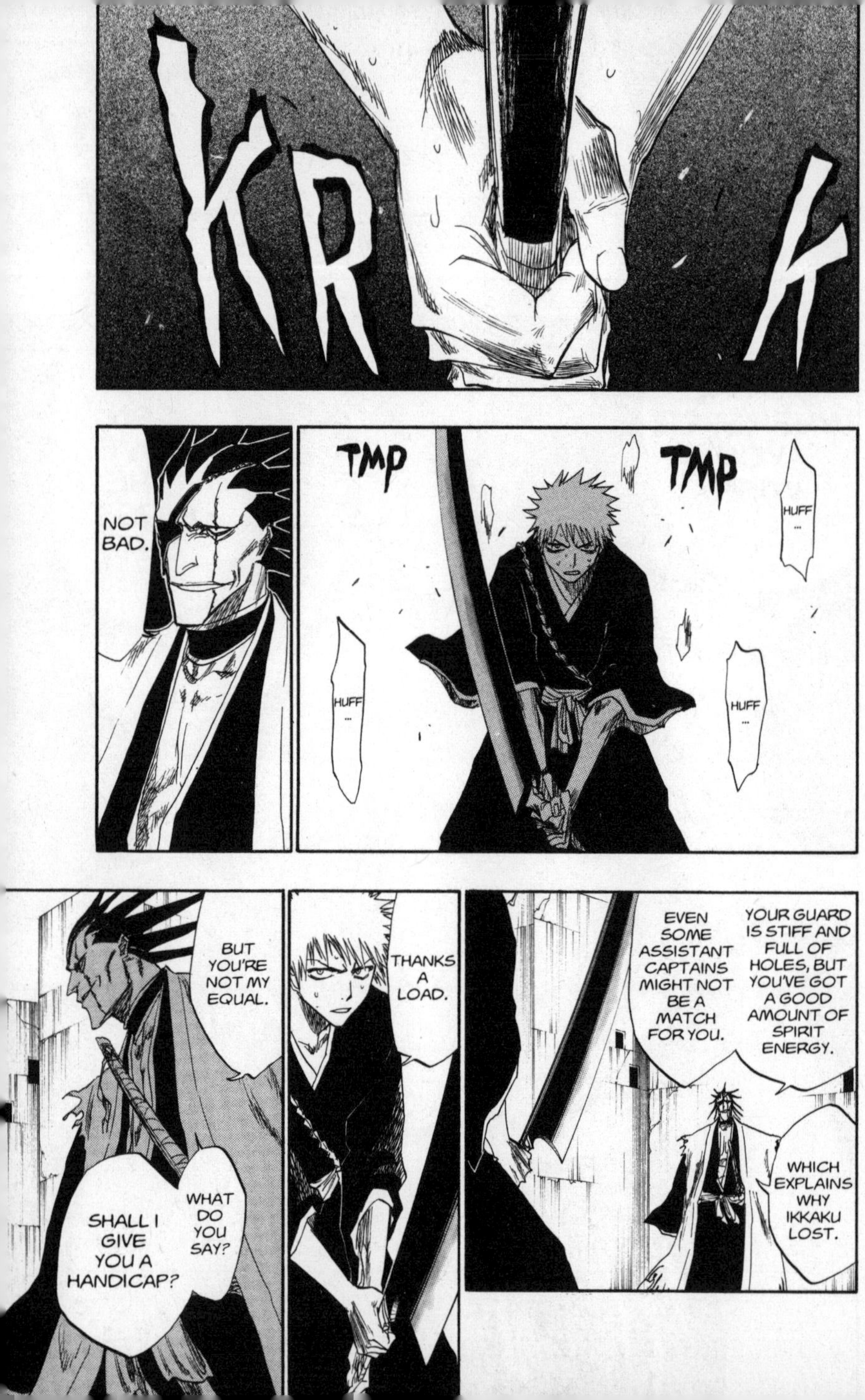
KRK
TMP
TMP
HUFF...
HUFF...
HUFF...
NOT BAD.
YOUR GUARD IS STIFF AND FULL OF HOLES, BUT YOU'VE GOT A GOOD AMOUNT OF SPIRIT ENERGY.
EVEN SOME ASSISTANT CAPTAINS MIGHT NOT BE A MATCH FOR YOU.
WHICH EXPLAINS WHY IKKAKU LOST.
THANKS A LOAD.
BUT YOU'RE NOT MY EQUAL.
WHAT DO YOU SAY?
SHALL I GIVE YOU A HANDICAP?

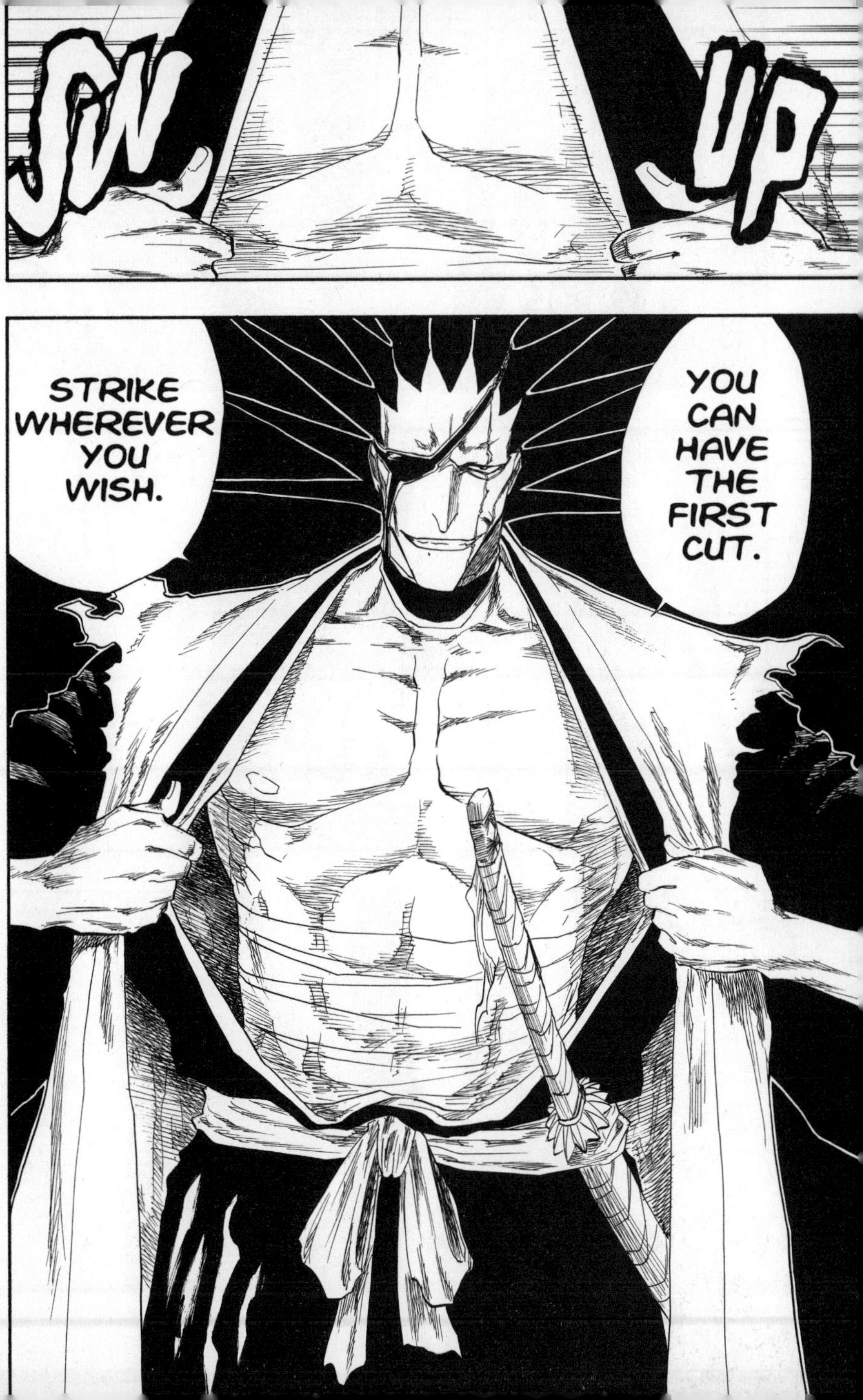
SHN
UP
YOU CAN HAVE THE FIRST CUT.
STRIKE WHEREVER YOU WISH.

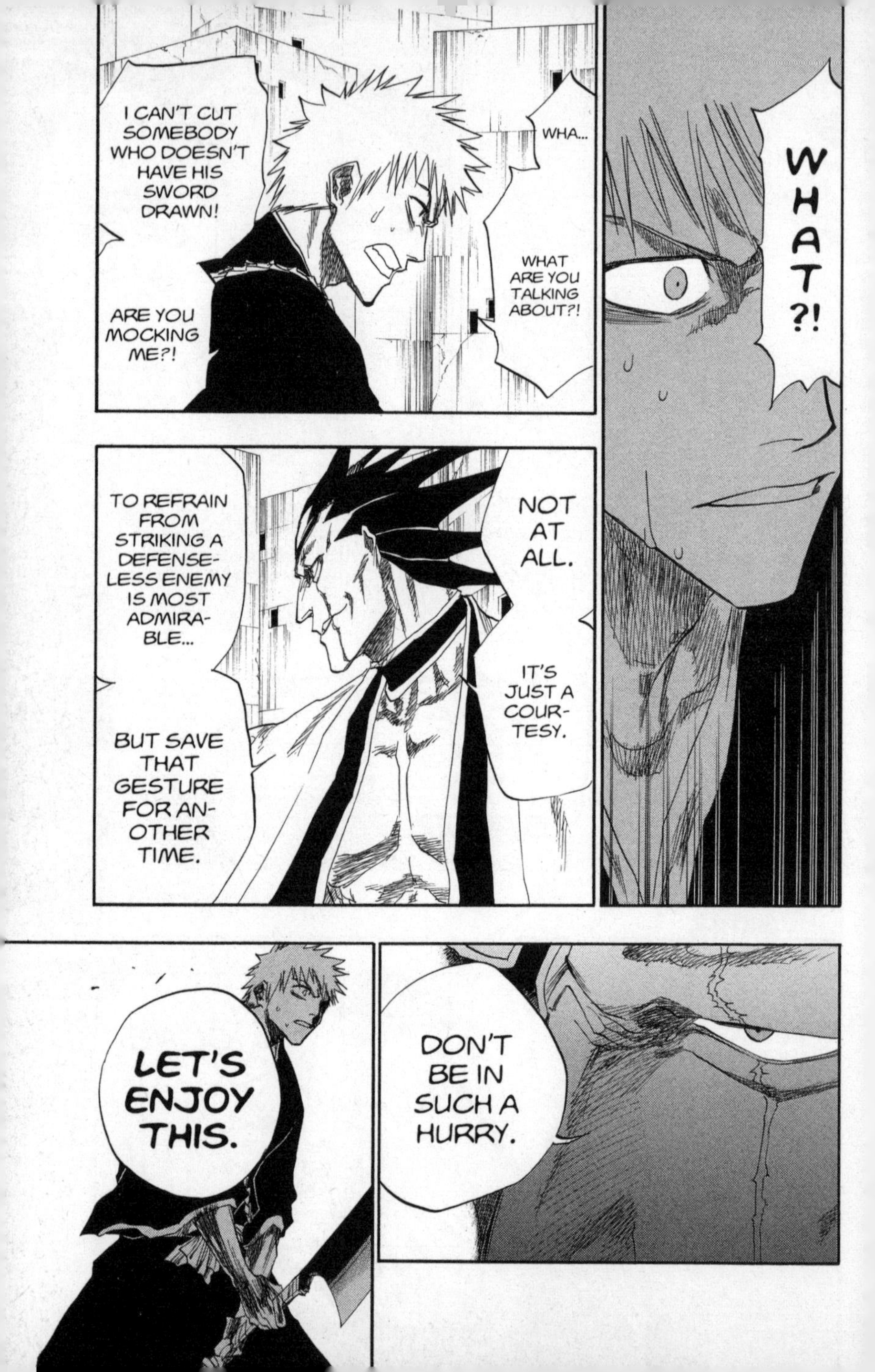
WHAT?!
WHA...
WHAT ARE YOU TALKING ABOUT?!
I CAN'T CUT SOMEBODY WHO DOESN'T HAVE HIS SWORD DRAWN!
ARE YOU MOCKING ME?!
NOT AT ALL.
IT'S JUST A COURTESY.
TO REFRAIN FROM STRIKING A DEFENSELESS ENEMY IS MOST ADMIRABLE...
BUT SAVE THAT GESTURE FOR ANOTHER TIME.
DON'T BE IN SUCH A HURRY.
LET'S ENJOY THIS.

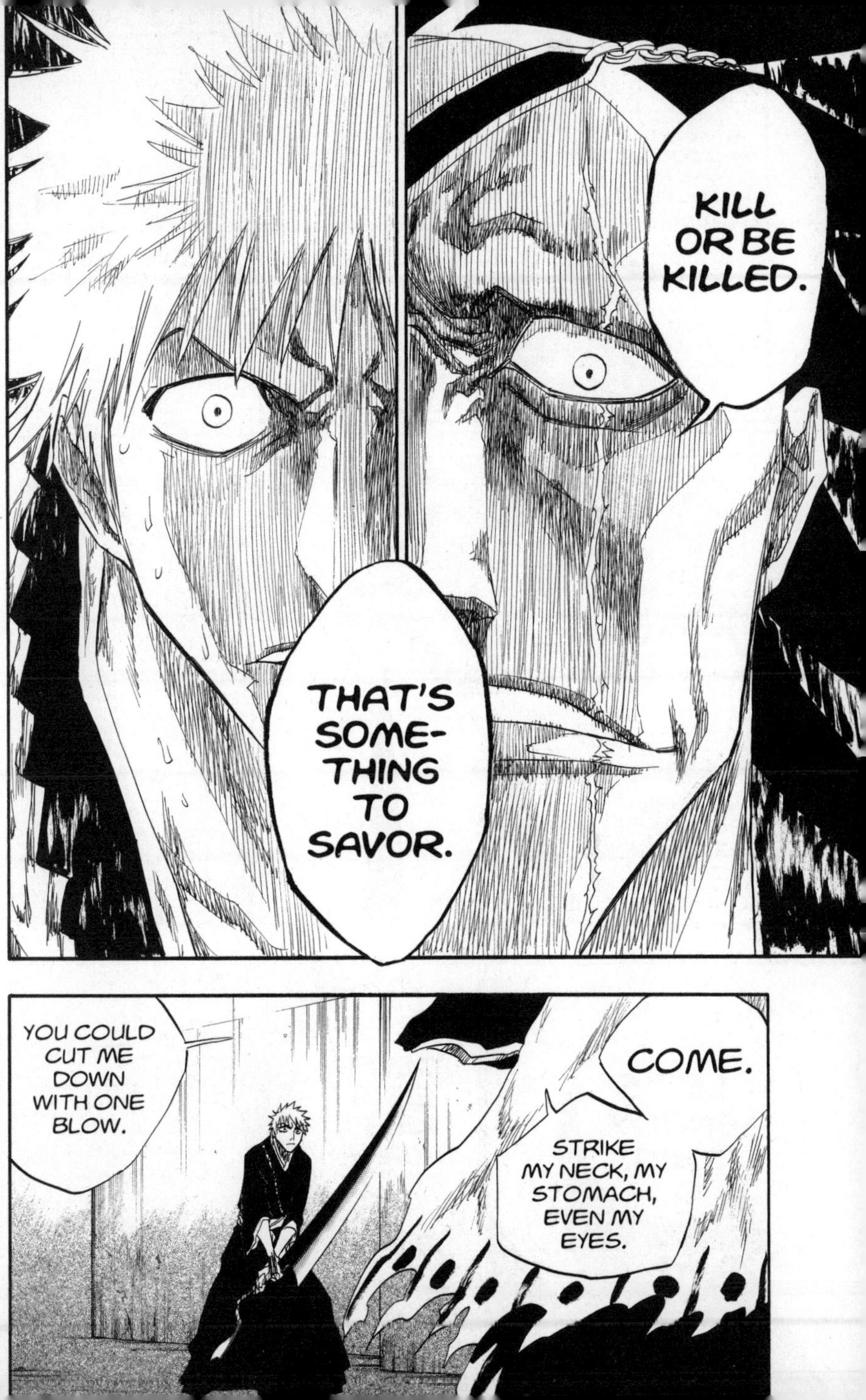
KILL OR BE KILLED.
THAT'S SOME-THING TO SAVOR.
COME.
STRIKE MY NECK, MY STOMACH, EVEN MY EYES.
YOU COULD CUT ME DOWN WITH ONE BLOW.

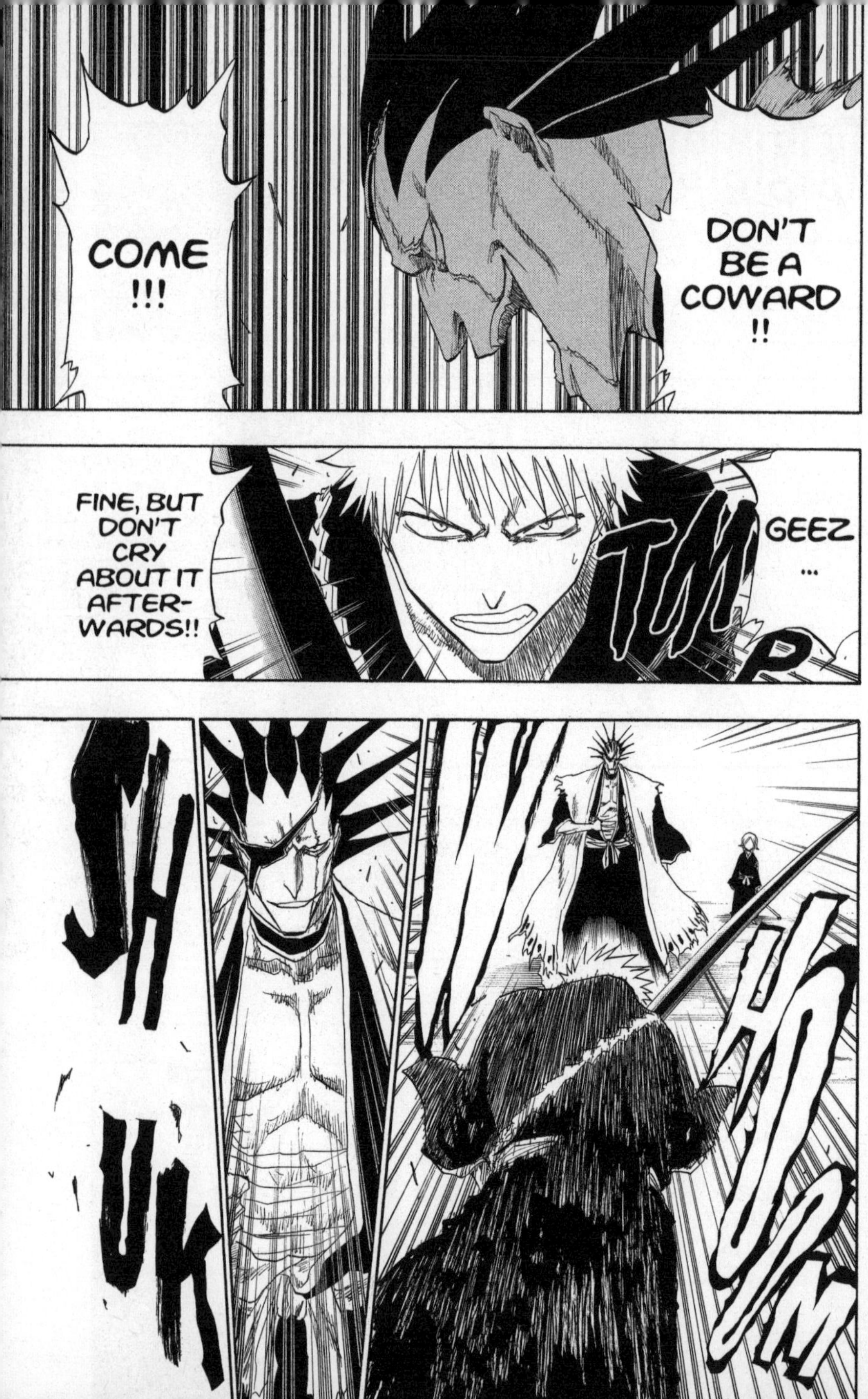
DON'T BE A COWARD !!
COME !!!
GEEZ ...
TMP
FINE, BUT DON'T CRY ABOUT IT AFTER-WARDS!!
HOOM
SHUK

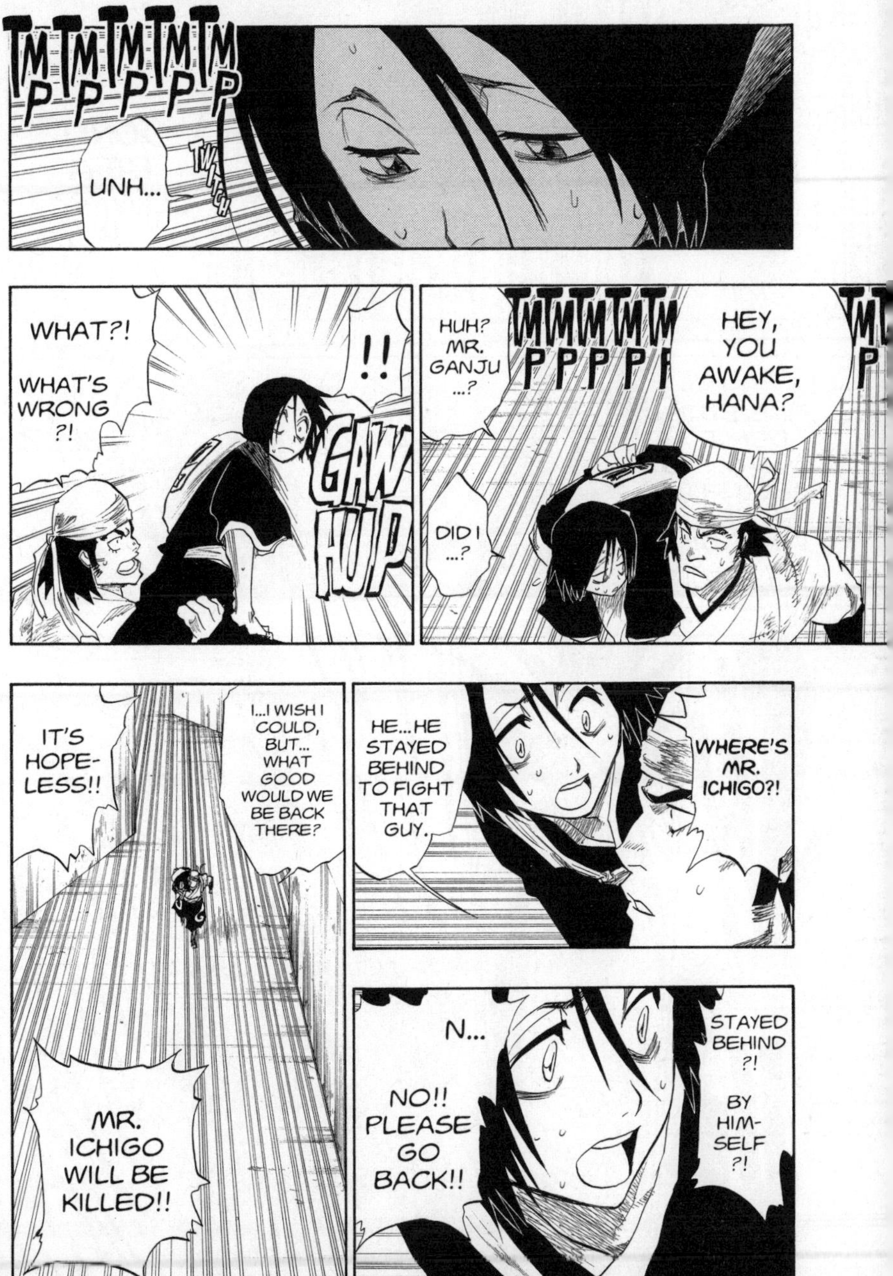
TMP TMP TMP TMP TMP
UNH...
TWITCH
TMP
HEY, YOU AWAKE, HANA?
TMP TMP TMP TMP TMP
HUH? MR. GANJU ...?
DID I ...?
!!
GAW HUP
WHAT?!
WHAT'S WRONG ?!
WHERE'S MR. ICHIGO?!
HE... HE STAYED BEHIND TO FIGHT THAT GUY.
STAYED BEHIND ?!
BY HIM-SELF ?!
N...
NO!! PLEASE GO BACK!!
I...I WISH I COULD, BUT... WHAT GOOD WOULD WE BE BACK THERE?
IT'S HOPE-LESS!!
MR. ICHIGO WILL BE KILLED!!

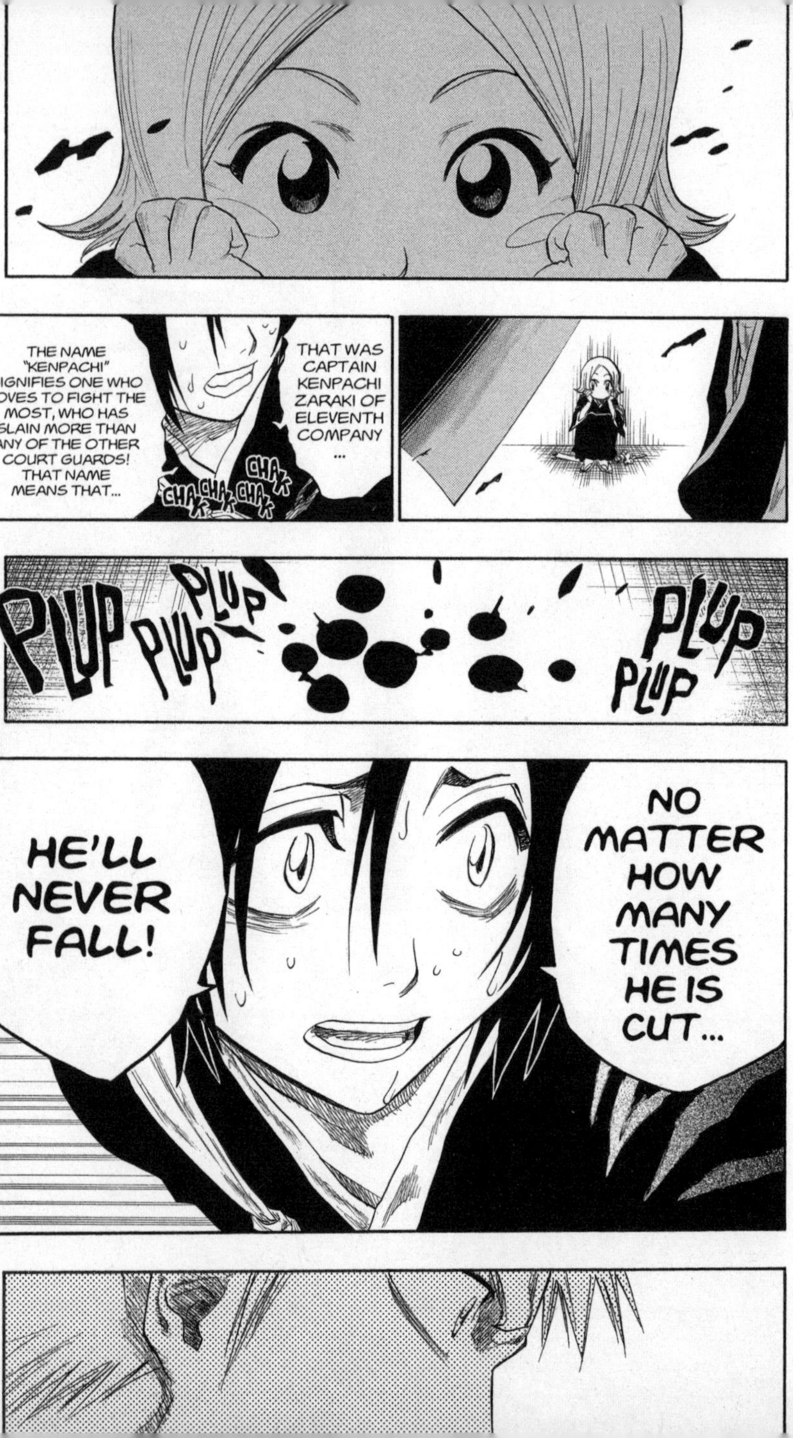
THAT WAS CAPTAIN KENPACHI ZARAKI OF ELEVENTH COMPANY ...
THE NAME "KENPACHI" SIGNIFIES ONE WHO LOVES TO FIGHT THE MOST, WHO HAS SLAIN MORE THAN ANY OF THE OTHER COURT GUARDS! THAT NAME MEANS THAT...
CHAK CHAK CHAK CHAK
PLUP PLUP
PLUP PLUP
PLUP
NO MATTER HOW MANY TIMES HE IS CUT...
HE'LL NEVER FALL!

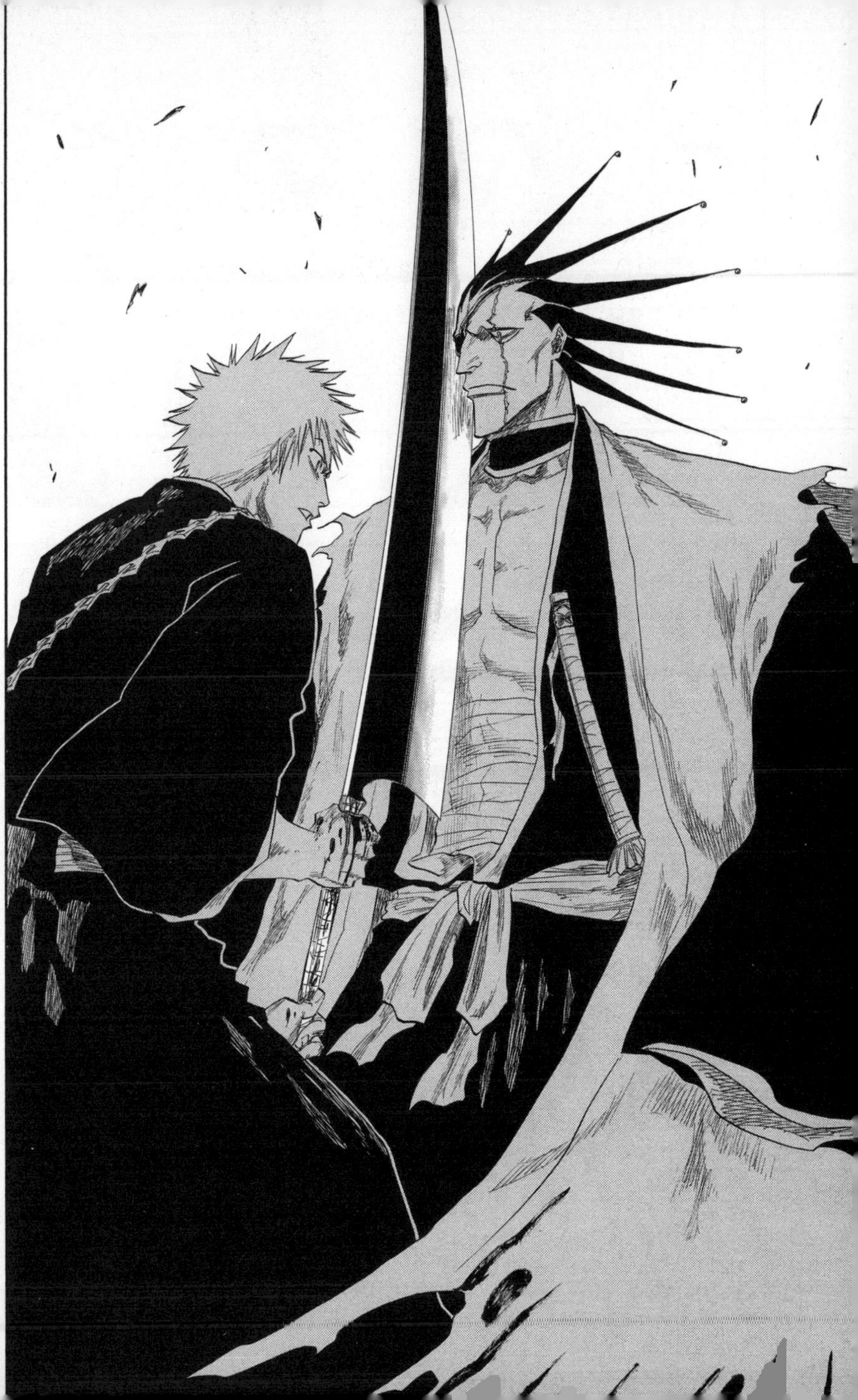

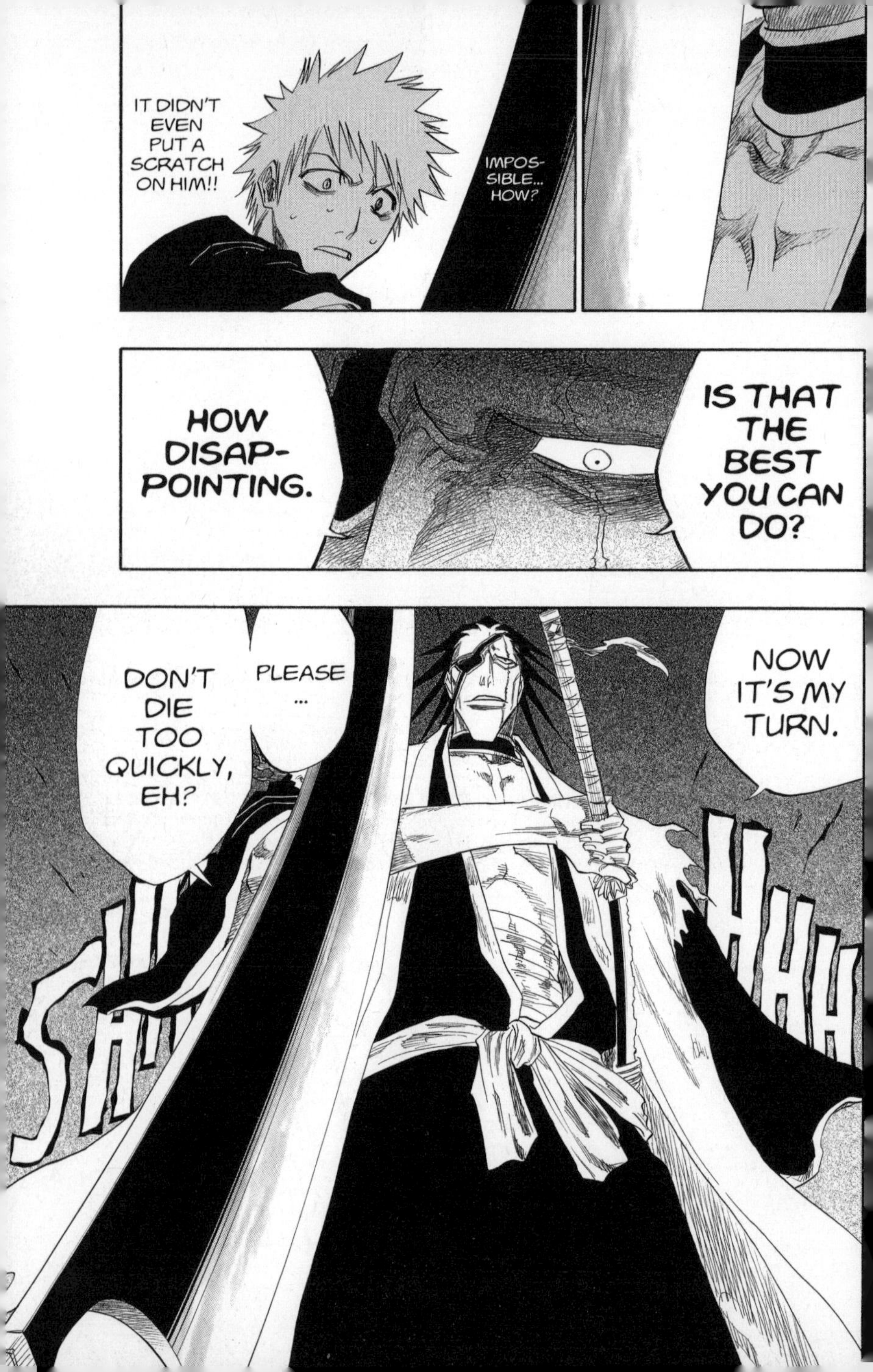
IMPOSSIBLE... HOW?
IT DIDN'T EVEN PUT A SCRATCH ON HIM!!
IS THAT THE BEST YOU CAN DO?
HOW DISAPPOINTING.
NOW IT'S MY TURN.
PLEASE...
DON'T DIE TOO QUICKLY, EH?

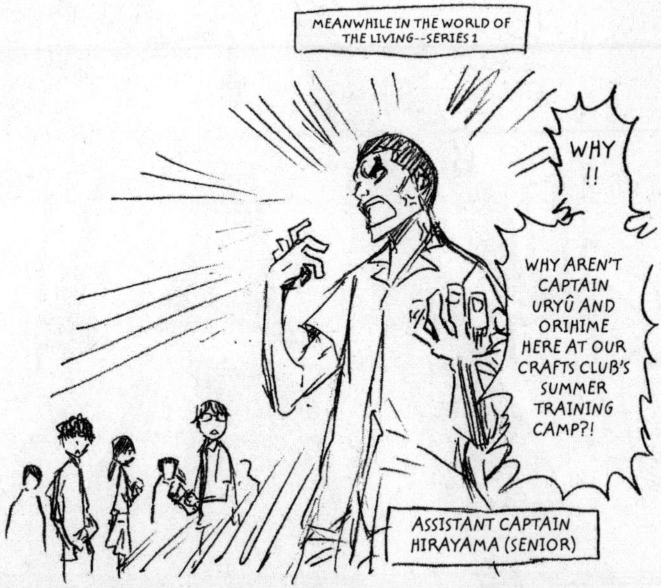
MEANWHILE IN THE WORLD OF THE LIVING--SERIES 1
WHY !!
WHY AREN'T CAPTAIN URYÛ AND ORIHIME HERE AT OUR CRAFTS CLUB'S SUMMER TRAINING CAMP?!
ASSISTANT CAPTAIN HIRAYAMA (SENIOR)

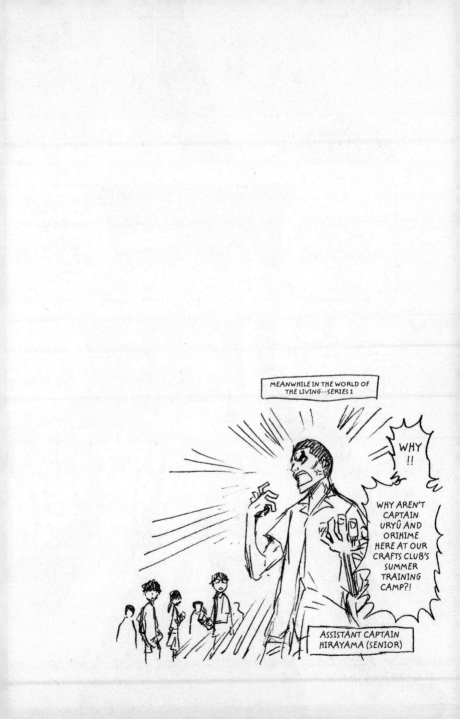

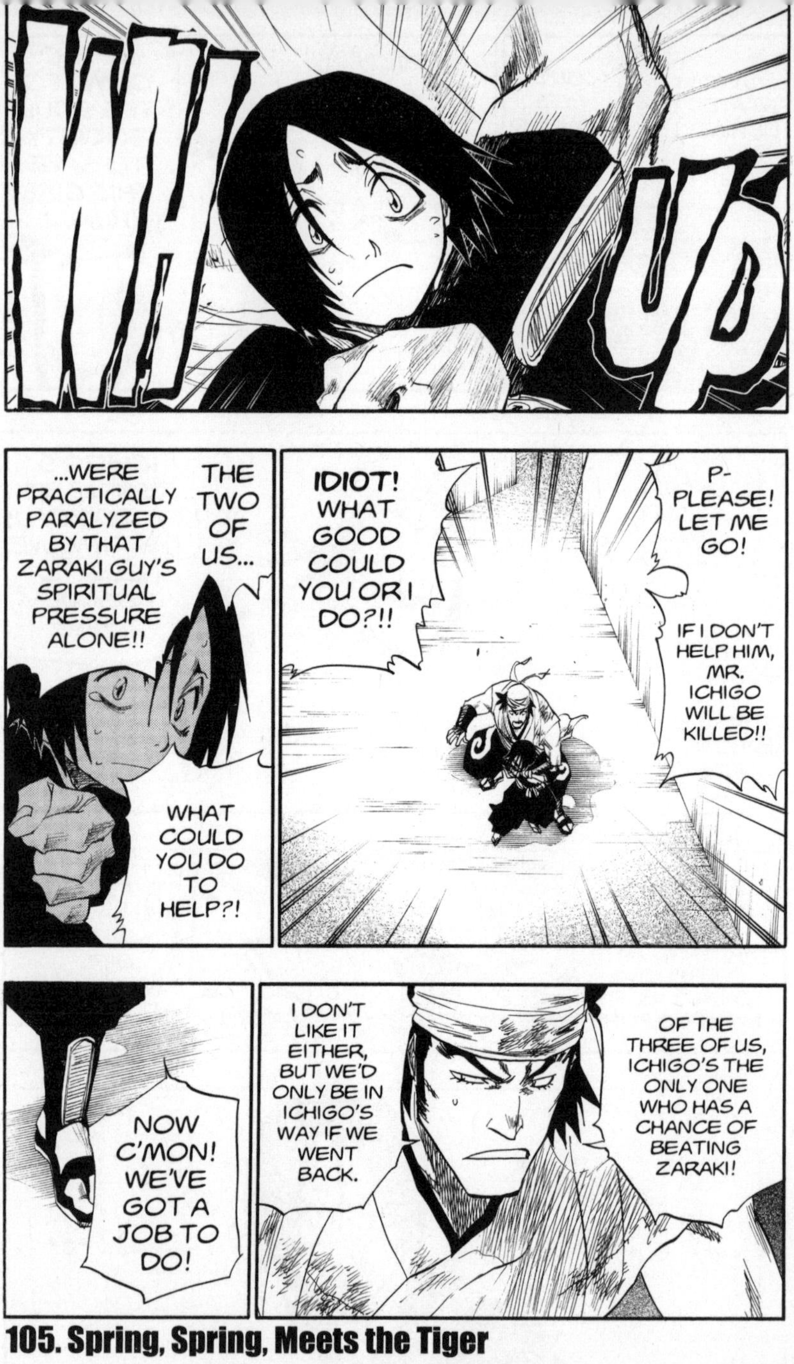
WHUD
P- PLEASE! LET ME GO!
IF I DON'T HELP HIM, MR. ICHIGO WILL BE KILLED!!
IDIOT! WHAT GOOD COULD YOU OR I DO?!!
THE TWO OF US...
...WERE PRACTICALLY PARALYZED BY THAT ZARAKI GUY'S SPIRITUAL PRESSURE ALONE!!
WHAT COULD YOU DO TO HELP?!
OF THE THREE OF US, ICHIGO'S THE ONLY ONE WHO HAS A CHANCE OF BEATING ZARAKI!
I DON'T LIKE IT EITHER, BUT WE'D ONLY BE IN ICHIGO'S WAY IF WE WENT BACK.
NOW C'MON! WE'VE GOT A JOB TO DO!

105. Spring, Spring, Meets the Tiger

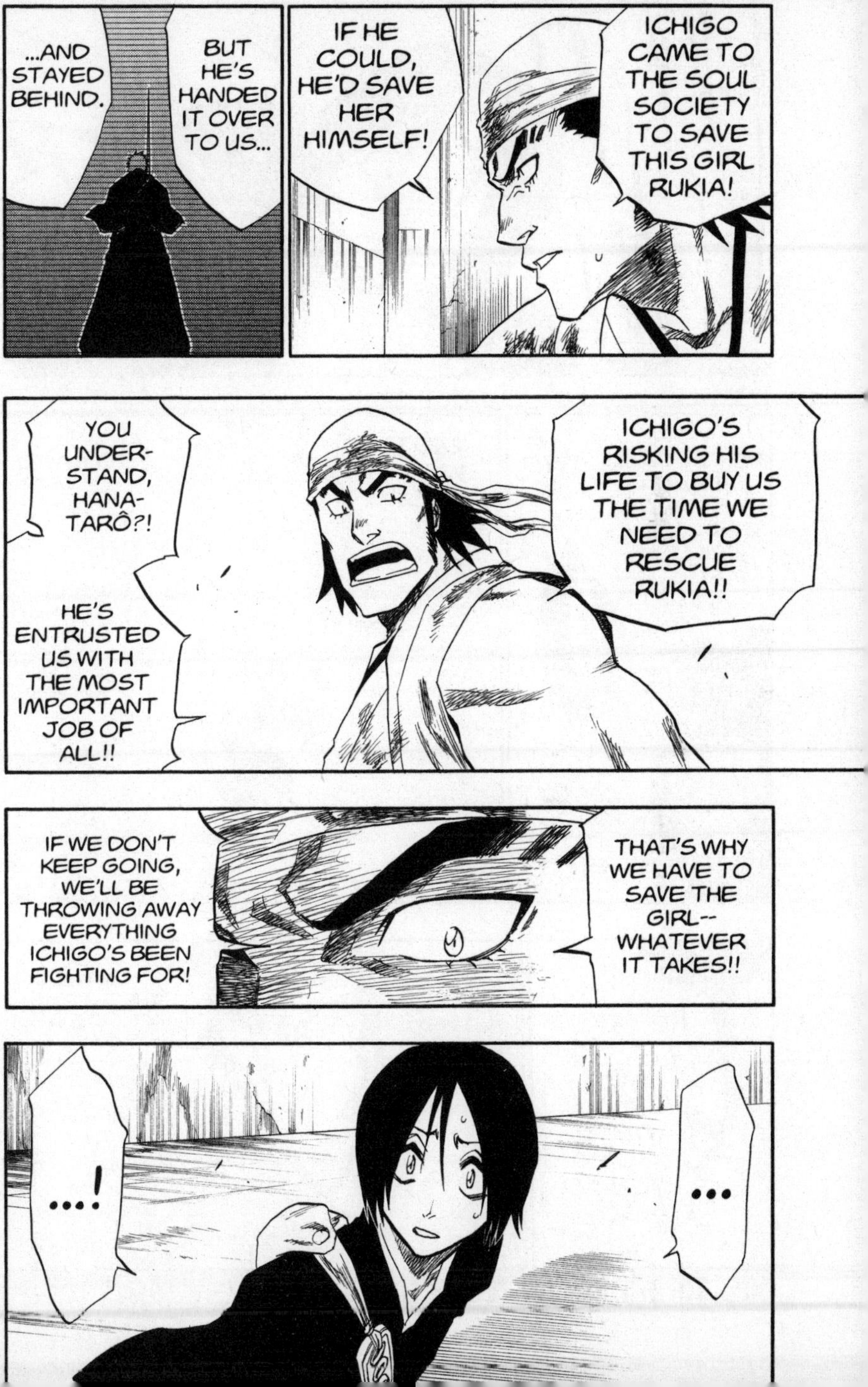
ICHIGO CAME TO THE SOUL SOCIETY TO SAVE THIS GIRL RUKIA!
IF HE COULD, HE'D SAVE HER HIMSELF!
BUT HE'S HANDED IT OVER TO US...
...AND STAYED BEHIND.
ICHIGO'S RISKING HIS LIFE TO BUY US THE TIME WE NEED TO RESCUE RUKIA!!
YOU UNDER-STAND, HANA-TARÔ?!
HE'S ENTRUSTED US WITH THE MOST IMPORTANT JOB OF ALL!!
THAT'S WHY WE HAVE TO SAVE THE GIRL-- WHATEVER IT TAKES!!
IF WE DON'T KEEP GOING, WE'LL BE THROWING AWAY EVERYTHING ICHIGO'S BEEN FIGHTING FOR!
...
...!

READ THIS WAY

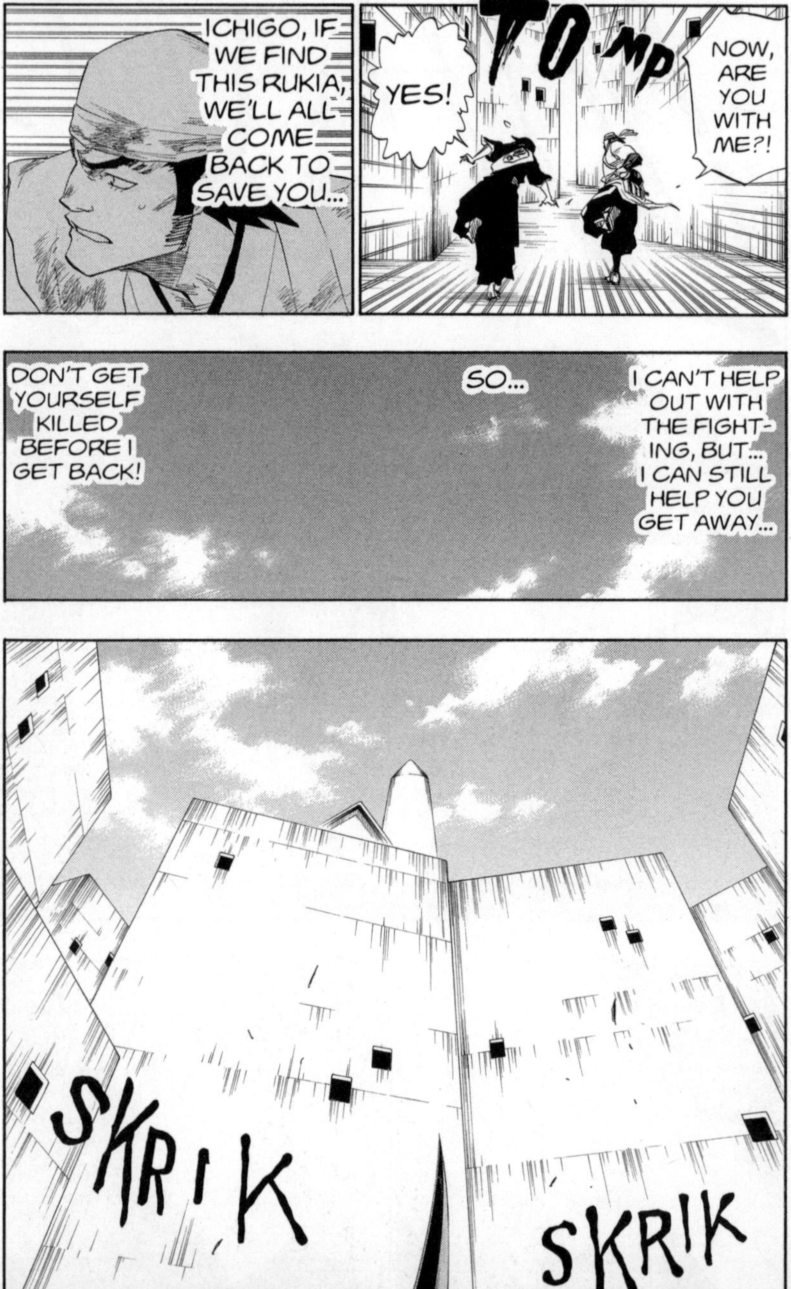
NOW, ARE YOU WITH ME?!
TOMP
YES!
ICHIGO, IF WE FIND THIS RUKIA, WE'LL ALL COME BACK TO SAVE YOU...
I CAN'T HELP OUT WITH THE FIGHT-ING, BUT... I CAN STILL HELP YOU GET AWAY...
SO...
DON'T GET YOURSELF KILLED BEFORE I GET BACK!
SKRIK
SKRIK

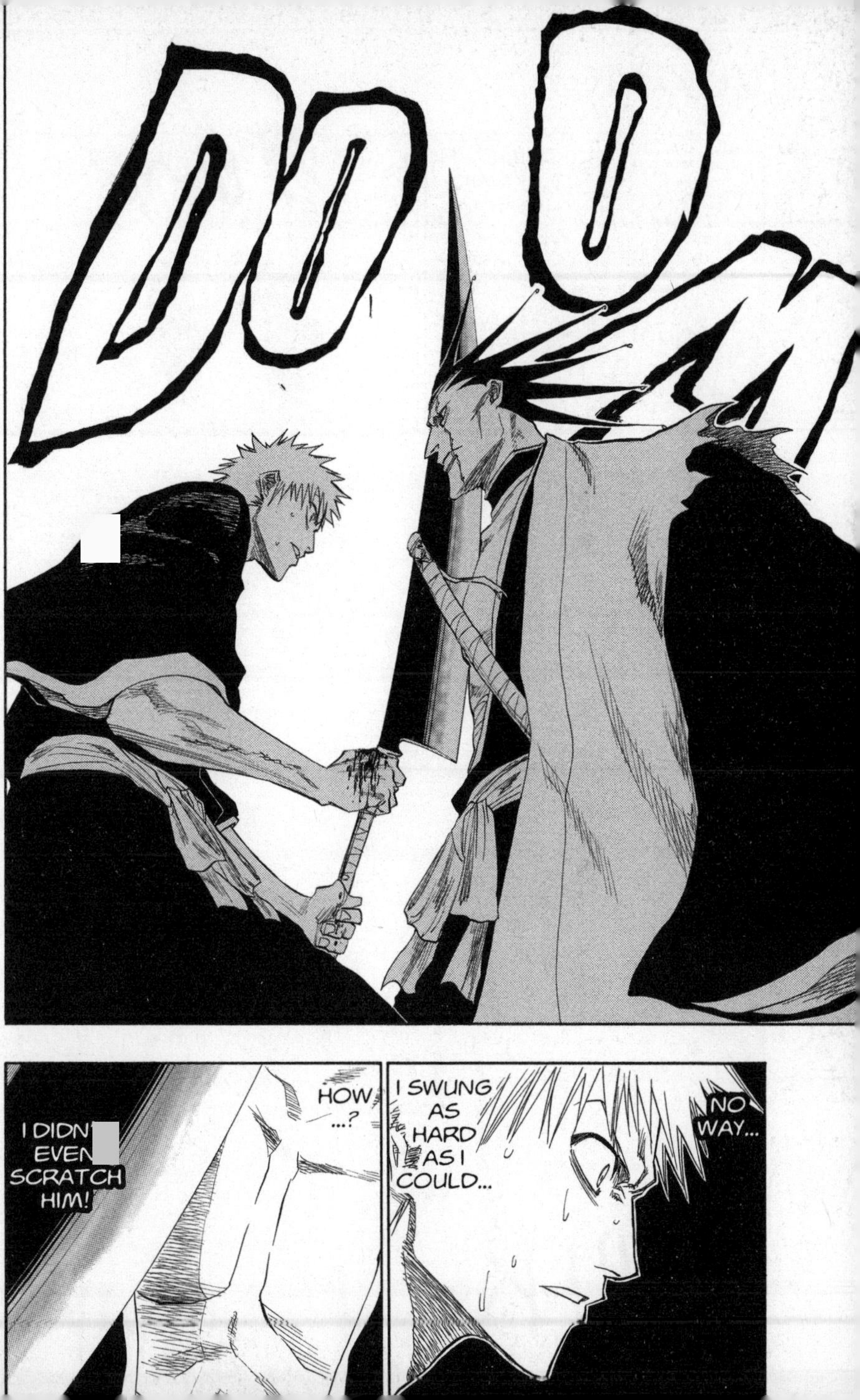
DOOM
NO WAY...
I SWUNG AS HARD AS I COULD...
HOW ...?
I DIDN'T EVEN SCRATCH HIM!

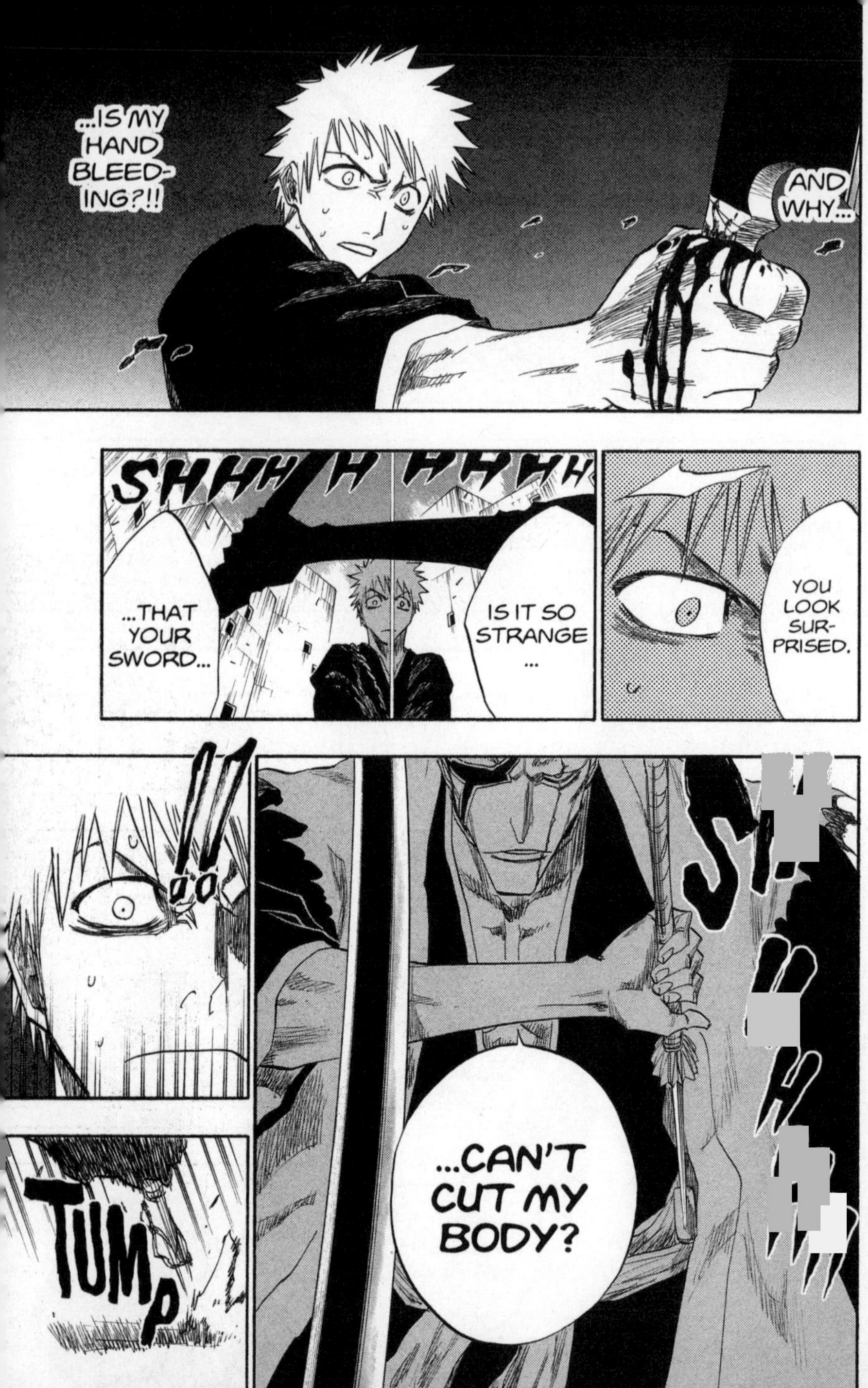
AND WHY...
...IS MY HAND BLEED-ING?!!
YOU LOOK SUR-PRISED.
IS IT SO STRANGE ...
SHHHHHHHHH
...THAT YOUR SWORD...
...CAN'T CUT MY BODY?
!!
TUMP

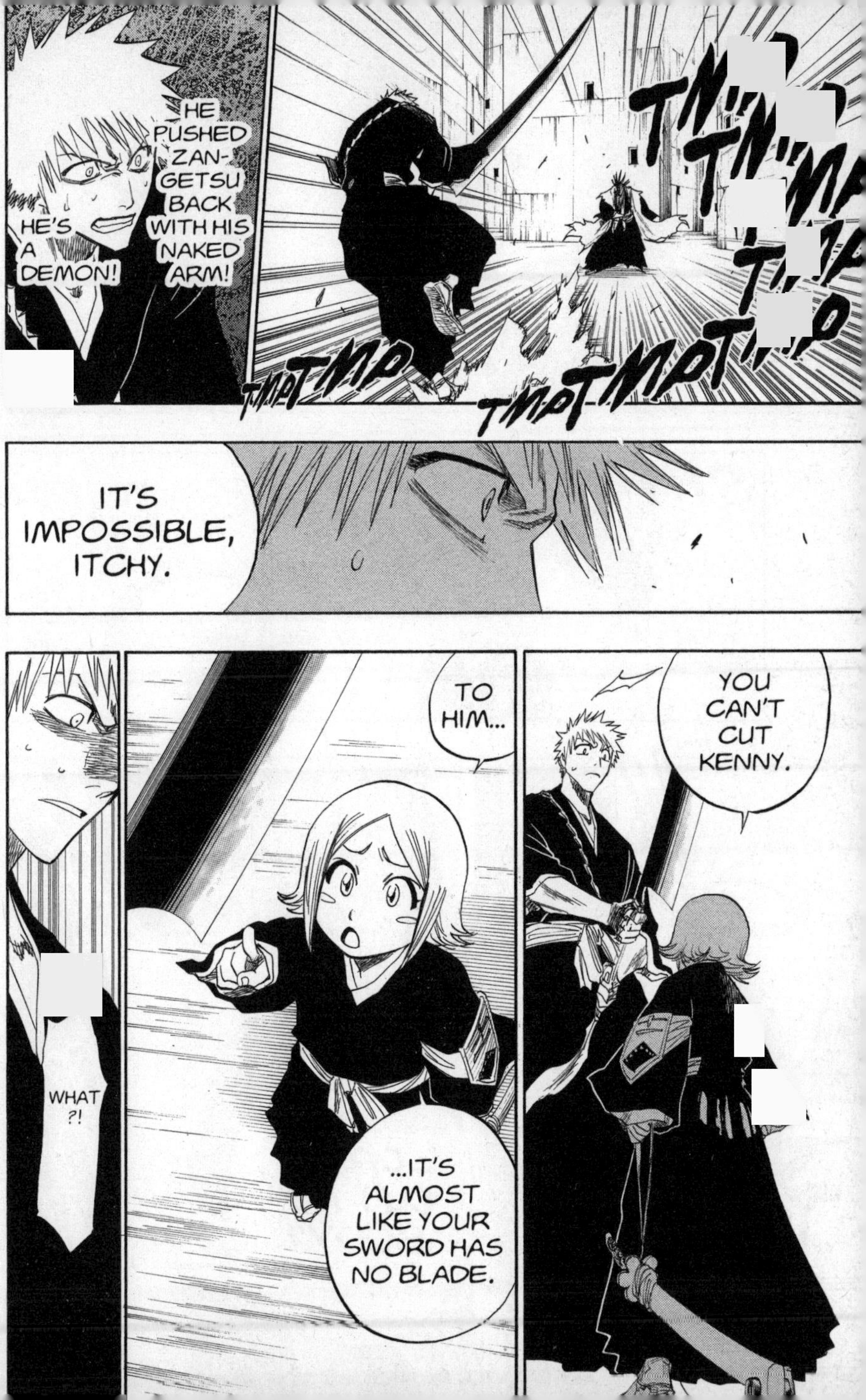
HE PUSHED ZAN-GETSU BACK WITH HIS NAKED ARM!
HE'S A DEMON!
IT'S IMPOSSIBLE, ITCHY.
YOU CAN'T CUT KENNY.
TO HIM...
...IT'S ALMOST LIKE YOUR SWORD HAS NO BLADE.
WHAT?!

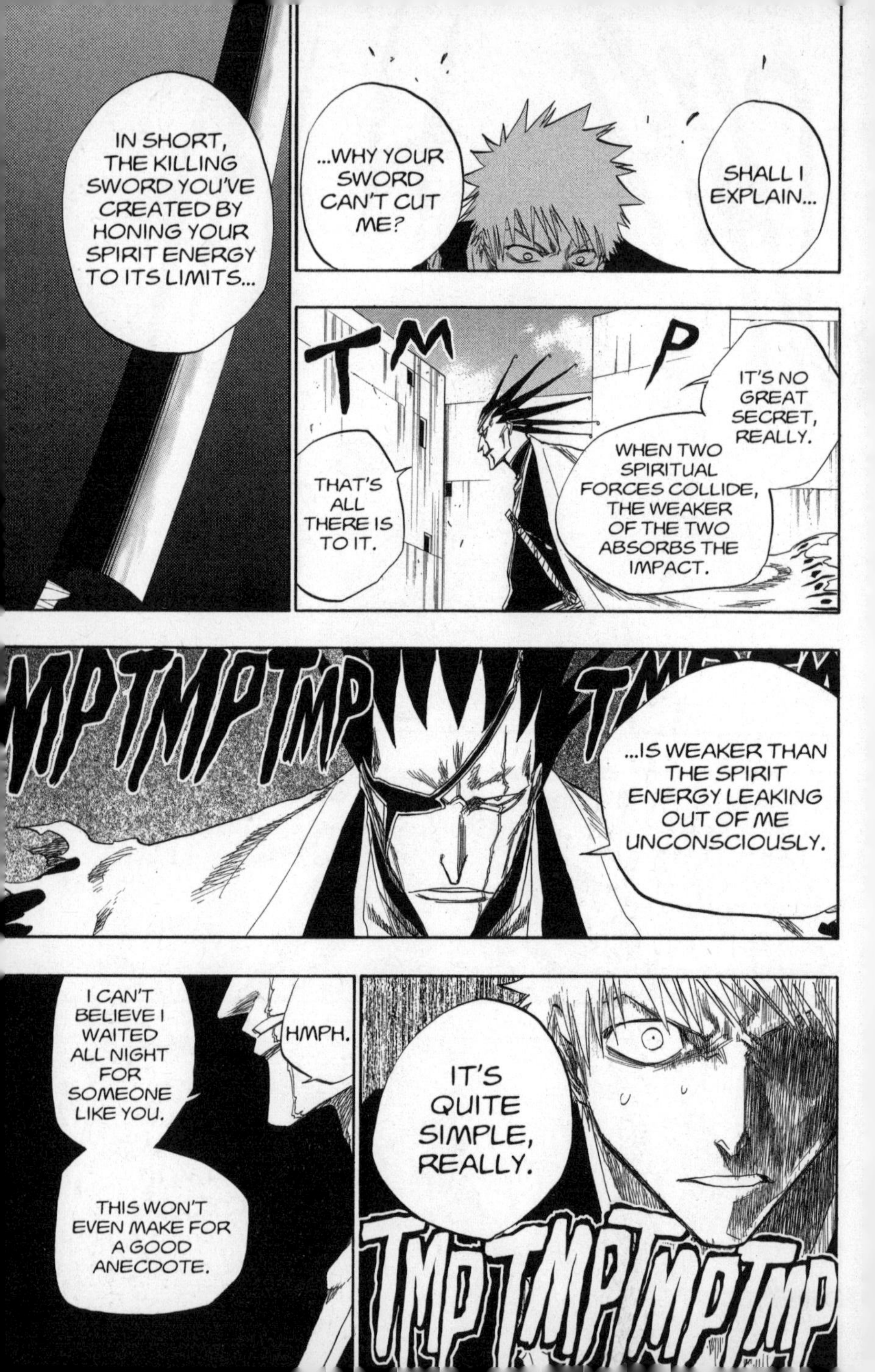

SHALL I EXPLAIN...
...WHY YOUR SWORD CAN'T CUT ME?
TMP
IT'S NO GREAT SECRET, REALLY.
WHEN TWO SPIRITUAL FORCES COLLIDE, THE WEAKER OF THE TWO ABSORBS THE IMPACT.
THAT'S ALL THERE IS TO IT.
IN SHORT, THE KILLING SWORD YOU'VE CREATED BY HONING YOUR SPIRIT ENERGY TO ITS LIMITS...
...IS WEAKER THAN THE SPIRIT ENERGY LEAKING OUT OF ME UNCONSCIOUSLY.
MP TMP TMP TMP
IT'S QUITE SIMPLE, REALLY.
TMP TMP TMP TMP
HMPH.
I CAN'T BELIEVE I WAITED ALL NIGHT FOR SOMEONE LIKE YOU.
THIS WON'T EVEN MAKE FOR A GOOD ANECDOTE.

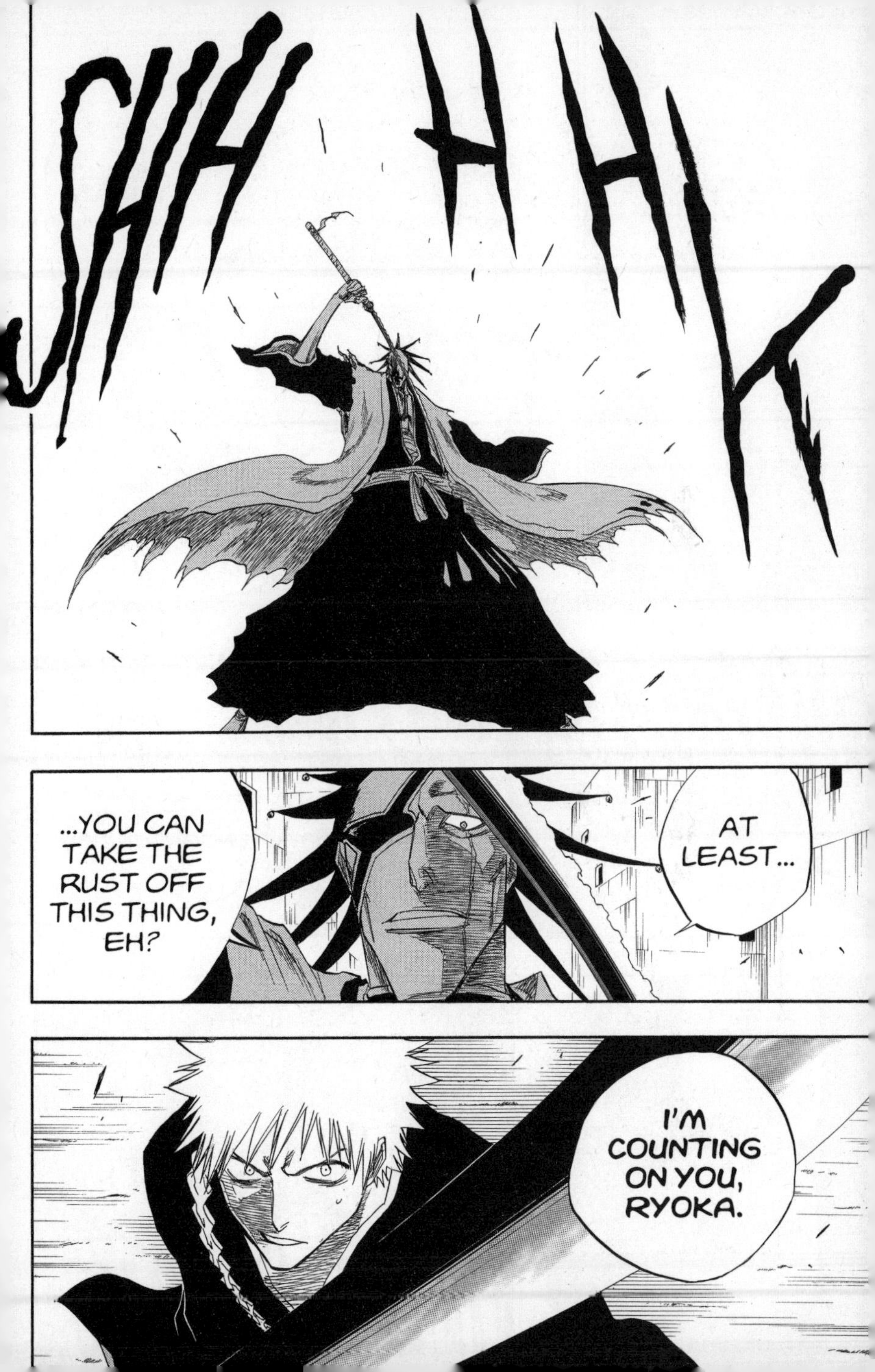
SHHHIK
AT LEAST...
...YOU CAN TAKE THE RUST OFF THIS THING, EH?
I'M COUNTING ON YOU, RYOKA.

105. Spring, Spring, Meets the Tiger

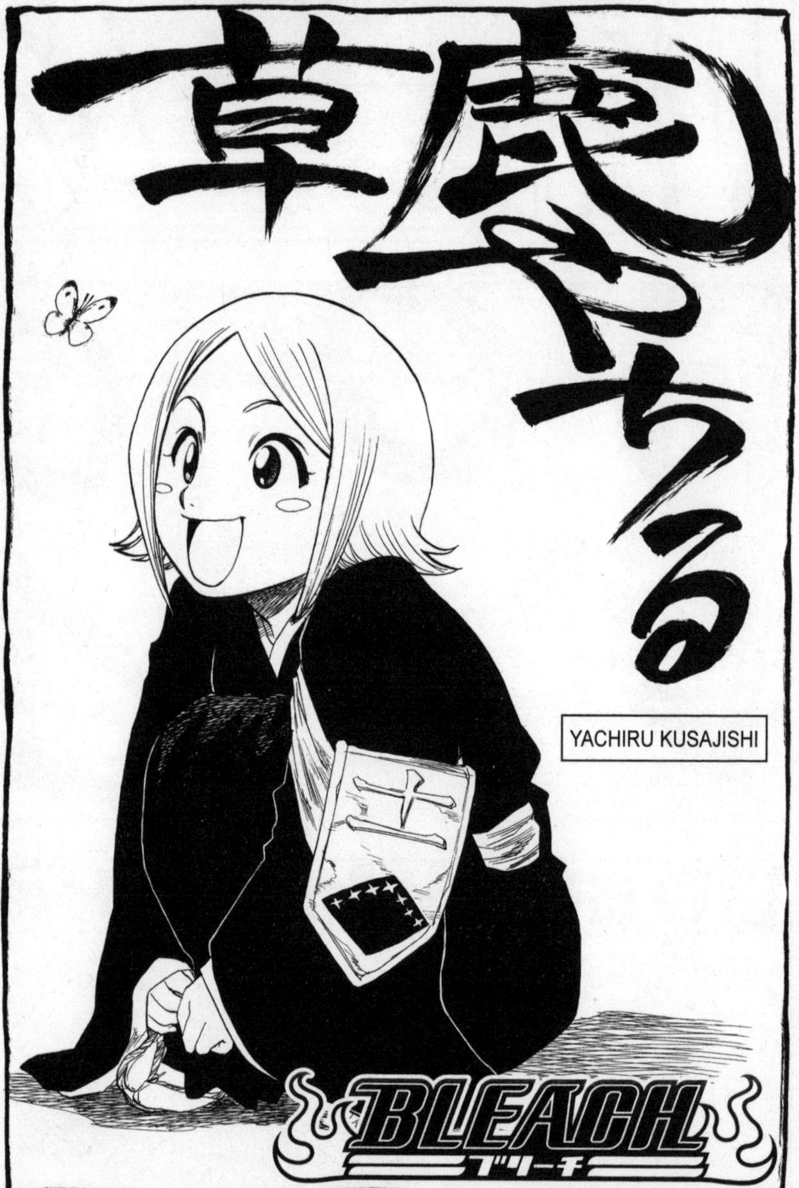
草鹿やちる
YACHIRU KUSAJISHI
BLEACH
ブリーチ

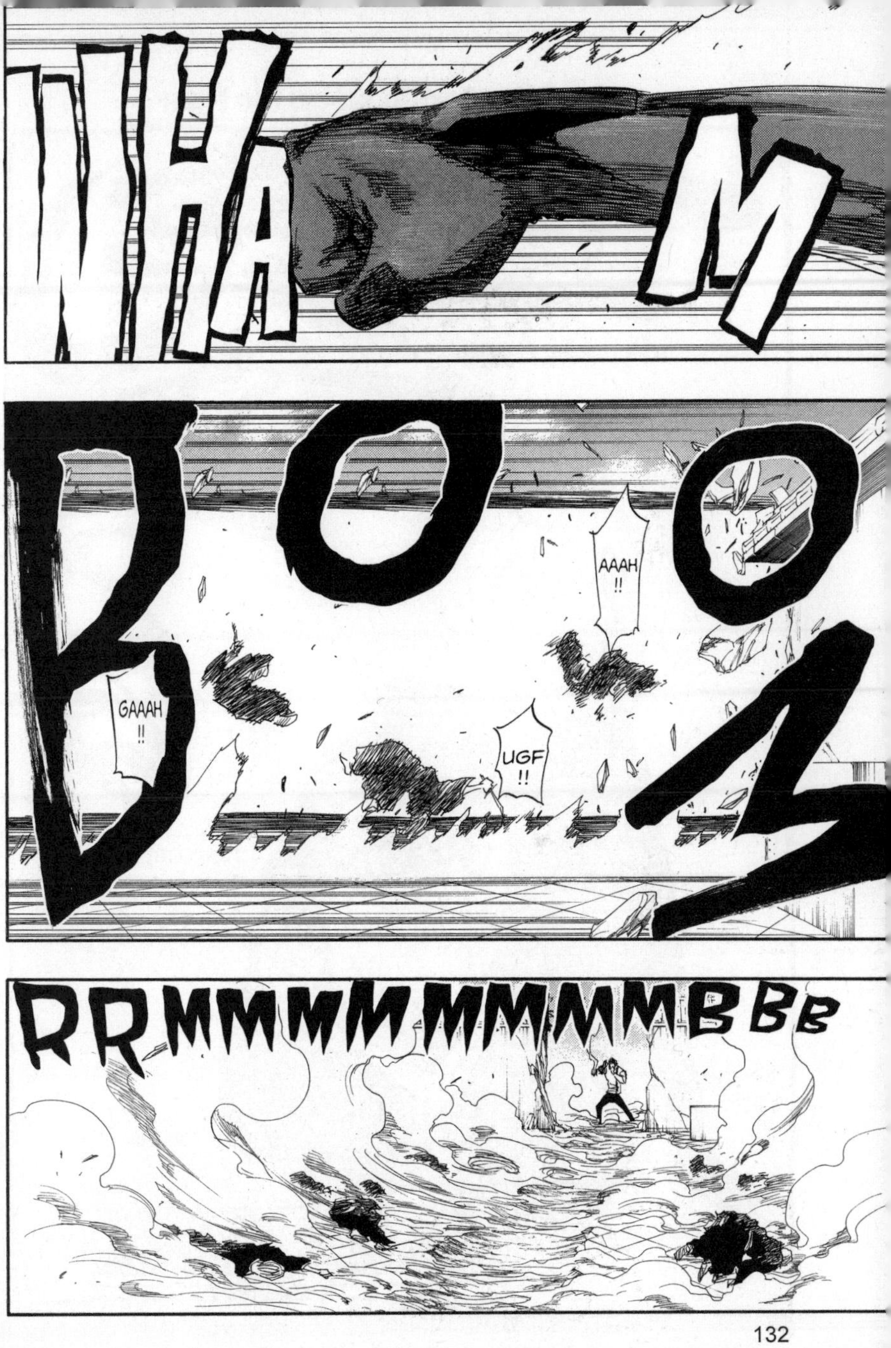
WHAM
BOOM
AAAH!!
UGF!!
GAAAH!!
RRMMMMMMMMMMBBB

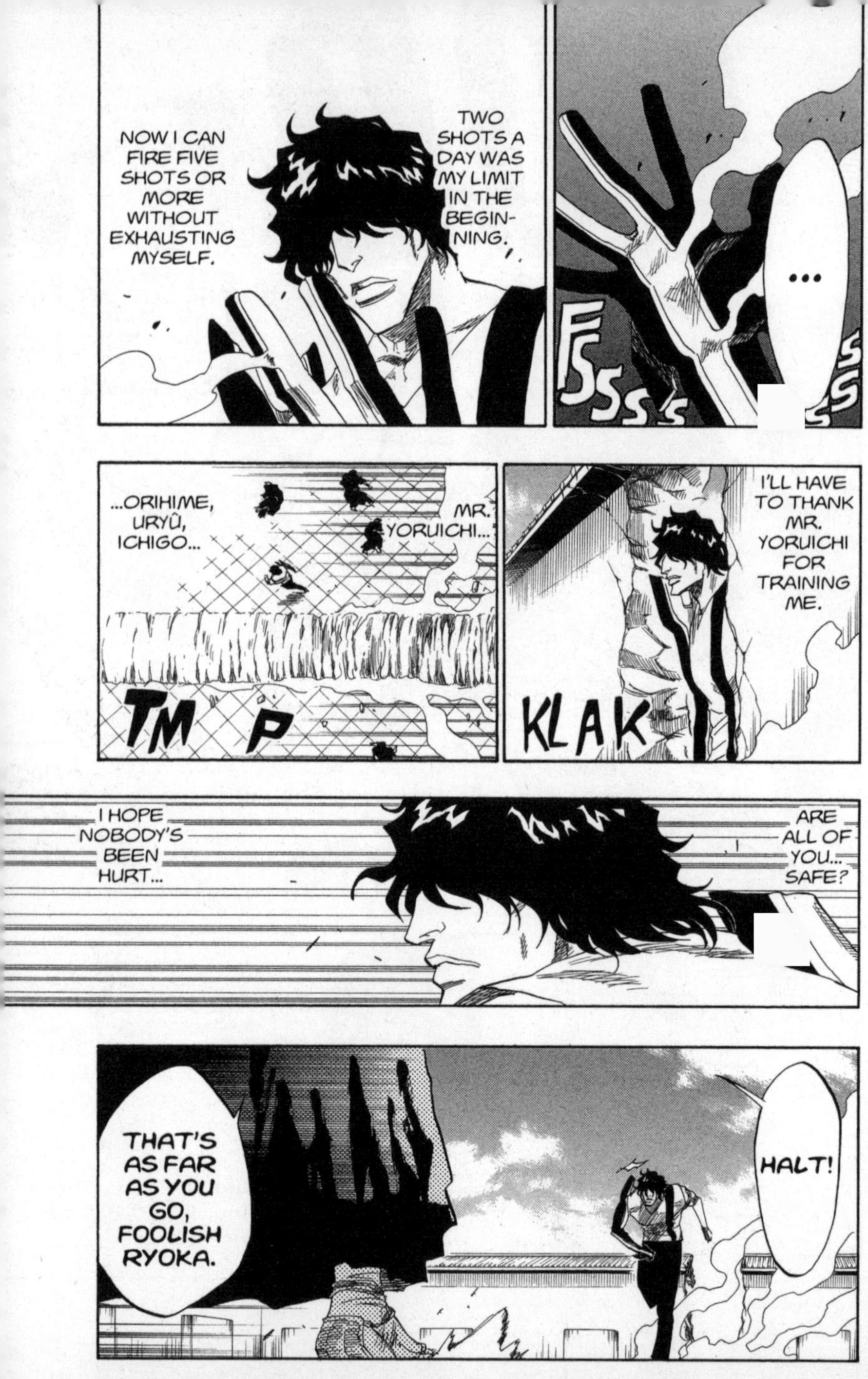
...
FSSSS
TWO SHOTS A DAY WAS MY LIMIT IN THE BEGINNING.
NOW I CAN FIRE FIVE SHOTS OR MORE WITHOUT EXHAUSTING MYSELF.
I'LL HAVE TO THANK MR. YORUICHI FOR TRAINING ME.
KLAK
MR. YORUICHI...
...ORIHIME, URYÛ, ICHIGO...
TMP
ARE ALL OF YOU... SAFE?
I HOPE NOBODY'S BEEN HURT...
HALT!
THAT'S AS FAR AS YOU GO, FOOLISH RYOKA.

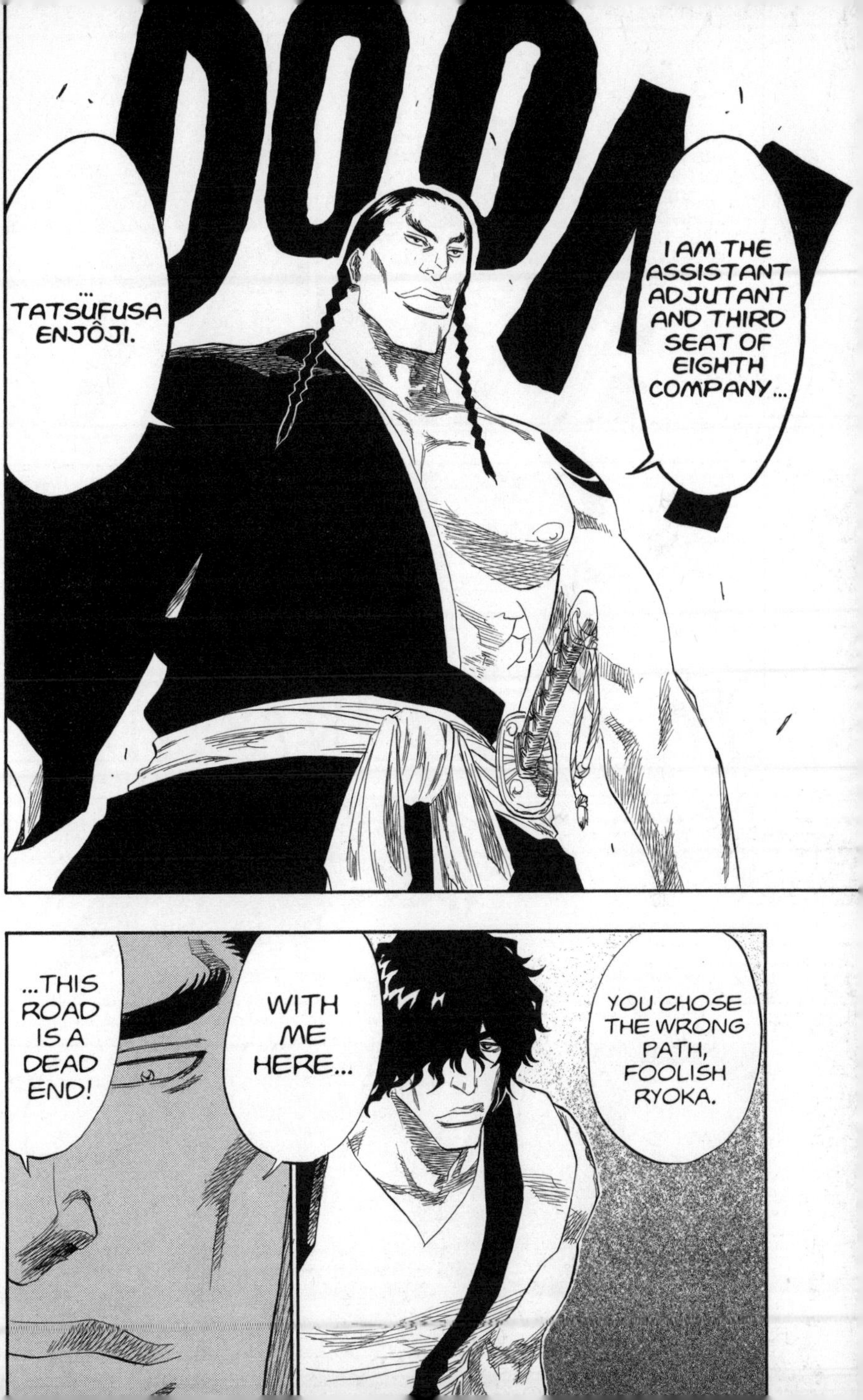
DOON
I AM THE ASSISTANT ADJUTANT AND THIRD SEAT OF EIGHTH COMPANY...
...TATSŪFUSA ENJÔJI.
YOU CHOSE THE WRONG PATH, FOOLISH RYOKA.
WITH ME HERE...
...THIS ROAD IS A DEAD END!

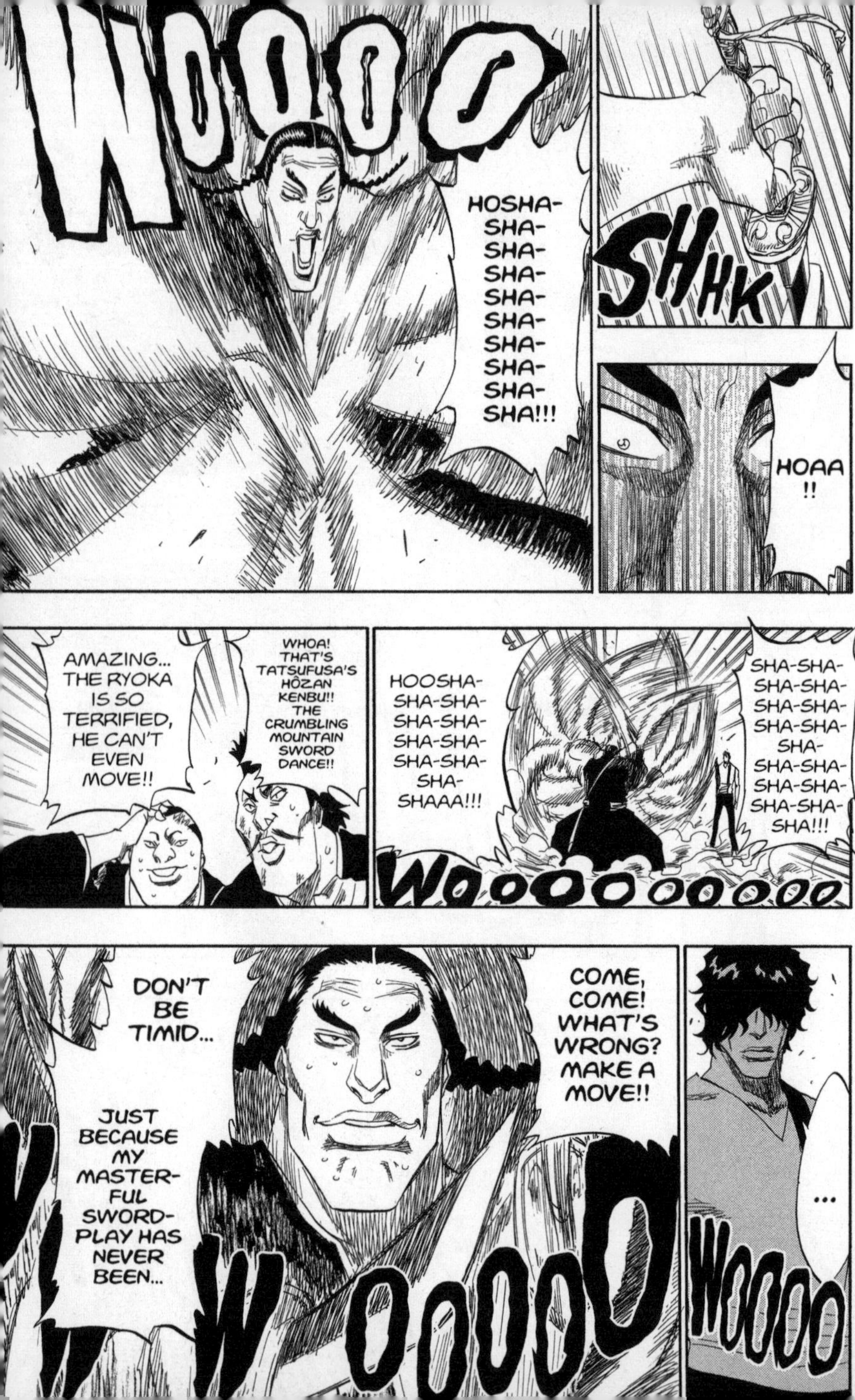
SHHK
HOAA!!
WOOOO
HOSHA-SHA-SHA-SHA-SHA-SHA-SHA-SHA-SHA-SHA!!!
SHA-SHA-SHA-SHA-SHA-SHA-SHA-SHA-SHA-SHA-SHA-SHA-SHA-SHA-SHA-SHA!!!
HOOSHA-SHA-SHA-SHA-SHA-SHA-SHA-SHA-SHA-SHA-SHAAA!!!
WOOOOOOOOOO
WHOA! THAT'S TATSUFUSA'S HÔZAN KENBU!! THE CRUMBLING MOUNTAIN SWORD DANCE!!
AMAZING... THE RYOKA IS SO TERRIFIED, HE CAN'T EVEN MOVE!!
...
WOOOO
COME, COME! WHAT'S WRONG? MAKE A MOVE!!
DON'T BE TIMID...
JUST BECAUSE MY MASTERFUL SWORDPLAY HAS NEVER BEEN...
WOOOOO

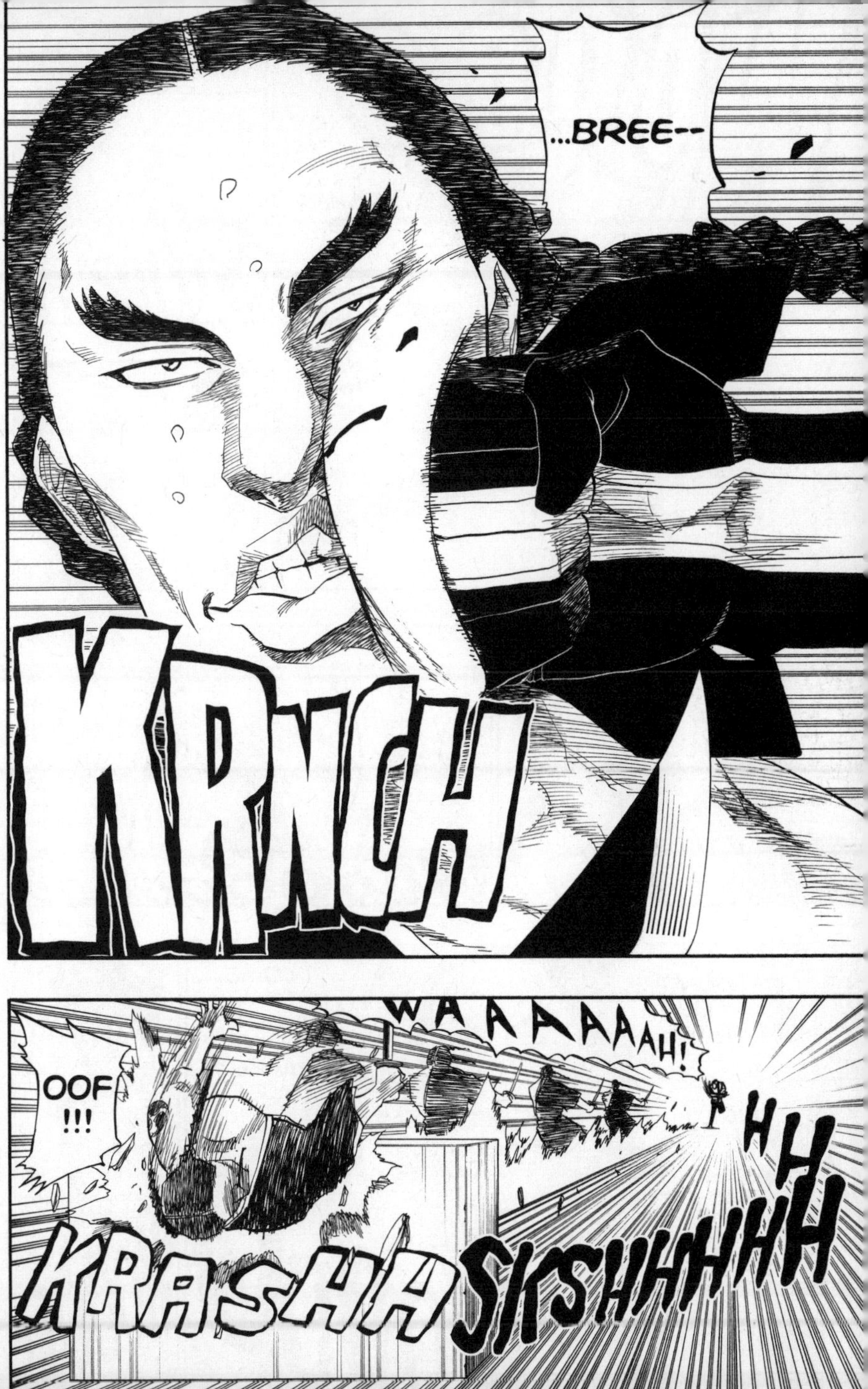
...BREE--
KRNCH
WAAAAAAH!
OOF !!!
HHH
SKSHHHHH
KRASHA

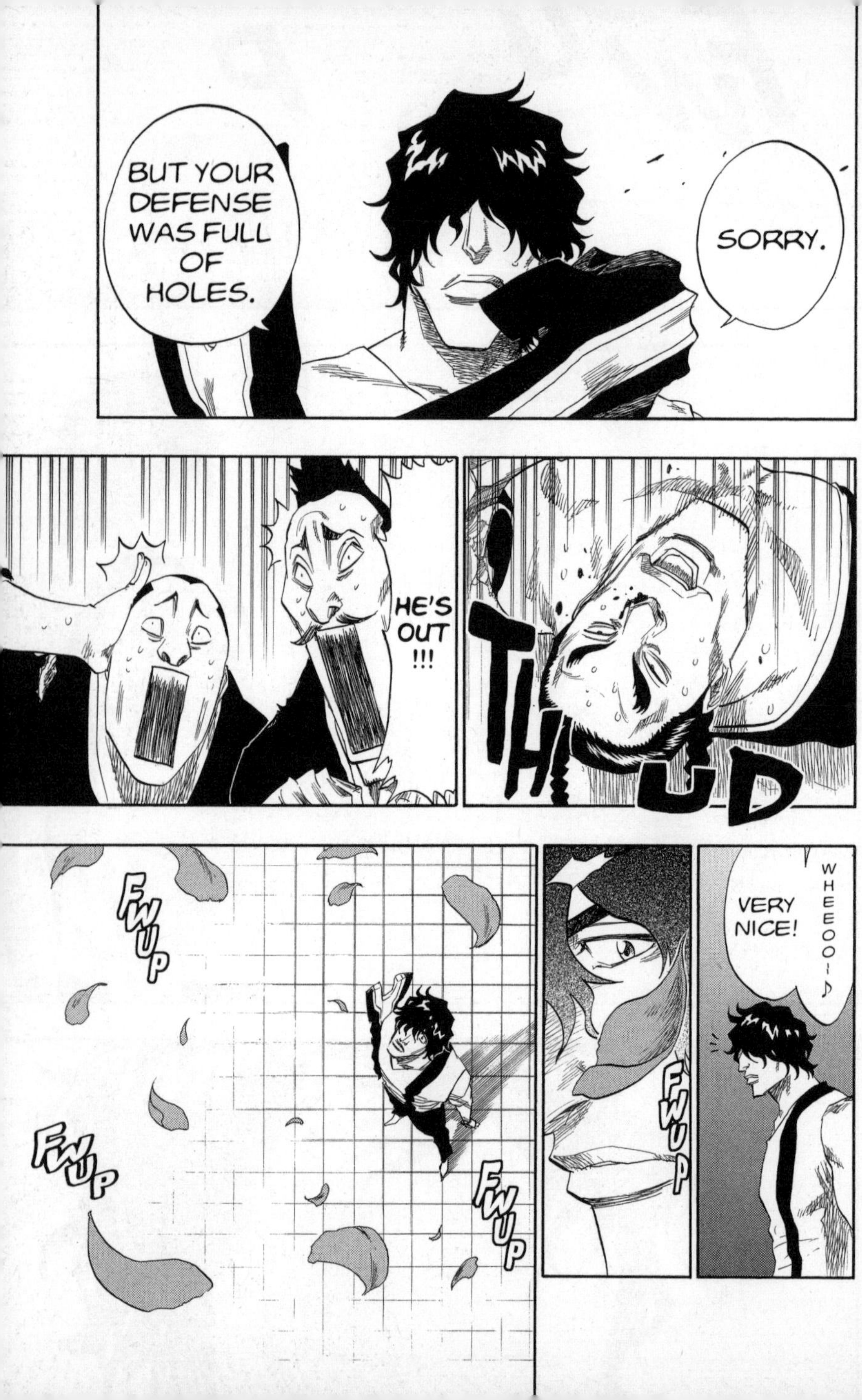
SORRY.
BUT YOUR DEFENSE WAS FULL OF HOLES.
THUD
HE'S OUT!!!
WHEEOO!♪
VERY NICE!
FWUP
FWUP
FWUP
FWUP

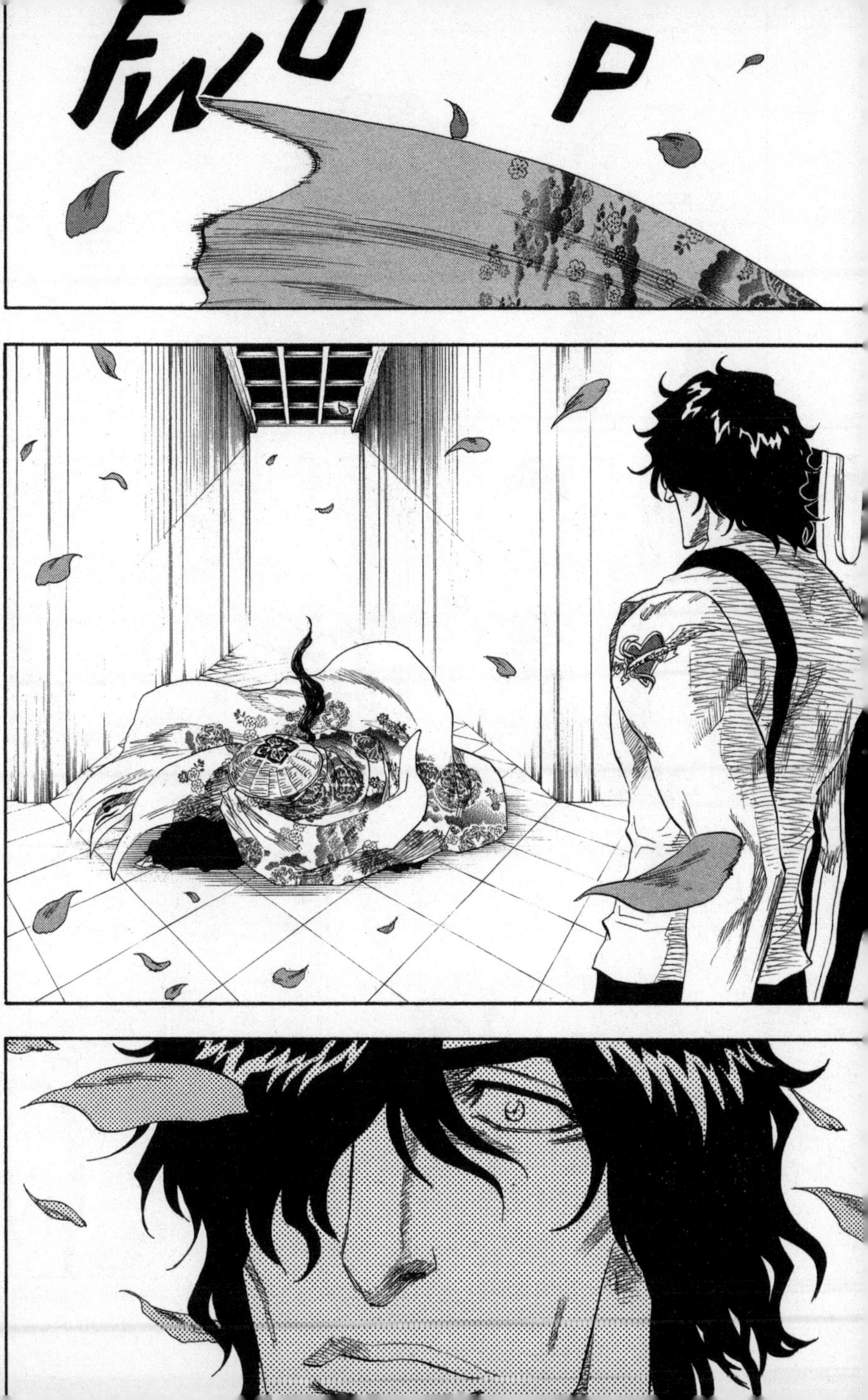
FWUP

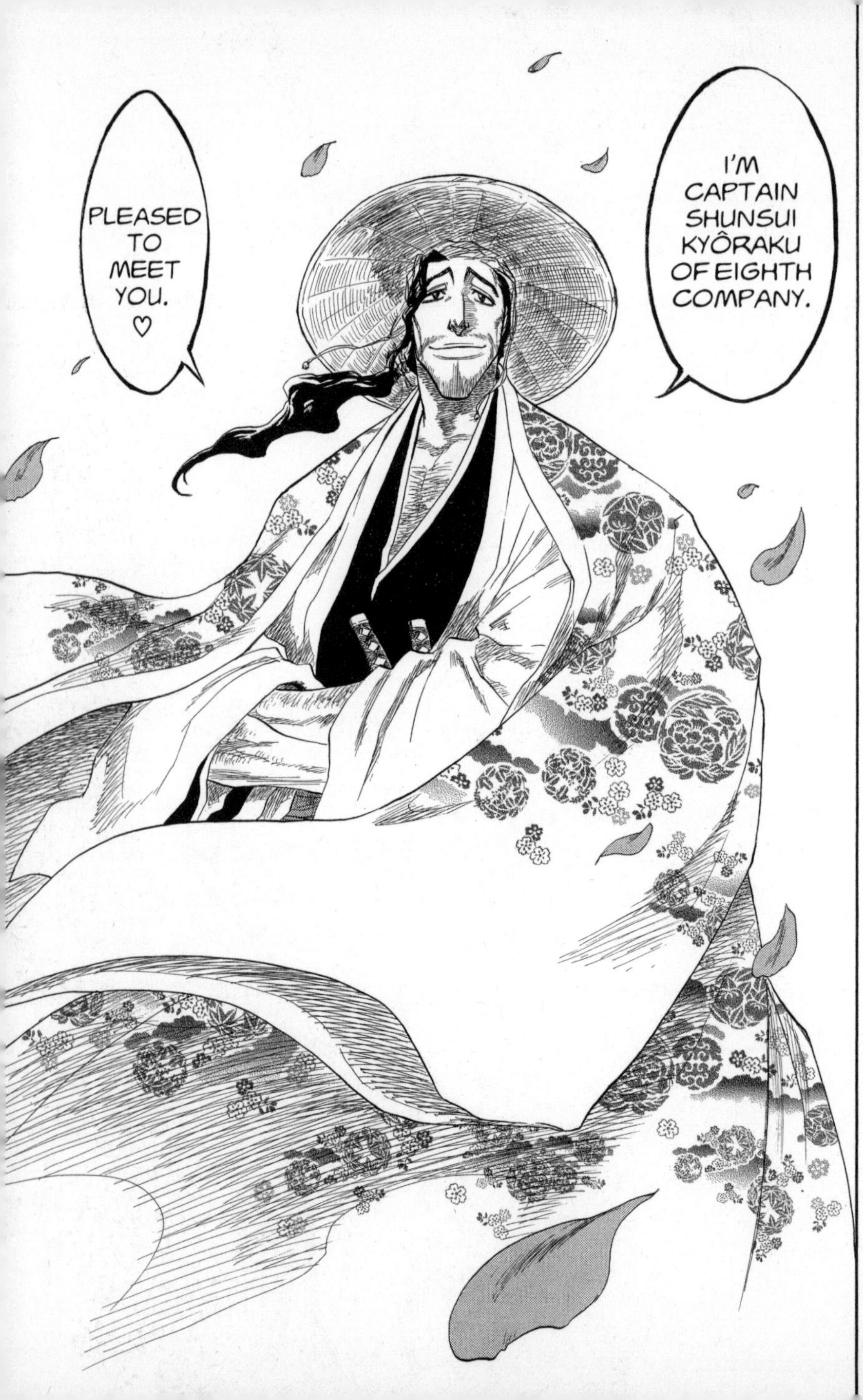
I'M CAPTAIN SHUNSUI KYÔRAKU OF EIGHTH COMPANY.
PLEASED TO MEET YOU. ♡

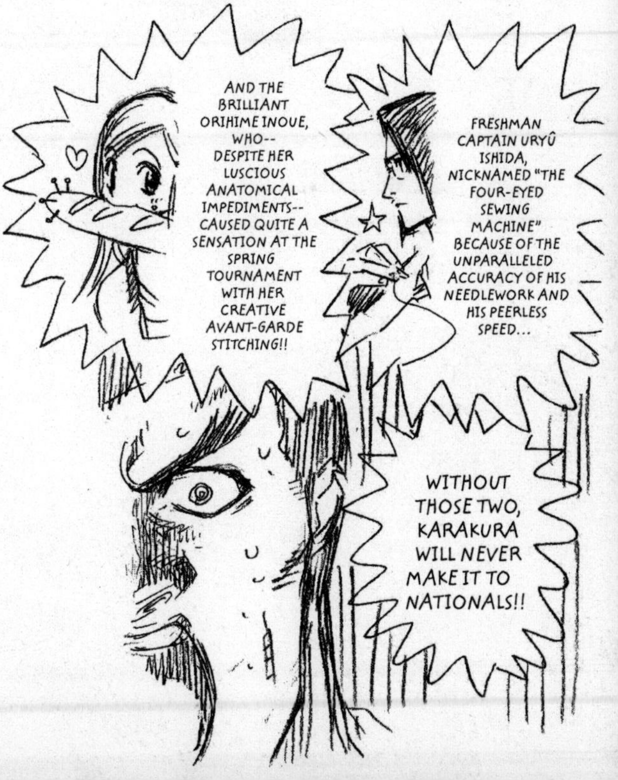
FRESHMAN CAPTAIN URYÛ ISHIDA, NICKNAMED "THE FOUR-EYED SEWING MACHINE" BECAUSE OF THE UNPARALLELED ACCURACY OF HIS NEEDLEWORK AND HIS PEERLESS SPEED...
AND THE BRILLIANT ORIHIME INOUE, WHO-- DESPITE HER LUSCIOUS ANATOMICAL IMPEDIMENTS-- CAUSED QUITE A SENSATION AT THE SPRING TOURNAMENT WITH HER CREATIVE AVANT-GARDE STITCHING!!
WITHOUT THOSE TWO, KARAKURA WILL NEVER MAKE IT TO NATIONALS!!

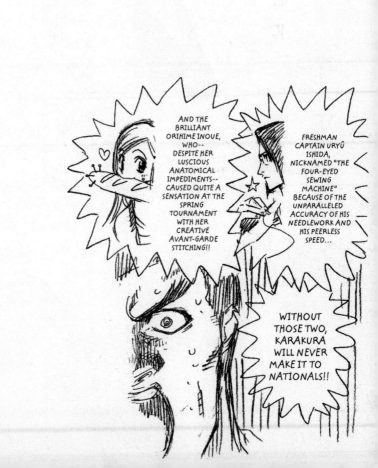

106. Cause to Confront

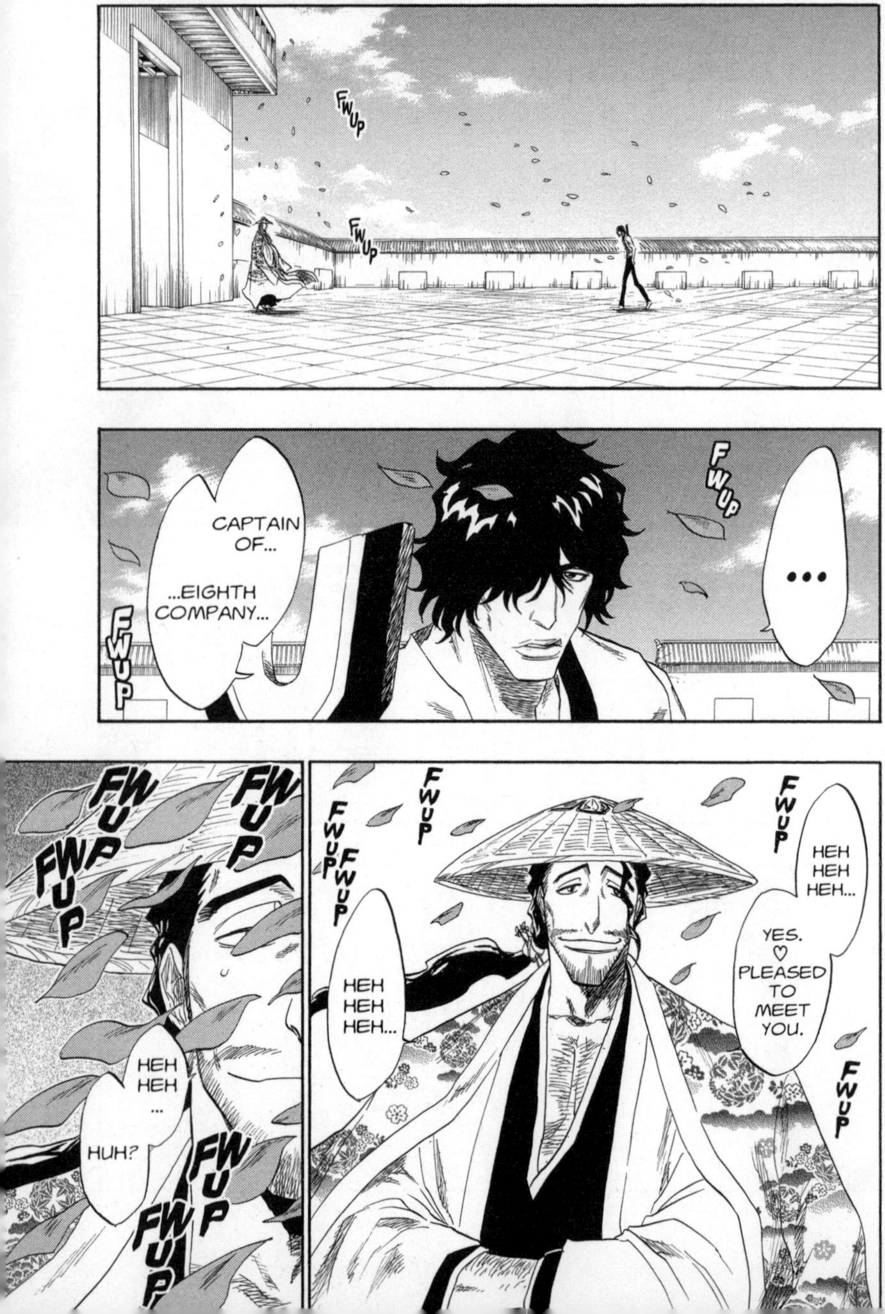
FWUP
FWUP
FWUP
...
CAPTAIN OF...
...EIGHTH COMPANY...
FWUP
FWUP
HEH HEH HEH...
YES. ♡ PLEASED TO MEET YOU.
FWUP
FWUP
FWUP
FWUP
HEH HEH HEH...
FWUP
FWUP
FWUP
FWUP
HEH HEH ...
HUH?
FWUP
FWUP

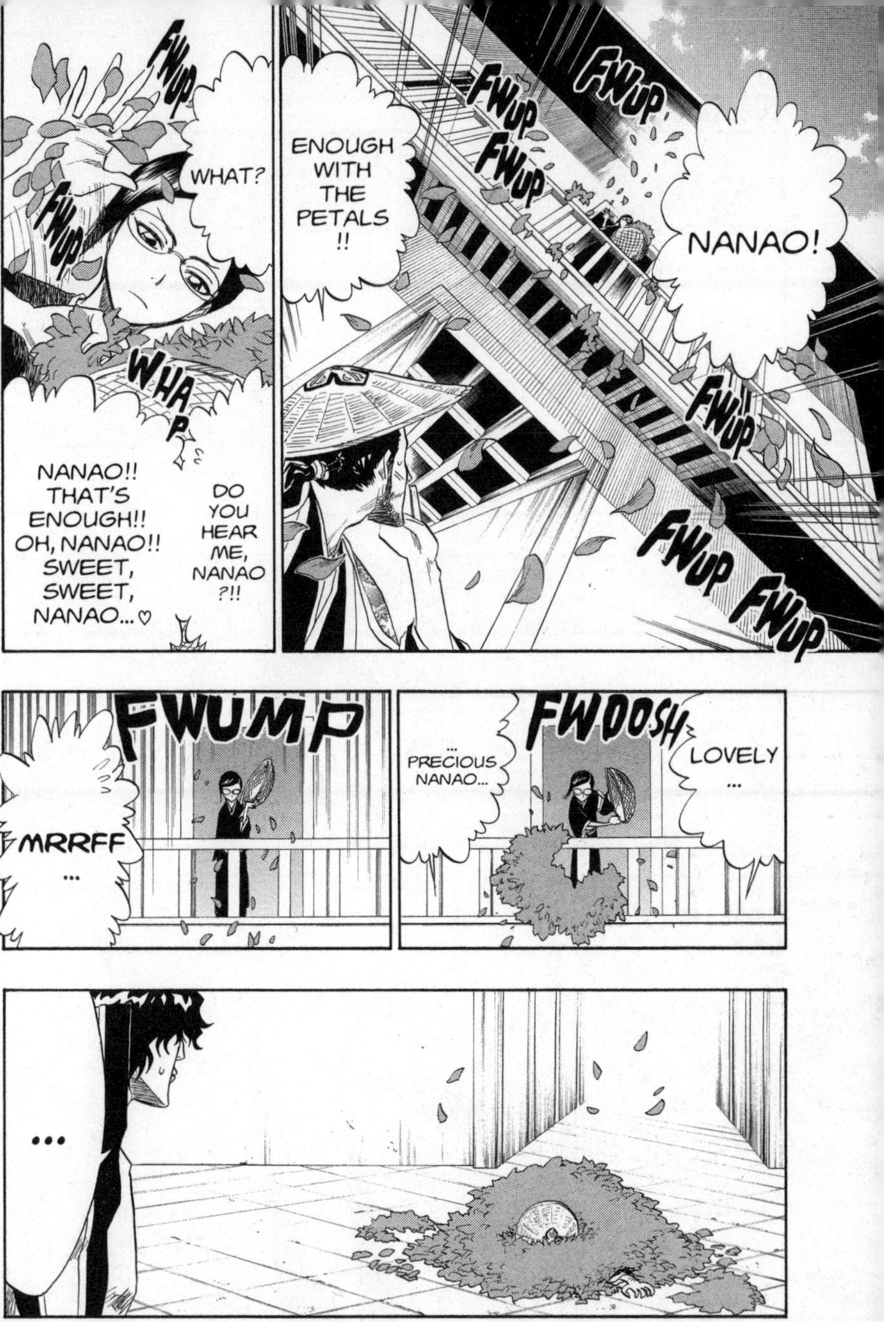
NANAO!
FWUP
FWUP
FWUP
FWUP
FWUP
FWUP
FWUP
ENOUGH WITH THE PETALS !!
WHAT?
FWUP
FWUP
WHAP
DO YOU HEAR ME, NANAO ?!!
NANAO!! THAT'S ENOUGH!! OH, NANAO!! SWEET, SWEET, NANAO...♡
LOVELY ...
... PRECIOUS NANAO...
FWOOSH
FWUMP
MRRFF ...
...

READ THIS WAY

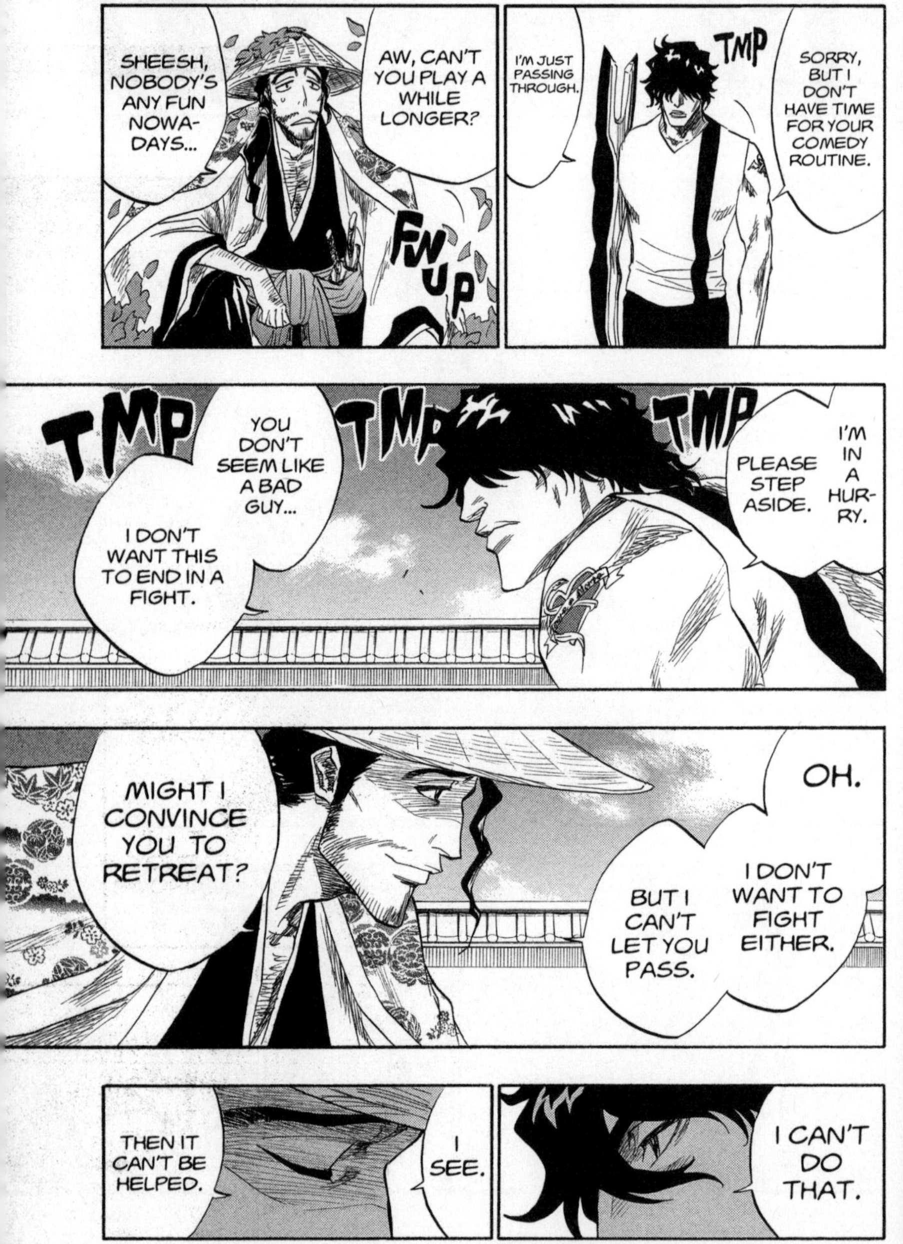
SORRY, BUT I DON'T HAVE TIME FOR YOUR COMEDY ROUTINE.
TMP
I'M JUST PASSING THROUGH.
AW, CAN'T YOU PLAY A WHILE LONGER?
SHEESH, NOBODY'S ANY FUN NOWA-DAYS...
FWUP
TMP
TMP
TMP
I'M IN A HUR-RY.
PLEASE STEP ASIDE.
YOU DON'T SEEM LIKE A BAD GUY...
I DON'T WANT THIS TO END IN A FIGHT.
OH.
I DON'T WANT TO FIGHT EITHER.
BUT I CAN'T LET YOU PASS.
MIGHT I CONVINCE YOU TO RETREAT?
I CAN'T DO THAT.
I SEE.
THEN IT CAN'T BE HELPED.

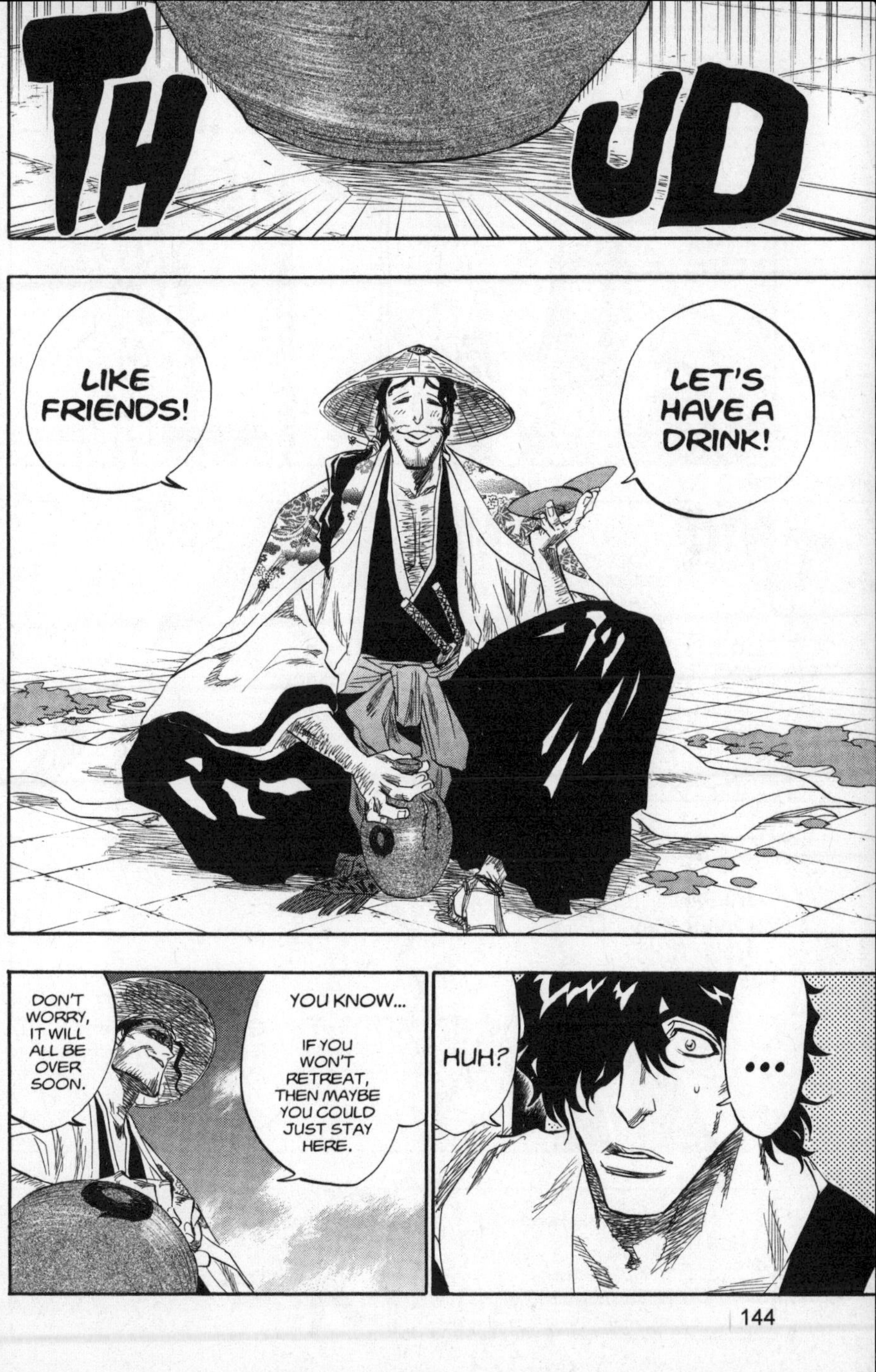
THUD
LET'S HAVE A DRINK!
LIKE FRIENDS!
...
HUH?
YOU KNOW...
IF YOU WON'T RETREAT, THEN MAYBE YOU COULD JUST STAY HERE.
DON'T WORRY, IT WILL ALL BE OVER SOON.

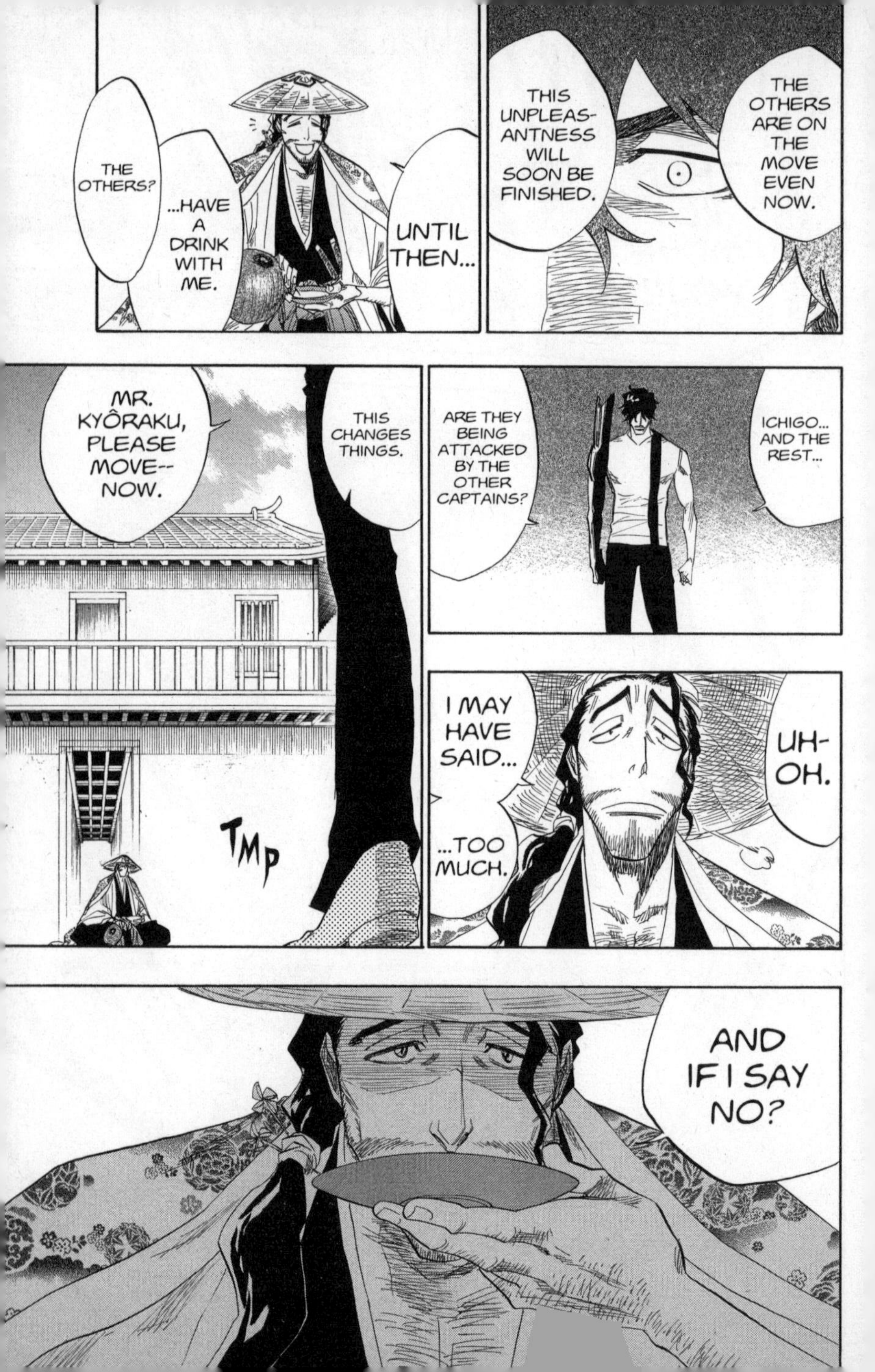
THE OTHERS ARE ON THE MOVE EVEN NOW.
THIS UNPLEAS-ANTNESS WILL SOON BE FINISHED.
UNTIL THEN...
...HAVE A DRINK WITH ME.
THE OTHERS?
ICHIGO... AND THE REST...
ARE THEY BEING ATTACKED BY THE OTHER CAPTAINS?
UH-OH.
I MAY HAVE SAID...
...TOO MUCH.
THIS CHANGES THINGS.
MR. KYÔRAKU, PLEASE MOVE--NOW.
TMP
AND IF I SAY NO?

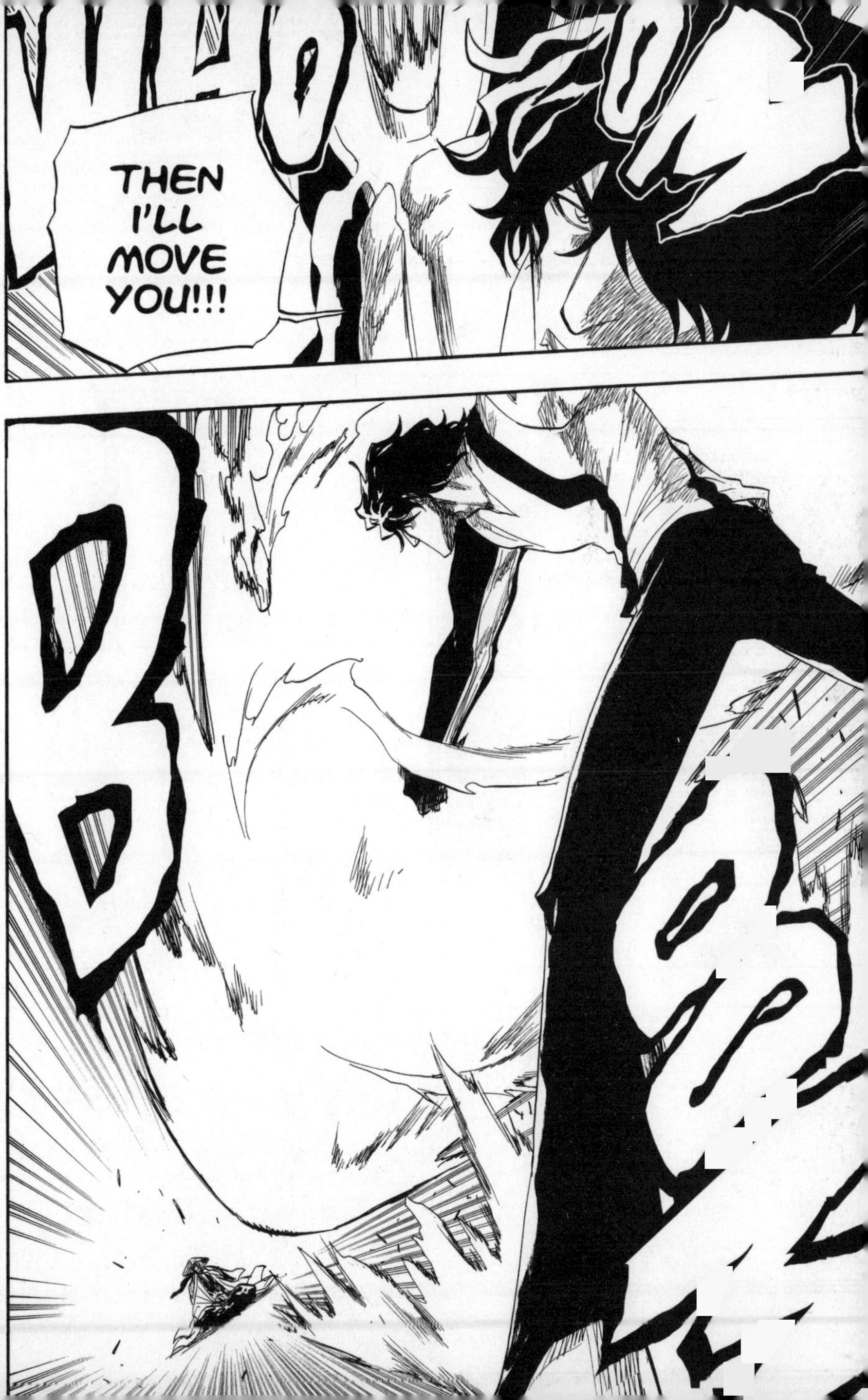
THEN I'LL MOVE YOU!!!

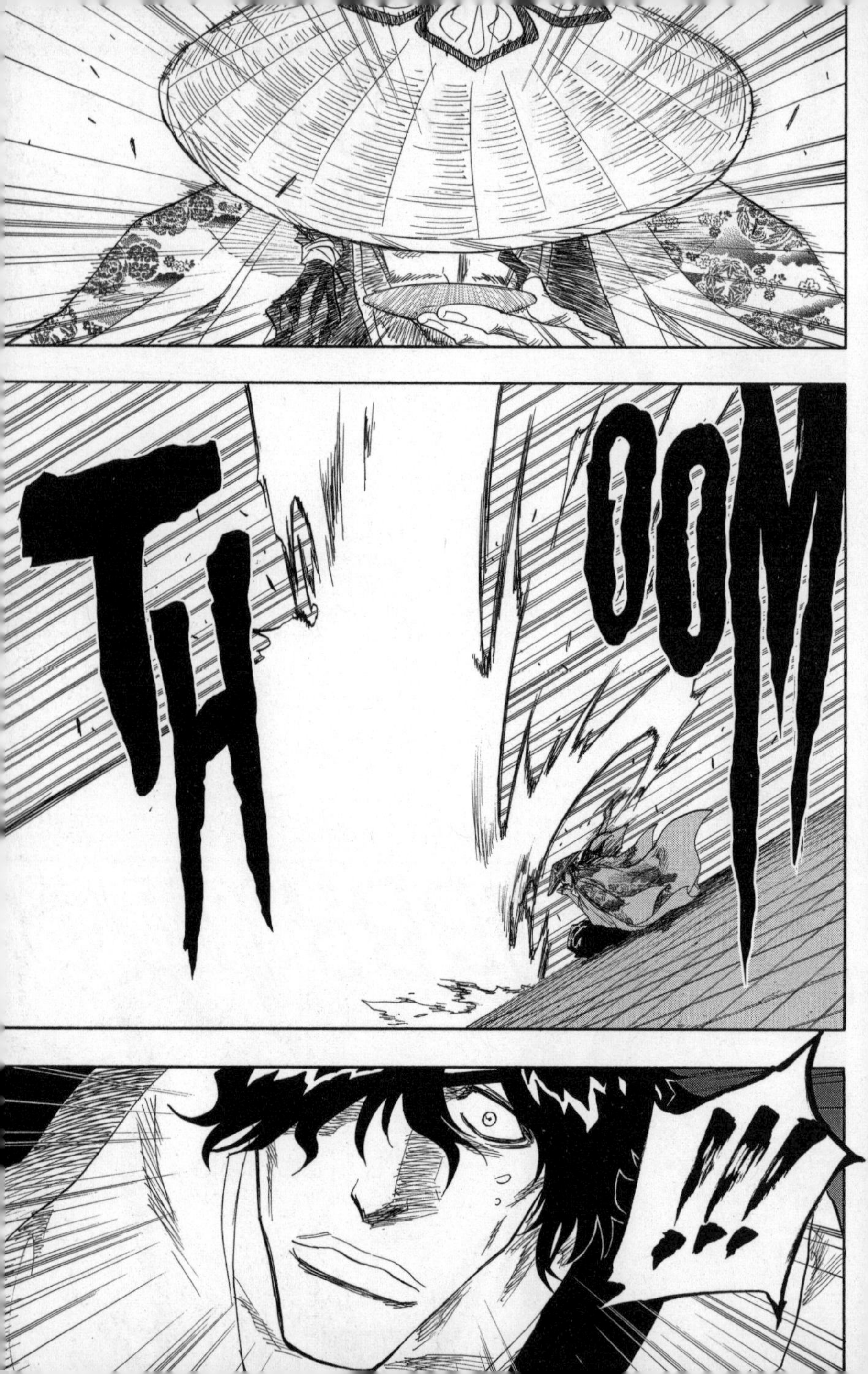
THOOM
!!!

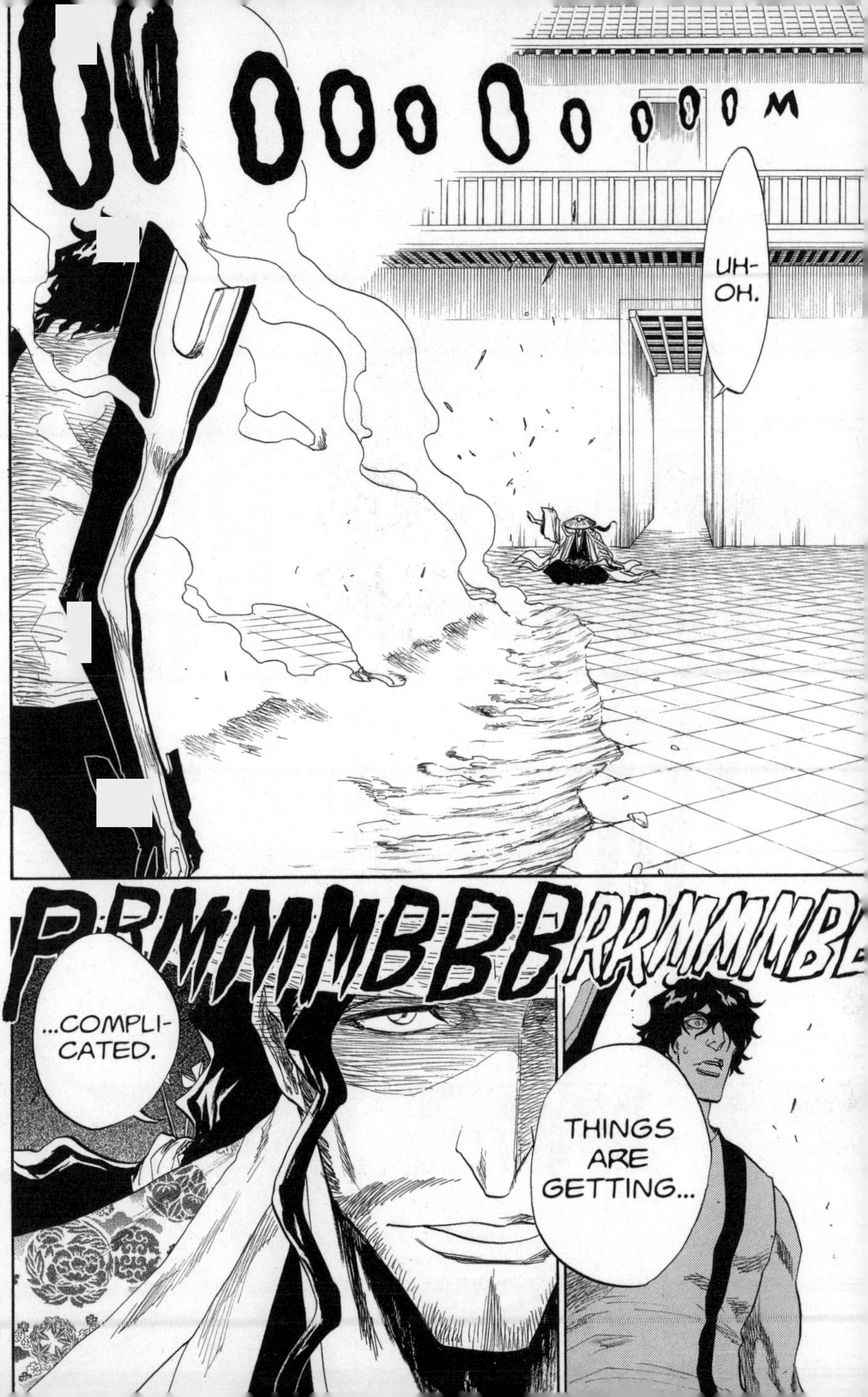
GOOOOOOOOOM
UH-OH.
PRMMMBBBRRMMMBL
THINGS ARE GETTING...
...COMPLICATED.

106. Cause to Confront

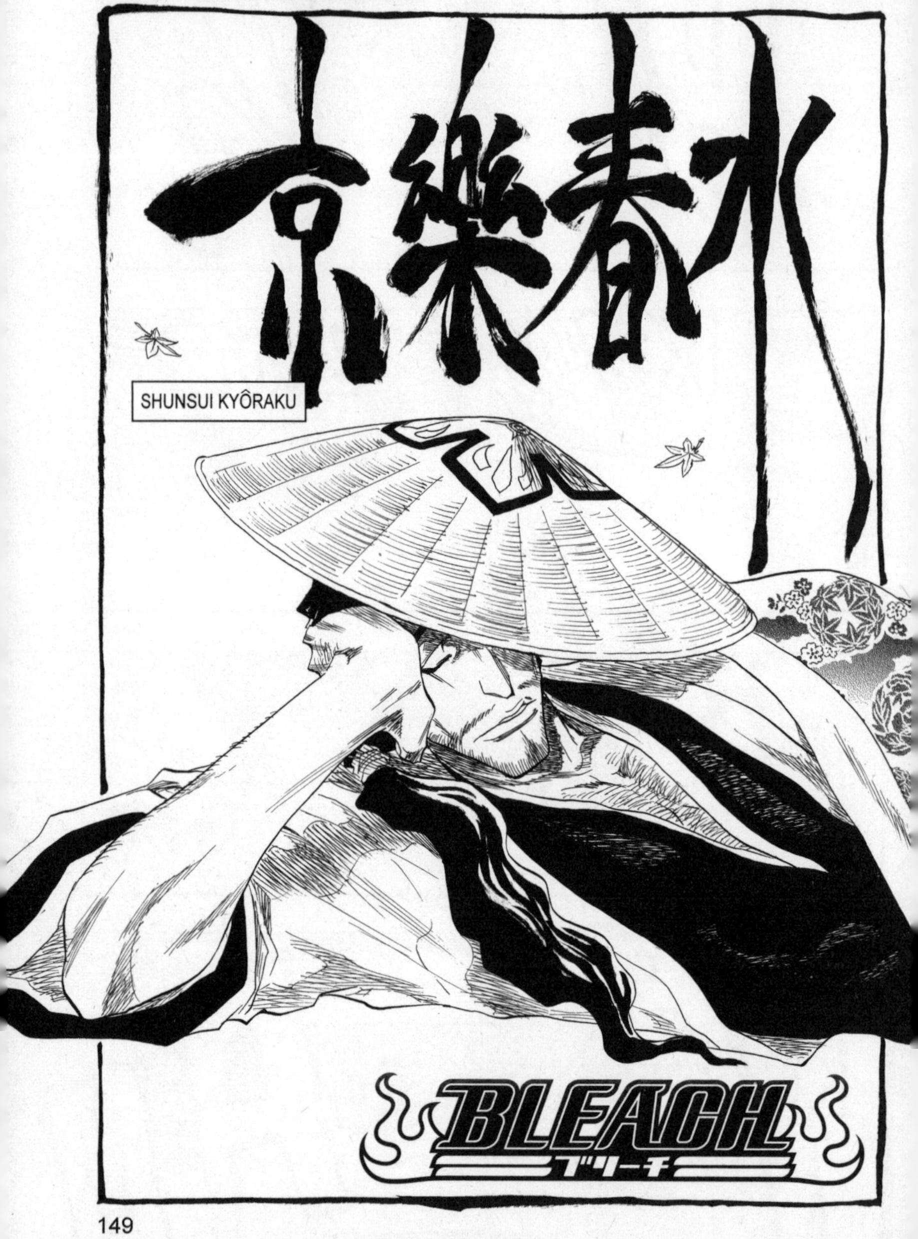
京樂春水
SHUNSUI KYÔRAKU
BLEACH
ブリーチ

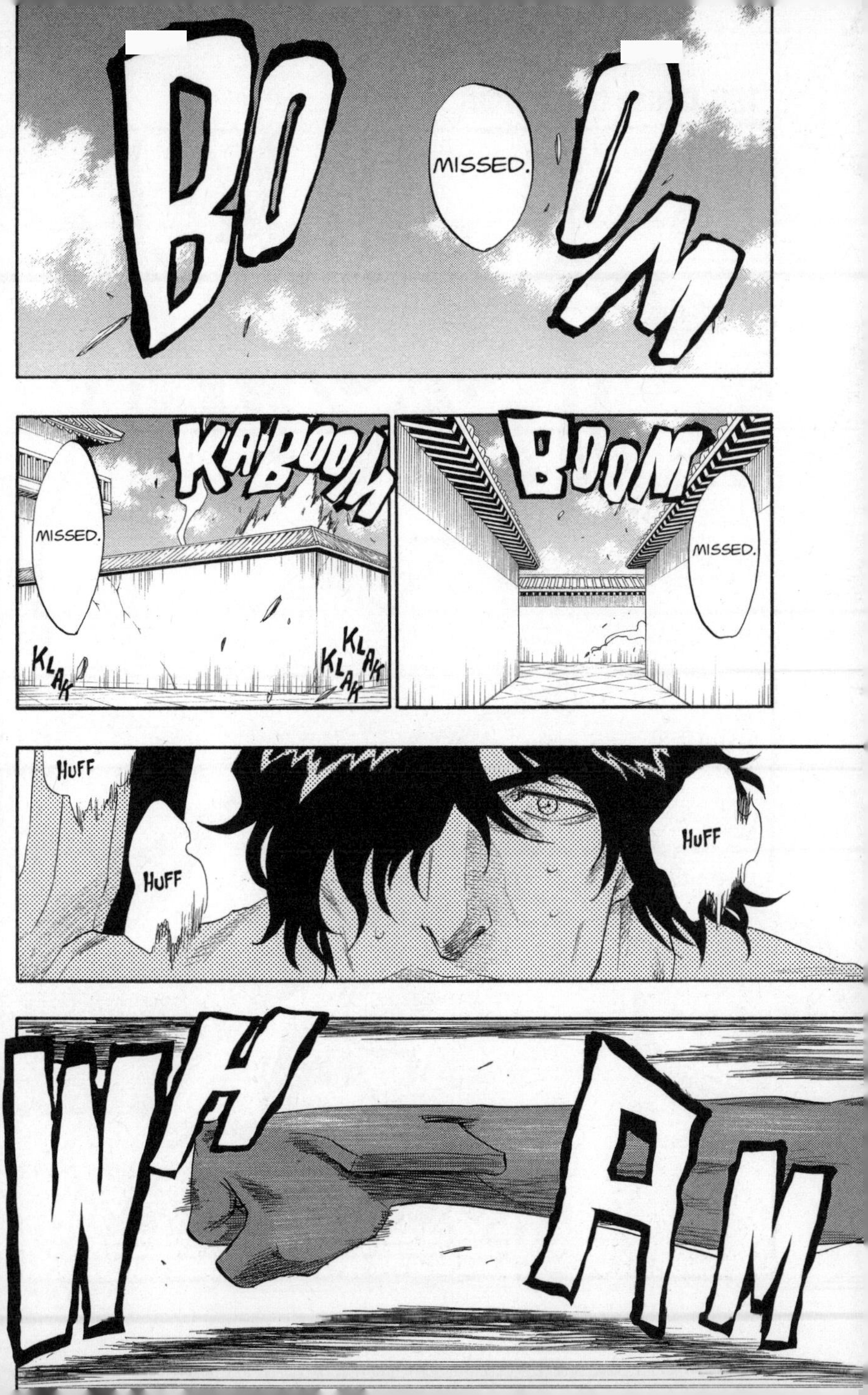
BOOM
MISSED.
BOOM
MISSED.
KA-BOOM
MISSED.
KLAK KLAK
KLAK
HUFF
HUFF
HUFF
WHAM

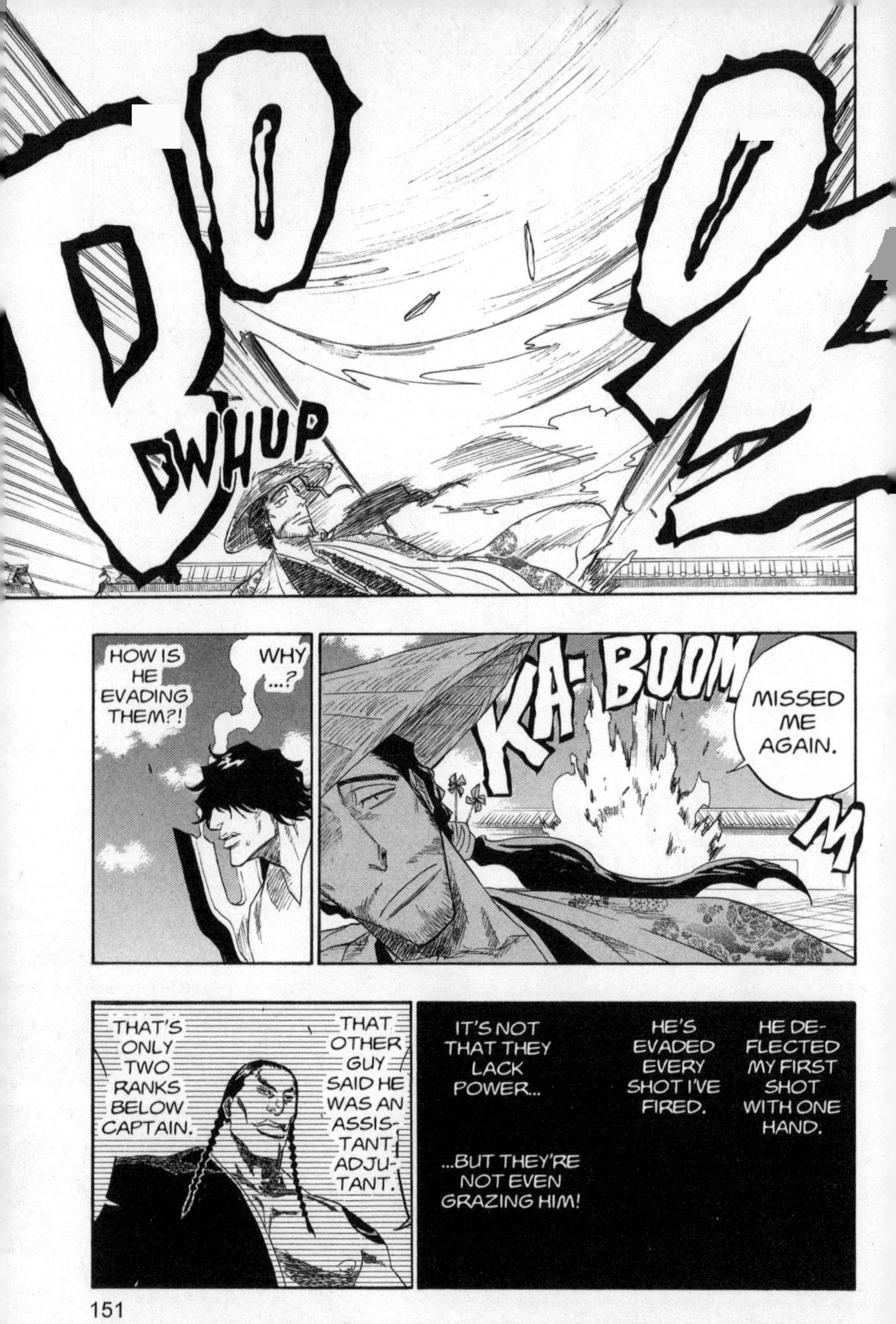
DWHUP
MISSED ME AGAIN.
KA-BOOMM
WHY ...?
HOW IS HE EVADING THEM?!
HE DE-FLECTED MY FIRST SHOT WITH ONE HAND.
HE'S EVADED EVERY SHOT I'VE FIRED.
IT'S NOT THAT THEY LACK POWER...
...BUT THEY'RE NOT EVEN GRAZING HIM!
THAT OTHER GUY SAID HE WAS AN ASSIS-TANT ADJU-TANT.
THAT'S ONLY TWO RANKS BELOW CAPTAIN.

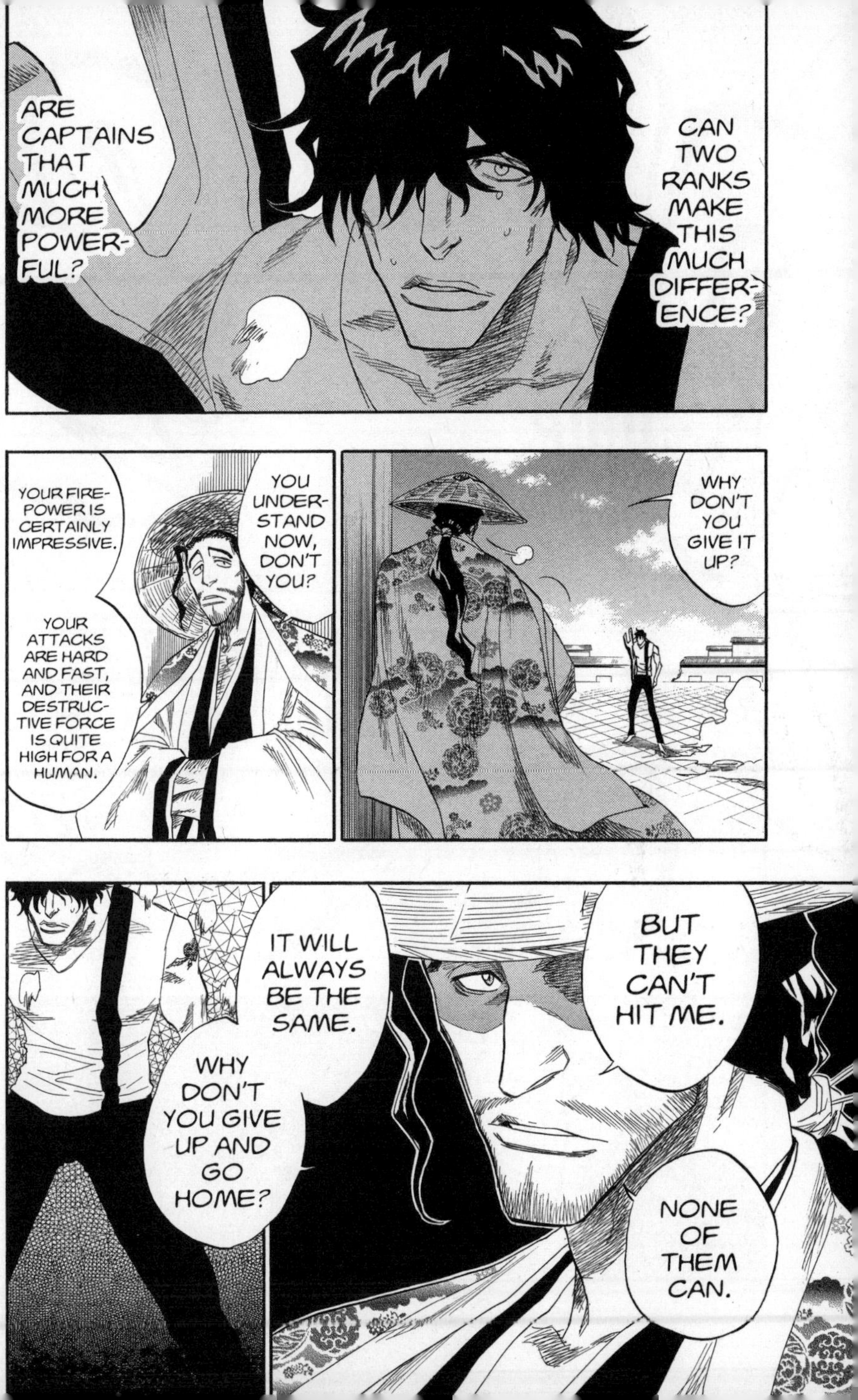
CAN TWO RANKS MAKE THIS MUCH DIFFERENCE?
ARE CAPTAINS THAT MUCH MORE POWERFUL?
WHY DON'T YOU GIVE IT UP?
YOU UNDERSTAND NOW, DON'T YOU?
YOUR FIREPOWER IS CERTAINLY IMPRESSIVE.
YOUR ATTACKS ARE HARD AND FAST, AND THEIR DESTRUCTIVE FORCE IS QUITE HIGH FOR A HUMAN.
BUT THEY CAN'T HIT ME.
NONE OF THEM CAN.
IT WILL ALWAYS BE THE SAME.
WHY DON'T YOU GIVE UP AND GO HOME?

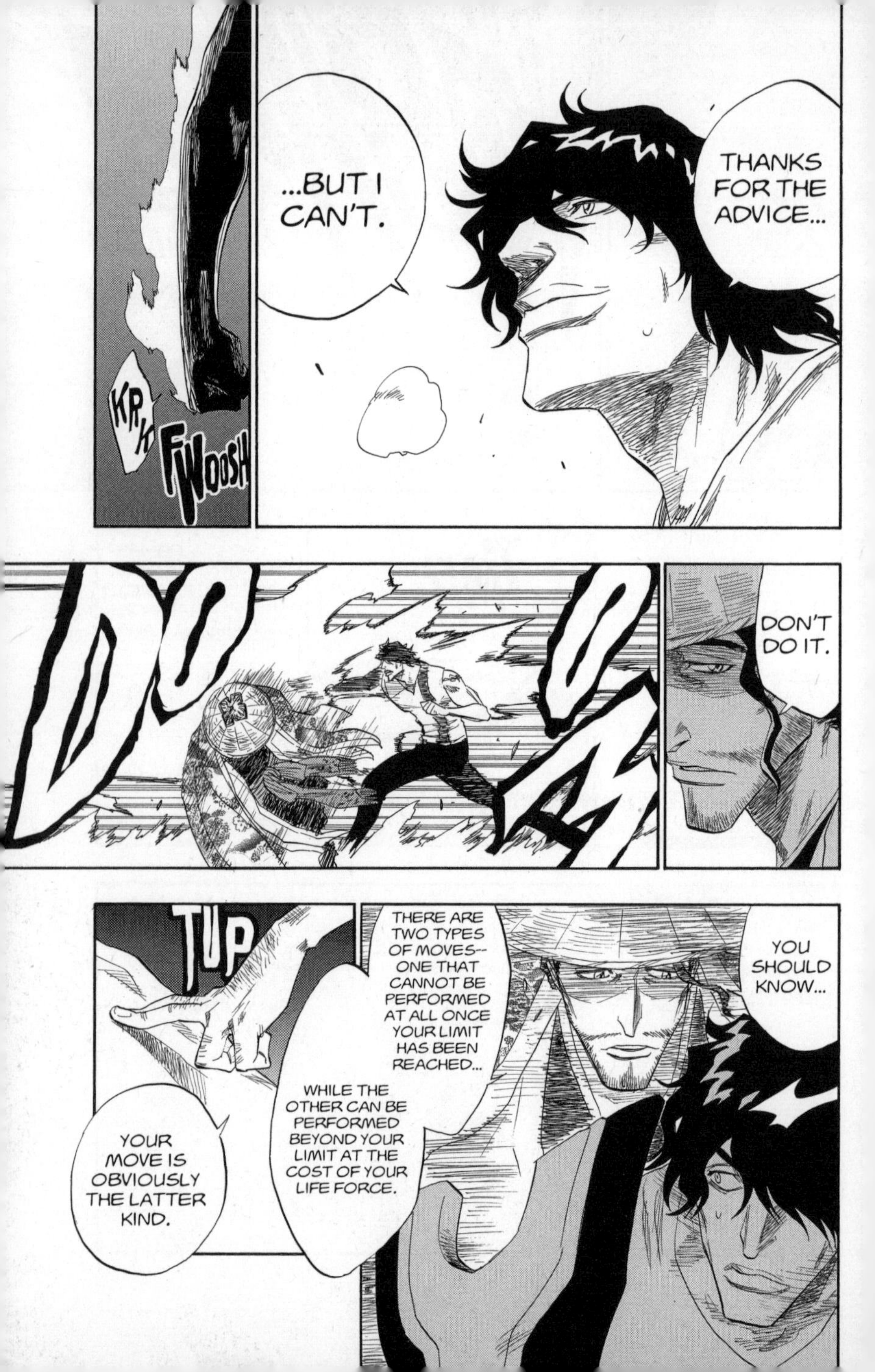
THANKS FOR THE ADVICE...
...BUT I CAN'T.
KRK
FWOOSH
DON'T DO IT.
DOOM
YOU SHOULD KNOW...
THERE ARE TWO TYPES OF MOVES-- ONE THAT CANNOT BE PERFORMED AT ALL ONCE YOUR LIMIT HAS BEEN REACHED...
WHILE THE OTHER CAN BE PERFORMED BEYOND YOUR LIMIT AT THE COST OF YOUR LIFE FORCE.
TUP
YOUR MOVE IS OBVIOUSLY THE LATTER KIND.

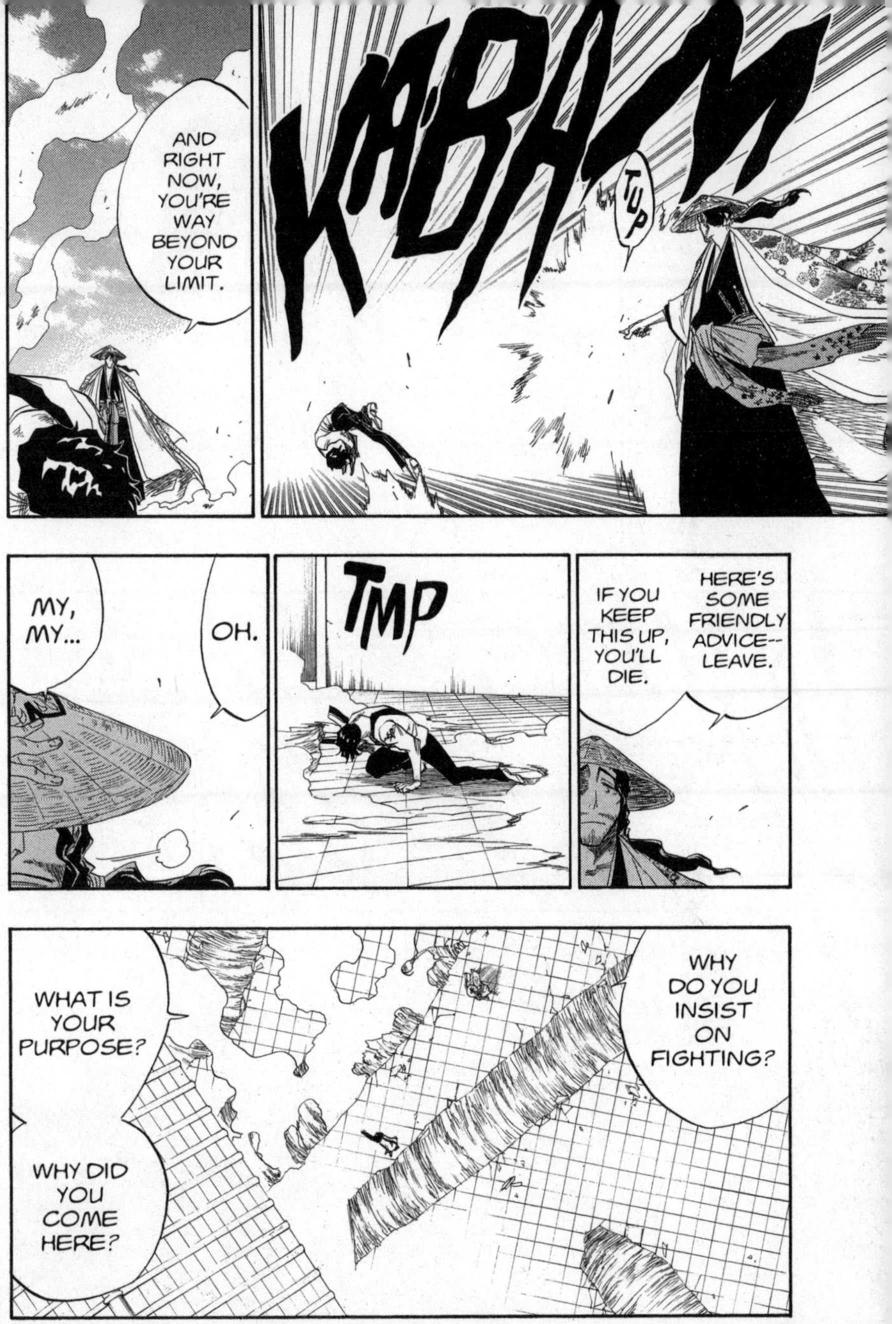
KABAM
TUP
AND RIGHT NOW, YOU'RE WAY BEYOND YOUR LIMIT.
HERE'S SOME FRIENDLY ADVICE--LEAVE.
IF YOU KEEP THIS UP, YOU'LL DIE.
TMP
OH.
MY, MY...
WHY DO YOU INSIST ON FIGHTING?
WHAT IS YOUR PURPOSE?
WHY DID YOU COME HERE?

READ THIS WAY

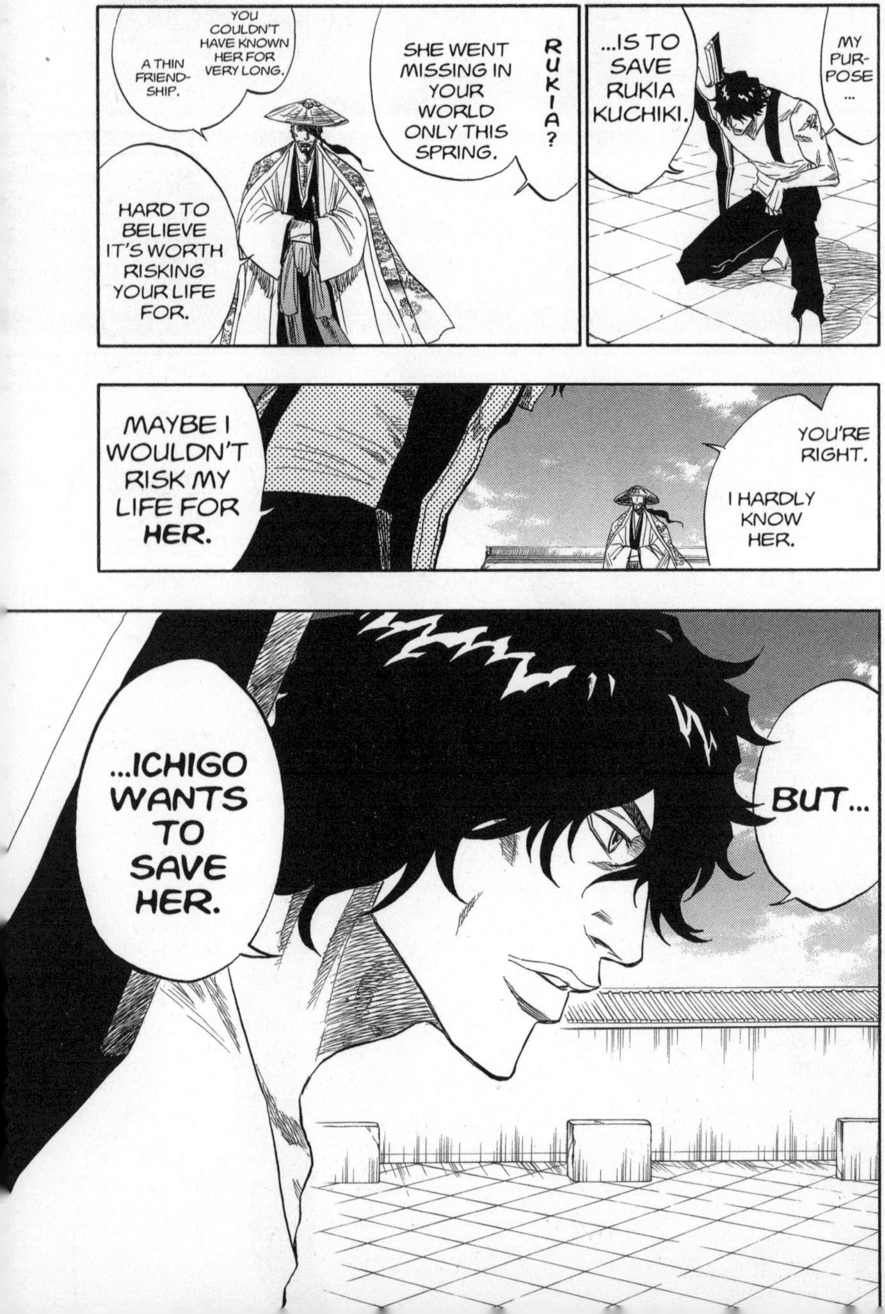
MY PURPOSE...
...IS TO SAVE RUKIA KUCHIKI.
RUKIA?
SHE WENT MISSING IN YOUR WORLD ONLY THIS SPRING.
YOU COULDN'T HAVE KNOWN HER FOR VERY LONG.
A THIN FRIENDSHIP.
HARD TO BELIEVE IT'S WORTH RISKING YOUR LIFE FOR.
YOU'RE RIGHT.
I HARDLY KNOW HER.
MAYBE I WOULDN'T RISK MY LIFE FOR HER.
BUT...
...ICHIGO WANTS TO SAVE HER.

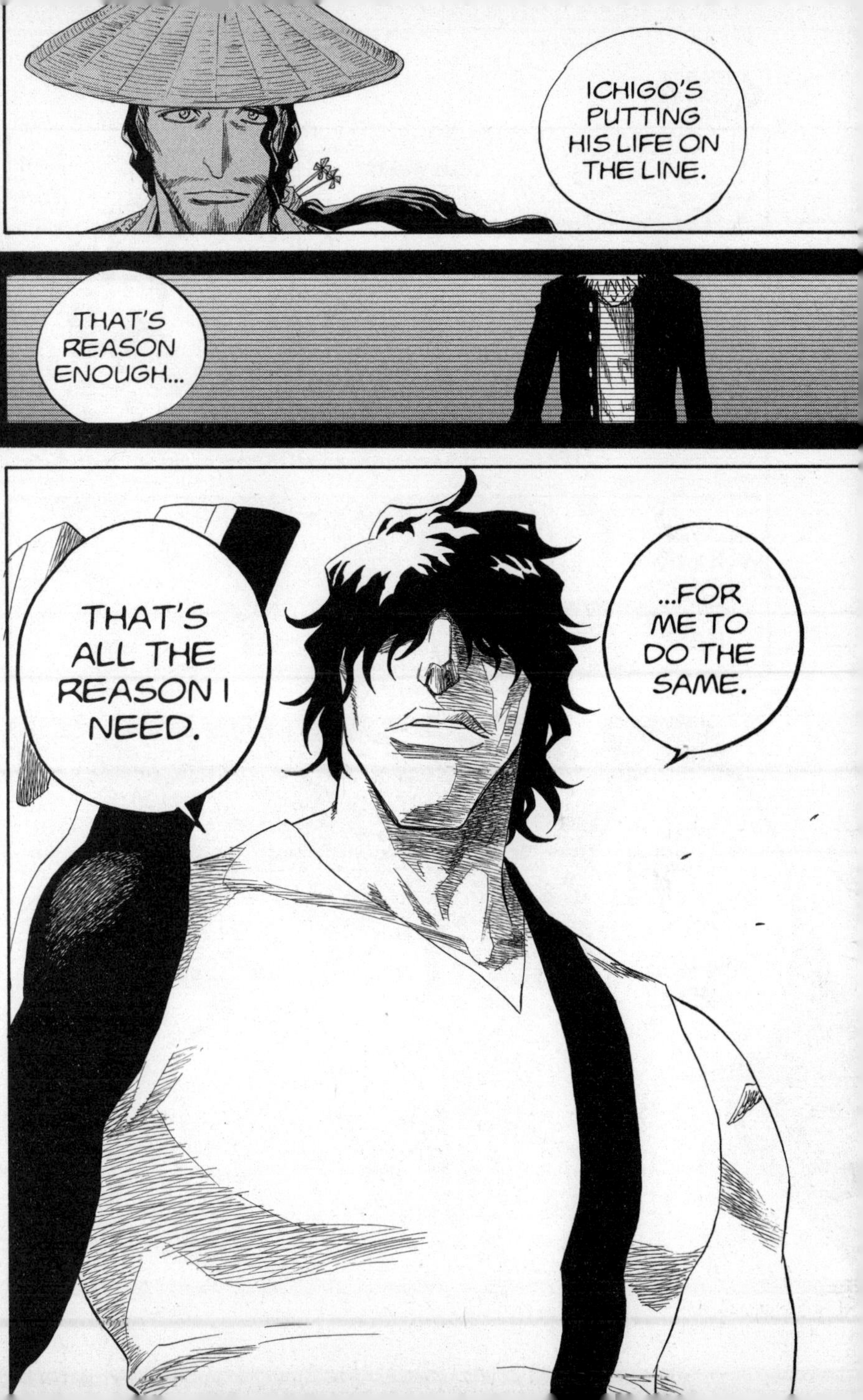
ICHIGO'S PUTTING HIS LIFE ON THE LINE.
THAT'S REASON ENOUGH...
...FOR ME TO DO THE SAME.
THAT'S ALL THE REASON I NEED.

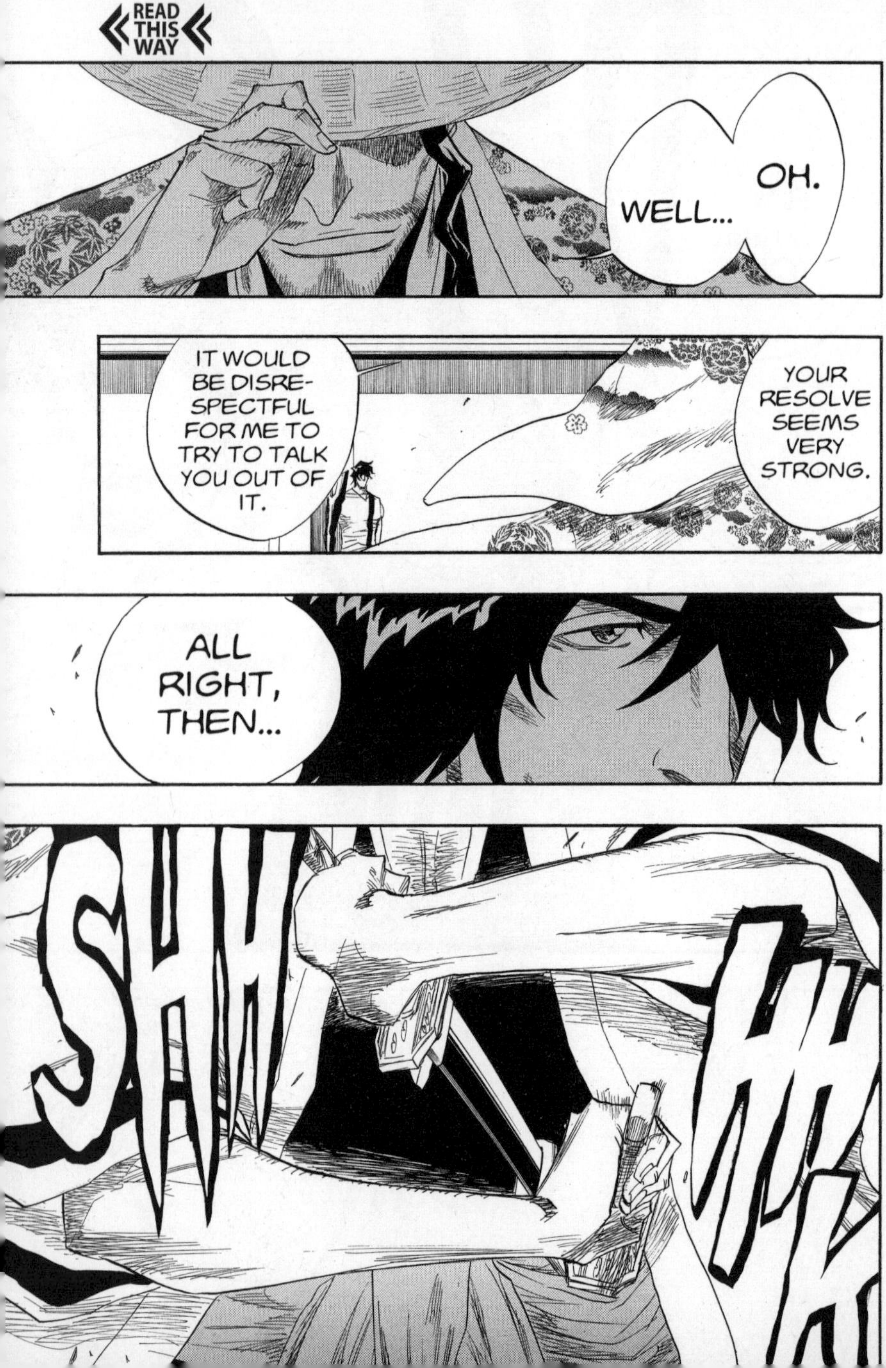
READ THIS WAY
OH. WELL...
YOUR RESOLVE SEEMS VERY STRONG.
IT WOULD BE DISRESPECTFUL FOR ME TO TRY TO TALK YOU OUT OF IT.
ALL RIGHT, THEN...

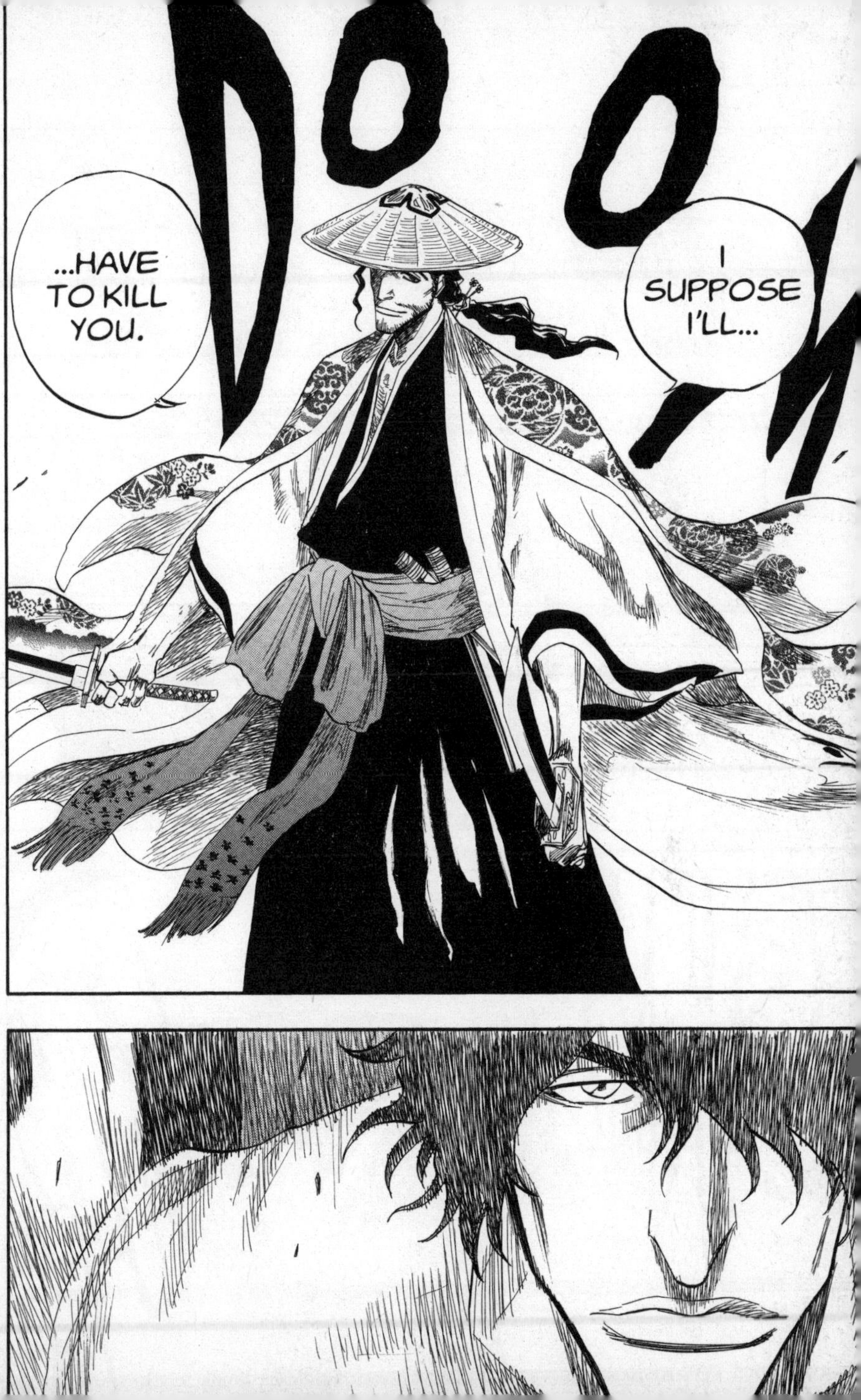
I SUPPOSE I'LL...
DOOM
...HAVE TO KILL YOU.

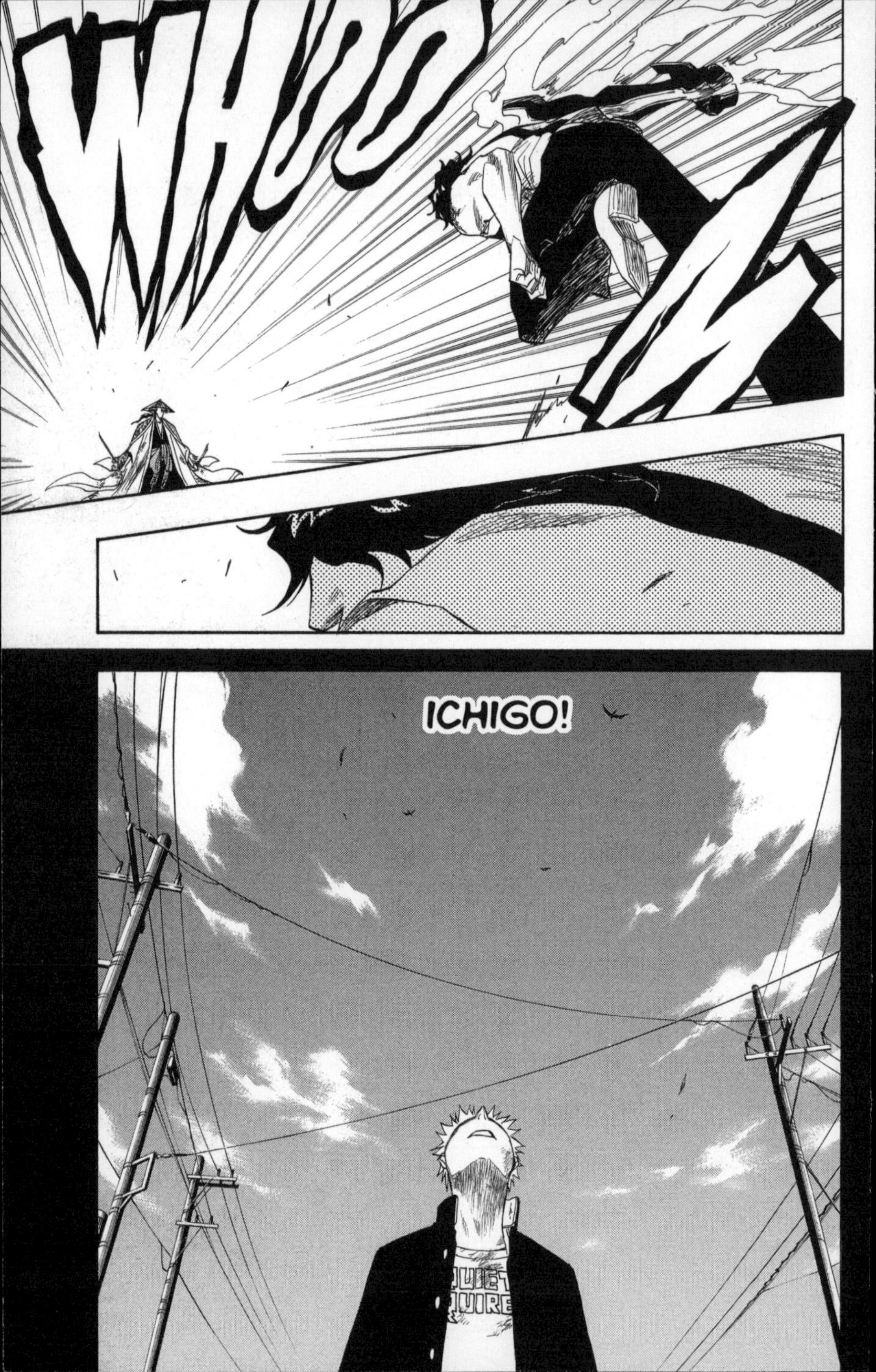
ICHIGO!

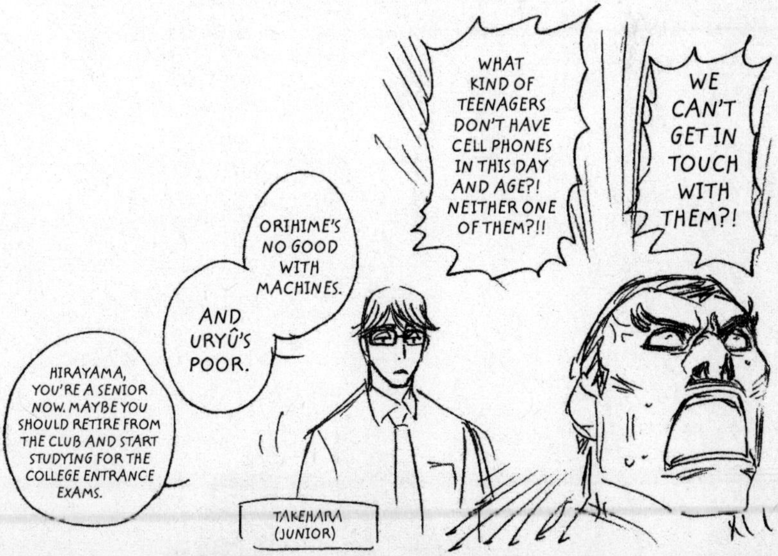
WE CAN'T GET IN TOUCH WITH THEM?!
WHAT KIND OF TEENAGERS DON'T HAVE CELL PHONES IN THIS DAY AND AGE?! NEITHER ONE OF THEM?!!
ORIHIME'S NO GOOD WITH MACHINES.
AND URYÛ'S POOR.
TAKEHARA (JUNIOR)
HIRAYAMA, YOU'RE A SENIOR NOW. MAYBE YOU SHOULD RETIRE FROM THE CLUB AND START STUDYING FOR THE COLLEGE ENTRANCE EXAMS.

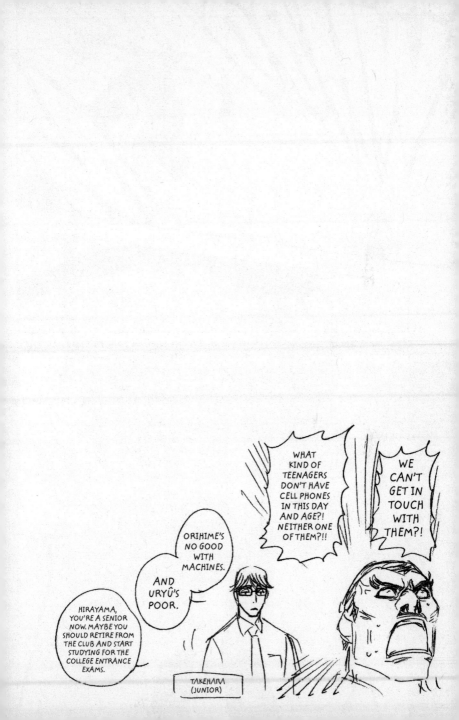

107. Heat in Trust

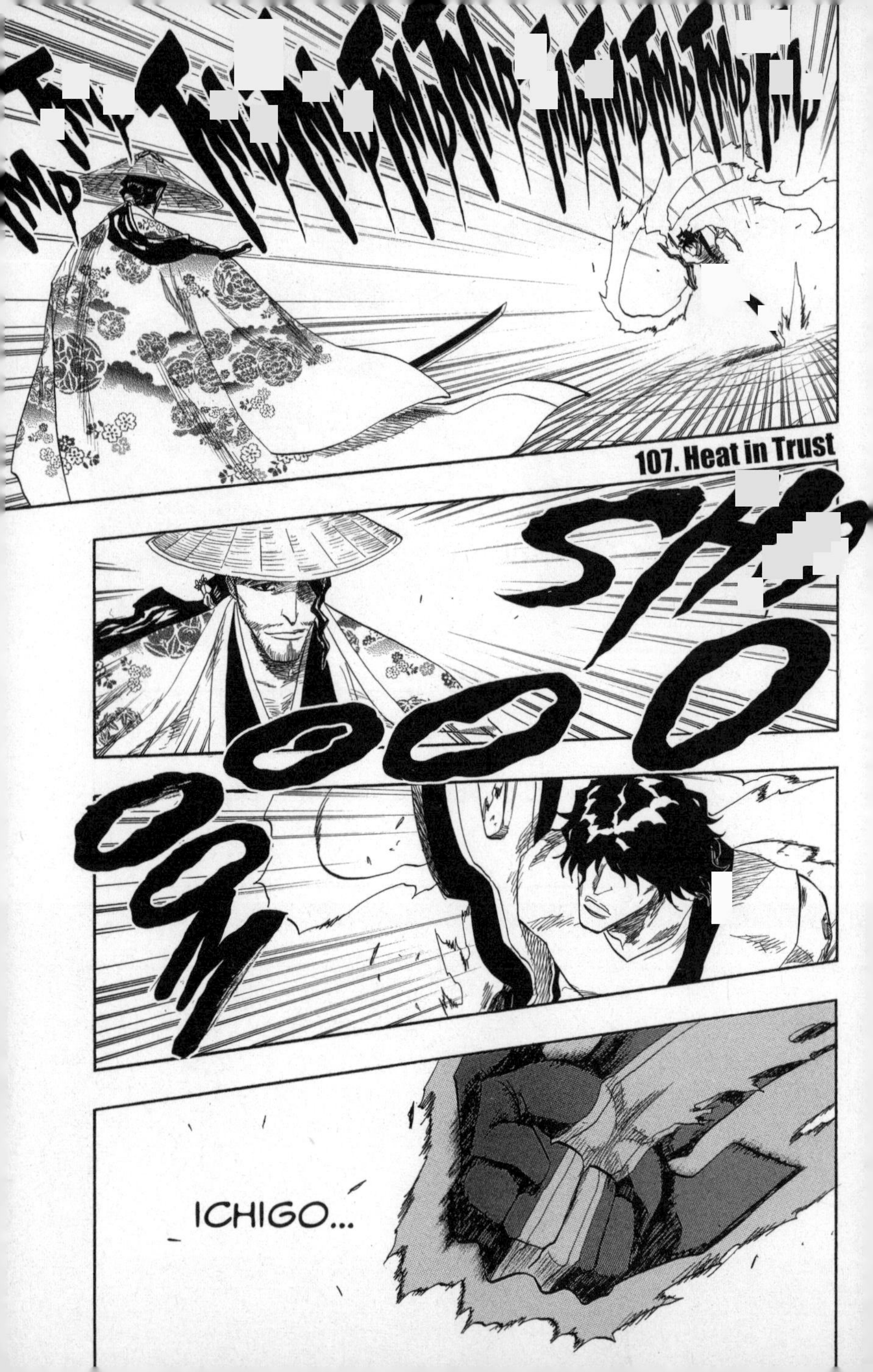
ICHIGO...

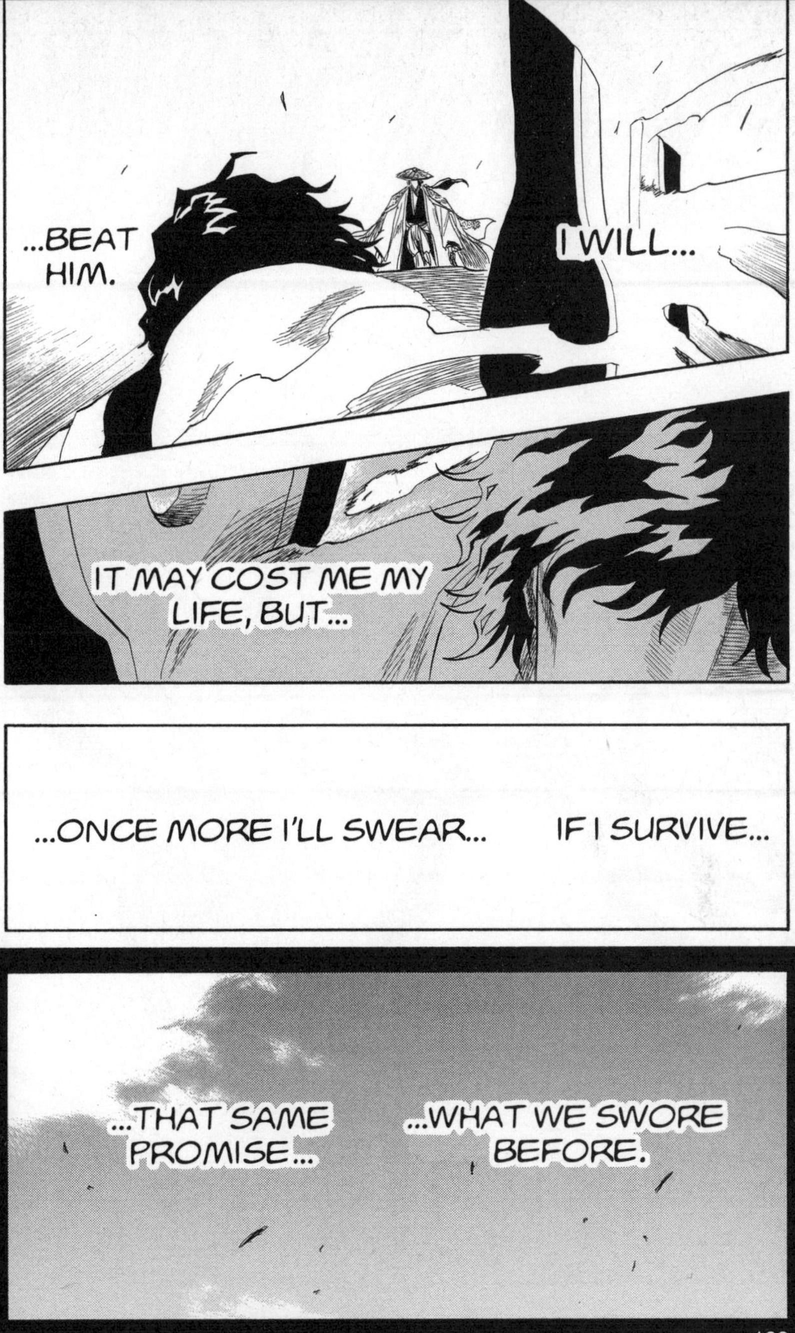
I WILL...
...BEAT HIM.
IT MAY COST ME MY LIFE, BUT...
IF I SURVIVE...
...ONCE MORE I'LL SWEAR...
...THAT SAME PROMISE...
...WHAT WE SWORE BEFORE.

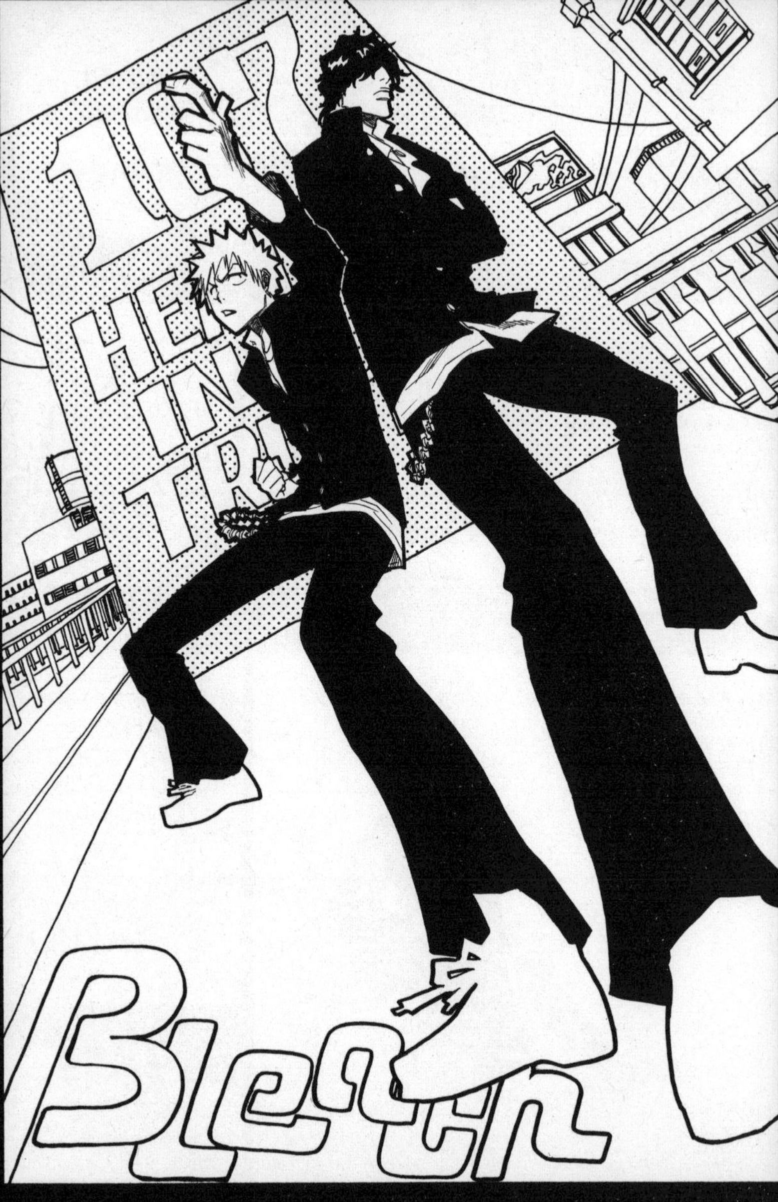
107
Bleach

107. Heat in Trust

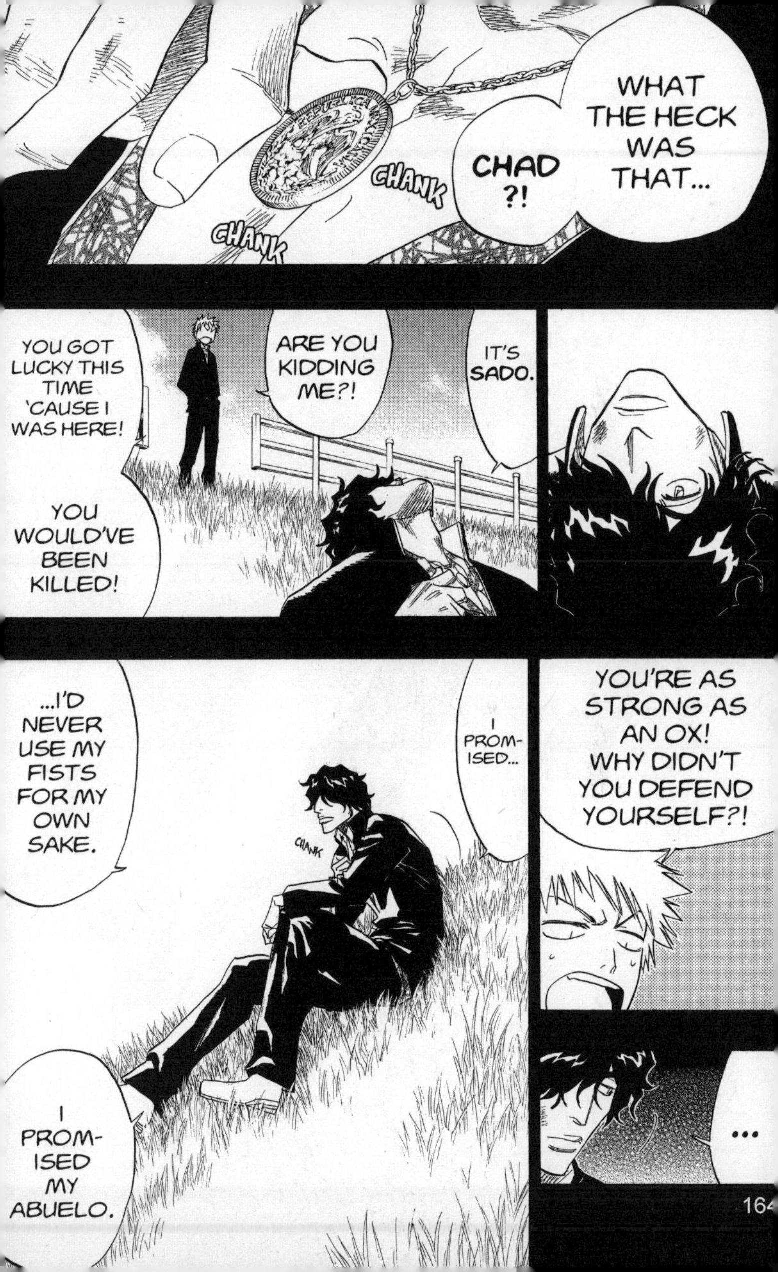
WHAT THE HECK WAS THAT...
CHAD?!
CHANK
CHANK
IT'S SADO.
ARE YOU KIDDING ME?!
YOU GOT LUCKY THIS TIME 'CAUSE I WAS HERE!
YOU WOULD'VE BEEN KILLED!
YOU'RE AS STRONG AS AN OX! WHY DIDN'T YOU DEFEND YOURSELF?!
...
I PROM-ISED...
CHANK
...I'D NEVER USE MY FISTS FOR MY OWN SAKE.
I PROM-ISED MY ABUELO.

READ THIS WAY

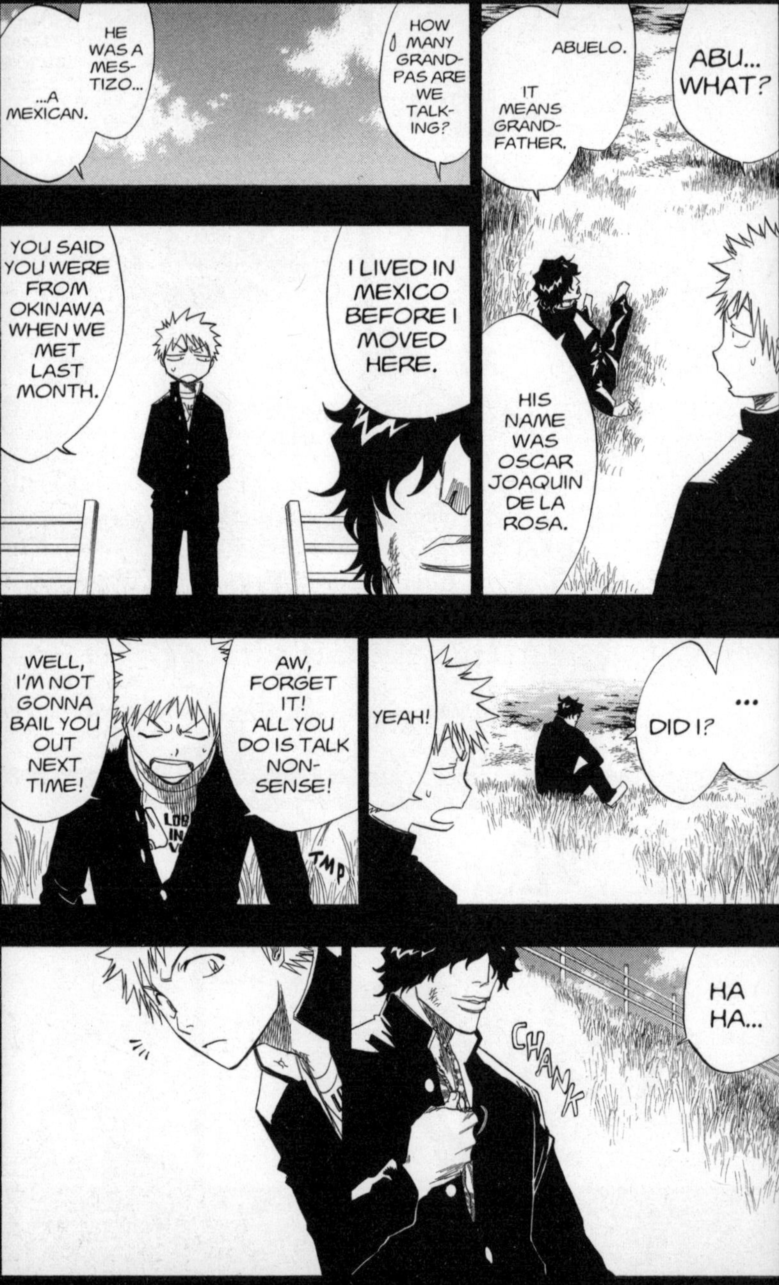
ABU... WHAT?
ABUELO.
IT MEANS GRANDFATHER.
HIS NAME WAS OSCAR JOAQUIN DE LA ROSA.
HOW MANY GRANDPAS ARE WE TALKING?
HE WAS A MESTIZO...
...A MEXICAN.
I LIVED IN MEXICO BEFORE I MOVED HERE.
YOU SAID YOU WERE FROM OKINAWA WHEN WE MET LAST MONTH.
... DID I?
YEAH!
AW, FORGET IT! ALL YOU DO IS TALK NONSENSE!
TMP
WELL, I'M NOT GONNA BAIL YOU OUT NEXT TIME!
HA HA...
CHANK

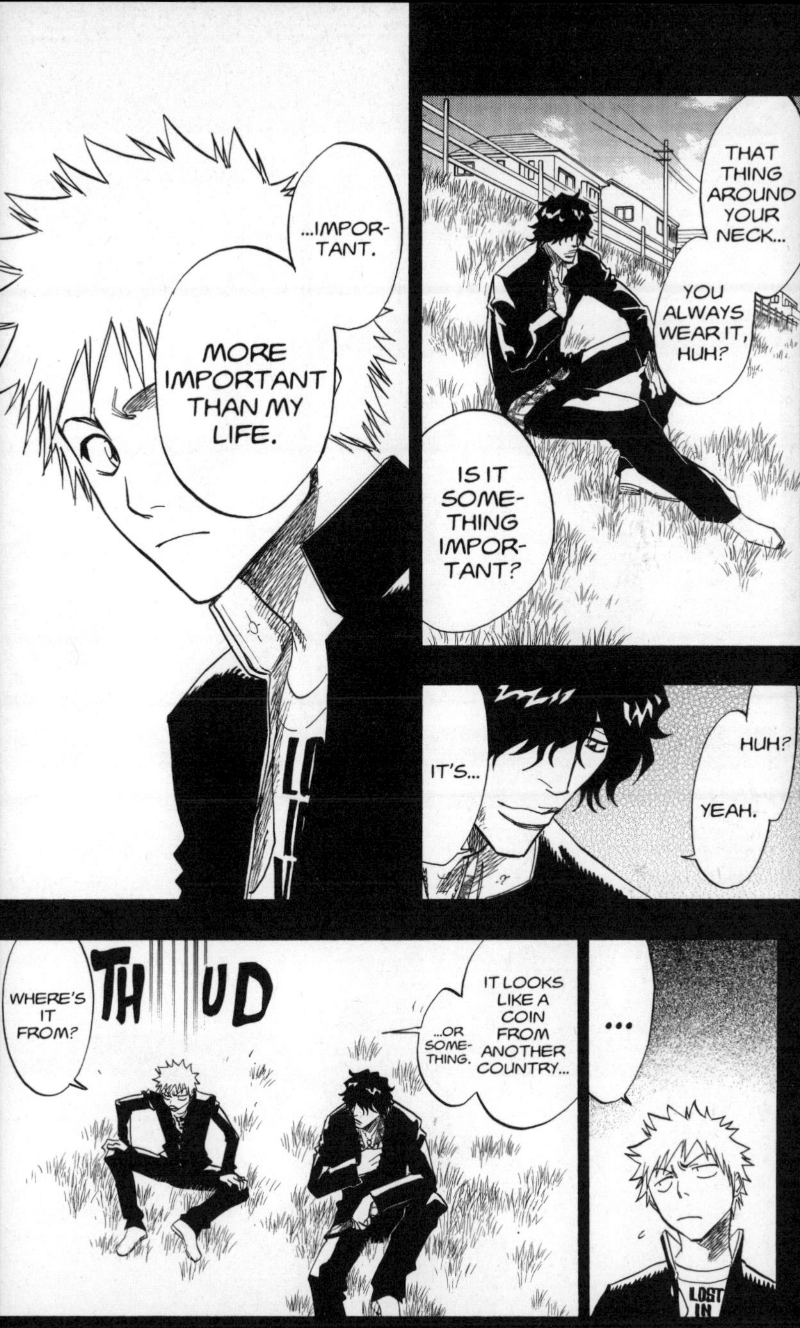
THAT THING AROUND YOUR NECK...
YOU ALWAYS WEAR IT, HUH?
IS IT SOMETHING IMPORTANT?
HUH?
YEAH.
IT'S...
...IMPORTANT.
MORE IMPORTANT THAN MY LIFE.
...
IT LOOKS LIKE A COIN FROM ANOTHER COUNTRY...
...OR SOMETHING.
THUD
WHERE'S IT FROM?
LOST IN

READ THIS WAY

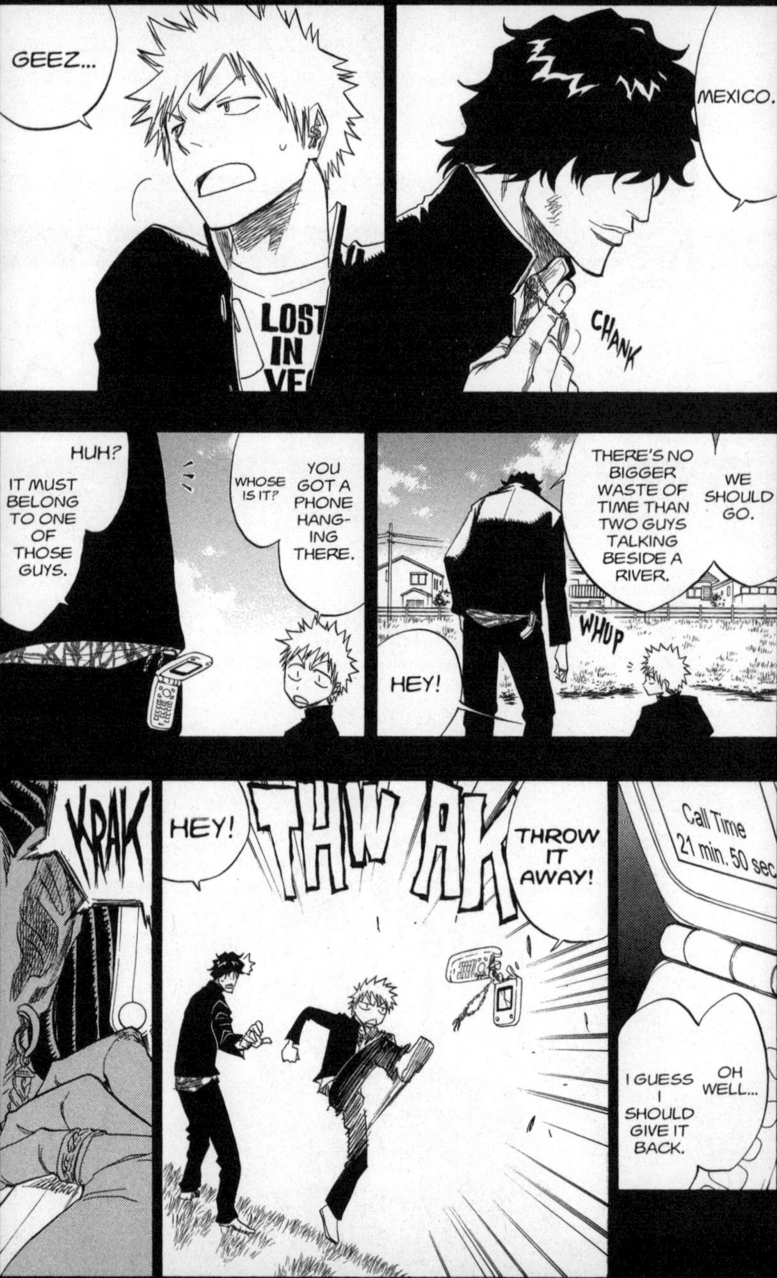
MEXICO.
CHANK
GEEZ...
LOST IN
WE SHOULD GO.
THERE'S NO BIGGER WASTE OF TIME THAN TWO GUYS TALKING BESIDE A RIVER.
WHUP
HEY!
YOU GOT A PHONE HANGING THERE.
WHOSE IS IT?
HUH?
IT MUST BELONG TO ONE OF THOSE GUYS.
Call Time
21 min. 50 sec
OH WELL...
I GUESS I SHOULD GIVE IT BACK.
THROW IT AWAY!
THWAK
HEY!
KRAK

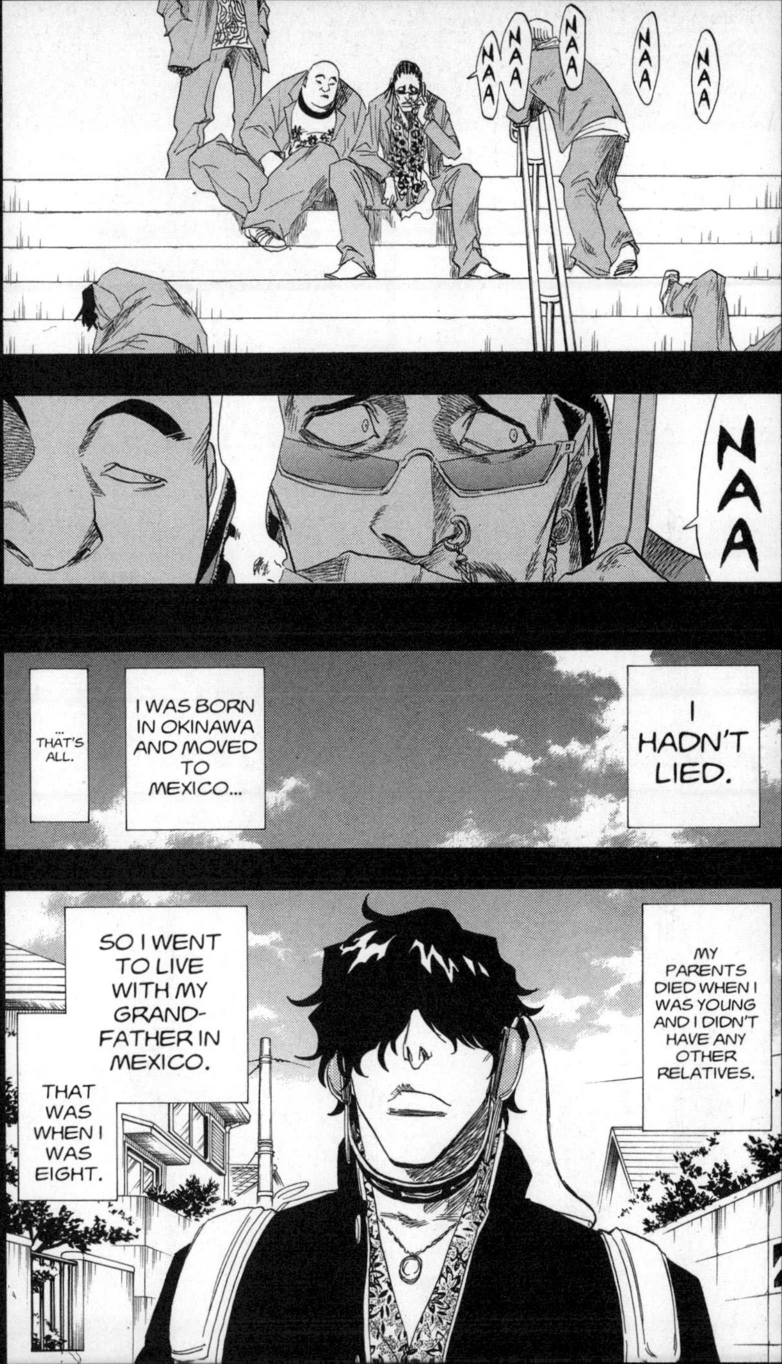
NAA
NAA
NAA
NAA
NAA
NAA
I HADN'T LIED.
I WAS BORN IN OKINAWA AND MOVED TO MEXICO...
... THAT'S ALL.
MY PARENTS DIED WHEN I WAS YOUNG AND I DIDN'T HAVE ANY OTHER RELATIVES.
SO I WENT TO LIVE WITH MY GRAND-FATHER IN MEXICO.
THAT WAS WHEN I WAS EIGHT.

READ THIS WAY

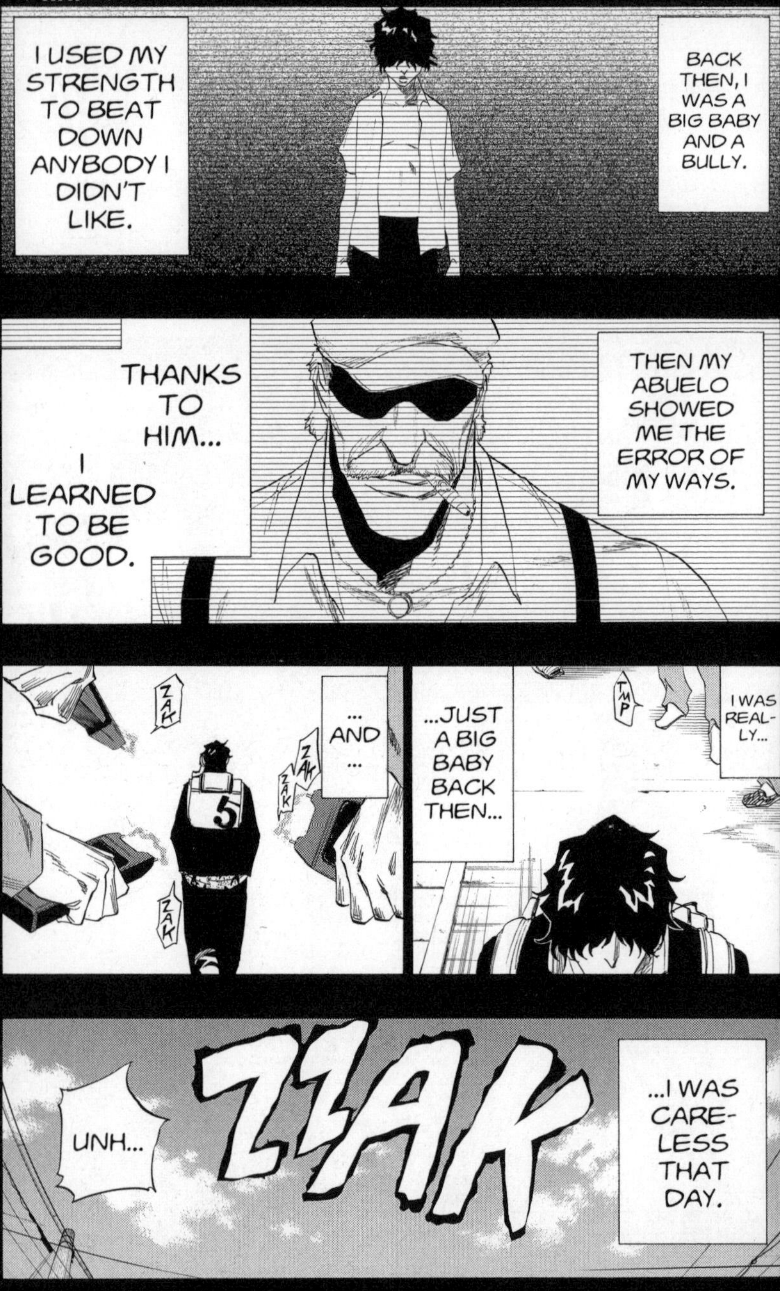
BACK THEN, I WAS A BIG BABY AND A BULLY.
I USED MY STRENGTH TO BEAT DOWN ANYBODY I DIDN'T LIKE.
THEN MY ABUELO SHOWED ME THE ERROR OF MY WAYS.
THANKS TO HIM...
I LEARNED TO BE GOOD.
I WAS REAL-LY...
TMP
...JUST A BIG BABY BACK THEN...
... AND ...
ZAK
ZAK
ZAK
ZAK
...I WAS CARE-LESS THAT DAY.
ZZAK
UNH...

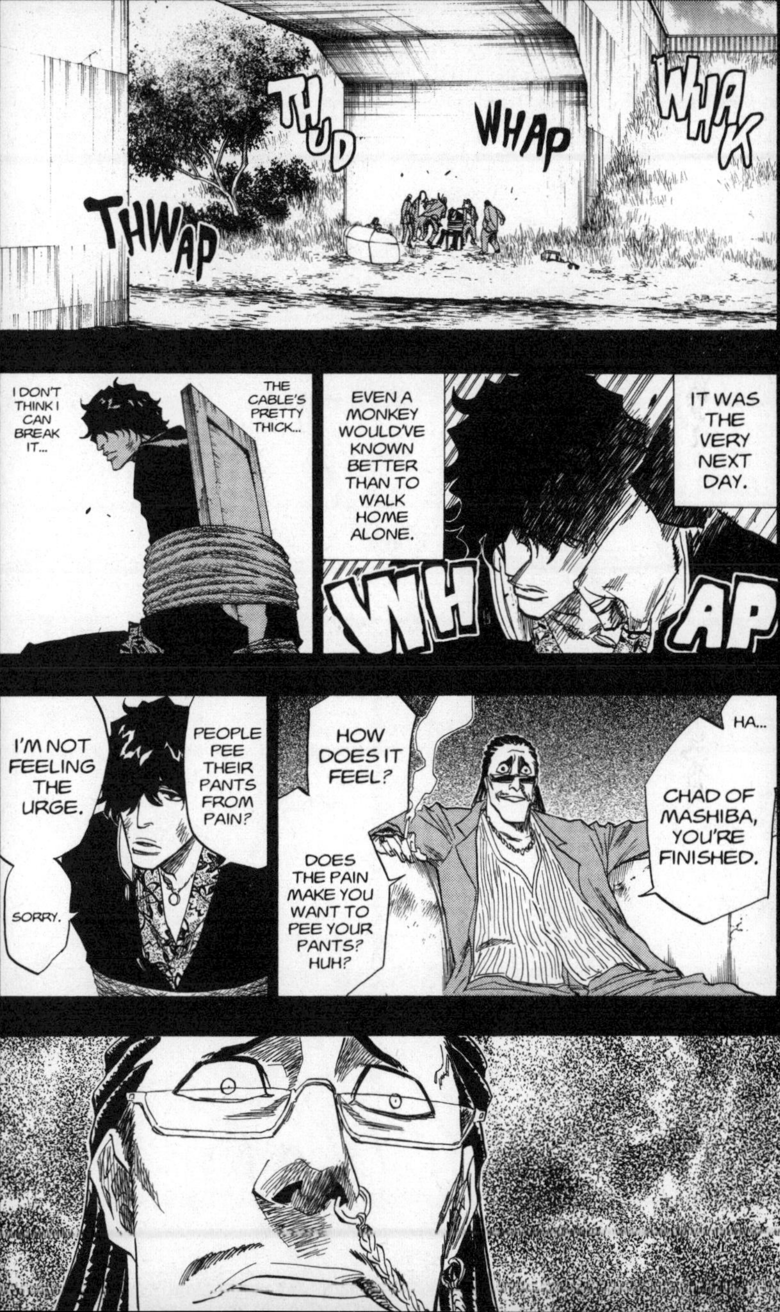
WHAK
WHAP
THUD
THWAP
IT WAS THE VERY NEXT DAY.
EVEN A MONKEY WOULD'VE KNOWN BETTER THAN TO WALK HOME ALONE.
WHAP
THE CABLE'S PRETTY THICK...
I DON'T THINK I CAN BREAK IT...
HA...
CHAD OF MASHIBA, YOU'RE FINISHED.
HOW DOES IT FEEL?
DOES THE PAIN MAKE YOU WANT TO PEE YOUR PANTS? HUH?
PEOPLE PEE THEIR PANTS FROM PAIN?
I'M NOT FEELING THE URGE.
SORRY.

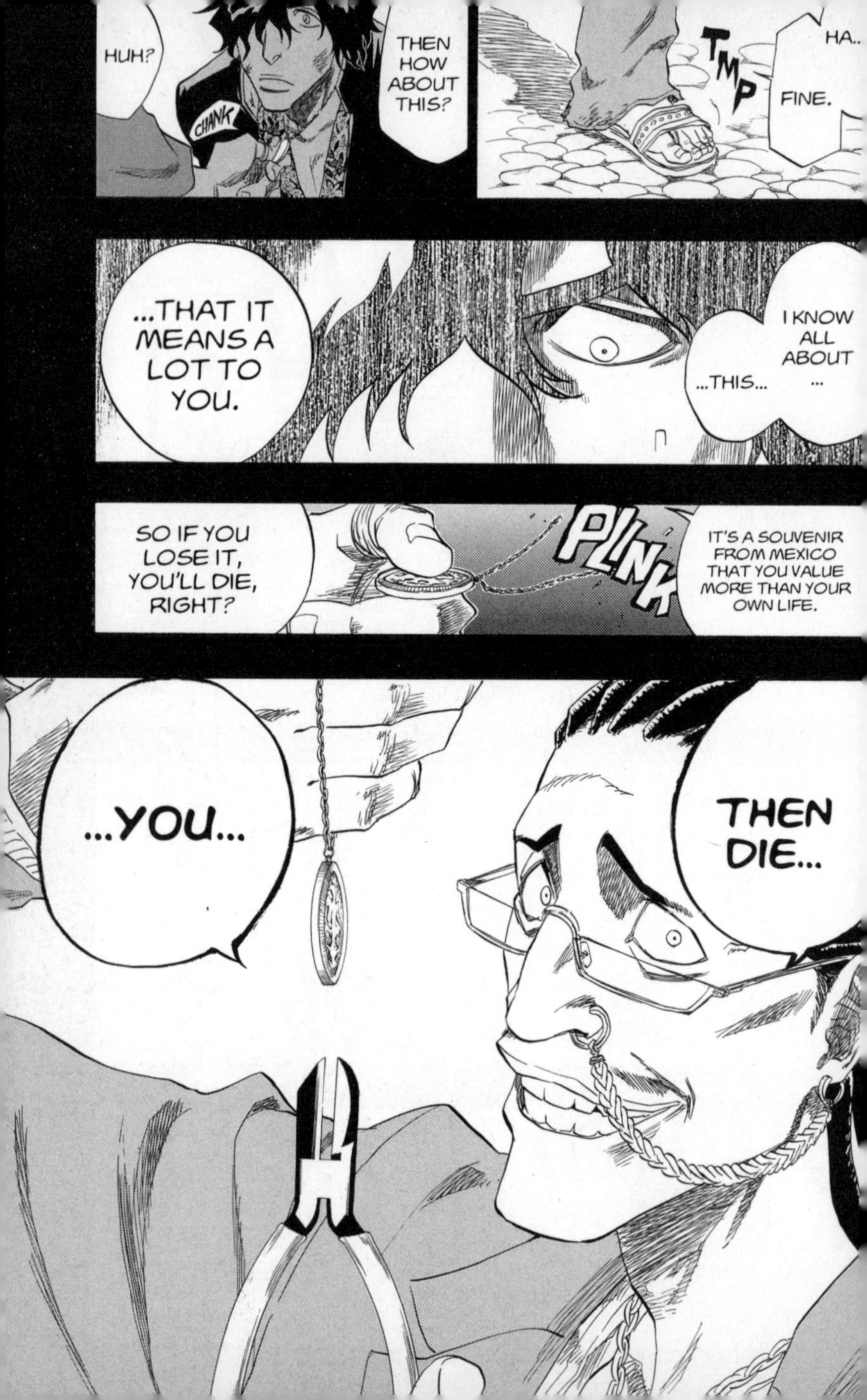
HA..
FINE.
TMP
THEN HOW ABOUT THIS?
HUH?
CHANK
I KNOW ALL ABOUT ...
...THIS...
...THAT IT MEANS A LOT TO YOU.
IT'S A SOUVENIR FROM MEXICO THAT YOU VALUE MORE THAN YOUR OWN LIFE.
PLINK
SO IF YOU LOSE IT, YOU'LL DIE, RIGHT?
THEN DIE...
...YOU...

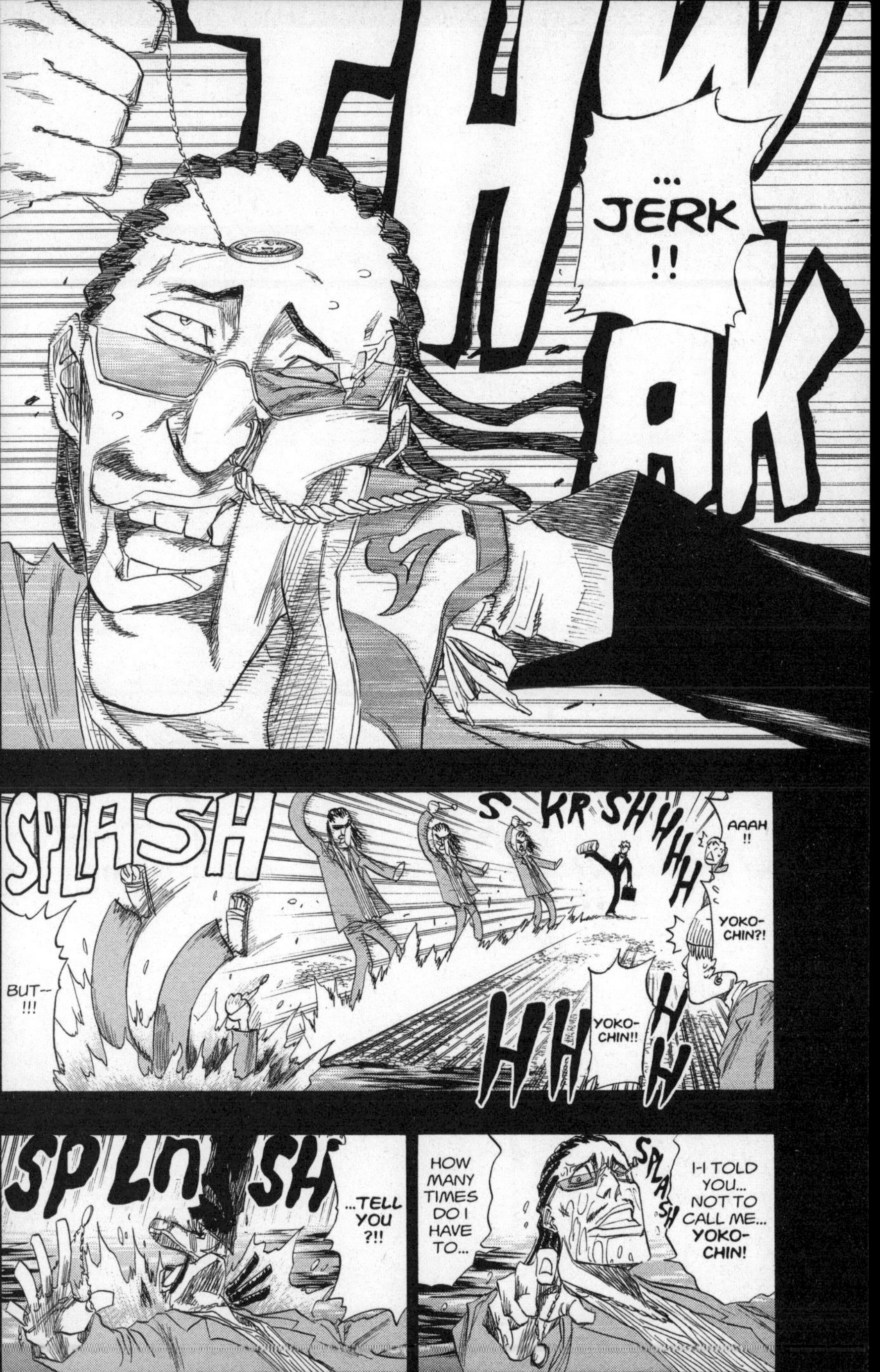

...JERK !!
THWAK
AAAH !!
YOKO-CHIN?!
YOKO-CHIN!!
BUT-- !!!
SPLASH
I-I TOLD YOU... NOT TO CALL ME... YOKO-CHIN!
SPLASH
HOW MANY TIMES DO I HAVE TO...
...TELL YOU ?!!
SPLASH

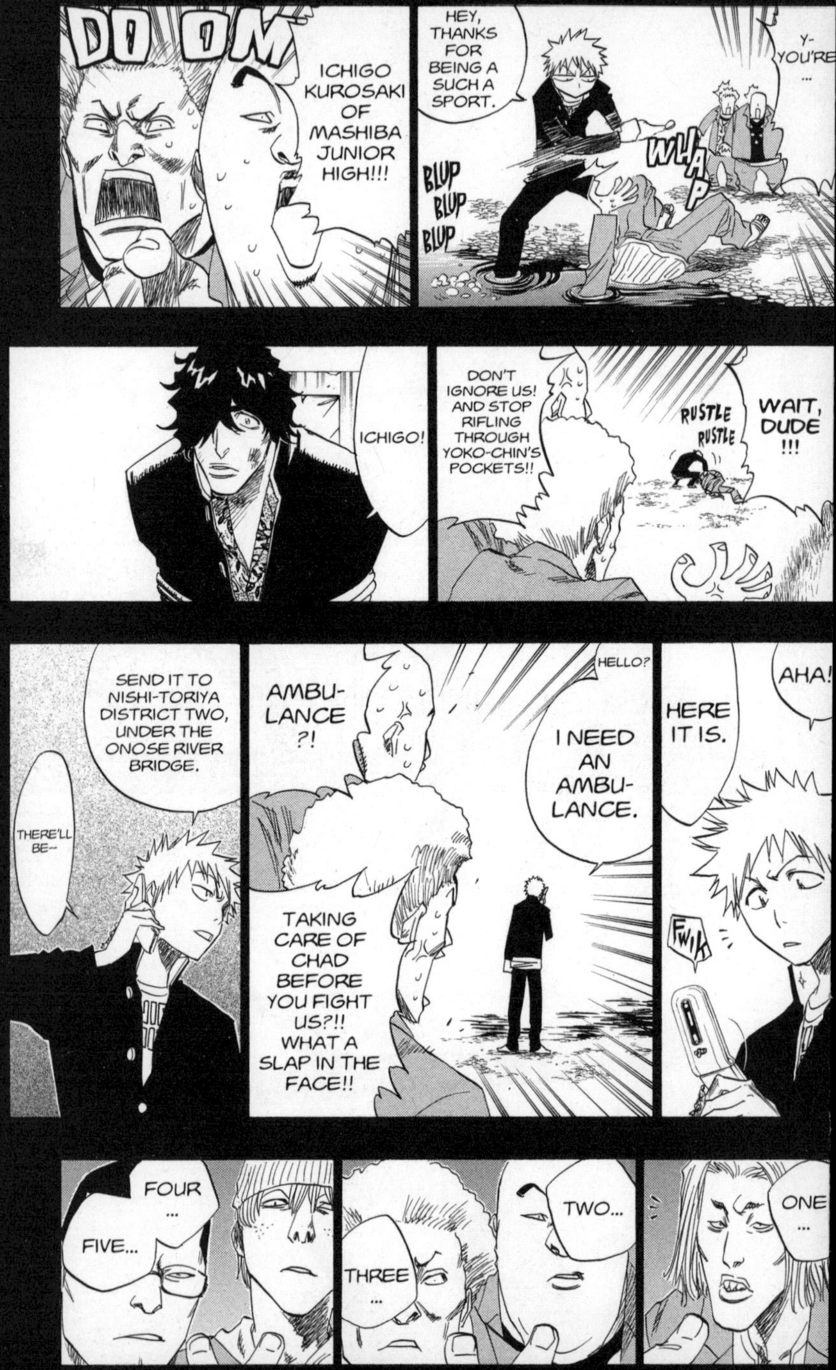
Y-YOU'RE...
HEY, THANKS FOR BEING A SUCH A SPORT.
WHAP
BLUP BLUP BLUP
DO OM
ICHIGO KUROSAKI OF MASHIBA JUNIOR HIGH!!!
WAIT, DUDE!!!
RUSTLE RUSTLE
DON'T IGNORE US! AND STOP RIFLING THROUGH YOKO-CHIN'S POCKETS!!
ICHIGO!
AHA!
HERE IT IS.
FWIK
HELLO?
I NEED AN AMBULANCE.
AMBULANCE?!
TAKING CARE OF CHAD BEFORE YOU FIGHT US?!! WHAT A SLAP IN THE FACE!!
SEND IT TO NISHI-TORIYA DISTRICT TWO, UNDER THE ONOSE RIVER BRIDGE.
THERE'LL BE--
ONE...
TWO...
THREE...
FOUR...
FIVE...

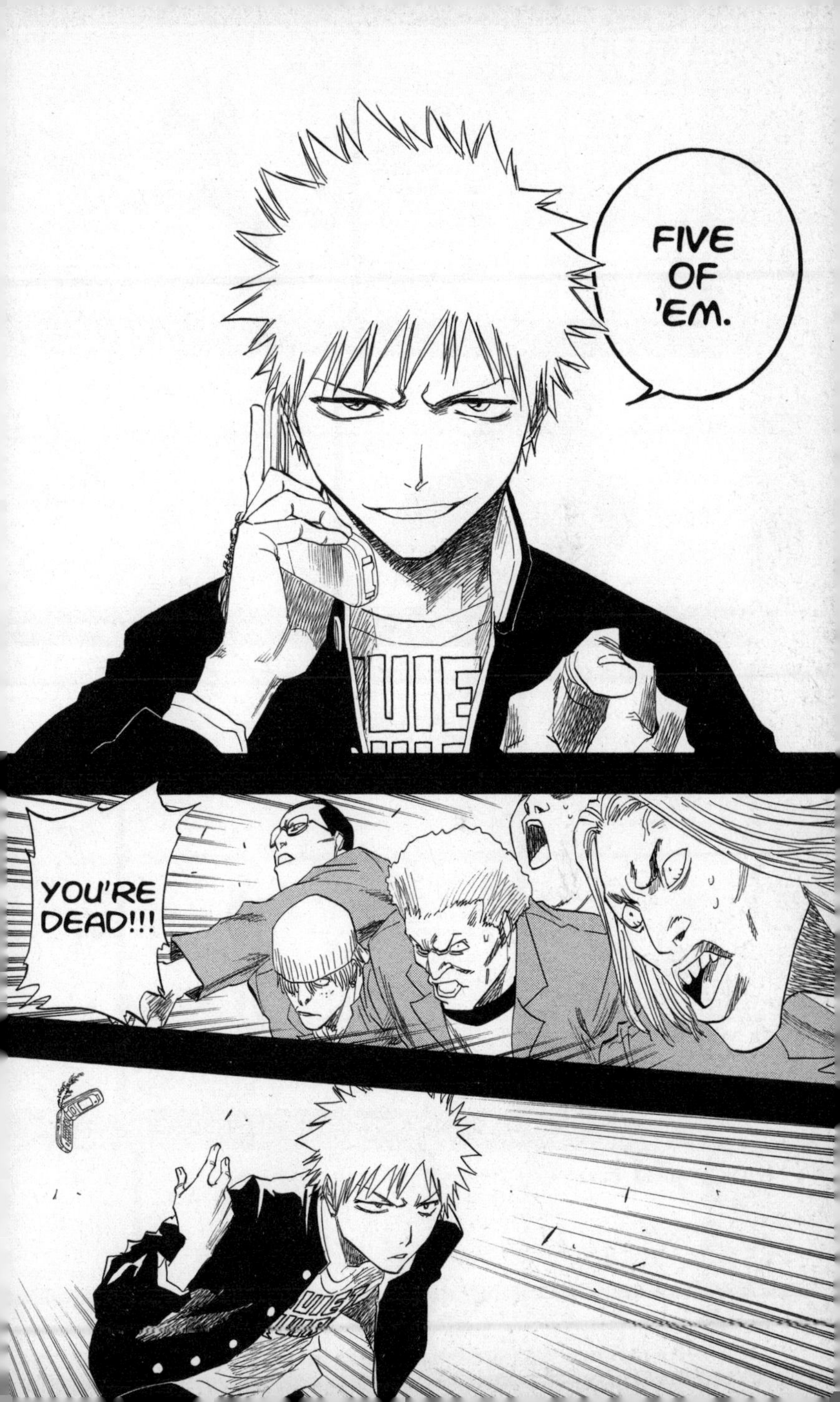
FIVE OF 'EM.
YOU'RE DEAD!!!

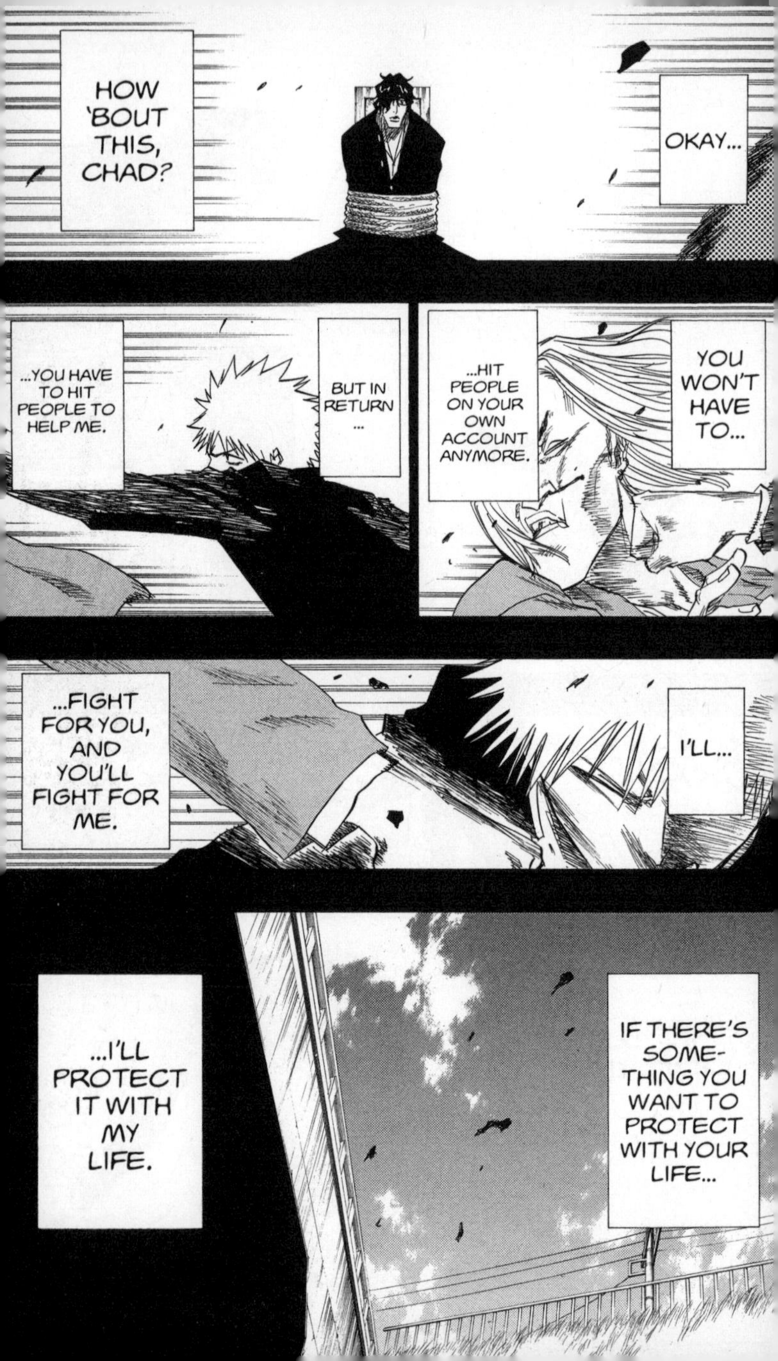
OKAY...
HOW 'BOUT THIS, CHAD?
YOU WON'T HAVE TO...
...HIT PEOPLE ON YOUR OWN ACCOUNT ANYMORE.
BUT IN RETURN ...
...YOU HAVE TO HIT PEOPLE TO HELP ME.
I'LL...
...FIGHT FOR YOU, AND YOU'LL FIGHT FOR ME.
IF THERE'S SOME-THING YOU WANT TO PROTECT WITH YOUR LIFE...
...I'LL PROTECT IT WITH MY LIFE.

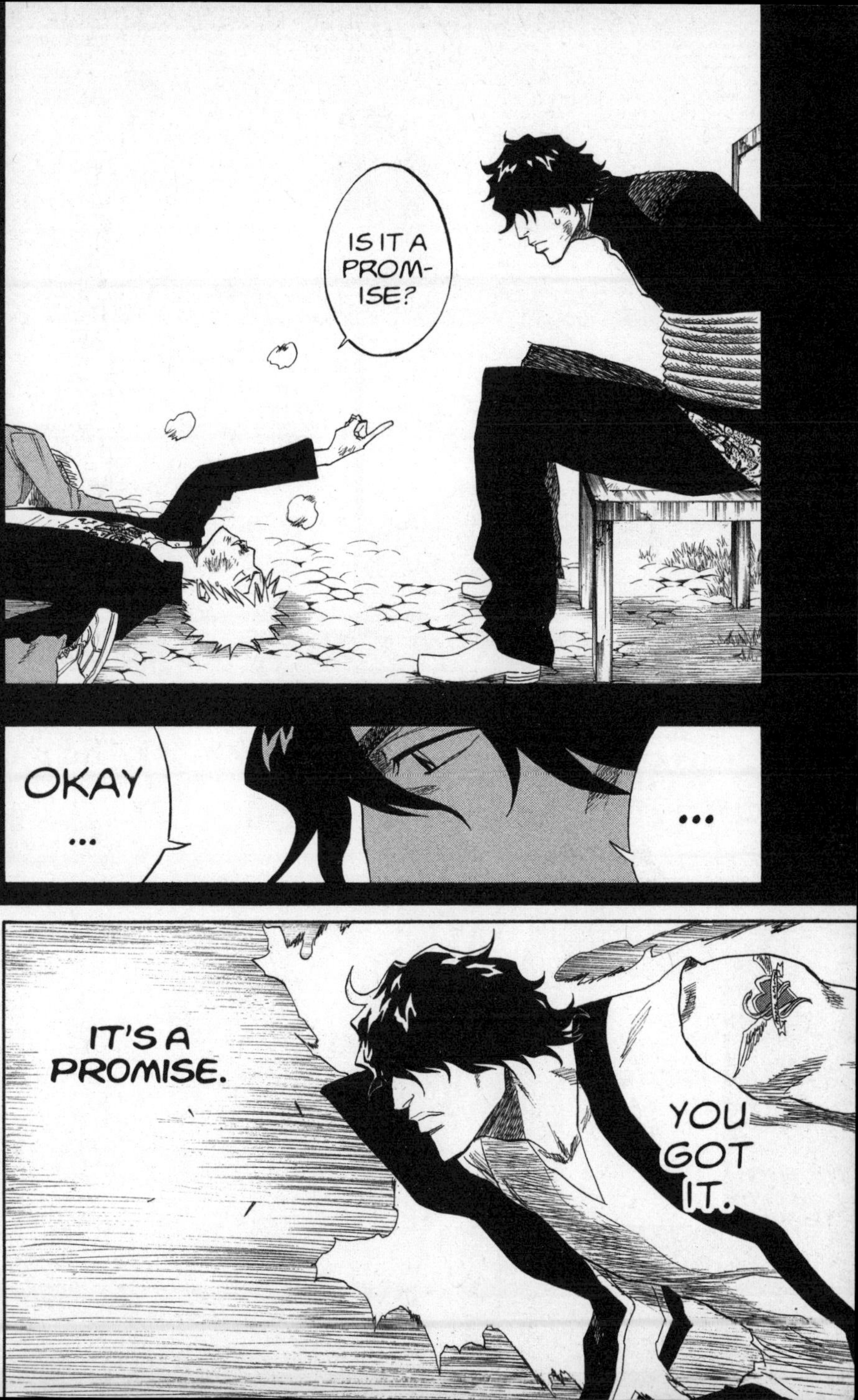
IS IT A PROMISE?
...
OKAY ...
YOU GOT IT.
IT'S A PROMISE.

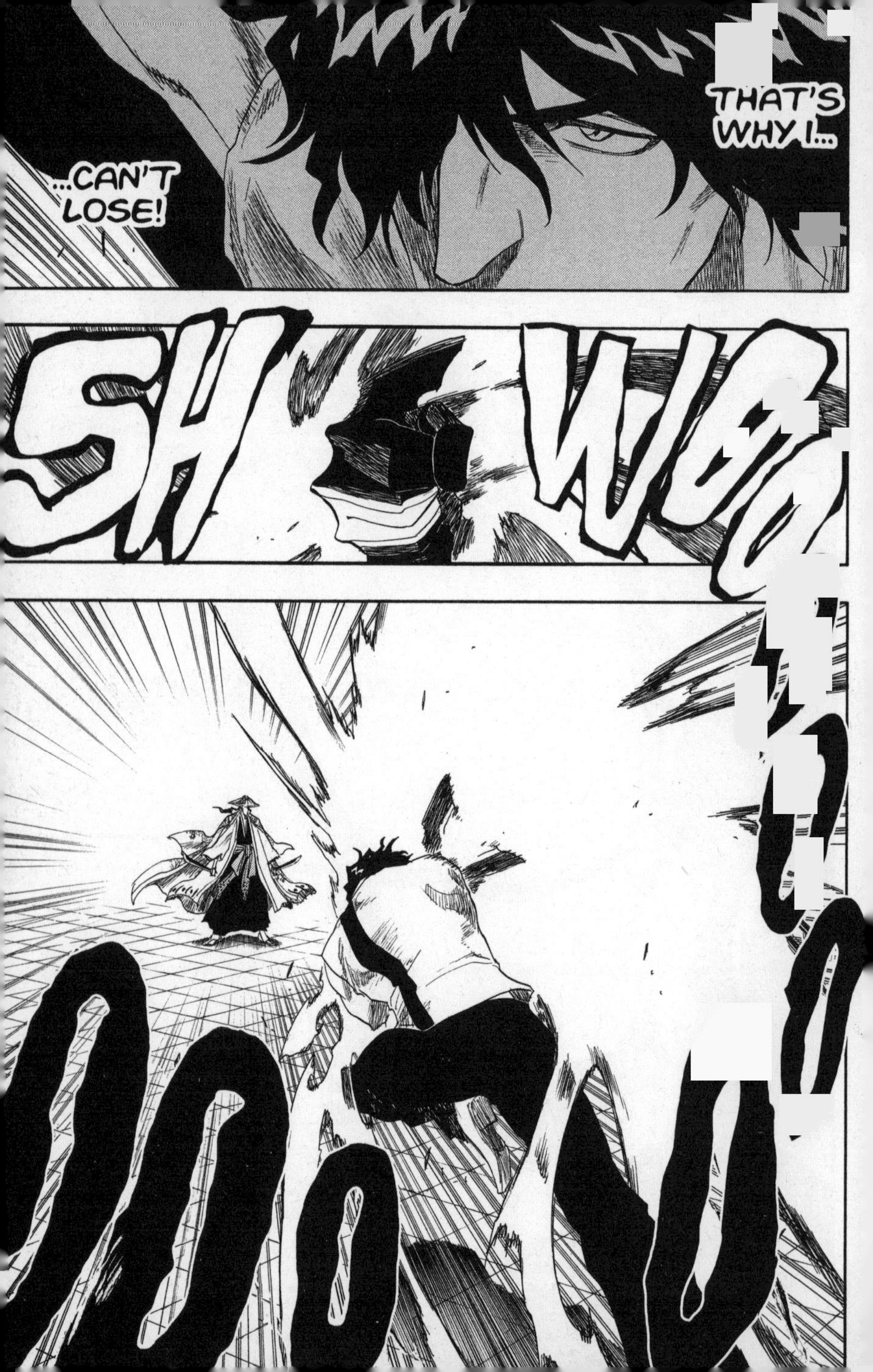
THAT'S WHY I...
...CAN'T LOSE!
SH WOOOOO

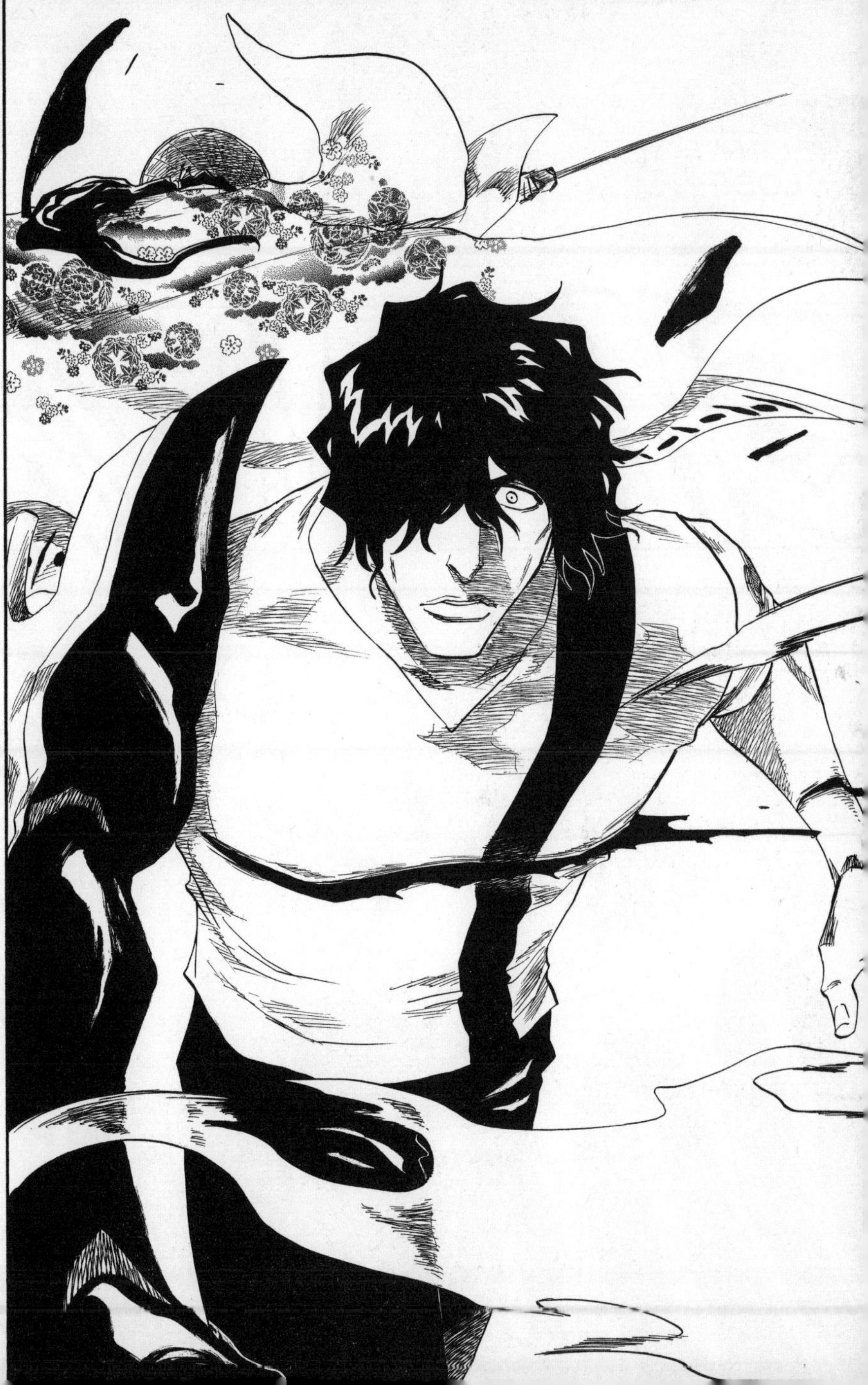

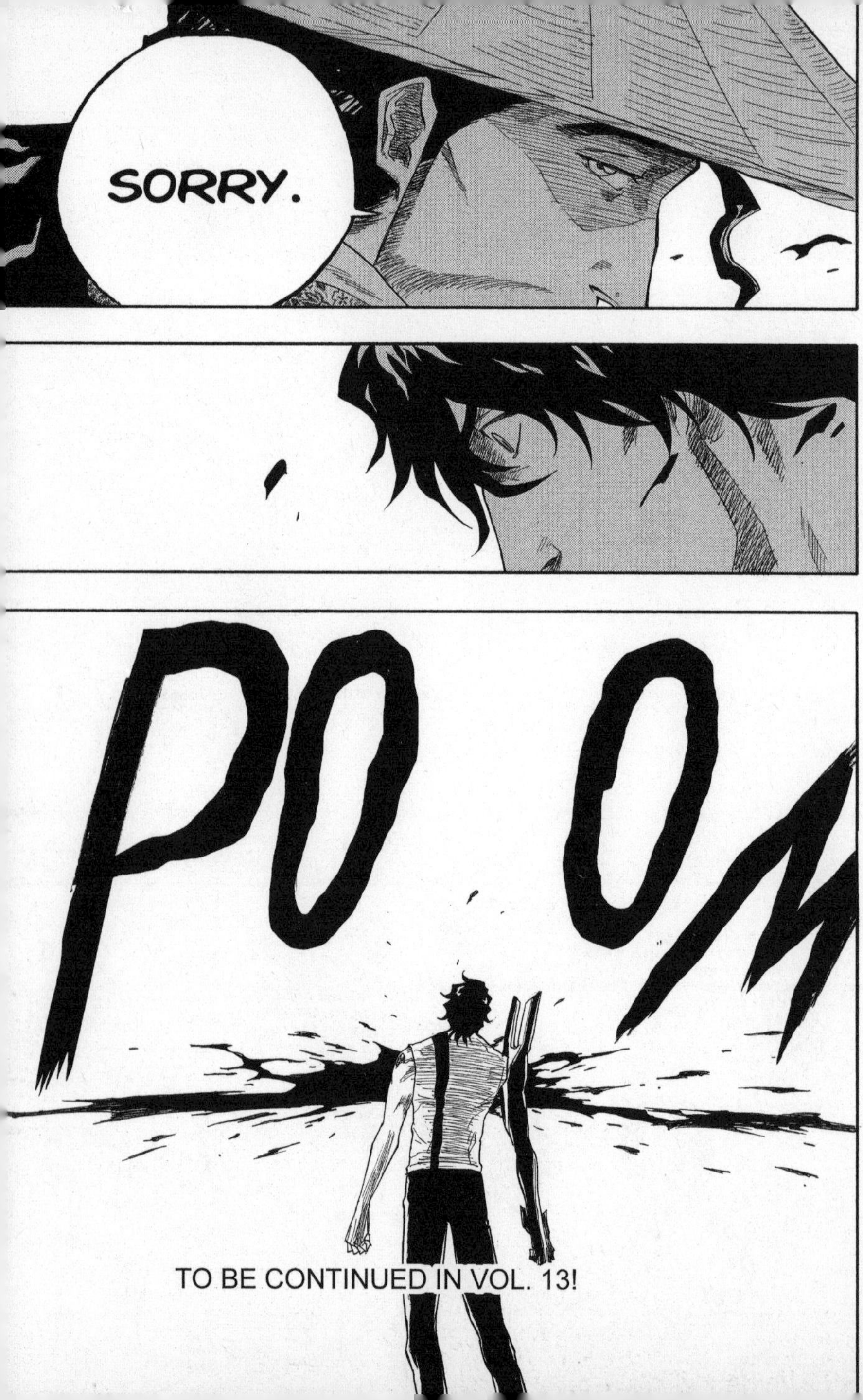
SORRY.
POOM
TO BE CONTINUED IN VOL. 13!

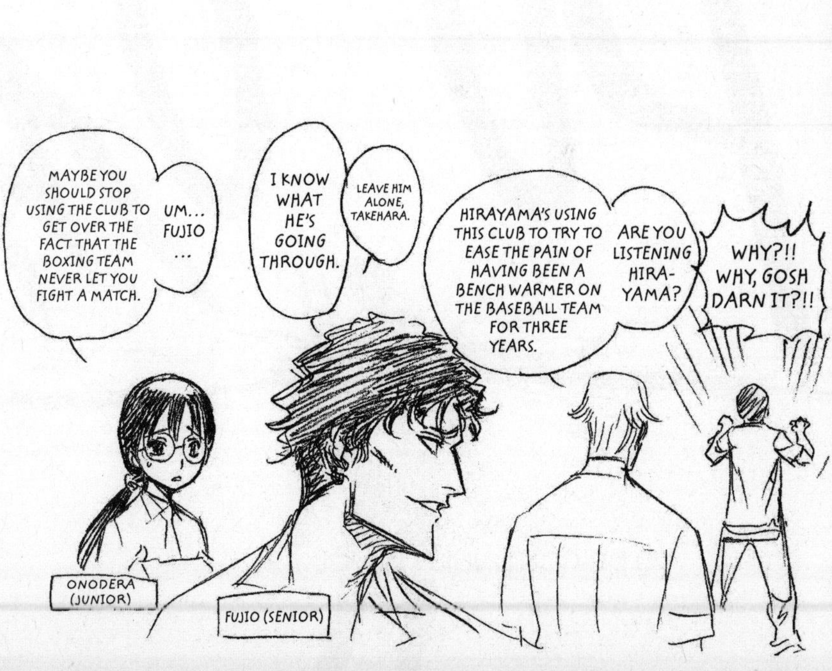
WHY?!! WHY, GOSH DARN IT?!!
ARE YOU LISTENING HIRA-YAMA?
HIRAYAMA'S USING THIS CLUB TO TRY TO EASE THE PAIN OF HAVING BEEN A BENCH WARMER ON THE BASEBALL TEAM FOR THREE YEARS.
LEAVE HIM ALONE, TAKEHARA.
I KNOW WHAT HE'S GOING THROUGH.
UM... FUJIO ...
MAYBE YOU SHOULD STOP USING THE CLUB TO GET OVER THE FACT THAT THE BOXING TEAM NEVER LET YOU FIGHT A MATCH.
FUJIO (SENIOR)
ONODERA (JUNIOR)

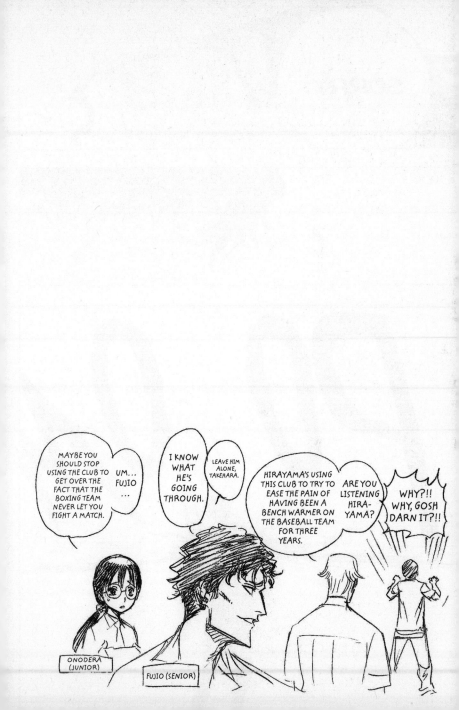

ラジコンベイビー

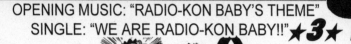

RADIO-KON★BABY!!

OPENING MUSIC: "RADIO-KON BABY'S THEME"
SINGLE: "WE ARE RADIO-KON BABY!!" ★3★

YO! HOW YOU GUY'S DOING?! IT'S BEEN A WHILE, HUH?!! TO TELL YOU THE TRUTH, I WAS SWEATING--I THOUGHT WE WERE FINISHED AFTER THE SECOND EPISODE!! BUT THE SUPER-POPULAR "RADIO-KON BABY"--THE FIRST THING TO GET CUT WHEN THERE ARE PAGE NUMBER CONSIDERATIONS--IS BACK FOR ITS THIRD INSTALLMENT!! OUR GUEST TODAY IS URYÛ ISHIDA!! THANK YOU VERY MUCH!!

...HELLO.

HEY!! WHAT'S THE MATTER, FOUR-EYES?!!

HURRY UP AND SIT DOWN!! OKAY, THE FIRST QUESTION IS... BUT BEFORE THAT, I GOTTA TELL YOU!! BECAUSE URYÛ'S IN THE CRAFTS CLUB, THERE WERE A BUNCH OF QUESTIONS ABOUT FIXING MY EARS AND RIPPING ME APART AND STUFF!! LISTEN UP!! I WOULDN'T LET THIS GUY LAY A FINGER ON MY BEAUTIFUL BODY!! GOT THAT, FOUR-EYES?! AND I DIDN'T SAY THAT TO SET UP A JOKE!!!

O-OKAY. I DON'T REALLY WANT TO ANYWAY.

Q CAN URYÛ'S CAPE FLY?

ERI FUKADA--OITA

WHAT A QUESTION. DID I EVER SAY IT COULD FLY?

MAYBE SHE'S SEEN TOO MANY FLYING CAPES IN MOVIES AND STUFF. OR MAYBE SHE'S JUST MAKING FUN OF YOU.

!!

Q I THOUGHT ARCHERS ALWAYS HOLD A BOW WITH THEIR LEFT HANDS REGARDLESS OF WHETHER THEY'RE LEFT- OR RIGHT-HANDED, BUT YOU HOLD IT WITH YOUR RIGHT. IS THAT SOME KIND OF QUINCY THING?

CHIMO--TOKYO

I DO?

IN VOLUME 5 YOU SAID YOUR FAVORITE FOOD WAS MACKEREL STEWED IN MISO THAT YOU COOK YOURSELF. DOES THAT MEAN YOU LIVE ALONE? AND WHAT OTHER FOODS DO YOU LIKE?

KITE WATANABE-- HOKKAIDO

GEEZ. WHAT A JERK.

NO.

I HAVE A QUESTION FOR URYÛ. WHAT WAS YOUR NICK-NAME AS A CHILD? ACTUALLY, CAN I CALL YOU "U-CHAN"?

AIKO ISHIMURA-- NIIGATA

WHY? IT'S BEEN WORK-ING FINE SO FAR...

THEN YOU'VE BEEN SHOOT-ING YOUR BOW WITHOUT REALLY KNOWING THE PROPER WAY? DUDE, THAT'S DANGER-OUS...

WELL...I WAS NEVER IN AN ARCHERY CLUB OR ANYTHING SO I DON'T REALLY KNOW WHAT'S RIGHT. ARE YOU SUP-POSED TO HOLD A BOW WITH YOUR LEFT HAND?

WHAT ?!

WAIT, IT'S NOT "QRACY," IT'S "QUINCY." THE LENGTH OF THE CAPE IS A MATTER OF INDIVIDUAL TASTE. MY MASTER ALWAYS SAID THAT A LONGER CAPE WAS COOLER.

YOUR CAPE IS SHORT AND YOUR MASTER'S WAS LONG. DOES THE LENGTH OF THE CAPE INDICATE THE STRENGTH OF A QRACY?

YÛMA-- HIROSHIMA

SO YOU'RE BASI-CALLY JUST A HOUSE-WIFE.

IT'S NOT REALLY MY FAVORITE, BUT I'M GOOD AT MAKING CHIKUZEN-NI. THAT'S CHICK-EN STEWED WITH TARO, BURDOCK, AND KONJAK*.

*KONJAK IS KONNYAKU, A GELATINOUS SUBSTANCE MADE FROM INDONESIAN POTATOES.

YOU REALLY ARE A JERK. OH WELL, THEN WHAT OTHER FOODS DO YOU LIKE?

WHAT DO YOU CARE? IT'S A PRIVATE MATTER. I DON'T WANT TO DISCUSS IT.

SERI-OUSLY? WHY? YOUR PAR-ENTS LIVE FAR AWAY OR SOME-THING?

YES, I LIVE ALONE.

HERE IT IS! THE BIGGEST QUESTION OF ALL!! THE SUSPICION THAT URYÛ ISHIDA IS UNCOOL!!!

WHY IS YOUR FASHION SENSE SO BAD?

YAKINIKU YASSAN-- OSAKA

DO YOU FEEL COMFORT-ABLE WITH YOUR SENSE OF FASHION?

SEIKÔ MATSUOKA-- YAMAGUCHI

...

I DUNNO? MAYBE YOU JUST DIDN'T MAKE A STRONG IMPRESSION ON THE READERS.

LIKE I SAID, IT'S NOT "QRACY," IT'S "QUINCY"! WHY DO SO MANY OF YOU REMEMBER IT INCORRECTLY?! WERE THESE QUESTIONS CHOSEN INTENTIONALLY?!

DESPITE EVERYTHING YOU'VE SAID, ARE YOU INTO QRACY COSTUMES?

NANAE KUDO-- HOKKAIDO

Q

WHEN YOU WERE LITTLE, YOU SAID, "WILL THIS TRADITIONAL QUINCY COSTUME EVER BE UPDATED? IT'S REALLY UNCOOL." WHAT KIND OF COSTUME WOULD YOU HAVE LIKED?

SEIYA IIDA--NIIGATA

SEE?! SEE?! WELL?! HUH?! EVEN **YOU** THOUGHT THE CAPE WAS UNCOOL! THEN WHAT COSTUME WOULD YOU HAVE LIKED TO WEAR? HUH? SAY SOMETHING, MR. URYÛ "I'M NOT UNCOOL" ISHIDA!!

HMPH!!!

WELL, THERE SURE SEEMS TO BE A CONSENSUS REGARDING YOUR COOLNESS FACTOR HERE.

THAT'S INSULTING! THE ONLY REASON PEOPLE THINK THAT IS BECAUSE ICHIGO KEEPS SAYING MY CLOTHES ARE FUNNY! I DON'T THINK I'M SO UNCOOL...

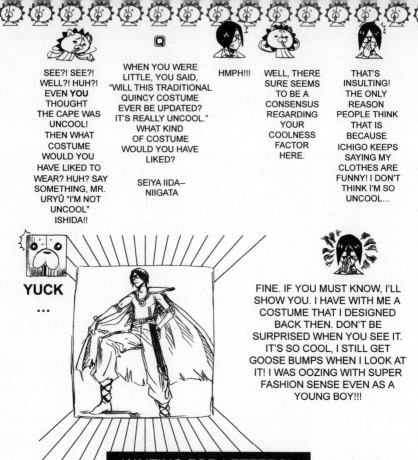

FINE. IF YOU MUST KNOW, I'LL SHOW YOU. I HAVE WITH ME A COSTUME THAT I DESIGNED BACK THEN. DON'T BE SURPRISED WHEN YOU SEE IT. IT'S SO COOL, I STILL GET GOOSE BUMPS WHEN I LOOK AT IT! I WAS OOZING WITH SUPER FASHION SENSE EVEN AS A YOUNG BOY!!!

YUCK...

WAITING FOR LETTERS!

ANY KIND OF QUESTION WILL DO!! BUT IF YOU SEND US A NAUGHTY QUESTION, PLEASE INCLUDE A RADIO NAME AS WELL AS YOUR REAL NAME, OTHERWISE THE KIDS AT SCHOOL WILL KNOW YOU'RE A PERV!! OUR NEXT GUEST WILL BE KISUKE URAHARA!! (UNCONFIRMED)

SEND YOUR QUESTION, NAME, ADDRESS, AGE, AND TELEPHONE NUMBER TO THE ADDRESS BELOW!!
SHONEN JUMP C/O VIZ MEDIA, LLC
★P.O. BOX 77010, SAN FRANCISCO, CA 94107★

● ATTN: "BLEACH" RADIO-KON BABY!! ●

SINGLE: "GOOD NIGHT, RADIO-KON BABY!" ENDING THEME MUSIC: WILLIE THE LION SMITH, "THE PANIC IS ON"

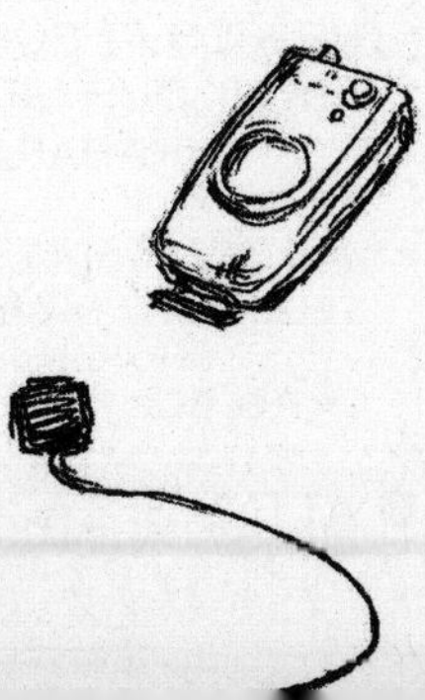

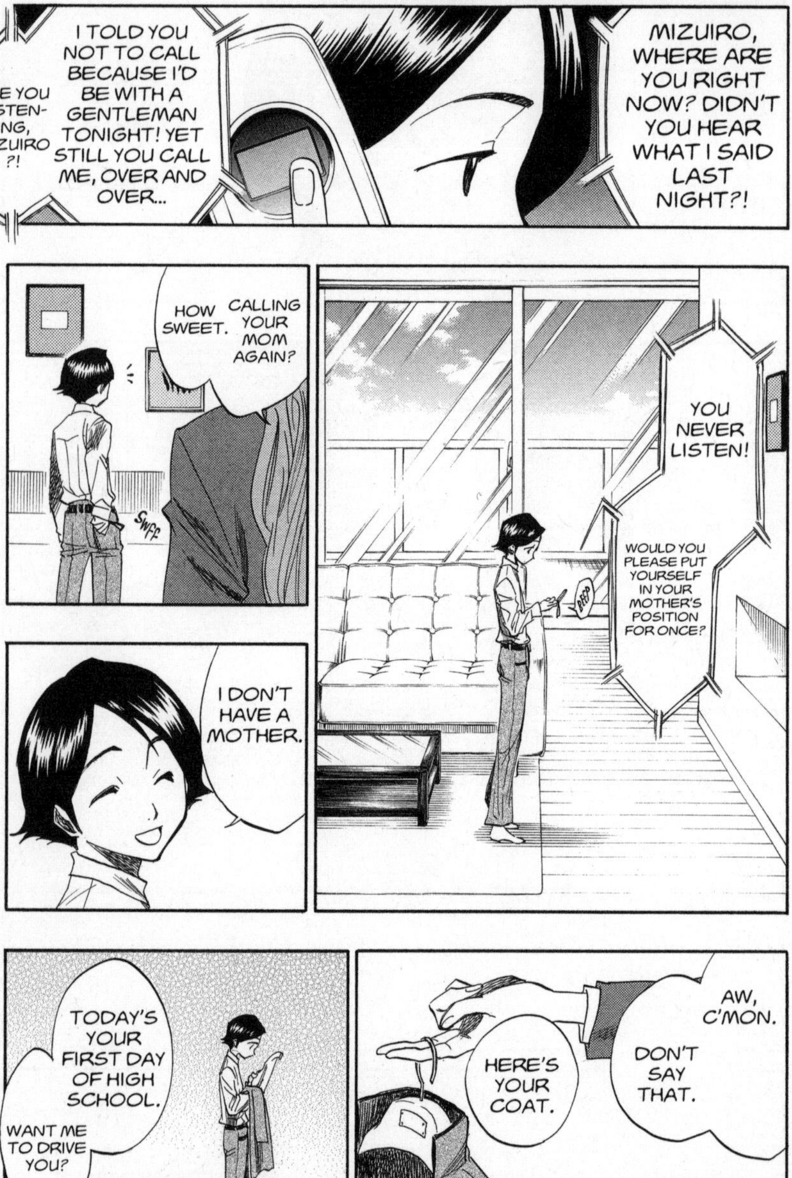
MIZUIRO, WHERE ARE YOU RIGHT NOW? DIDN'T YOU HEAR WHAT I SAID LAST NIGHT?!
I TOLD YOU NOT TO CALL BECAUSE I'D BE WITH A GENTLEMAN TONIGHT! YET STILL YOU CALL ME, OVER AND OVER...
ARE YOU LISTEN-ING, MIZUIRO ?!
YOU NEVER LISTEN!
WOULD YOU PLEASE PUT YOURSELF IN YOUR MOTHER'S POSITION FOR ONCE?
BEEP
CALLING YOUR MOM AGAIN?
HOW SWEET.
SWFF
I DON'T HAVE A MOTHER.
AW, C'MON.
DON'T SAY THAT.
HERE'S YOUR COAT.
TODAY'S YOUR FIRST DAY OF HIGH SCHOOL.
WANT ME TO DRIVE YOU?

0.8. a wonderful error

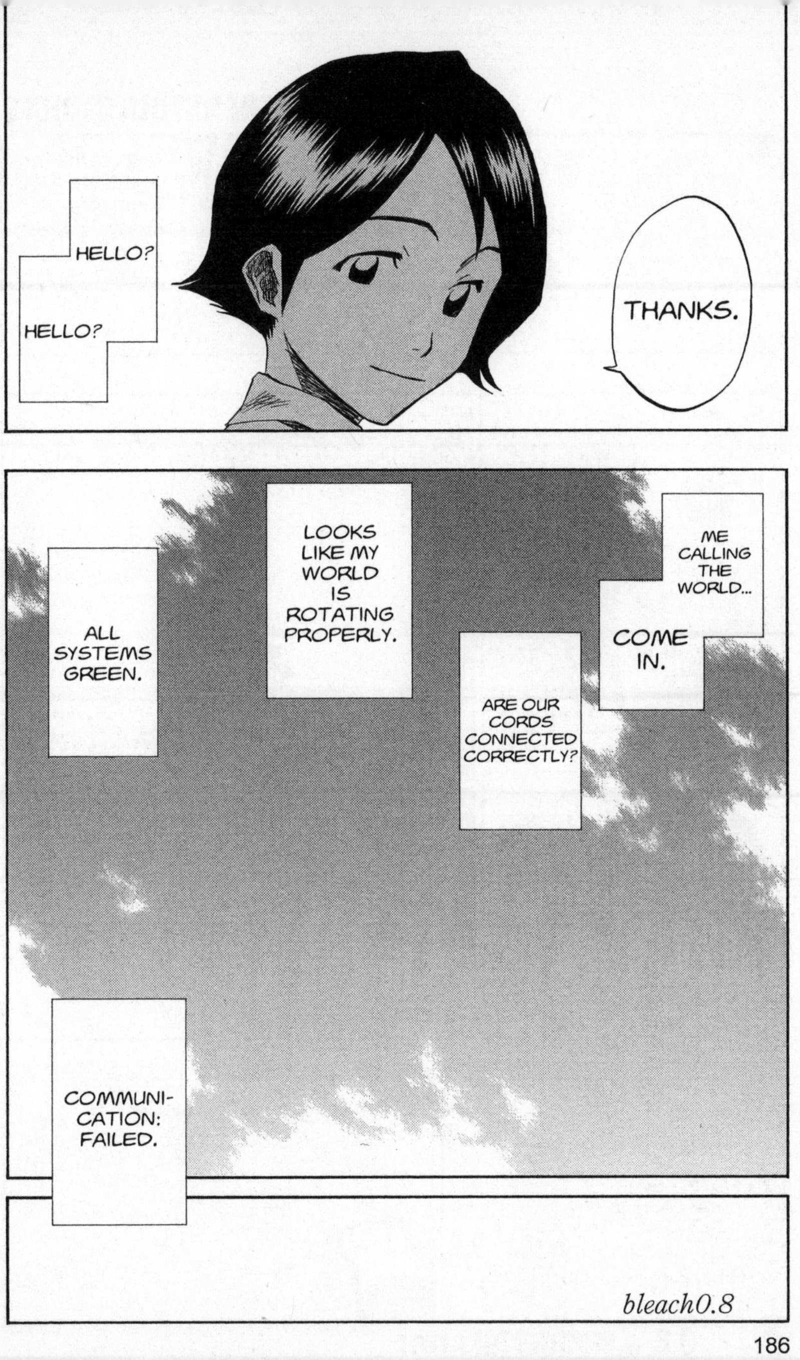
THANKS.
HELLO? HELLO?
ME CALLING THE WORLD... COME IN.
ARE OUR CORDS CONNECTED CORRECTLY?
LOOKS LIKE MY WORLD IS ROTATING PROPERLY.
ALL SYSTEMS GREEN.
COMMUNICATION: FAILED.
bleach0.8

READ THIS WAY

a wonderful error

TITE KUBO

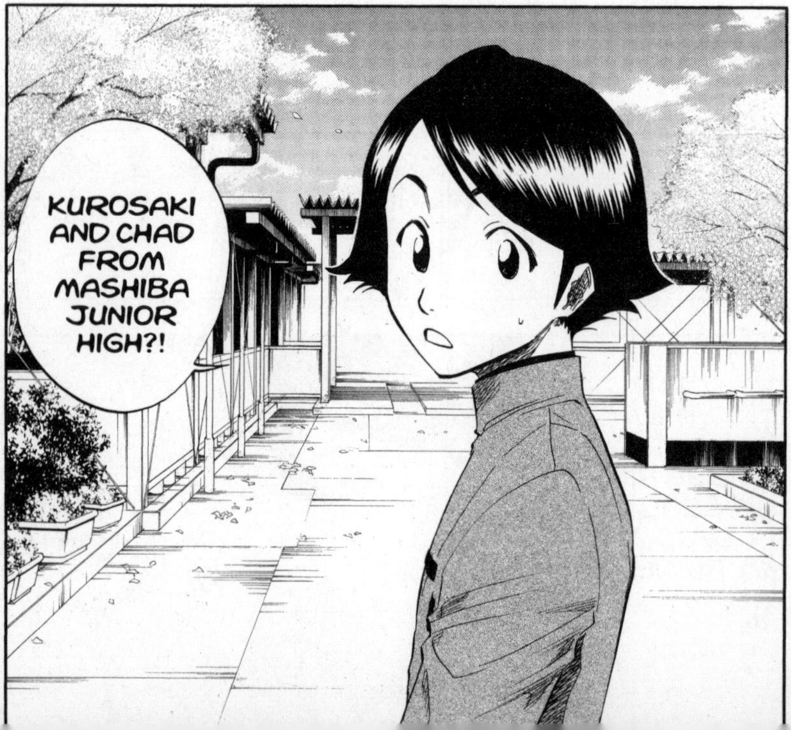
KUROSAKI AND CHAD FROM MASHIBA JUNIOR HIGH?!

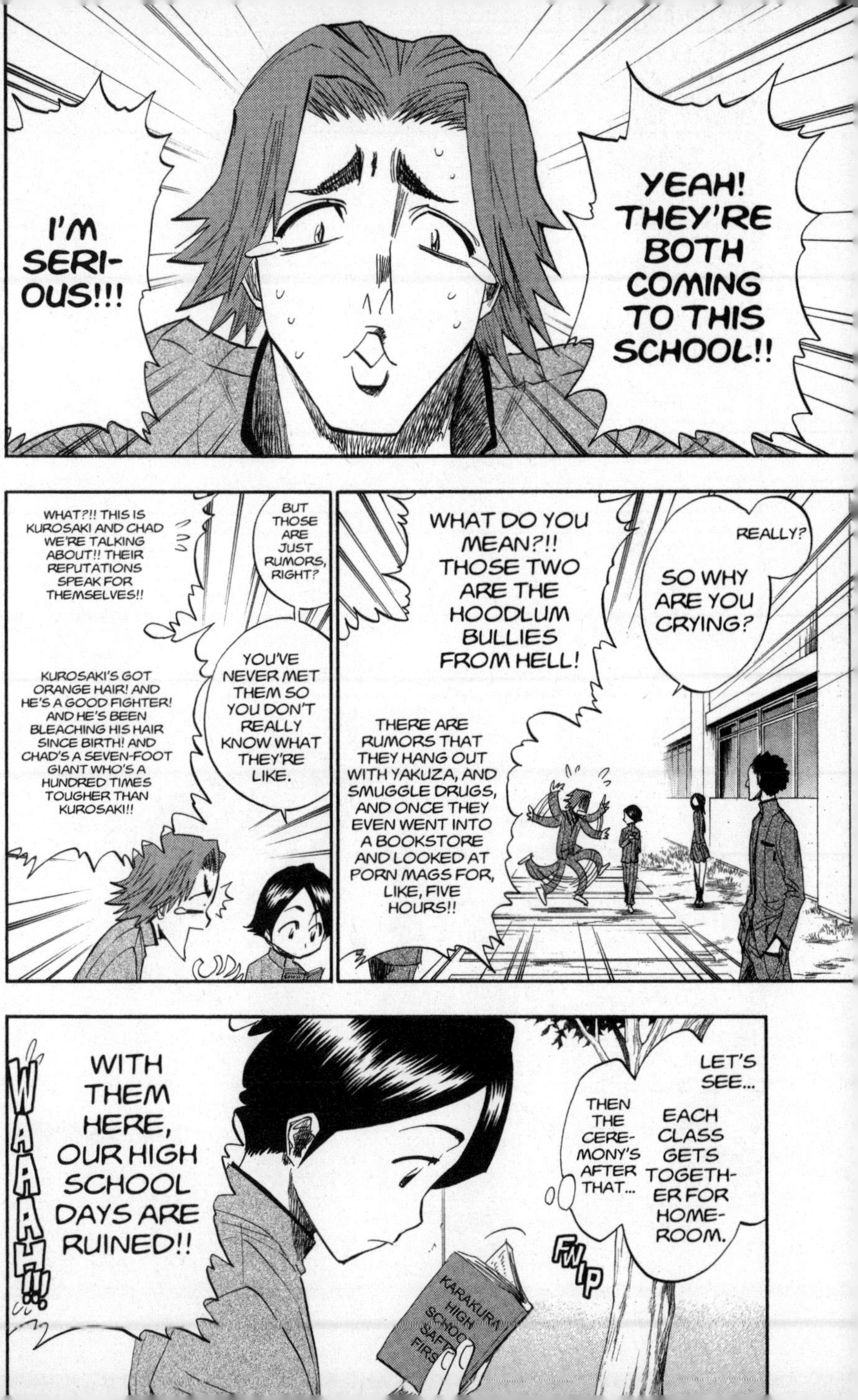
YEAH! THEY'RE BOTH COMING TO THIS SCHOOL!!
I'M SERI-OUS!!!
REALLY?
SO WHY ARE YOU CRYING?
WHAT DO YOU MEAN?!! THOSE TWO ARE THE HOODLUM BULLIES FROM HELL!
THERE ARE RUMORS THAT THEY HANG OUT WITH YAKUZA, AND SMUGGLE DRUGS, AND ONCE THEY EVEN WENT INTO A BOOKSTORE AND LOOKED AT PORN MAGS FOR, LIKE, FIVE HOURS!!
BUT THOSE ARE JUST RUMORS, RIGHT?
WHAT?!! THIS IS KUROSAKI AND CHAD WE'RE TALKING ABOUT!! THEIR REPUTATIONS SPEAK FOR THEMSELVES!!
YOU'VE NEVER MET THEM SO YOU DON'T REALLY KNOW WHAT THEY'RE LIKE.
KUROSAKI'S GOT ORANGE HAIR! AND HE'S A GOOD FIGHTER! AND HE'S BEEN BLEACHING HIS HAIR SINCE BIRTH! AND CHAD'S A SEVEN-FOOT GIANT WHO'S A HUNDRED TIMES TOUGHER THAN KUROSAKI!!
LET'S SEE...
EACH CLASS GETS TOGETH-ER FOR HOME-ROOM.
THEN THE CERE-MONY'S AFTER THAT...
FWIP
WITH THEM HERE, OUR HIGH SCHOOL DAYS ARE RUINED!!
WAAAAH!!!

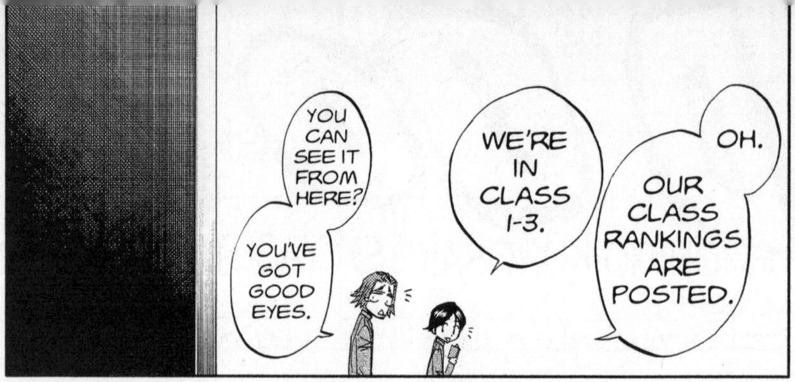
OH.
OUR CLASS RANKINGS ARE POSTED.
WE'RE IN CLASS 1-3.
YOU CAN SEE IT FROM HERE?
YOU'VE GOT GOOD EYES.

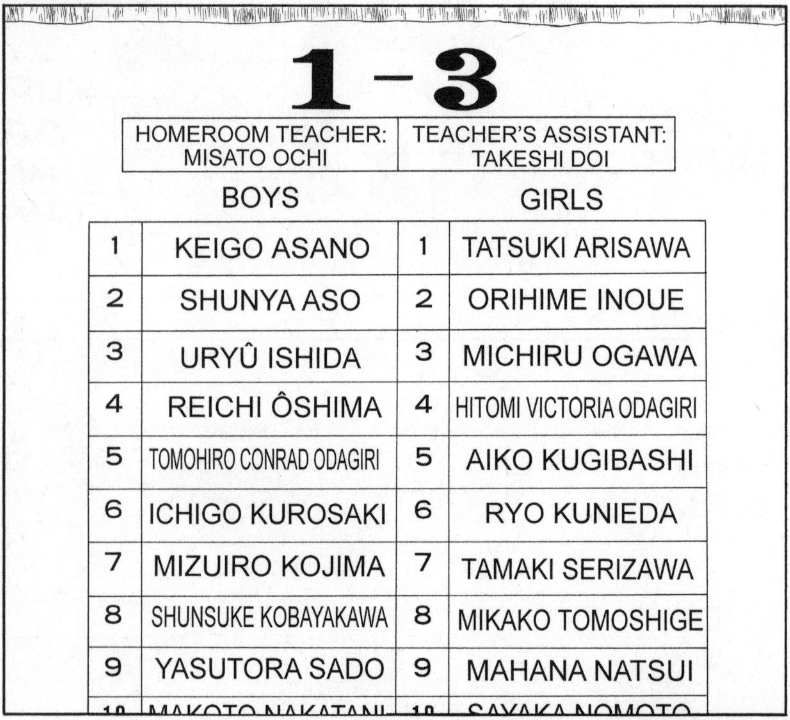

1-3

HOMEROOM TEACHER: MISATO OCHI	TEACHER'S ASSISTANT: TAKESHI DOI

BOYS		GIRLS	
1	KEIGO ASANO	1	TATSUKI ARISAWA
2	SHUNYA ASO	2	ORIHIME INOUE
3	URYÛ ISHIDA	3	MICHIRU OGAWA
4	REICHI ÔSHIMA	4	HITOMI VICTORIA ODAGIRI
5	TOMOHIRO CONRAD ODAGIRI	5	AIKO KUGIBASHI
6	ICHIGO KUROSAKI	6	RYO KUNIEDA
7	MIZUIRO KOJIMA	7	TAMAKI SERIZAWA
8	SHUNSUKE KOBAYAKAWA	8	MIKAKO TOMOSHIGE
9	YASUTORA SADO	9	MAHANA NATSUI
10	MAKOTO NAKATANI	10	SAYAKA NOMOTO

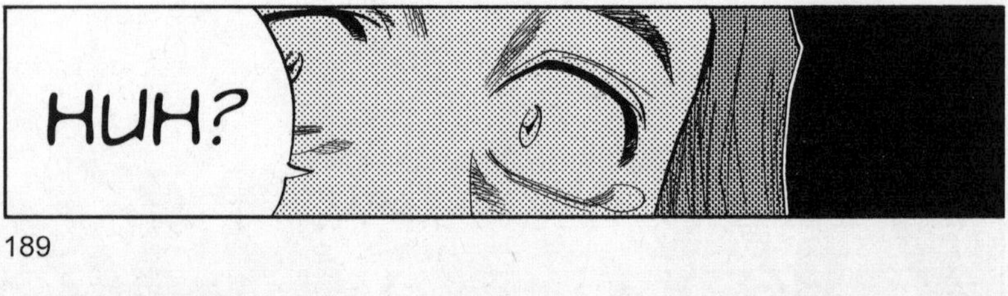
HUH?

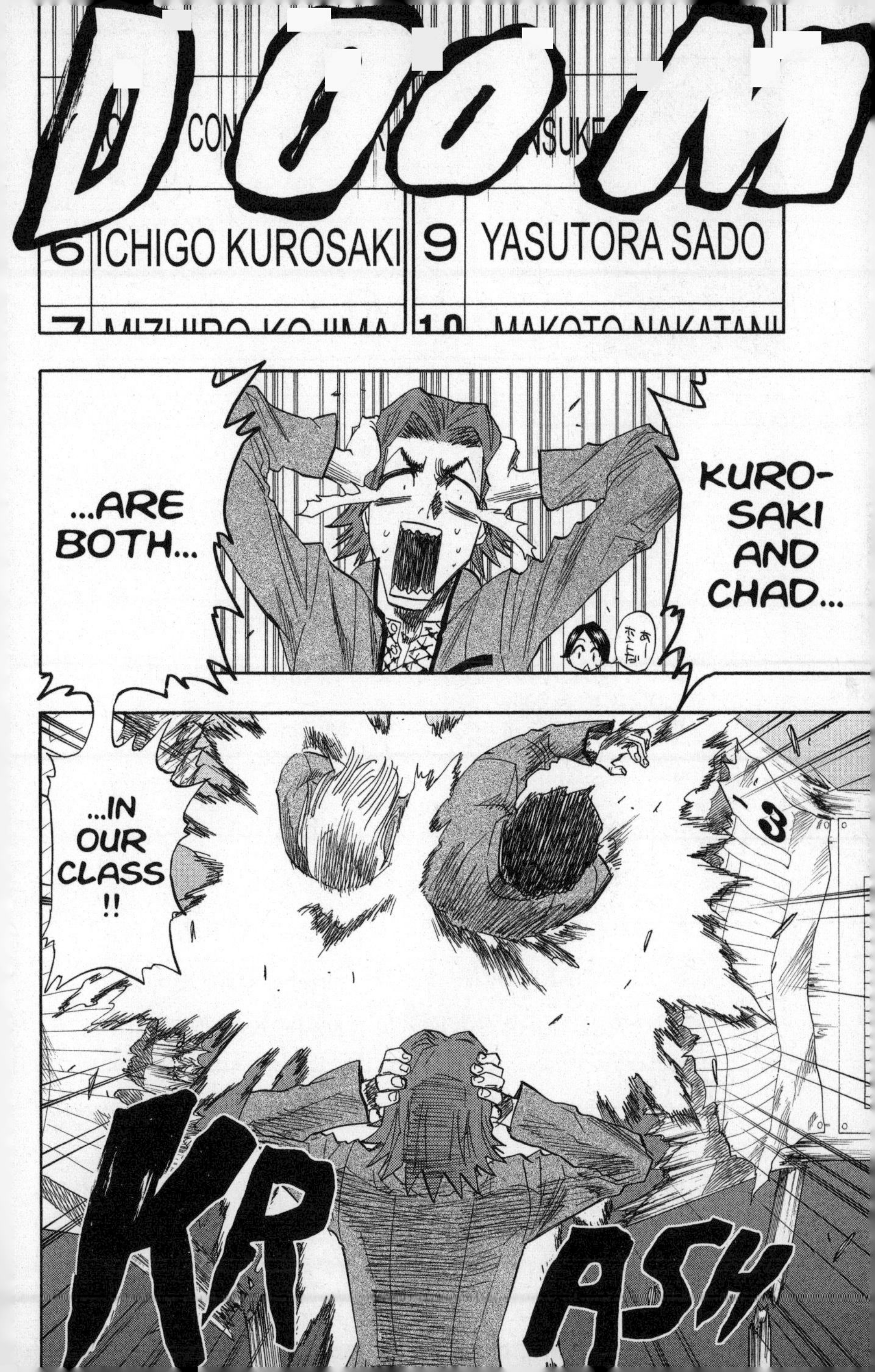
DOOM
6 ICHIGO KUROSAKI
9 YASUTORA SADO
KURO-SAKI AND CHAD...
...ARE BOTH...
...IN OUR CLASS !!
KRASH

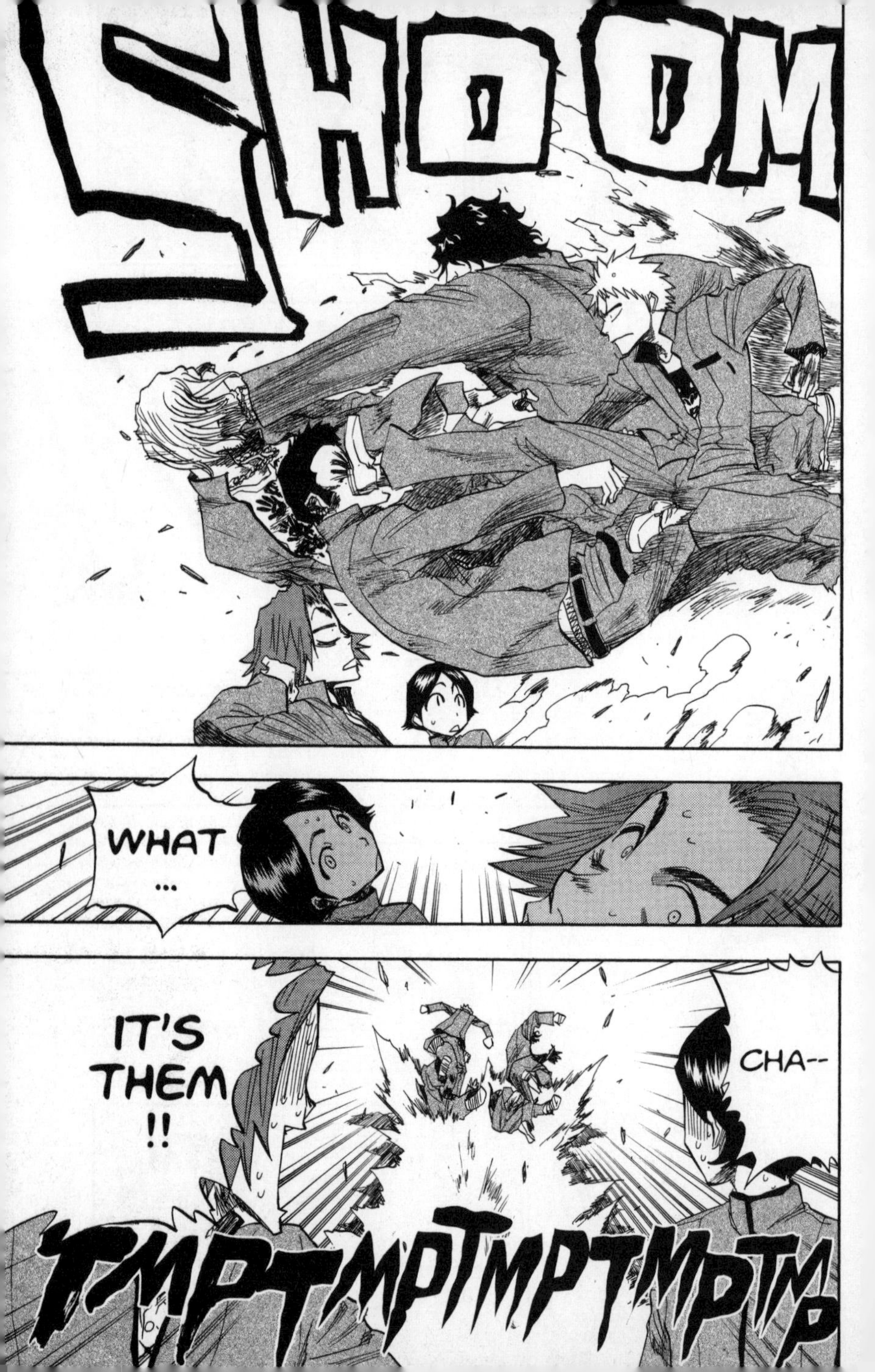
VHOOM
WHAT ...
CHA--
IT'S THEM !!
TMPTMPTMPTMPTMPTMP

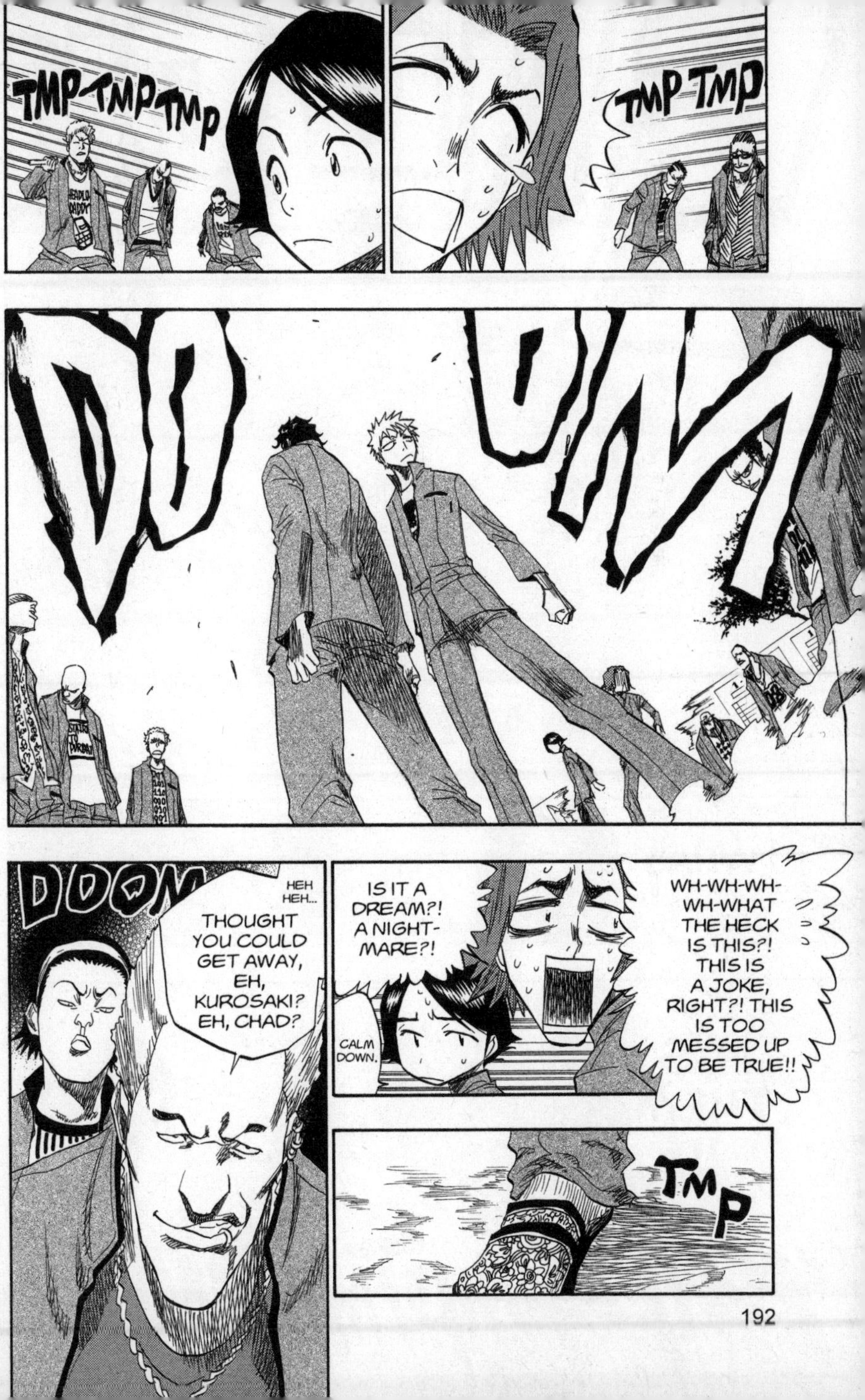
TMP TMP
TMP-TMP TMP
DOOM
WH-WH-WH-WH-WHAT THE HECK IS THIS?! THIS IS A JOKE, RIGHT?! THIS IS TOO MESSED UP TO BE TRUE!!
IS IT A DREAM?! A NIGHTMARE?!
CALM DOWN.
TMP
DOOM
HEH HEH...
THOUGHT YOU COULD GET AWAY, EH, KUROSAKI? EH, CHAD?

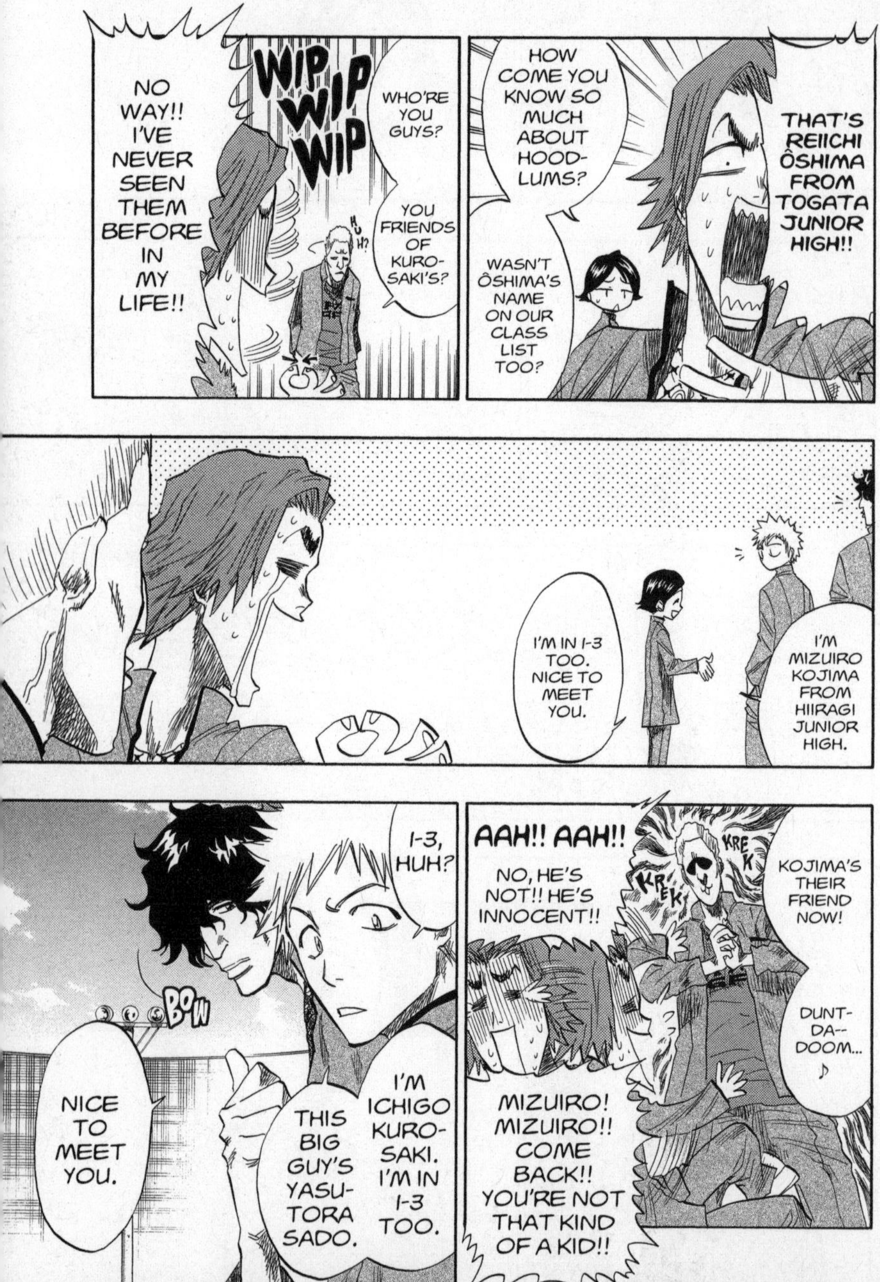
THAT'S REIICHI ÔSHIMA FROM TOGATA JUNIOR HIGH!!
HOW COME YOU KNOW SO MUCH ABOUT HOOD-LUMS?
WASN'T ÔSHIMA'S NAME ON OUR CLASS LIST TOO?
WHO'RE YOU GUYS?
YOU FRIENDS OF KURO-SAKI'S?
HUH?
WIP WIP WIP
NO WAY!! I'VE NEVER SEEN THEM BEFORE IN MY LIFE!!
I'M MIZUIRO KOJIMA FROM HIIRAGI JUNIOR HIGH.
I'M IN 1-3 TOO. NICE TO MEET YOU.
KOJIMA'S THEIR FRIEND NOW!
KREK
KREK
AAH!! AAH!!
NO, HE'S NOT!! HE'S INNOCENT!!
DUNT-DA--DOOM... ♪
MIZUIRO! MIZUIRO!! COME BACK!! YOU'RE NOT THAT KIND OF A KID!!
1-3, HUH?
I'M ICHIGO KURO-SAKI. I'M IN 1-3 TOO.
THIS BIG GUY'S YASU-TORA SADO.
BOW
NICE TO MEET YOU.

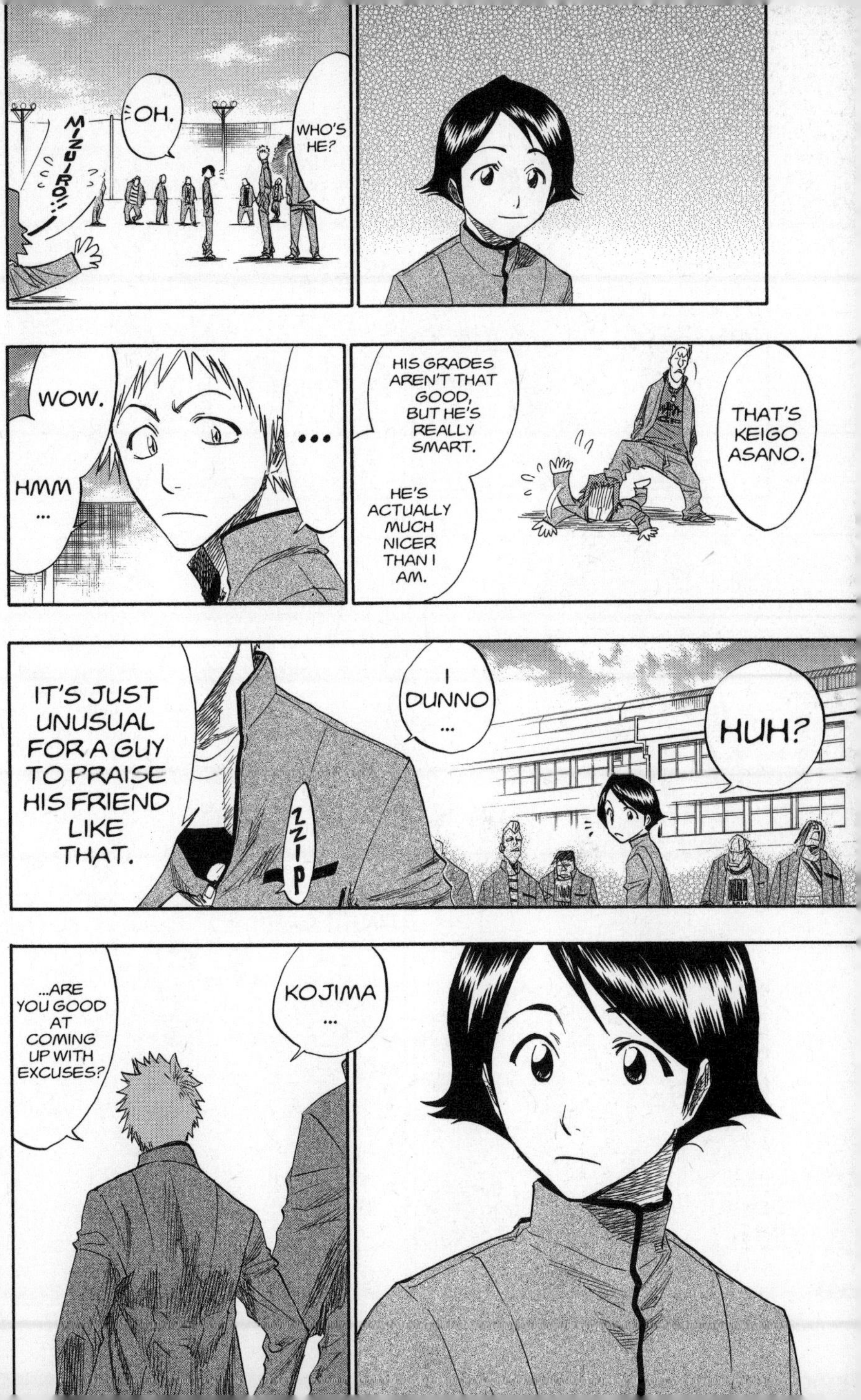
WHO'S HE?
OH.
MIZUIRO!!
THAT'S KEIGO ASANO.
HIS GRADES AREN'T THAT GOOD, BUT HE'S REALLY SMART.
HE'S ACTUALLY MUCH NICER THAN I AM.
...
WOW.
HMM ...
HUH?
I DUNNO ...
ZZIP
IT'S JUST UNUSUAL FOR A GUY TO PRAISE HIS FRIEND LIKE THAT.
KOJIMA ...
...ARE YOU GOOD AT COMING UP WITH EXCUSES?

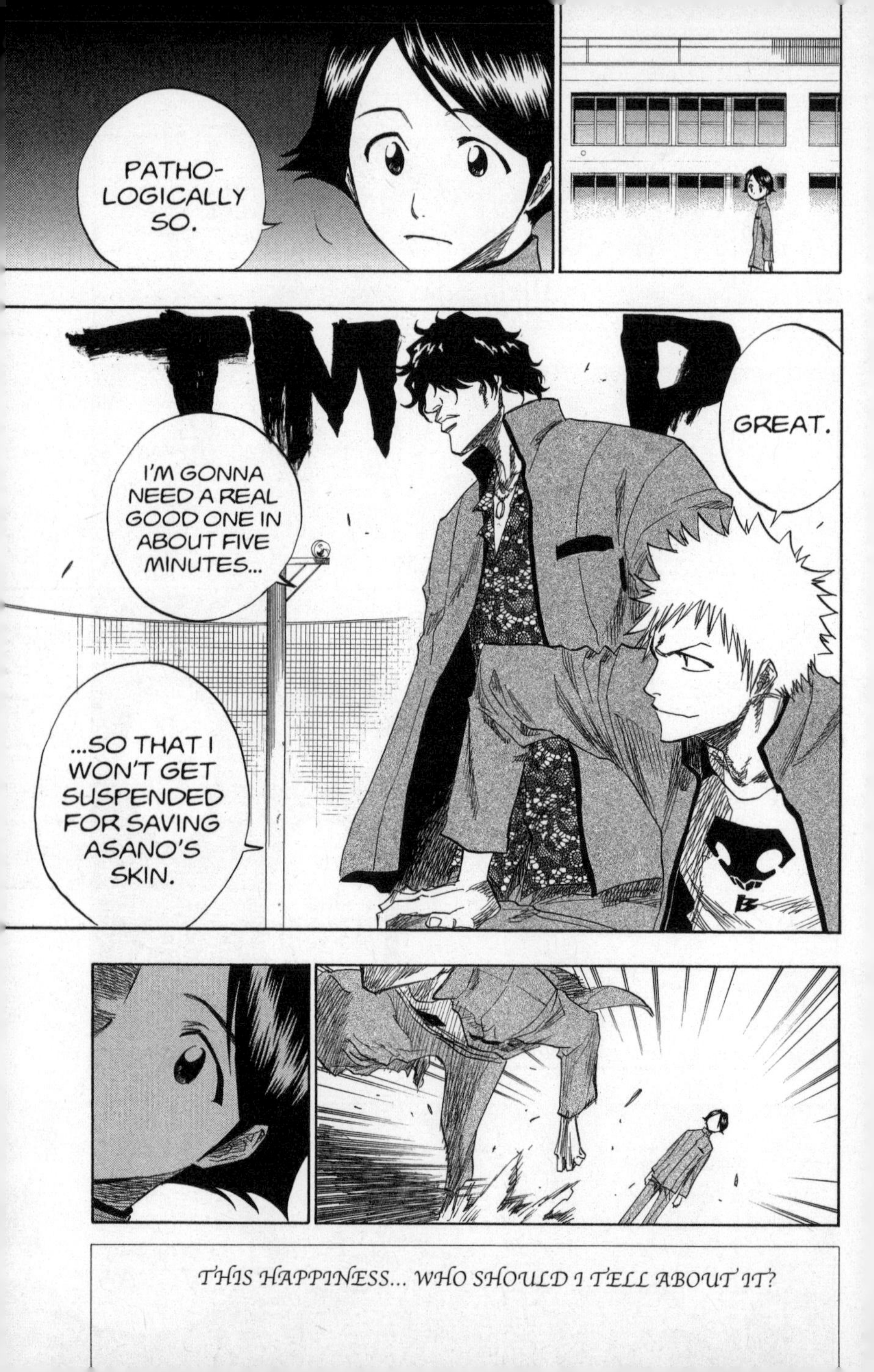
PATHOLOGICALLY SO.
TMP
GREAT.
I'M GONNA NEED A REAL GOOD ONE IN ABOUT FIVE MINUTES...
...SO THAT I WON'T GET SUSPENDED FOR SAVING ASANO'S SKIN.
THIS HAPPINESS... WHO SHOULD I TELL ABOUT IT?

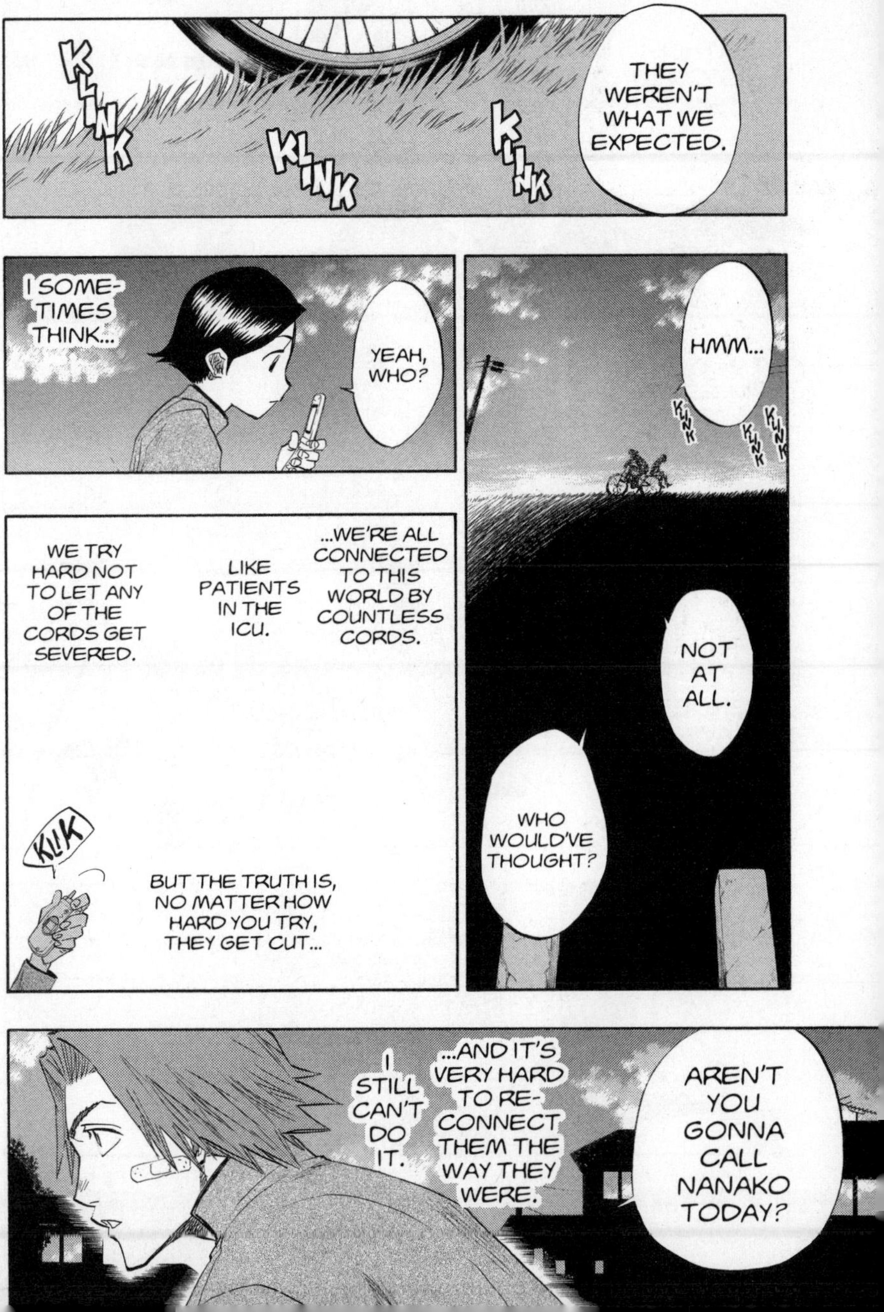
THEY WEREN'T WHAT WE EXPECTED.
KLINK
KLINK
KLINK
HMM...
KLINK
KLINK
KLINK
NOT AT ALL.
WHO WOULD'VE THOUGHT?
YEAH, WHO?
I SOMETIMES THINK...
...WE'RE ALL CONNECTED TO THIS WORLD BY COUNTLESS CORDS.
LIKE PATIENTS IN THE ICU.
WE TRY HARD NOT TO LET ANY OF THE CORDS GET SEVERED.
KLIK
BUT THE TRUTH IS, NO MATTER HOW HARD YOU TRY, THEY GET CUT...
AREN'T YOU GONNA CALL NANAKO TODAY?
...AND IT'S VERY HARD TO RECONNECT THEM THE WAY THEY WERE.
I STILL CAN'T DO IT.

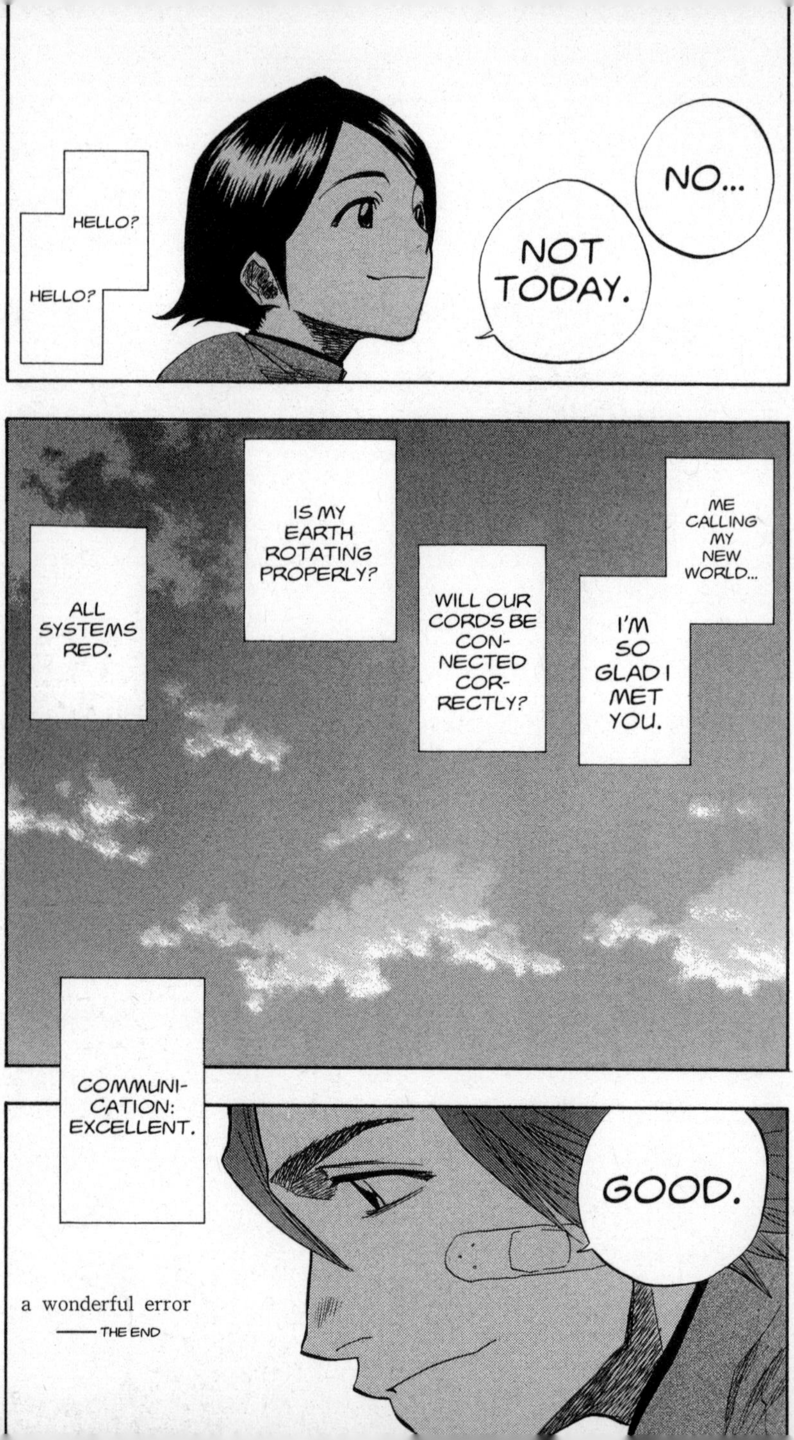
NO...
NOT TODAY.
HELLO?
HELLO?
ME CALLING MY NEW WORLD...
I'M SO GLAD I MET YOU.
WILL OUR CORDS BE CON-NECTED COR-RECTLY?
IS MY EARTH ROTATING PROPERLY?
ALL SYSTEMS RED.
GOOD.
COMMUNI-CATION: EXCELLENT.
a wonderful error
—— THE END

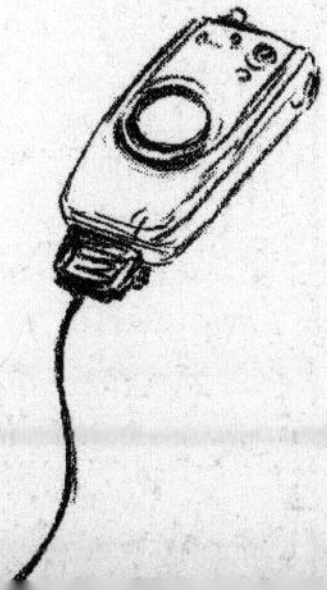